THE *Pony Club* BOOK

Contents

When Flying Hooves Ruled the Road *Valerie Watson*   4
Spring Ride *Carole Vincer*   11
The Horse from the Sea *Louise E. Johnson*   12
What's Wrong? *Maggie Raynor*   16
From Weston Park to World Gold *Judith Draper*   18
Did you Know?   24
Tina and Tinker   26
Double Meanings   26
Summer Ride *Carole Vincer*   27
The Man who loved Cowboys and Indians *Beth Carnes*   28
Tom and Trampus   37
Cooking for your Pony *Lisa Jones*   38
The Zebroids of Sangare *Diana Wilson*   40
Autumn Ride *Carole Vincer*   43
The Girl who didn't like Ponies *Elisabeth Beresford Illustrated by Sally Bell*   44
Personal Pony Presents *Lisa Jones*   48
King Harry's Saddle *Barbara Cooper*   50
Just What He Needs   54
Spooky Tales *Valerie Watson*   56
Winter Ride *Carole Vincer*   59
Faithful Friends *Christine Morgan-Owen*   60
Answers   63
Acknowledgments and Picture Credits   63

When Flying Hooves Ruled the Road

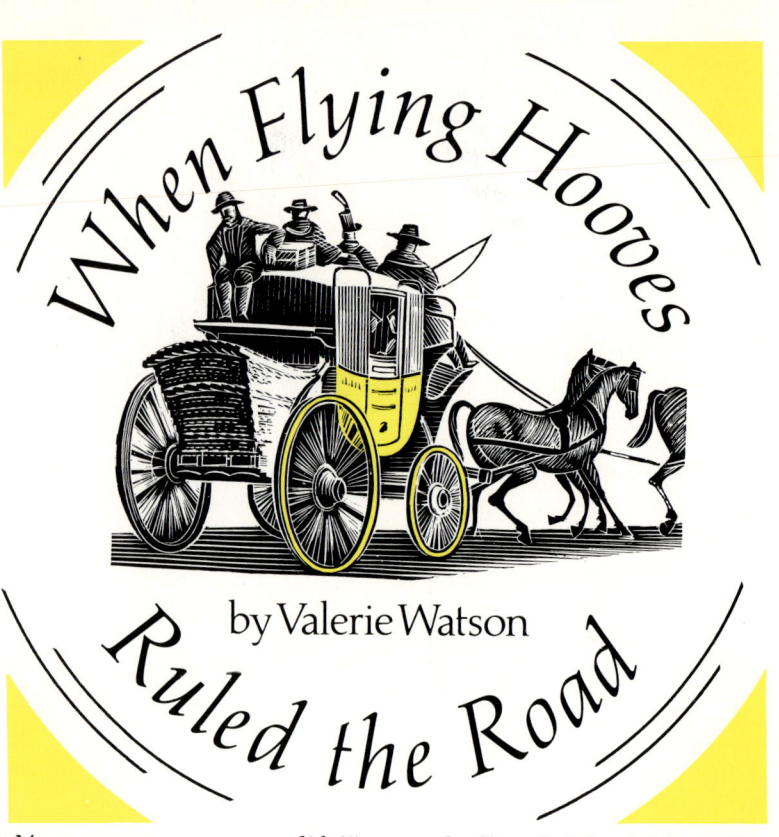

by Valerie Watson

"Stand and deliver! Your money or your life!" The shouting comes from some way off but has a terrifying effect on the passengers. The ladies shriek, and cling together. The men try to look out of the windows, but as the coach driver shouts and whips on his horses, the whole vehicle lurches from side to side and everyone is thrown about. The horses are wild-eyed and straining, but they can go no faster. The highwaymen are gaining, the wildness of the chase in their eyes. They are masked and armed with glistening swords and deadly pistols. The coachdriver realises that there is no hope. Two of the highwaymen ride along-side the leading horses and grab the reins. For the passengers, time moves like treacle as the coach slowly comes to a halt.

Can you imagine the horror of being held up like that? To the people of the 17th and 18th Century it was as frightening as it is today when an aircraft is hi-jacked. Fortunately for us, hi-jacks are fairly rare – but for our ancestors the chances of being robbed and killed were considerable. In fact, if you were going on a journey by stagecoach in the mid-17th Century, you stood a fifty per cent chance of being held up by highwaymen. No wonder so many people made wills before setting off on a journey!

There has always been crime on the road. Until the second half of the last century only rich people used to travel long distances and very often they would take their money and jewels with them. Stagecoaches, which were not the quickest of vehicles, were easy prey for thieves, and offered rich pickings. By the 18th Century the roads were full of coaches and horsedrawn vehicles; during the summer season, in one day forty or more coaches would travel on the London to Brighton Road alone.

Highwaymen would lurk in a hideaway at a place where the coach was at its most vulnerable. A steep hill was ideal. The passengers would climb out in order to lighten the horses' load. Then when coach and passengers were half way up, the highwaymen would strike. One of the most notorious of these spots was Shooter's Hill on the Dover Road. Other favourite places were wide open spaces and waste land, such as Hounslow and Hampstead Heath and Finchley Common near Central London, and bleak Witham Common on the Great North Road. All over Britain there are open places and stretches of woodland whose names are linked with the activities of highwaymen – and also with their timely ends. Many of them were caught and hanged and, as a lesson to others, their corpses were left to decay by the roadside – at crossroads and on hills. Have you noticed names such as 'Gibbet Hill' or 'Gibbet Cross' when you have been driving to a show? In the past it must have been revolting to see all those corpses – but people felt that the villains deserved their fate.

In my local hunting country there are two woods called Cutpercy and The Hangings. I often wonder if any of the vicious 'cut-purses' who hid in the wood (now named after them) ended up on the gallows at The Hangings.

"Highway robbery" became the organised crime of the day. All coaches had to stop at inns for the passengers to rest and to change the horses. Some inn-keepers did deals with the highwaymen, and for a share of the spoils would give them valuable information about the passengers and what they were taking on the journey. Wealthy travellers riding on coaches which changed horses at The Talbot Inn in Newark would unknowingly be in danger. The landlord of The Talbot was in league with "Swift Nick" one of the most notorious and feared highwaymen of the North of England.

The landlord at The Bell at Hounslow was also part of a desperate gang. In June 1698 he cheerily sent the Dover Stage on its way. Secretly he had sent out a message to his fellow-crooks that there were six people on the coach and that it was well worth looting. The highwaymen attacked the coach at Shooter's Hill in south-east London, killed one of the passengers, and stole £300 which was a fortune in those days.

Probably the most dangerous area for travellers was within a twenty-mile radius of London. As long ago as the 14th Century, King Edward I ordered the clearing of 200 foot swathes on either side of the roads to remove cover for criminals. His grandson Edward III repeated the operation. As the population increased and the roads became busier – so did the foot-pads, cut-purses and highwaymen. Many of them were caught, and in the twelve years between 1759 and 1771, 250 highwaymen were hanged at Tyburn, in London, alone. 'Tyburn Tree' (the gallows) stood at the western end of what is now Oxford Street, near Marble Arch.

As highwaymen were clearly a menace to society, why do we have such romantic ideas about them? Most of them were vicious thugs: much more likely to chop off a lady's finger in order to steal her ring than to kiss her hand and/or to charmingly ask her to donate a piece of jewellery for a good cause.

The answer to the question lies in the mid-1600s after the English Civil War when a number of impoverished royalist gentlemen began to rob travellers. It is from them that has grown the romantic idea of the charming and courtly 'Gentlemen of the Road'. A few highwaymen did have a polite way of behaving. Claude Duval,

Downhill. The Dover Mail on the Dover Road. Note the guard's scarlet, blue and gold uniform.

who was probably the first 'Gentleman of the Road' is said to have danced a 'coranto' with a young lady on Hounslow Heath while his thugs held her husband captive with a pistol to his head. Ladies of fashion thought that this was very romantic, and hundreds of them mourned when Duval was finally caught and hanged at Tyburn in 1670.

Some highwaymen were not men at all, but women. Mary Frith, known as 'Moll Cutpurse' was never caught – though many people suspected her. She was too clever for her pursuers, and when she died in 1659 at the great age of 75 it was discovered that she had amassed a huge fortune through her secret profession.

The most famous highwayman of them all has to be Dick Turpin who with his beautiful mare, Black Bess, became a legend in his own lifetime. Bess must have been quite a horse, for she and Turpin are said to have galloped all the way from London to York in the middle of the night – escaping arrest several times by jumping the tollgates. When she reached York, Bess collapsed and died, and without her Turpin was soon caught.

In the early days, stage travel was really awful. The coaches were bumpy, cold and draughty. To stand up to the horrendous roads they had to be very solidly constructed. They had broad wheels which made the ruts in the road worse and worse. The heaviest coaches could weigh up to four tons and were pulled by teams of eight horses, with teamsters walking beside them cracking their whips.

In bad weather a coach could get stuck in the mud for days. The average speed was two miles an hour, and some journeys took weeks to complete. As time went by, coach design improved, but the roads were still muddy tracks full of potholes. What with the risk of accidents, highwaymen and the miserable conditions, travel was not for the faint-hearted.

Things could have remained like this for a great deal longer but for a man called John Palmer, who was very upset that his mail took so long to arrive. He pointed out that it was having a very bad effect on the commerce of the country, and he was right. The postboys, who rode mules, didn't really take the job of getting letters and packages to their destinations very seriously. Not only were they slow, but 'things' happened to them. They were robbed. They got lost. They were waylaid. And sometimes they lost their postbags. In other words, if you sent a letter, the chances of it arriving were fairly slim.

Palmer had the bright idea of combining the jobs of the coach and the postboy.

The new vehicles would be called 'Post Coaches' and would be fast, light coaches, fitted with the newly invented steel springs which would make them a lot more comfortable for the passengers.

The first trial was from Bristol to London in 1784. The coach left Bristol at 4 o'clock on the afternoon of 2nd August and reached the General Post Office in Lombard Street, London at 8 o'clock the next morning: a fast time for those days. The experiment proved to be a great success.

Thanks to The Turnpike Act and to civil engineers such as 'Blind Jack' Metcalf, John L. McAdam and Thomas Telford, the network of roads began to improve. In fact the average speed of the fastest mail-coach was soon to be 10 miles per hour: which is a fast trot and canter all the way. The Post Coach changed horses every 7 to 10 miles and the grooms were very quick to 'turn a team round'. On a mail run it took no longer than five minutes to change the four horses. The Quicksilver, the only named Mail Coach, which ran from London to Falmouth, could cover the leg to Exeter (176 miles) in 16 hours allowing for changes and stops for meals. (In 1887 the Mail service was revived for a few weeks to beak a railway monopoly, and it was discovered that the train was only one mile per hour faster than coach and horses!)

The Post Office provided a guard who was in charge of the coach and responsible for keeping to time. He sat on a rear seat with the mail and valuables in a locker under his feet, and he carried pistols and a blunderbuss. No one was allowed to sit beside him, and only three people were allowed on top of the coach, as the guard must have a clear view. Not surprisingly, the Mail was never robbed, but the stagecoaches (which also now employed guards) were constantly molested by highwaymen.

Travellers could travel 'post haste' with the mail by paying a higher fare than on the stage, but with little fear of attack. However, there was a snag: the mail had to come first. If anything unforeseen happened, such as an accident or delay, the guard had orders to unharness the horses and to ride on with his bags, leaving the passengers stranded on the road.

All guards had to be very strict about keeping time. Each guard had a long horn called a 'Yard of Tin' which he was allowed to use only for letting people know that the mailcoach was in the vicinity (and not for playing popular tunes!) When 250 yards from a toll-gate, he would blow loud blasts on his horn and if the toll-keeper didn't have his gates open for the Mail to fly

No time to stop! The mailbags are handed through the inn window as the mailcoach speeds by.

through, there would be trouble. The fine for anyone delaying the Mail was 40 shillings. As well as not having to pay tolls, the Mail was also entitled to claim right of way.

The arrival of a stage-coach was announced by a blast on the guard's 'key-bugle' but, like all other traffic, coaches had to halt at toll-gates and to pay to go through.

The mailcoach brought glamour and drama into the lives of country people. They would look up from their work in the fields and wave when one went by. In times of national trouble the guards would be given a supply of printed handbills, which they would distribute as they travelled from town to town. People could set their clocks by the Mail, and the atmosphere must have been electric when these wonderful coaches in their livery of red, black and gold with the royal arms on their panels came clattering up the High Street.

Roads were getting better and better: more than 20,000 miles were maintained under the supervision of the turnpike system. And now the emphasis was on speed. Innkeepers prided themselves on running the fastest service, and sometimes coaches – especially the mailcoaches – would race each other. The highwaymen were all but gone, but now passengers were prey to a new danger – accidents caused by speed. The Quicksilver once overturned as she was leaving Brighton and pitched her outside passengers into gardens and on to spiked railings.

In 1820 the Chester Mail and the Holyhead Mail raced each other down the hill into St Albans. The road was wide enough and the Chester mail soon gained the lead – but the coachman was so excited that he waved his hat at the other driver, and lost control. His lead-horses flew in front of the Holyhead team, and there was an awful collision. One of the Holyhead

Uphill. The **Brighton Comet**, *with a full load of passengers, makes its way over the Sussex Downs.*

passengers was killed instantly, and another broke his arm and leg. Both drivers were charged with murder, but were only sent to prison for a year or two – which in those days was a very lenient sentence.

Coach-horses had to be really 'corned up' and fit to reach the required speeds – and sometimes accidents happened because the coachman couldn't hold them. On one occasion, all eleven outside passengers were seriously hurt and one was killed when the coachman couldn't hold his fresh team. They crashed into a wagon coming from the other direction.

The coaching inns in towns became very important. They were meeting-places and parcel depots and they offered large stabling facilities. In the High Streets of market towns all over England and Wales you will find large inns with arched entrances into car parks, which used to be the stable-yards. Many innkeepers owned their own mail and stagecoaches and became very rich. The most famous of them all was Mr Chaplin who kept The Swan and The Spread Eagle in Gracechurch Street, London. He owned 70 coaches and 1,800 horses (a third of which he changed every year to keep up the quality of his service) served 68 routes, and employed 2,000 people. His most famous coach was *The Brighton Comet;* the most newsworthy was the Exeter Coach, which was attacked by an escaped lioness in 1816 near the Pheasant Inn between Salisbury and Stockbridge.

Although it was cheaper to travel by night, it was far more dangerous – partly because of the dark and partly because they used horses of inferior quality.

Unlike the mailcoaches, which were very 'official', stagecoaches were painted in bright colours, with the name, destination and sometimes decorative pictures on the panels: such as running foxes or crossed whips – anything to advertise the coach's speed.

Many of the artists employed to decorate coaches went on to become famous painters: the best known being James Herring. For seven years he worked at the Doncaster Coach depot during which time he painted the famous *London-Doncaster Highflyer*. Once 'discovered', Herring was commissioned by Queen Victoria and members of the aristocracy, and he is now regarded as an English Old Master.

The stagecoaches had wonderful names and their performances were really phenomenal. The *Tallyho* from London to Birmingham covered 109 miles in 7½ hours, at an average of 14½ miles per hour. A century before, it had taken two and a half days to complete the journey.

The Star could run from London to Cambridge and back in a day. *The Red Rover* was one of the most exciting coaches to see as it sped towards Manchester. The coach was red, the driver wore red, and the horses' harness was red: much much more colourful than the *Manchester Defiance*. *The Beehive* was advertised as being 'lighted with wax' because it carried lamps inside and out. *The Shrewsbury Wonder* was well named. 150 horses were kept for this coach alone and it was driven by a man called Sam Hayward. Although there were accidents, on the whole coachmen were extremely skilled and Hayward was one of the best. People would come to watch him gallop down the steep hill of Wyle Cop, turn the horses in their own length, and drive them through the narrow archway of The Lion at a smart trot. The arch was so narrow that the outside passengers all had to duck.

The speed and glamour of the road and the skill of coachmen such as Hayward inspired young men of fashion to learn to drive a 'Four-in-Hand'. Many of them even wore the same type of clothes as coachmen, and before long, boots, breeches and great-coats with lots of capes became 'all the rage'.

Some of these young men took it so seriously that they became professional coachmen – much to the horror of their families. One of them was Harry Stevenson, educated at Eton and Cambridge, who turned professional and operated a Brighton run in his own coach, *The Age*, which was said to have eclipsed all other coaches in elegance and comfort. Stevenson had a team of roans, a team of skewbalds, a team of chestnuts and a team of dun horses.

The fittings on their harness were silver-plated and on the journey his servants rode with the passengers and served refreshments.

The heyday of coaching – when roads were good and crime had diminished – only lasted for

Reading Telegraph *coaches passing each other on their way up and down to London.*

The Horse from the Sea

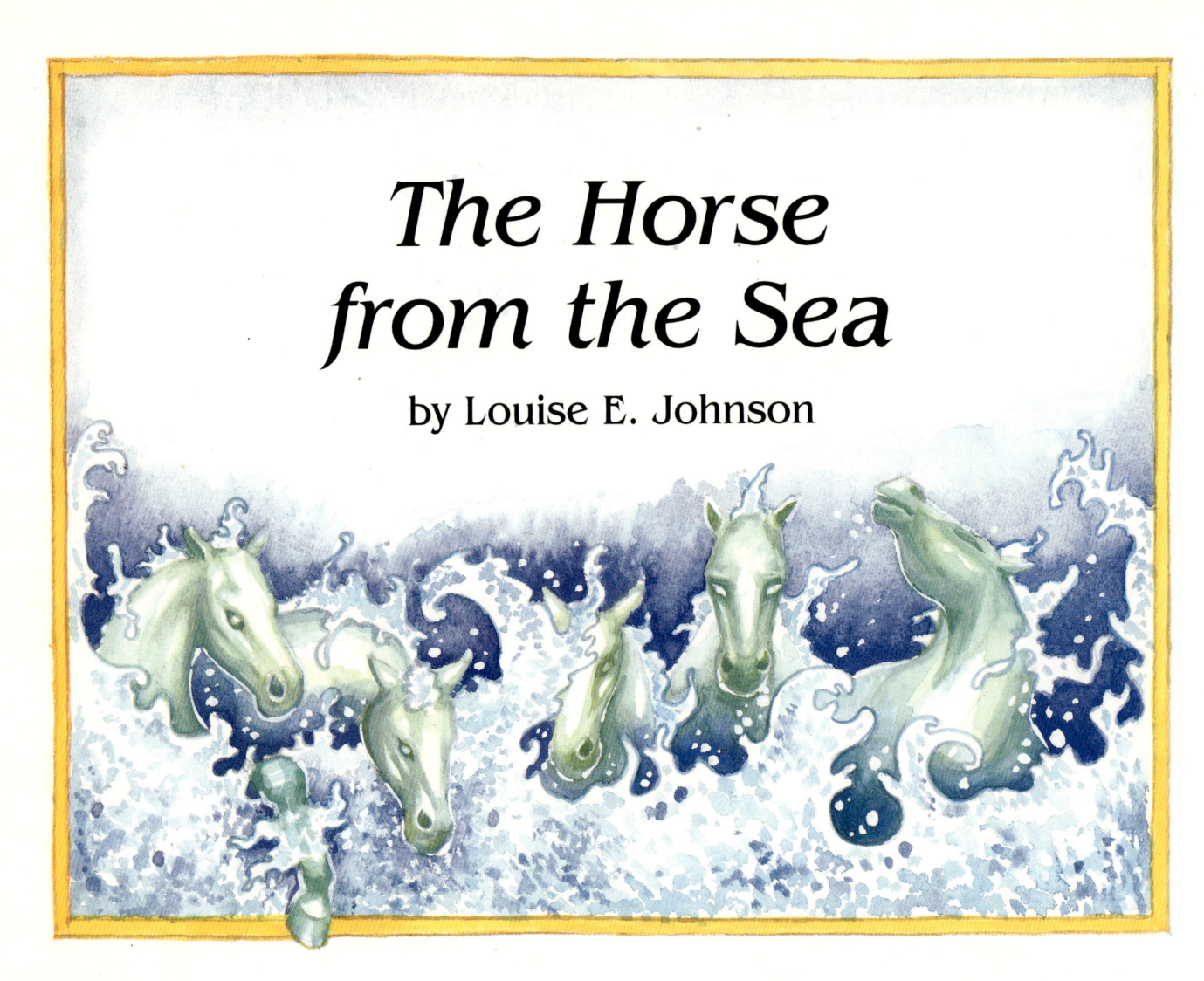

by Louise E. Johnson

The girl lived with her father in a small, grey, flinty cottage by the sea. It sat on a cliff-top overlooking a bay with a narrow strip of sandy beach. The cottage had a garden at the front where her father kept a few hens. In a nearby field was a small flock of her father's sheep.

The girl went to a village school across the fields. She did not have many friends, but she did not care. She felt that the sea and the wind were her friends and she was sure that they whispered out her name. She grew to know the sea in its many moods, and loved it best when the wind came whistling into the bay; when ragged clouds chased across the sky, and 'white horses' raced along the wave-tops. 'White horses' were what her father liked to call the wave-caps whipped up by the wind. Of course, she knew that there were not really horses out there amongst the waves, but sometimes if she stared hard enough she imagined that she could glimpse the toss of a foamy mane and hear horses whinnying.

One evening as darkness fell, a strong gale began blowing in from the sea. The girl, pressing her nose against the cold glass of her bedroom window, could see the waves rising wildly in the bay and flecks of foam illuminated in the moonlight, for there was a full moon in the sky. 'What a night for white horses,' she whispered to herself, her breath misting the glass.

Some hours later, after her father had gone to bed and the cottage was in darkness, she lay listening to the rushing wind outside. A sudden impulse to watch the wild sea made her climb from her bed and look out of the window again. She caught her breath in wonder – for there in the garden, standing in the moonlight, was a horse. His pale body gleamed as if wet, and he had a peculiar luminous quality like a sunlit sea. As the gusting wind blew against his body, clouds of vapour were swept up around him, and she saw that he was transparent: for through him the grass of the lawn was dimly visible. Then she realised that the frothy mane that curled along his neck was flecked foam. He was fashioned from the sea itself.

She crept through the cottage and quietly lifted the front door-latch. Outside, the rushing wind tangled her hair and tugged at her nightdress. The horse from the sea looked at her with green, watery, unblinking eyes. The girl walked slowly towards him, her hand outstretched, sure that this must be a dream and that she would wake up any minute. But her hand touched his wet nose, her fingertips passing through its silvery substance. The horse looked at her and blew through his nostrils. His breath smelt of a fresh sea-wind, and was just as cold. She put her hand in his mane, and the foam curled around her fingers.

Without thinking, she climbed upon his broad back. Her body sank comfortably into his, and she was kept buoyant by his watery substance. Looking down, she could see the grass passing dimly beneath his body.

The horse turned, scattering flecks of foam. The hen-house door had blown open, and the hens, who had come out to investigate, ran squawking back inside. The horse leaped over the wall, and the startled sheep, who had been huddling close to each other for shelter, scattered, bleating in fright. The girl laughed at the sheer wonder of it all, the wind stinging her face, the horse powerful beneath her. She had ridden bareback before, but this was quite different, like something out of a dream. It was almost as if she were a part of his rushing form.

He galloped straight towards the edge of the cliff and leaped towards the sea. The girl opened her mouth in a silent scream. The horse's foamy mane flew in her face and her hair spread out behind her. For one heartstopping moment they plunged through the darkness towards the billowing sea. Then the horse landed amongst the waves, scattering spray, and began to gallop along the wave-tops out, far out, to sea.

The girl rode on his back, the sea passing beneath her, the stars spinning overhead, and the gale blowing about them. She was not afraid, but lost in the exhilaration of the moment. Soon the shore was out of sight.

But then the gale began to die down, and as it did so, the horse started to return slowly into the sea from which he had been spawned. The girl cried out in terror as she realised that once the horse had gone there would be nothing between her and the cold, dark depths beneath.

Now the horse was wading up to his knees as his legs began to dissolve back into seawater, and the girl's toes were touching the freezing wave-caps. The horse seemed to understand her plight – for he turned and headed back towards the shore. But the wind was losing its force more and more quickly, and as it dropped, the horse's strength waned, too. Now he was swimming, and the girl's legs were being dragged into the cold sea. She clung to the horse's watery neck, feeling that with every passing moment he seemed less solid, the shore further away.

She was beginning to despair, and thinking how foolish she had been to believe that the sea and the wind were her friends – for they were wild, untameable elements that took little notice of living creatures.

A breeze left behind by the gale passed above them, and the horse flung back his watery head and called out – his mournful cry like that of a whale in the ocean's depths.

The breeze spun around the horse and girl, whipping her hair upwards. The horse began to re-form a little, and struck out more strongly towards the shore. But the breeze did not have the power of the gale, and the shore was still a long way off. The girl was now so cold and tired that she lost track of time, but she still clung to the horse's neck.

Suddenly, she felt sand beneath her feet. With a last desperate effort the horse had flung himself on to the beach. As the girl scrambled to get away to safety she looked back and saw the shape of his head briefly silhouetted against the moon, before it curled under a wave and was gone.

Afterwards, the girl could not remember returning to the cottage, and was never sure that the whole thing had not been a fantastic dream. But, dream or reality, the events of that night always remained in her mind, and in later life the liveliest horse, the fastest gallop, seemed feeble indeed compared with that wild, starlit ride across the windswept sea.

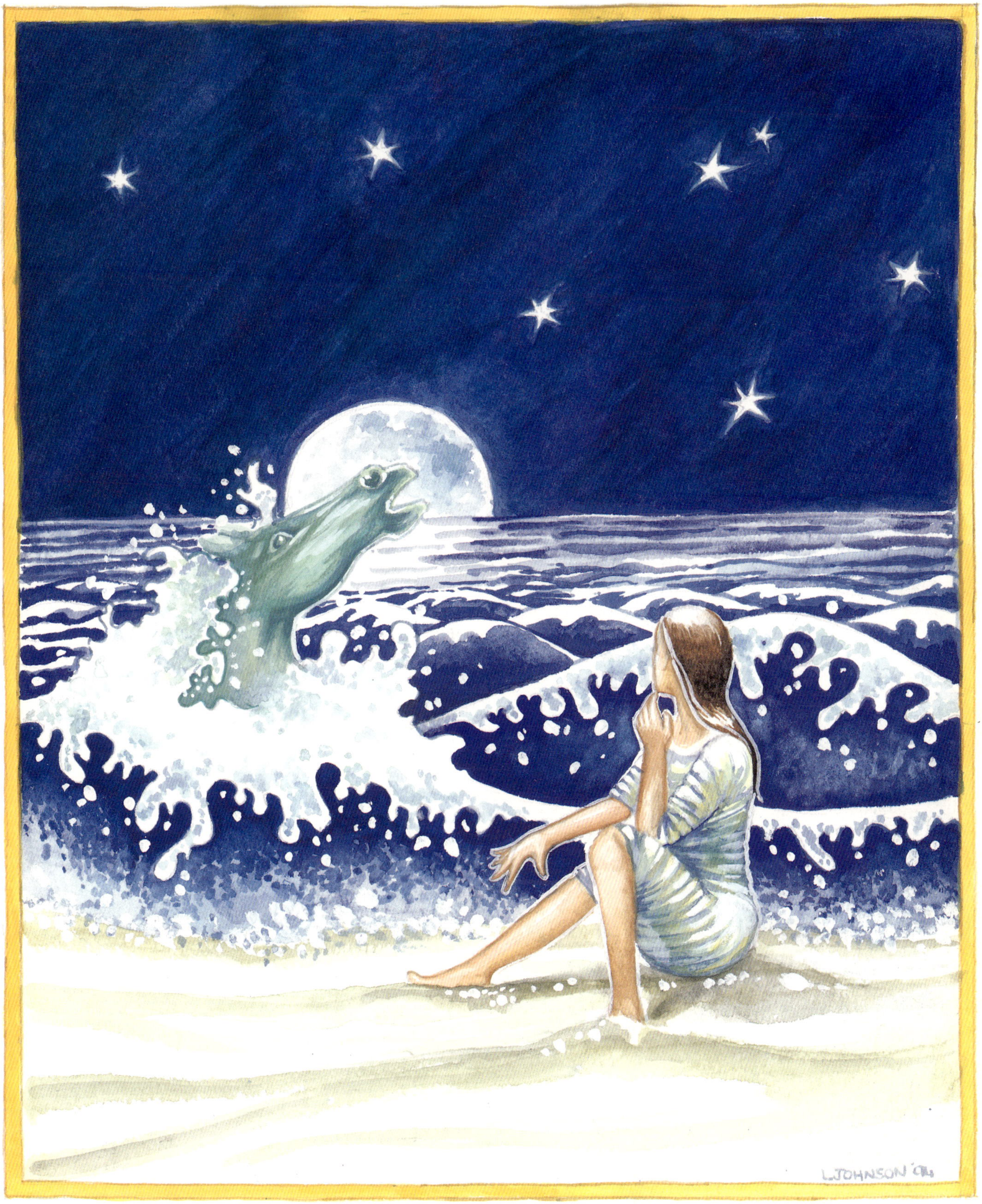
L.JOHNSON '94

Melissa and Sparky are trotting down the centre-line at their first Riding Club Preliminary Dressage Competition. How many mistakes has Melissa made in Sparky's tack and her own clothes?

What's

Philip and Gunner are competing in their first Riding Club Hunter Trials. How many mistakes can you find in their tack and clothing?

Wrong?

BY MAGGIE RAYNOR

Samantha and Cloudy are ready to go into the ring for their first 'Condition and Turnout' class. How many mistakes can you find?

Daniel and Larkspur have just come home after a 15-mile fun ride. Daniel is saying goodbye to Larkspur before leaving him for the night. How many mistakes in his stable-management can you find?

Answers on page 63.

FROM WESTON PARK TO WORLD GOLD

BY JUDITH DRAPER

Ask any international rider what they most dream of winning, and the answer is sure to be 'an Olympic gold medal'. In 1992 Karen Straker knew that her brilliant three-day event horse Get Smart had a good chance of making that dream come true at the Olympic Games in Barcelona.

'Smart' was performing brilliantly and while many other horses were failing to do their best because of the fierce heat, Karen knew that the Spanish weather would not bother her tough partner.

Sadly, they came home without either an individual or a team medal. For Karen – and probably for Get Smart, too, if he could talk – it was the most frustrating time of her riding career.

Being in a team, of course, brings special responsibilities. Riders have to follow the advice given to them by the team selectors and advisors. In Barcelona, following her instructions to take certain slow routes on the cross-country in order to get safely round the course, cost Karen and Get Smart the chance of winning an individual medal, perhaps even the gold.

Get Smart had done a superb dressage test to finish with the third-best score. He was close enough to win a medal if all went well on cross-country day. After walking the course Karen had planned to take all the fast routes on the cross-country, except for the last of the three water jumps. But while she was in the ten-minute box she was told that she must take all the slow routes. Luckily for Karen there was a long delay before she could start because a previous competitor had had a fall. It gave her time to persuade the selectors that she should take as many fast routes as possible, though she did agree to go the slow way at the first two water jumps.

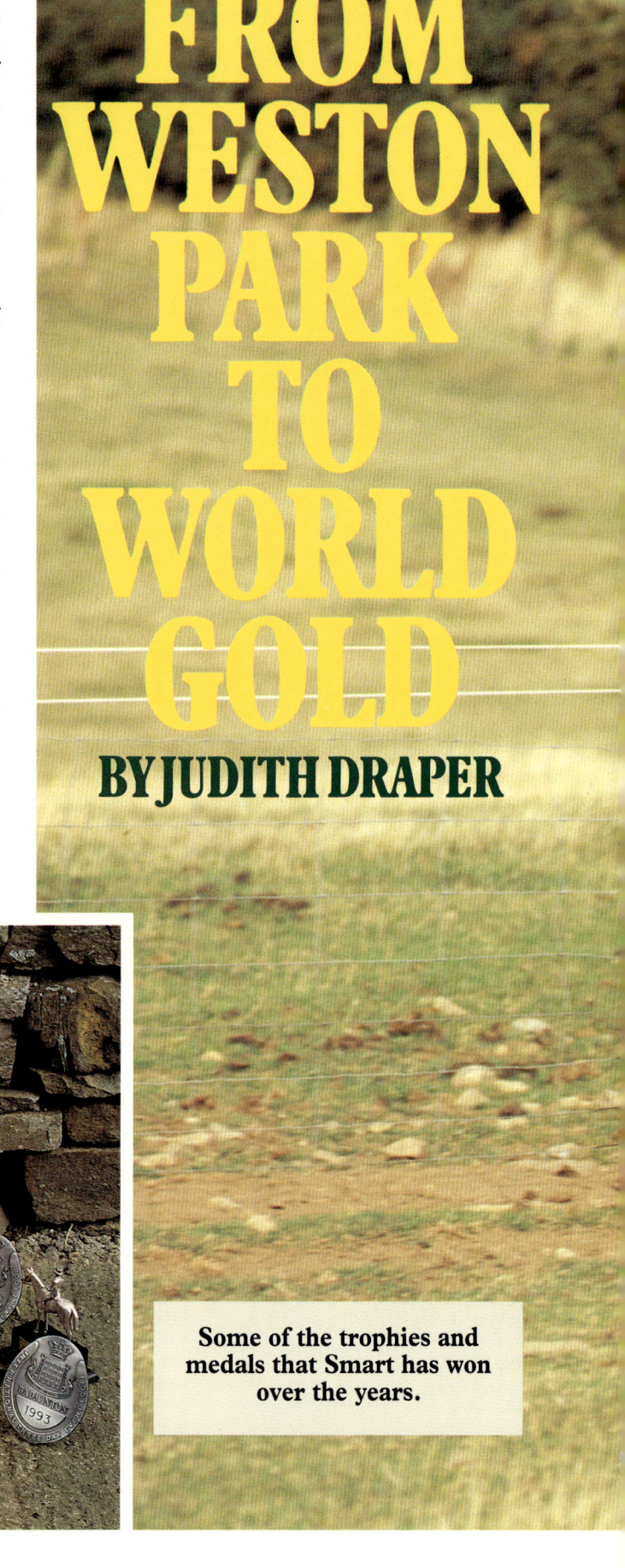

Some of the trophies and medals that Smart has won over the years.

Fit and free. Smart having a great time galloping in the field after returning home from the Barcelona Olympics.

"Smart just after we bought him as a 4 year-old. Mum re-broke him – hence the lungeing kit. We called him 'Get Smart' because you need to be smart to stay on him!"

Smart was ready to run for his life, and she found it very frustrating to have to keep hooking him back when she knew he could take everything in his stride.

Smart cruised round the cross-country, but time penalties dropped him to eighth place. With just one fence down in the show jumping he finally finished an honourable sixth, leaving Karen to wonder what might have been if Smart had been allowed to 'go for it'.

'I felt terrible for a long time afterwards,' she said. 'It was a real setback in my life. I would much prefer, rightly or wrongly, to give it a crack and either fall at the first fence and have people say, well she had a go, or to go and win it. I think people respect you much more for it.'

Such disappointments are, of course, all part of being a rider, and although Karen said it took her a long time to get over it, she and Smart have bounced right back. Since then, they have won a team gold medal and an individual bronze in the World Championships, and as Get Smart will be only 16 in 1996, Karen is hopeful of taking him to the next Olympics in Atlanta.

If that plan comes off, it will be their third Olympic Games together – a remarkable achievement for a partnership that started at Pony Club level many years ago when Karen was a teenager.

It was because of their involvement with the Pony Club that the Strakers found 'Smart' in the first place. It was 1984 and Karen, who was then an Associate, and her mother, Elaine, were teaching the Hurworth branch at a farm near Northallerton. One of the sons of the owner of the farm was riding Smart. He had only just been broken in and he was being hacked around and was half joining in with the Pony Club ride.

'When I asked if he would jump a telegraph pole he bobbed up over it with no worry at all,' Karen recalls. 'We liked him straight away because of his outlook on life. He had only been ridden for about four days and there he was, out in a field full of children and ponies, having a great time. He was a really bouncy horse, with a very cheeky character.' He also had good conformation and wonderful movement – ideal for an event horse. The Strakers were so impressed that they bought him.

As he was only four and had been ridden so little, Mrs Straker decided to start training him again from scratch. She gave him lots of work on the lunge before Karen began to school him under saddle. He has always been a fun-loving horse and right from the start he enjoyed a good buck and a squeal whenever he had the chance. That is why then named him Get Smart: you had to be smart to stay on him!

Smart learned so quickly that he was soon taking part in Pony Club competitions, and as a five-year-old he qualified to go to Weston Park for the Horse Trials Championships.

'I always think that Pony Club competitions are a great grounding for a horse,' Karen said. 'That level of competition – hunter trialling and Pony Club one-day eventing – is fantastic for a young horse.' She and Smart finished second in the Associates' section at Weston Park, the first step in her new horse's eventing career.

When he was six, Smart won the novice two-day event at Holker Hall and finished sixth at Osberton. The highlight of his seven-year-old season was his first attempt at a major three-day event, Burghley.

'He had done Gatcombe,' Karen remembers, 'and finished third, but at Thirlestane Castle, his final run before Burghley, we had a fall. By this time he was becoming really cocky. He could see the finish from about two fields away and just ran away with me at the last few

Karen and Smart at Pony Club Championships, Weston Park, 1985. They finished second in Associates. Smart was only five, and very bold.

fences. He really put his foot down. At the second-last fence I tried to regain a bit of control but he just kept motoring on and we met it on a corker of s stride and fell. I broke my wrist and sprung my collarbone. So I went to Burghley with my wrist in plaster.

'He had become so big for his boots that I think he needed a bit of a comedown and that mistake had really done him good. He went beautifully round Burghley and we finished 12th.

Right from the start Smart found everything easy. He is by a Thoroughbred stallion named Garnered out of a 14.2hh pony mare called Samantha and seems to have the best qualities of both parents. He stands 16hh and can gallop into a fence or trot into it, depending on the situation. He can be as nimble as a cat and put in an extra stride at the last moment, or take off from a long stride. He has never found show jumping difficult and only has the occasional fence down. And because of his good natural paces he can be brilliant at dressage.

'He's got natural talent and flare so he finds the movements easy. It's just a question of keeping him together, because he loves to have fun and can be a naughty character,' said Karen.

By 1988, when he was eight, he was ready to make his first appearance at Badminton. The selectors told Karen that if Smart went well there, she might even be put on the long list for the Olympic Games.

'That hadn't even crossed my mind,' she said. 'It was a great surprise for someone even to *say* it, let alone for it to happen.' Smart went like a dream at Badminton, finishing fifth, and Karen's name was put on the Olympic long list with both Get Smart and her other top horse Corriwack, who had won at Punchestown, in Ireland, that spring.

At the final trial, Smart finished second and Corriwack was fourth. As a result, Karen was selected to go to the Olympics, which were being held in Seoul, capital of South Korea, in the autumn.

'Smart and I were always number five, always the bridesmaids in the back row behind Ginny Leng (now Elliot), Mark Phillips, Ian Stark and Lorna Clarke,' she admits. 'The selectors sort of left the fourth place between Lorna and me, but it didn't take the brains of an archbishop to work out that she would be preferred to me because she was so experienced. I had only ever been to junior and young rider championships, never to a senior one. Imagine being with Ginny, Mark, Lorna and Ian in your first team – they were all *seriously* high powered and it was very frightening.'

Then Lorna's horse knocked himself in his box and suddenly Karen was in the team.

'The selectors didn't tell us until the day of the opening ceremony. It was my birthday [17 September], *and* the Olympic opening ceremony, *and* Smart and I had been selected for the team. It was a big day!'

Get Smart went really well in the dressage, finishing ninth behind the eventual winner, Charisma, ridden by New Zealand's Mark Todd. Then the horses had to be

"Smart's first One-Day event as a 5 year-old: Brougham Horse Trials, Cumbria; Novice Class. He was brilliant from the word go!"

transported a long distance to the cross-country course. Karen and Get Smart had never experienced anything like this before, and found it very strange. Karen also found it rather strange that everyone was so tense.

'I enjoy what I do,' she said, 'and suddenly everyone was nervy and I wondered what was the matter with them.' The first drama came when Mark Phillips' horse, Cartier, was withdrawn after the steeplechase. This meant that all three remaining riders had to complete if the British team was to have a chance of winning a medal.

'The 10-minute box was hell on earth – worse than Pony Club camp!' said Karen. 'One person was telling me one thing, another person was telling me another. All I wanted to do was get out of there and get on with it. The only piece of information we *didn't* get was that there was a bit of a hole on the right-hand side of the water and horses had been lurching into it.'

Get Smart was going well until that fence, number 24 of the 32 on the course. Unfortunately he jumped in and went right, could not get his front end up and Karen fell into the water. She was quickly back on board, but riding on a wet saddle is like sitting on a bar of soap, and when Smart hit the next fence, she very nearly fell off. Hanging on grimly on one side, she struggled to avoid another fall inside the penalty area.

The fence judge, trying to help, started to 'shoo' at Smart to get him going again and out of the penalty area. Unfortunately Smart misunderstood. Thinking there might be a packet of Polo mints on offer – he will do anything for anybody if they give him Polo mints – he started to go *towards* the fence judge instead of away. In the end Karen clambered back into the saddle without

21

"Badminton '94. The first time that Smart *performed* in the dressage. Look at the concentration on his face! Normally the hounds in the Park upset him, but that year we didn't bump into them!!"

touching the ground and the pair finished the course. She rode the rest of the way with her hands wrapped round the breastplate, just in case.

Smart jumped an excellent clear round in the show jumping and finished 19th individually. Britain won the team silver medal.

'If we hadn't parted company in the water, it would have been glorious gold for the team,' she recalls. But that is all part of the sport, and for a pair with no experience at senior championship level, Smart and Karen had done well.

The following year, 1989, Smart went to the European Championships at Burghley, though he and Karen were not selected for the team which won the gold medals. They just failed to win an individual medal, finishing fourth.

In 1990 the first ever World Equestrian Games were held, in Stockholm, Sweden. Karen and Smart were members of the British team which won the silver medals. They were again placed 19th individually, though Karen feels sure they would have been higher if she had not been told that she must jump the right-hand side of the big water complex.

'I wanted to jump to the left. I knew the other route was not the right one for me. Because I didn't believe that I was doing the right thing, Smart sensed my uncertainty and stopped. It wasn't his fault.'

Twelve months later they finally won gold, at the European Championships in Punchestown, where the British team were absolutely unbeatable and Smart took the individual bronze.

Everyone in the horse world has their ups and downs and 1993, the year after the Barcelona Olympics, was not a good one for Get Smart. Normally well behaved in the dressage, he has always been naughty at Badminton and he was particularly wild that year, ruining his chances by 'blowing up' in the arena. Then later in the season he had a fall at Gatcombe and cut his elbow with his hind foot.

'The cut went right into the muscle,' Karen recalled. 'He had to have nine stitches inside, and 11 outside. The amazing thing was that he was never lame. He would trot and canter around and not seem to feel it. But because it was in such a bad place, the stitches popped open again and then when he moved the cut opened and you could hear the air being sucked in and coming out again – it was like walking in wet wellies.' The selectors kept hoping that it would heal in time for the European Championships but Karen knew it was impossible.

After going brilliantly across country at Badminton the next year he was lying second. But he had unluckily cut his pastern at the Luckington Lane crossing and although he passed the vet the next day Karen thinks that the three mistakes which he made in the show jumping were caused because he was feeling sore.

However, he had done enough to earn a place in the British team for the second World Equestrian Games, held in The Hague in Holland. The all-woman team won the gold medals, and Karen and Smart achieved the highlight of their career so far by taking the individual bronze.

In fact, if Smart had not rolled a pole off the very last show jump, they would have won the silver. But Karen has no regrets. In fact, she was rather pleased to have collected five penalties.

Barcelona. The will to win is on their faces – but they were under orders to back-pedal.

The Hague. Waving to the crowd after show-jumping their way to the individual bronze which helped the British team to win the gold.

'If we had been clear,' she explained, 'we would have missed winning the individual gold by 0.4 of a penalty. I don't think I could have lived with myself if I'd just missed out like that. Anyway, the team gold was fantastic and special.'

As for the future, Karen has the 1996 Olympics firmly in her sights.

'Smart will be 16, but he is still as bouncy as ever and game for a laugh. The heat won't be a problem for him.'

One thing this super-brave horse does need, though, is to have people around him whom he loves.

'When we bought him he was quite insecure – he had been through the sales and had probably been roughly treated. When we first got him home if he was left on his own and mum or I went to stand with him, he would grab hold of our coat and hold on to it as if to say, don't go. He's still a bit like that.'

DID YOU

SSHH!

That according to a Lincolnshire superstition, if you see a white dog you should stay silent until you have also seen a white horse.

That Philip Astley, who founded the first circus in London in 1779, owned a horse named Billy whose many talents included being able to wash his feet in a bucket, unsaddle himself – and wait at table!

That the official world high jump record for a horse is 8 ft 1¼ in (2.47 m), set in 1949 in Chile by an ex-racehorse called Huaso, ridden by Captain Alberto Larraguibel Morales.

That according to superstition you can cure yourself of nightmares by placing a stallion's teeth under your pillow.

That the world's tallest living horse is Bovington Black King, a Shire gelding born in 1984 in Devon. He stands 19.2 hh (1.98 m). The tallest horse ever recorded, another Shire gelding named Sampson (later renamed Mammoth), stood 21.2 hh!

That the smallest breed of horse in the world is the Fallabella, which may stand as little as 14-15 in (33.5-38 cm) at the withers. The breed is named after the Argentinian family who developed it.

KNOW

That the world speed record for a horse is 43.2 mph (69.62 km/h). It was set in Mexico City in 1945 by a four-year-old racehorse named Big Racket.

That grey horses are said to be lucky, while skewbalds are considered unlucky.

That the official world long-jump record for a horse is 27 ft 6¾ in (8.40 m). This record is held by a horse with the unusual name of Something, who cleared this length in Johannesburg, South Africa, in 1975, when ridden by André Ferreira.

That the famous show jumper Milton, ridden by John Whitaker, is the only horse in the world (outside racing) to have won more than £1 million in prize money.

That finding a horseshoe in the road is said to bring you luck. Luckiest of all is one from the hind leg of a grey mare.

That the oldest horse on record was Old Billy. He was born in Lancashire in 1760, spent most of his life working on the canals, and died at the age of 62.

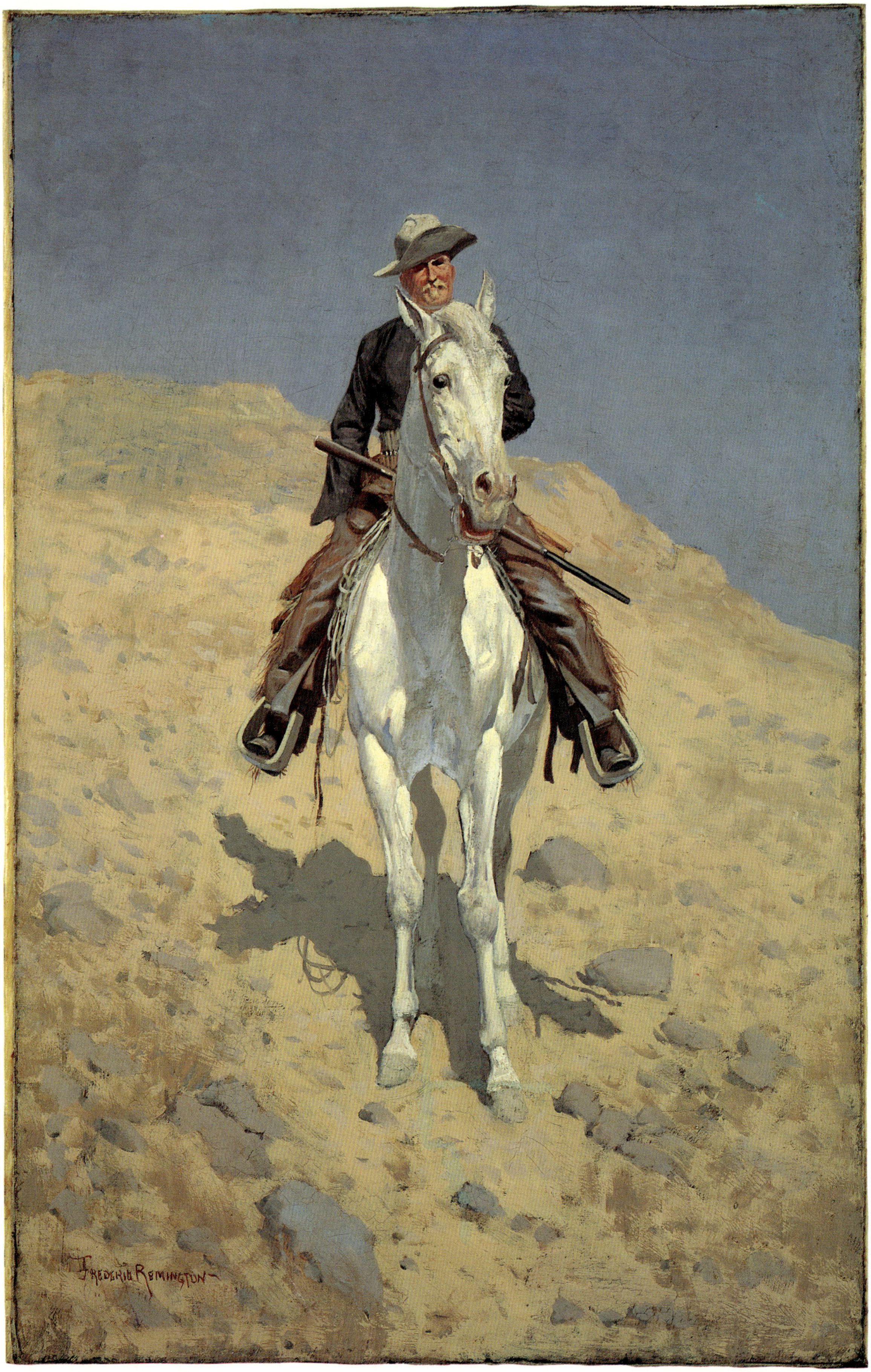
FREDERIC REMINGTON

THE MAN WHO LOVED COWBOYS & INDIANS

Frederic Remington, 1861–1909

By Beth Carnes

The young man was a strapping big fellow, sandy-haired, and only nineteen years old. This was his first trip into the wild, open and beautiful country of the West, the frontier of what was then called "the Montana Territory," but it was to set him on the course for the next 28 years of his life as the artist who brought the powerful images of the American frontier to the rest of the world.

Self-Portrait on a Horse
"What success I have had," Remington told a reporter, "has been because I have a horseman's knowledge of a horse. No-one can draw equestrian subjects unless he is an equestrian himself." This is Remington's only known finished self-portrait, showing him dressed as a cowpuncher.
c. 1890. Oil on canvas.
Sid Richardson Collection of Western Art, Fort Worth, Texas.

The young man was Frederic Remington, whose very name has become synonymous with the American West. While he was to become famous world-wide for his black and white illustrations, his huge paintings and his life-size bronzes, on this first trip he was employed as a cowboy and ranch cook.

It was a long way from upstate New York, where Frederic had been born into a comfortable household. His father was a staunch Republican journalist who had started his own newspaper as a way of advancing the causes of the Republican party. Young Frederic was sent at age fifteen to military school where, when not spending his free time with youthful pranks, he began to develop the artistic talents which led to his career.

His letters to friends of the period were highly illustrated with his visions of cowpunchers, Indians, and desperados. Although the young Remington was quite shy and bashful, "Bud" as he was called by his schoolmates, made lasting friendships while at

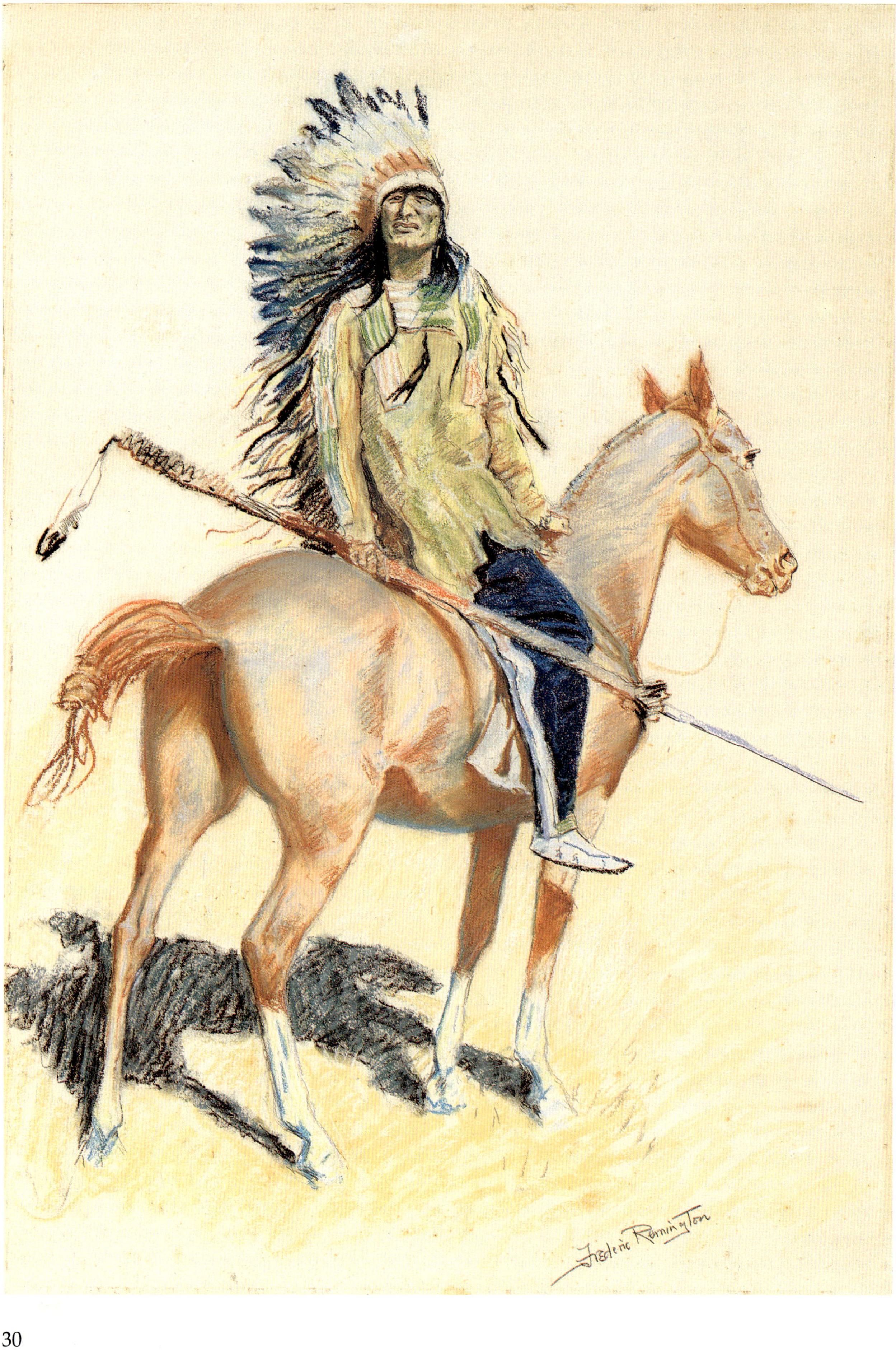
Frederic Remington

school, in part owing to his happy and generous disposition. It was also his artistic abilities that brought him friendship. "We soon found that he had a talent for drawing," wrote one of his fellow cadets, "which made him in demand at all gatherings of the cadets, who delighted in his caricatures of the cadet officers and teachers."

By the spring of 1878, Remington was considering what college to enter and what career to follow. He wrote to his uncle, "I am going to try and get into Cornell College this coming June and if I succeed will be a Journalist. I mean to study for an artist anyhow, whether I ever make a success of it or not." But when the fall came, he entered Yale University's School of Fine Arts, probably because Cornell's curriculum included neither journalism nor art. Here he began to refine his art and develop his talent.

A Sioux Chief
Remington's Indian portraits were remarkable for their detail and accuracy. Notice the ease with which the Chief sits his horse in full regalia.
1901. Pastel on art board.
Sid Richardson Collection of Western Art, Fort Worth, Texas.

But in 1879 his father died, and after much careful deliberation Remington quit Yale. This was likely due in large part to financial considerations. His legal guardianship was granted to his uncle Lamartin Remington, who was decidedly opposed to having any men artists in the family. As a result, young Remington began an unsatisfying series of jobs such as a clerk in the New York Governor's office.

He met and fell in love with a local beauty, Eva Caten, and asked for her hand in marriage. Consent was "withheld," however, which young Remington took as a reflection of his limited future prospects. This was the motivation that led him West to seek his fortune.

However, when he returned home to Albany it was without riches, at least in the sense of money or gold or land deeds. But he did return with suitcases bulging with lively sketches and drawings of what he had seen in his travels, and he was filled with ideas and excitement for a career as an illustrator. His first interview with the editor of *Harper's Weekly* was a success and he sold one of his sketches. The sketch was redrawn by William Rogers, an experienced illustrator, and appeared as a full page illustration in *Harper's Weekly*. Rogers credited Remington, though, and Frederic told Rogers later, "It was you who introduced me to the public. That was my first appearance and I was mighty glad I fell into the hands of an artist who knew a cowboy saddle and a Western horse."

The sale of one sketch did not exactly launch his career, so at the age of twenty-one Remington moved to Kansas to try his hand at sheep ranching – sheep being considerably less expensive to buy than cattle. At first Kansas depressed him: the endless flat prairie in cold March was hardly an inspiring sight. Although the sheep-ranch grew and he enjoyed a certain degree of prosperity, Remington came to know that it was not the life for him, and he moved to Kansas City, Missouri – with Eva (who he called 'Missie') accompanying him as his wife.

Kansas City in the mid-1880s was the largest cattle market in the West – a busy, bustling city and no longer a frontier town. Remington wanted to benefit from the town's economic boom, and used the last of his inheritance to invest in a saloon. He passed much of his time in leisure activities and sports, especially boxing and riding, while always filling his sketchbooks with drawings and illustrations.

Remington spent two years in Kansas City, until his luck soured: the saloon moved locations and through some legal wrangling he lost his entire investment. The family finances grew desperate and Missie returned to New York while Frederic again travelled West to gather new material for another stab at becoming an illustrator for Eastern publishers.

Together again, he and Missie moved to Brooklyn, New York, where he began to make the rounds of publishers. He received only a lukewarm response and so headed West once more, probably on assignment from *Harper's*. This trip was the turning point for Frederic. He travelled to St Louis, and then through Colorado, New Mexico, Arizona, and even into Mexico, in search of the legendary Indian Geronimo. Although he never met Geronimo face to face, Frederic came away deeply impressed by what he'd seen. He said, "Let anyone who wonders why the troops do not catch Geronimo but travel through a part of Arizona and Sonora and then he will wonder

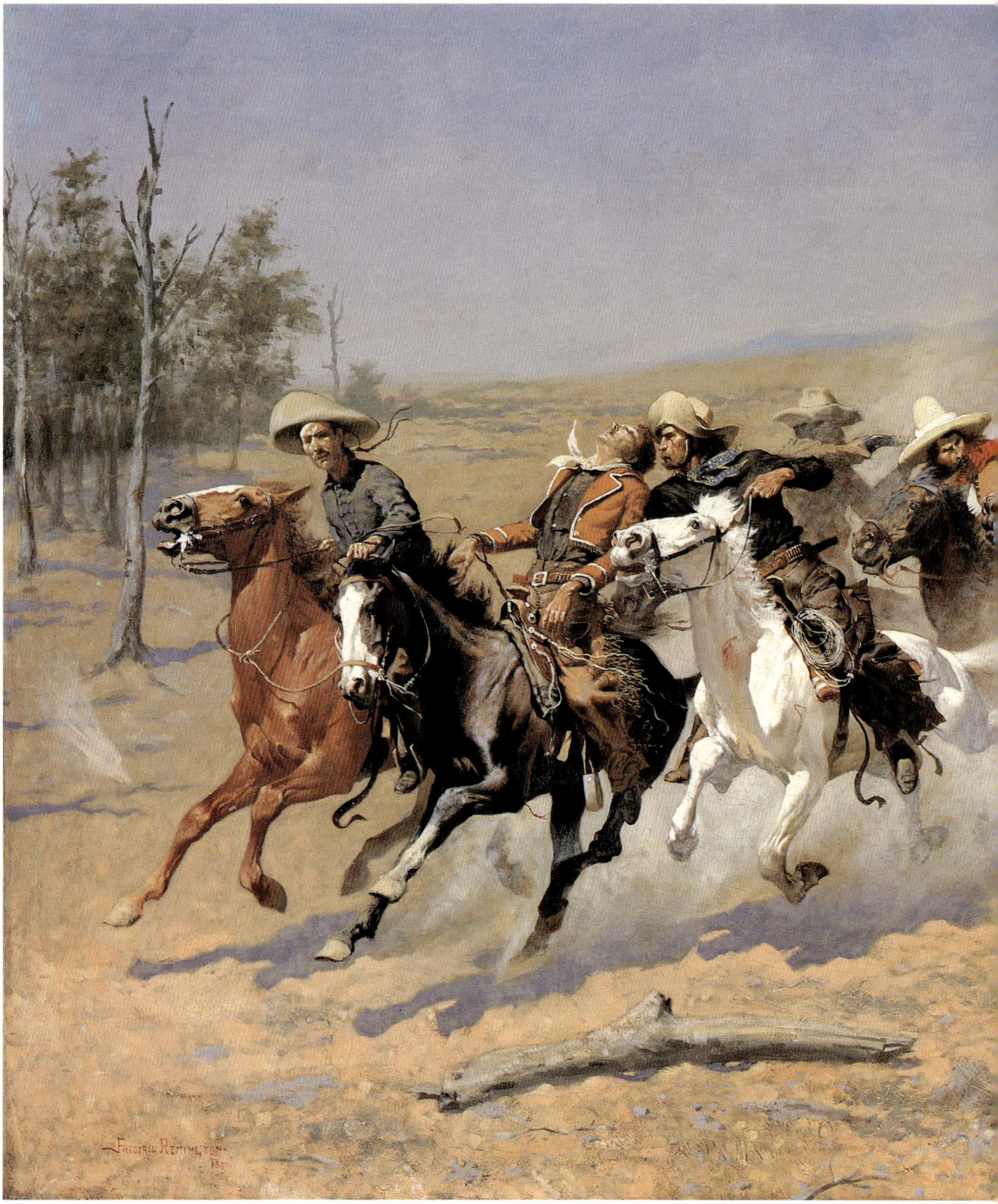
FREDERIC REMINGTON

A Dash for the Timber

Of all the dangers faced by white men in the West, the most fearsome was attack by Indians. Here, a group of cowboys race from an attack by an Apache war party to the small stand of timber, the preferred defensive position. Will they make it?

1889. Oil on canvas. Amon Carter Museum, Fort Worth.

that they even try. Let him see the desert wastes of sand devoid of even grass, bristling with cactus . . . let the sun pour down white hot upon the blistering sand about his feet and it will be plainer. Let him see a part of those jagged mountains . . ."

On this return trip, success finally caught up with him. His drawings and illustrations began to be published in magazines, including *Outing* where the jubilant editor, an old friend from Yale called Poultney Bigelow, purchased Frederic's entire portfolio. Said Bigelow, "Here was the real thing . . . Mexican ponies, cowboys, cactus, lariats and

---

The Bronco Buster (Large Version)
This dramatic image of the cowboy on a bucking horse was the subject of Remington's first and probably most popular bronze. After creating a smaller version (23¼" by 15⅝") in 1895, he created this one, about half again as large (32½" x 18"). Breaking horses for riding in this way was considered the most efficient, though risky, method in the Old West.
1909. Bronze. Amon Carter Museum, Fort Worth.

---

sombreros. No stage heroes these, no carefully pomaded hair and neatly tied cravats; these were the men of the real rodeo, parched in alkali dust, blinking out from barely opened eyelids under the furious rays of an Arizona sun."

At this point, Frederic worked in watercolours for exhibition, and pen and ink for illustration. Although he claimed that pen and ink was never natural for him, these early works are fresh and lively. They attracted the attention of President Theodore Roosevelt, who pressed Frederic into illustrating a series of articles he was writing about his early life ranching and hunting in the West. This collaboration began a lasting friendship between the two New Yorkers "cut from the same cloth," sharing the experience of youthful wanderlust in the West.

The magazines now wanted all the illustrations and drawings that he could supply, as people everywhere were fascinated by the images of the American West. By 1889, he had truly received the recognition he sought and had become one of the most famous American illustrators.

To fill the demand, he continued to travel West armed with his sketchbooks and camera, travelling through Colorado, New Mexico and Texas and throughout the Indian Territory. He rode with the Tenth Cavalry through the Apache lands of Arizona and came to admire the soldiers who had such hard duty. Along the way, he also wandered among the Pueblo and Navajo Indian tribes of New Mexico (who he found a little "tame" as subjects, owing to their more peaceable societies), and the Cheyenne, Kiowa, Wichita and Comanche of Oklahoma.

Frederic prided himself on his stamina and toughness against the harsh elements. But he also wrote home to Missie, "Here I am at last – leave in the morning by stage for Fort Sill . . . The mosquitoes like to have eaten me up – there is not one square inch on my body that is not bitten – and oh oh oh how hot it is here – I have sweat and sweat my clothes full . . . I am dirty and look like the devil and feel worse . . . Well all this is very discouraging but it's an artist's life. I have no idea how long this thing will take, for these Indians are scattered all over the earth but I 'touch and go.' I came to do the wild tribes and I do it."

His perseverance paid off. In the public's mind the name 'Frederic Remington' and the West became one. His lively and vigorous style based on first hand "I-was-there" knowledge made him the expert on the West for editors and writers. By the end of 1890 over four hundred of his pictures had appeared in magazines and he had illustrated several books, too, including Theodore Roosevelt's *Ranch Life and the Hunting-Trail* and a new edition of Longfellow's *Song of Hiawatha*. Perhaps more amazingly, he had accomplished this in just three years after becoming an artist as a full time occupation, especially when one considers his somewhat shaky start!

His paintings and illustrations offered a sympathetic portrayal of Indians, rather than depicting them as "savages," as was the more popular view. His renderings of trappers and soldiers and cowboys all have a gritty realism about them, not glamorous or idealized. The qualities of the hot, dusty landscape with the brightness of the sun are to be found throughout his work.

The Cheyenne
While working on this powerful bronze, Remington was on crutches, the result of a fall from his horse. In an invitation to a friend to visit, he wrote, "(Will) show you a mud of an Indian & pony which is burning the air – I think & hope he won't fall off as I did – he had a very teetery seat and I am nervous about even mud riders."
1901. Bronze. Amon Carter Museum, Fort Worth.

And central to much of his work is the horse. It was his talent for painting horses, both at rest and at full gallop, that brought him the greatest recognition. Aided by developments in photography, his horses in action are accurate as well as powerful images.

Along with his sketchbooks and photographs brought home from the West, Frederic collected a huge array of artifacts and paraphernalia to serve as artist's props when he worked at home. His studio was filled to overflowing, as was his attic. A visitor described the setting, "The trophies of his many visits and errands to the West hang all about the walls and litter the floors delightfully. Aces, clubs, saddles, spears, bows and arrows, shields, queer water-tight baskets, quaint rude rugs, chaparrajos, moccasins, head-dresses, miniature canoes, gorgeous examples of beadwork, lariats, and hundreds of sorts of curios from the desert and wilderness complete a collection that has been a mine of profit and a well-spring of pleasure to him."

In the mid-1890s Remington tried his hand at sculpture, or "mud" as he called it. His first piece was "The Bronco Buster", and when it was completed he took it to a foundry where it was reproduced in bronze. It was shortly before his thirty-fourth birthday that he copyrighted this first piece.

The public loved his new technique, and even today it is Remington's bronzes that are the favourites. For the artist himself, sculpture was about equal parts pleasure and hard work. "Great fun," he said. "Just see what can be done with it – isn't it wonderful. You can work for days, changing and rechanging as you like – the only limit is your time and patience."

As the nineteenth century came to a close, Remington continued to travel West, sometimes as often as three or four times in a year. But the West was changing from the wild frontier to something more settled and civilized, and Remington mourned its passing. He grumbled after one trip, "Shall never come West again. – It is all brick buildings – derby hats and blue overhauls – it spoils my early illusions –

The Smoke Signal
The Indians of the Plains used a highly sophisticated communication system based on codes relayed through smoke signals. By burning buffalo chips or grass, they could send detailed messages when out of sight of the recipient. Here, a group of Indians sends a message to far-away fellows, perhaps warning of impending danger or the location of a Buffalo herd.
1905. Oil on canvas. Amon Carter Museum, Fort Worth.

and they are my capital." While he did not keep this vow, it was clear that he had caught a magic moment in his work, one that would never again be returned to.

Remington's last show was in 1909, where his work was acclaimed and his reputation established. Only ten days afterwards, he was stricken with abdominal pains, and the day after Christmas 1909 he died. He was only forty-eight years old, but he left behind a legacy in paint and bronze that is greatly treasured to this day. Frederic Remington *is* the American West. Theodore Roosevelt said it best in his eulogy:

"The soldier, the cowboy and rancher, the India, the horse and cattle of the plains, will live in his pictures, I verily believe, for all time."

TOM AND TRAMPUS

"COME ON TRAMPUS. LET'S GO FOR A RIDE!"

"NO WAY!"

"TRAMPUS! TRAMPUS! OH WHY WON'T YOU LET ME CATCH YOU?"

"BECAUSE THE ONLY TIME YOU COME TO SEE ME IS WHEN YOU WANT A RIDE"

"WELL, I SUPPOSE I DO TAKE HIM FOR GRANTED. PERHAPS IF I MADE MORE OF A FUSS OF HIM..."

"THAT'S IT TRAMPUS YOU ENJOY YOURSELF. I'LL GROOM YOU NEXT"

"DELICIOUS!"

"NOW THAT I SPEND MORE TIME WITH YOU, TRAMPUS, I CAN CATCH YOU MORE OFTEN!"

"THAT'S BECAUSE FRIENDS NEED TO BE APPRECIATED"

The Zebroids of Sangare

BY DIANA WILSON

Grévy zebra. Note stripes, mane, ears.

The mean look is inherited from the father.

Just north of Nanyuki, on the edge of the Aberdare Mountains looking out to the snowcapped peaks of Mount Kenya, lies a magical place called Sangare, owned by Jane and Michael Prettejohn. Although it is a commercial ranch, producing top-class beef cattle and Angora goats, wild animals – such as elephant, buffalo, leopard, giant forest hog and antelope – abound and are allowed to co-exist side by side with the livestock.

It is here that the last remaining herd of zebroids in Africa have been bred. Zebroids are a cross between a zebra stallion and a mare; the resultant offspring is a striped hybrid mule, which like all mules is sterile.

Zebroid foals seem to adopt the background coloration of the mare, with the fine stripes of the stallion superimposed. They have all the hardiness, resistance to disease and tolerance to drought of their zebra father (as well as his irascible temper) but are larger in stature, like their mothers.

These fascinating creatures are difficult to break and train and are never very easy to

Dark brown mare with dun zebroid foal.

The patient look is inherited from the mother.

handle, as they are always inclined to be 'spooky'. Because of their straight shoulders and uncertain temperaments they are neither comfortable nor easy to ride, and they can buck like broncos in a rodeo! However, despite these disadvantages, their hardiness and sureness of foot – both up in the mountains and in dry, desert conditions – make them very useful as pack animals.

The first known zebroids were bred by Raymond Hook, who arrived in Kenya in 1908 and became well-known as a big-game hunter. He farmed for many years at Nanyuki, and in the 1930s he used the zebroids as pack-animals for safaris up Mount Kenya.

At Sangare the zebra stallion was a Grévy – a species who are bigger than their more common Burchell cousins, and who live in the semi-arid bush country of northern Kenya. Characteristically, the Grévy has much narrower stripes than other zebras and is easily identifiable by his crested mane and most unusual and delightful large, rounded ears.

The Grévy is now on the international list of

Zebroids used as packhorses on safari in the Aberdares.

Foal from palomino mare.

endangered species and has its own stud book, kept at Marwell Zoo in Hampshire. In association with other conservation-minded zoos throughout Europe and America, Marwell are in the process of producing a larger genetic pool for a breeding project. The Grévy stallions have to be caught as foals and brought up on a mare or with horses, and even then they will retain their basic wildness. Once a stallion is mature, he has to be kept just with his mares, as he would try to kill any other stallion or gelding with which he came in contact.

Sangare Ranch has a heard of country-bred mares, several of whom are palominos. From the Grévy stallion they have produced the most enchanting foals with pale golden coats overstamped with fine black stripes, and with large black-edged ears and beautiful 'mascara'-rimmed eyes.

Sadly, the stallion died in 1988, and so far they have not been able to find a replacement. There are now only five zebroids left in Kenya – four at Sangare and one in another part of the country.

Autumn Ride

Everywhere glows with the colours of autumn. Leaves carpet the ground. Birds disperse. The weather is changing and it is time for planting and sowing.

White mustard is being folded into the land as 'green manure'. Gulls follow the plough.

Some birds migrate. Others start to arrive.

Jay collects acorns

Hazel nuts

Fly agaric

Parasol

Shaggy ink cap

Fungi in the woods.

Horse chestnuts

The weasel is more bold.

Wasps are at their peak.

Common visitors.

Redwing

Brambling

Fieldfare

Berries in the hedgerow.

Blackberry

Rose hips

Hawthorn

Elderberry

Blackthorn (sloe)

Pheasants are being reared. Go quietly if you see a feeding hopper in the field or woods.

Heavy leaf carpet can obscure holes in the ground.

Tree branches may have fallen in the high winds.

Do not gallop down grassy rides when wet or soft, as it cuts them up.

43

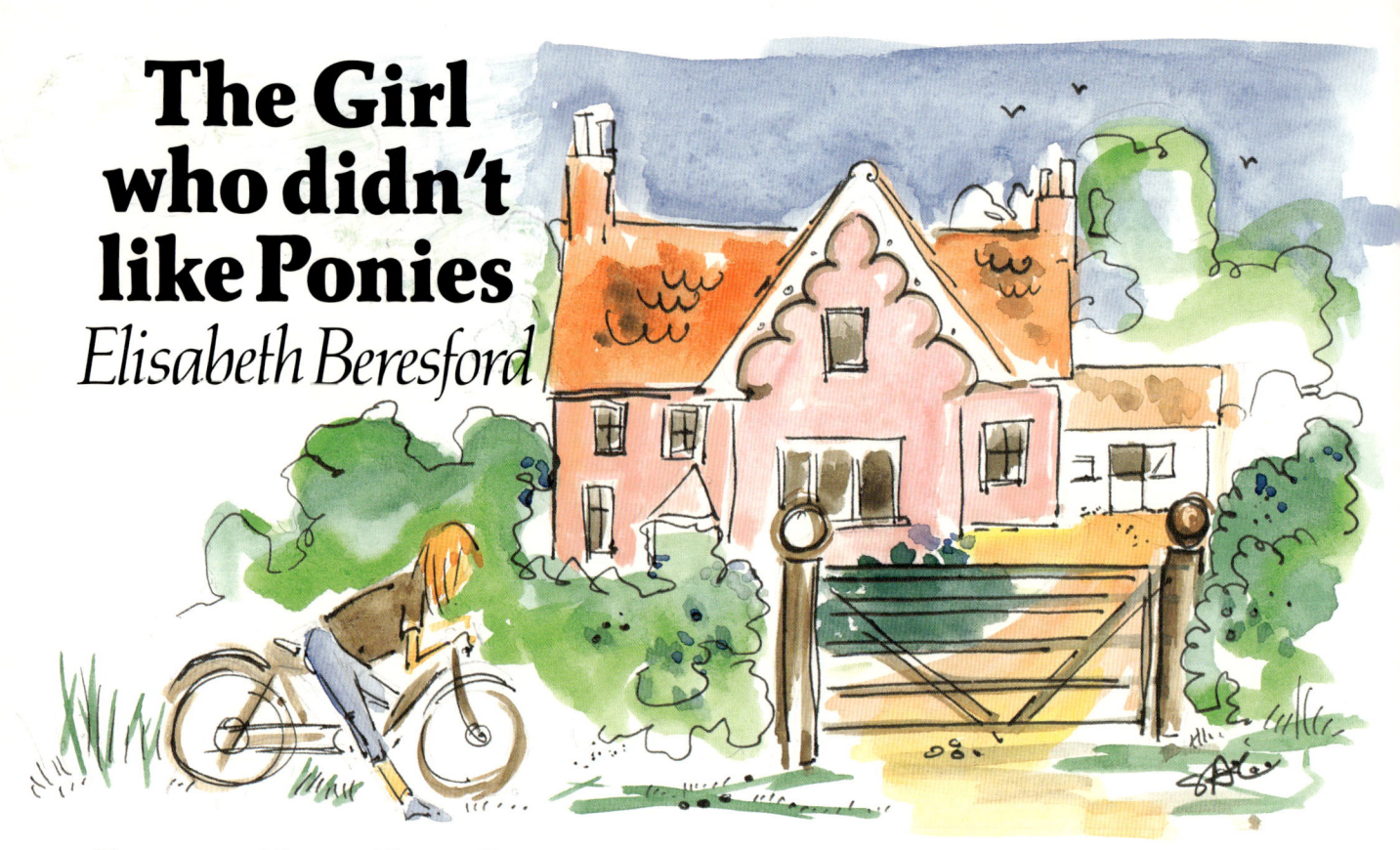

The Girl who didn't like Ponies
Elisabeth Beresford

Illustrated by Sally Bell

It was bad enough leaving Dalton Towers *and* starting a new school without Dads suddenly deciding that we should live in the country. The house was OK – a bit old and creaky – and, to begin with, Dads, who is quite tall, kept banging his head on the beams and doorways. There was a big garden and I had a look round it, because we'd never had a garden before. All my life we'd lived on the 15th floor of Dalton Towers and I missed the high-speed lift and watching the big jets coming in on their way to Heathrow Airport.

After living in a city I found the country quite dull. We moved in during the holidays, and we didn't know anyone. There were Mr and Mrs Bates who looked after things, but they didn't talk to me much so I was a bit low . . . until the day when Dads came back from his office with this big van following him up the drive.

"Hey, Bibi," he called out. "I've brought some friends back for tea."

This woman climbed down from the van. She had shiny curls and a jacket and breeches and boots. Two girls jumped down after her – and they were all curls and boots, too. The mother was called Mrs Bowen, the daughters were Bella and Emma – just the sort of names they *would* have. We walked round the garden, but nobody talked much until Bella asked:

"Would you like to meet Mr Manners?"

I just stared at her – I'm quite good at that – and she quickly continued:

"He's here, in the lorry . . ."

And she opened up the rear doors and let down a sort of platform thing, and the next minute she came out leading this animal.

"He's my very own pony," she said. "Mr Manners."

I'd never been so close to a big animal before. In fact even cats weren't allowed at the Towers, so I didn't know much about animals. But what I *did* know, right away, was that I didn't like ponies. This one had enormous teeth. He rolled his eyes, and he snorted at me.

"Isn't he beautiful?" said Bella. "With his lovely, lovely coat. Just feel how silky it is."

Not likely! I was looking at the pony's big, big *feet*. I didn't like him and he didn't like me: I could tell by the way he jerked his head away and looked at me sideways. I just wished that they'd all go away and leave me alone.

I thought things couldn't get worse, but they did.

The Bowens were all chattering away and it was "pony this" and something called "mounted games" and something else called "polocross" and what fun it all was, and somewhere in the background I heard Mrs Bowen say to Dads:

"Of *course* Bibi's shy. It's no wonder. We're all strangers to her. What she needs is a companion – her very own pony. We've got such a sweet little newcomer in the stables. We call him Archie because he comes from Archer's Farm."

"What a good idea," said Dads before I could get to him. "I'll buy him as a 'Welcome to our New Home' present. What do you say, Bibi: your very own pony?"

I didn't say anything, because I couldn't. I had already decided that I *didn't like* the boring old countryside. Now I *loathed* it. Mr Bates was grinning from ear to ear, because he'd been asked by Dads to clear our stable out. Dads went off in the car whistling. And I spent the next two days thinking about running away.

Then the van – sorry, *horse box* – arrived with all the Bowens in it – plus the famous Archie. It took both Bella and Emma to get him down the ramp. His legs were stiff as pokers, his ears were back, and his eyes were staring out of the back of his head. His coat was rough and his mane was a sort of stringy tangle.

"Isn't he *sweet*", cooed Bella, wrapping her arms around his neck and whispering in one of his laid-back ears. "Of course he's rather *shy*. He's not used to people yet. He hardly saw anybody on the farm and he's never been in a horsebox before . . ."

. . . She went rattling on and on, and Archie and I looked at each other sideways. It was a case of hate at first sight.

"Try him with an apple," said Mr Bates, handing me one.

Archie looked at it as if it was poisoned, and tossed his head and then stared straight in front of him. In a funny sort of way he reminded me of someone. Bella went chattering on to Mr Bates and I heard Dads say to Mrs Bowen:

". . . really do appreciate it. Bibi's never had much to do with animals of course – and, speaking of which, I gather that there was some sort of trouble near Archer's Farm the other night."

"It was some town boys tearing about on motor bikes. They didn't do much damage – just scared the animals. Which is bad enough, of course."

Then they saw that I was listening, and they changed the subject, back to Archie. They gave me lots of instructions and advice, but I knew that Mr Bates would be looking after him so I just nodded and went "mm mm".

Archie had gone very quiet. He was hanging his head and looking silly, and when Mr Bates offered him an apple he gobbled it up in one bite. Typical. The apple that *I* had offered obviously wasn't good enough for him.

"Well, we must be off. Come along girls," said Mrs Bowen. "Then, looking at me: "Once you and Archie get to know each other, Bibi, we'll be able to start work" (whatever that meant). "It'll be lovely for you."

She didn't sound too certain, and even Bella and Emma weren't quite as bouncy as usual. Dads was looking at me, and I managed to murmur "Thank you very much," etc, etc. I just wished that they wouldn't interfere. At that moment I would have given a year's pocket money to be back in Dalton Towers. It all made me feel quite sick. Then, to make it even worse, Archie pulled free from Mr Bates, turned round very fast and *butted* me. It was a really powerful shove and I went flying and landed on my knees, hands outstretched, with a terrific thud. Mr Bates had already fallen over backwards. Then Archie kicked out and sent a couple of buckets flying. It was Bella, of course, who managed to grab hold of him.

I was on my hands and knees trying to get up, Mr Bates was wheezing, Dads was apologising to everyone as if it had all been his fault and not the stupid pony's, and Bella was just looking at me as if I had just crawled out from one of the buckets. She must have let go of his mane, because he suddenly ducked his head down, and curled his lips. Then he *blew* at me.

At supper that night Dads was very quiet, and when Mrs Bates had cleared away he said in a very heavy sort of voice:

"I'm sorry, Bibi. It was a mistake moving here. I just thought that it would be nicer for you living in the country."

"It's all right," I – well – *growled*. My knees were still sore, and I'd been made to look an absolute idiot in front of the Perfect Bowens. And it was all the fault of that scruffy, obstinate, pig-headed, stupid pony.

Dads wasn't listening:

"I'll have to sell Archie. Mrs Bowen will arrange it, I'm sure".

It was just as if Archie had been a second-hand van or something. Still, it would be great to get rid of him. Just great.

"OK," I said, and shrugged.

I decided that I would go and tell Archie that he wouldn't be staying.

"Mind that you lock up properly when you come back in," Dads called. "I've got to go out for a couple of hours. The Bates' will be there if you want anything."

I knew that he was worrying about the motor-bike boys, so I promised to lock up, and after waving Dads off I went down to the stables. Mr Bates was there, leaning on the half-door and talking to Archie as if he were a person.

"You poor young pony. You're not going to have much of a time with Miss Sulky, I'm afraid. She's a townie through and through. It's not her fault, but you can see that she's scared to death of you. And you are of her, aren't you? And you're homesick into the bargain. Well, I expect they'll move you on. Have an apple, then, eh? Yes . . ."

I crept off into the dusk. Miss Sulky! I felt like being really cross, and crying, at the same time. And I never ever cry . . . well hardly ever. It was that beastly pony. It was all his fault. *Everything* was his fault: Dad's' sad face, and Bella Bowen giving me that look, and Mr Bates calling me Miss Sulky.

Then back in my bedroom just as I was going to clean my teeth I saw my face in the mirror. My mouth was right down at the corners. My hair was a real mess. And if my ears could have been laid back they would have been. It reminded me of something . . . or someone.

I didn't expect to get to sleep because I was so upset – but I must have dozed off, because one moment I was dreaming about dozens of ponies running in all directions, and the next I was wide awake with my heart pounding. In the distant there was a 'roar-roar-roar' and a lot of shouting: something I was used to in the city but not in the country.

I looked out of the window but there was no sign of Dads' car. The Bates' curtains were drawn, and I could hear the sound of their television.

I pulled on my jeans and a sweater and went down to have a look. There was a big silvery moon which made all the shadows very dark, and a bat flitted over my head. Then I saw them. The bike boys. There were three or four of them – it was difficult to see how many. They had broken the stable door open, and one of them was pulling and pulling. Immediately I knew what it was. They were trying to kidnap Archie. I should have thought "Good luck to them", but I didn't. I suddenly felt really angry. How dare they!

At that same instant there was a loud snorting noise from inside the stable, and the sound of clattering hooves. The bike boy fell backwards, just as I had done. And I knew exactly what Archie had been up to. He had butted the biker! More than that: his hooves were being put to good use. A bucket was flung into the air and after it came Archie, his feet flying, and his mane standing up on end.

The bikers were quite hefty but they scattered in all directions. Archie was behaving like a prize-winning bucking bronco. His feet and teeth were everywhere, and those bikers just couldn't get away fast enough. They weren't shouting and jeering now. They were really scared. In next to no time they were off down the lane and leaping on to their bikes.

I looked around for Archie. One of the bike boys had slammed the main gate, and I could see Archie gathering himself as though he were going to have a shot at jumping it. Somehow I managed to get to him, and to throw my arms around his obstinate, stupid neck. He was trembling and gasping and snorting. And so was I. We were really both in a state!

"You stupid pony", I panted. And he went "gasp gasp gasp" in my ear, nearly deafening me. So I did the same thing back to him and gave him a hug and slowly we both stopped trembling. Then he nudged at my pocket, hoping for a titbit, gave himself a little shake, trotted over to the gate, and stood looking at me.

I guessed what he was trying to tell me.

"You want to go home to Archer's Farm," I said. "It's like me and Dalton Towers. Only we're stuck here. And it really isn't *so* bad, is it? Well, it needn't be . . ."

Archie swung his head from side to side, and looked at me again. And there and then I knew exactly who he reminded me of. It was me! Or *I* made me think of *him*. It doesn't matter.

"Let's go and find an apple and have a bit of a chat," I said. I put my arm around his neck and rested my head on his mane as we ambled into the yard, just as Mr Bates appeared.

"My goodness. It's you two. Mrs Bates said that she thought she could near noises . . . But what have you been up to? It's way past your bedtime."

"Just been for a little walk," I replied.

The nicest presents are not necessarily the most expensive, and the ones that you make yourself will be particularly appreciated. Here are three presents which you can give to your friends from you and your pony. They will cost very little but will mean a lot!

Personal Pony Presents

Friendship Bracelet

You will need:

Some long strands of hair from a pony's tail.
Five skeins of embroidery thread. One of these should be exactly the same colour as the tail hair.
A safety pin.

How to make the bracelet:

1. Take the embroidery thread that is the same colour as the tail hair.
2. Cut a piece of the same length as the tail hair. Separate the strands of thread and put half of them aside.
3. Take the tail hair and add enough strands of thread so that it returns to its original thickness. You have to do this because horse hair on its own is too wiry and slippery to knot easily and it therefore causes the knot to be uneven.
4. Knot the hair and the thread tightly at the top to secure them.
5. Repeat, so that you have two identical strands.
6. Take two pieces of embroidery thread in each of the other colours and cut them to the same length as above.
7. Bunch the embroidery threads and horsehair threads and knot them together about 3cms (1⅛") from the top.
8. Push the point of the safety pin through the knot and pin the bunch of threads to something like the tablecloth to keep it secure while you work.
9. Flatten the bunch and arrange the threads so that the two colours are side by side. You are now ready to begin plaiting!
10. Take the left-hand thread (thread 1) and loop it across the thread to its right (thread 2). Tuck it under and through (*see illustration*) and then tighten the knot by pulling thread 1 upwards and thread 2 downwards.
11. Repeat this process, and then move to the next thread on the right (thread 3). Make another two knots before moving on to thread 4, and so on.
12. When you get to the end of the row a different thread will have become number 1, and you carry on until the bracelet is long enough to fit around a wrist.
13. To finish so that the end of the bracelet is neatly squared off, make four knots on thread 2, three knots on thread 3, two on thread 4, and one on thread 5. (In fact, the number of knots that you make on that first thread is up to you. You merely make fewer and fewer knots until you reach the end.) If you like, you can then plait the threads for a few centimetres so that it will fit around wrists bigger than your own.
14. Finally, knot the bracelet and fray any ends that protrude beyond the knot.

Note: Do not use the horsehair as threads 1 or 2, and make sure to keep the plaiting tight and even throughout.

Personal Pony Presents

Show-off Shoes

Next time the farrier comes to shoe your pony, ask him to remove the nails from the old shoes. You can turn them into good-luck gifts for your friends by spraying them with gold or silver paint and threading a pretty ribbon through the nail-holes. Then tie the ribbon into a double-knotted bow for hanging on a wall or door.

Pony Portrait

How about making a portrait of your pony by using hair from his moulting winter coat? If it's good enough, it might be accepted by a museum of modern art!

You will need:

A small paintbrush
Strong glue, such as Copydex or Elmer's, or wallpaper paste
A square of strong white paper or cardboard
A black felt or fibre-tip pen

How to make your portrait:

1. Draw an outline of your pony's shape on to the card, including any special markings.
2. Go and groom your pony and collect a pile of his hair from the brushes as you clean them.
   Note: If your pony has a white blaze or socks, or patches of different colours, be sure to collect enough of that hair, too.
3. Having made your pony feel nice and clean and helped him to get rid of his itchy winter coat you can now return to your drawing.
4. Dip the paintbrush in the sticky stuff and carefully spread it over the outline of socks and/or other markings.
5. Take the hair that matches the markings and press it firmly over the glue. You will need to apply it really thickly.
6. Fill in the rest of the colours, as above.
7. Shake off the surplus hair.
8. Finish off by sticking on some mane and tail hair, trimmed to size.
9. Use the felt-tip to draw in the hooves, eyes and nostrils.
10. If you prefer a less shaggy portrait, you can 'clip' the hair with a small pair of scissors.
11. You may decide that the portrait would look better with a background. If so, you can try using leaves, wool, hay, feed – or even bits of coloured paper!

King Harry's Saddle

The Battle of Agincourt, fought on 25th October, 1415 between the armies of King Henry V of England and Charles VI of France, was one of the greatest victories in military history. Thanks to the superiority of the English cavalry and the deadly skills of the longbowmen of South Wales, a French army of around 30,000 men was overwhelmed by a force of 6,000 British.

The battle began at 11 o'clock in the morning. By 2 o'clock in the afternoon – just three hours later – some 7,000 Frenchmen lay dead and 1,500 had been taken prisoner. The British losses amounted to no more than 500.

The story of Agincourt is vividly told in one of Shakespeare's greatest plays, *Henry V*. Reminders of the men who took part in the battle can still be seen today in brasses and effigies at churches throughout England – among them those of Thomas, Lord Camoys, at Trotton in West Sussex and Sir William Phelip (later Lord Bardolph) at St Mary's, Dennington, Suffolk. Many manuscripts

When Henry set sail with his army from Southampton on the 14th August 1415 he took 21,000 horses, of which 330 were for use of his personal retinue. Many horses and men died at the siege of Harfleur, which took place five weeks before Agincourt, and on the way inland. Among the King's horses killed in the battle were Lyard [black] Strickland, Bayard [bay] Chaucer, Morell [dark brown] Kene, Sorell [sorrel, = reddish brown] Tavistock and Grey Cornwell; all were probably named after knights who rode them in the battle.

Two scenes from the recent film of Henry V. (Left) Kenneth Branagh chose not to wear helmet or full armour; otherwise the battle was realistic. (Below). King Harry sits back in the saddle at the siege of Harfleur! (Right) The ruins of Kenilworth castle (near Pony Club HQ). Henry inherited the castle from his grandfather, John of Gaunt.

and 'rolls' (parchments) concerned with the battle have survived – some of them listing the names of the knights, squires and ordinary soldiers who took part. But by far the most personal, interesting and (for anyone who has an imagination) stirring reminder of Henry V and Agincourt is the King's war saddle, preserved at Westminster Abbey for over 570 years: the oldest known saddle in England.

Henry died in 1422, aged only 34, at Vincennes near Paris. His body was brought back to England and borne in solemn procession through crowds of his mourning subjects who lined the roads all the way form the coast of Kent to the Abbey in London. Here a chantry had been prepared to house his tomb, and until this century, his saddle, helmet and shield hung above the tomb.

Though in his play, Shakespeare *invented* some of the story, his portrayal of Henry as a brave, noble warrior and a much-loved king was based on eye-witness accounts written during the King's lifetime. So we know for sure that on the night before the battle he visited all the British camps, putting heart into his soldiers with encouraging words, and occasionally kneeling to pray with them. We know that on the day of the battle he rode a small grey horse and had a white charger in reserve; and that he wore around his helmet a crown richly encrusted with precious stones. And we know that during the battle he dismounted and fought on foot, shoulder to shoulder with his men-at-arms and archers.

The Saddle

Its measurements are 26½ inches long, 21½ inches wide, 15½ inches high in front, 13 inches high at the back.

The *tree* consists of two hardwood (probably oak) boards, or 'side-bars', set at an angle to each other. They were designed to keep the weight of the rider (particularly when wearing armour) off the horse's spine.

The side-bars were riveted to the wooden *bow* (pronounced as in 'bow-wow') in front and to the *cantle* behind. On the front of each of the side-boards are two iron staples with pierced heads, to which the breast-piece was probably attached. At the cantle end, on each side, are single staples, which probably secured the crupper. The high bow protected the rider from lance thrusts and from arrows. The cantle was curved inward to give him support, and to prevent him from being unhorsed.

Connecting the bow and cantle is the seat, made of canvas stuffed with straw (or hay, according to some descriptions). The seat is raised 5 inches above the tree, allowing space for a padded numnah or folded woollen cloth.

Stapled to the tree on either side are large, rectangular, faceted buckles, which secured the stirrup-leathers. Under the nearside buckle are the remains of two leather straps (with zig-zag pattern) to which the double girths were attached.

Needs

How well do you know just what your pony needs to keep him happy and safe? Here is a game to test you. All you have to do is to choose the correct answer.

6 Your pony is quidding. You need to:
   (a) feed him bran mashes only?
   (b) call the horse dentist or vet to attend to his teeth?
   (c) wash his mouth out with salty water?

7 Your fit, stabled pony has returned from an event and tomorrow he will have a 'day off'. What will his supper be:
   (a) carrots because he has been so good?
   (b) just hay?
   (c) a bran mash?
   (d) oats and sugar-beet to replace energy?

8 When you visit your pony one evening, he is uncomfortable, looking at his belly and sometimes kicking it. He clearly needs the vet and when you telephone, it can help if you have an idea what the trouble is. Has he:
   (a) lice?
   (b) colic?
   (c) windgall?
   (d) strangles?

9 You have borrowed a pony for the holidays. He is looking poor and has been kept on sour pasture with many other ponies. He needs:
   (a) to go straight on to a high protein diet?
   (b) peace and quiet in a field on his own?
   (c) to be wormed immediately, then kept on a regular worming routine?
   (d) a good bath?

10 Your pony has been working hard during the winter and is starting to lose condition. You decide that he needs to be clipped. He lives outside, but has a good shelter. Which clip is best for him:
   (a) blanket clip?
   (b) hunter clip?
   (c) full clip?
   (d) belly and gullet clip?

Answers on page 63.

Spooky Tales

Horses have long been credited with the ability to see ghosts, as well as with other strange spiritual powers. Until quite recently country people believed that these powers made horses open to the influence of evil spirits. So to protect working horses from the 'Evil Eye', farmers used to hang brasses and bells from the harness. The brasses were made in traditional anti-evil-spirit shapes such as the sun or a crescent moon.

Unless nursing a sick horse, people are unlikely to visit their stables during the 'haunting hours' of night – so there have been very few sightings of riderless ghost horses, either out of doors or in stables. The only recorded sighting is in a sunken lane leading to Welwyn village in Hertfordshire. Why the horses swirl in panic like great wafts of smoke, and why they appear headless, no-one really knows. One theory is that their appearance may be linked to a bloody battle which took place near by in AD1002, when the local Saxons rose up against the Danes.

Most phantom horses are seen, ridden by their master, carrying out very gruesome or mournful tasks . . . doomed to repeat over and over again something which once really took place. For example, at night-time on many battle sites people living locally hear the pounding of hooves, the call of bugles, the shouts of soldiers, and the neighing of horses. This often happens near Kineton in Warwickshire on the anniversary of the Battle of Edgehill, which took place on 23 October 1642 during the Civil War.

Another haunting Civil War story is that of Alice Birch and Charles Clifford, two young lovers who were fleeing from the Roundheads. They fled from the house in Goodrich near Ross-on-Wye in Herefordshire, where they had been hiding, and were drowned while trying to cross the River Wye. On some nights, it is said, the ghost of their gallant horse can be seen in its hopeless attempt to reach the bank.

Quite a few ghosts haunt the places where they have committed some foul deed. Many years ago the wild young Lord Dacre murdered a gamekeeper in the woodlands of Herstmonceux Castle in Sussex. His spirit, on horseback, haunts the grounds, but whereas ghostly horses are generally black or white, people who have witnessed the Dacre apparition all agree that the horse is a beautiful rich chestnut. The ghost wears a rust-coloured riding cloak and has large brass spurs on his high boots.

Many spirits linger where something sad has happened to them, and some stay because they can't bear to leave. This must be the case with the famous jockey Fred Archer, who in his time was as famous as Lester Piggott. He won the Derby four times, and died in 1886 when he was only twenty-nine years old.

A jockey riding a strange white horse has been seen many times on Newmarket Heath. It began to appear soon after Archer died, and was seen by many people who knew him. This ghost has been blamed for dozens of unexplained mishaps on the Newmarket course, especially when horses have swerved violently for no apparent reason. On race days, many jockeys and punters alike have seen a strange white form hovering alongside the galloping horses.

People see ghosts when they least expect to, and if many different people see the same ghost the experts take the story seriously, and they collect and record all the details. Over the years there have been hundreds of recorded sightings involving horses and carriages. One strange fact is common to all the sightings: the phantom horses are generally headless!

One of the saddest, and most frightening stories, is associated with Queen Anne Boleyn, mother of Queen Elizabeth I, who was beheaded at the Tower of London on 19 May 1536. On the anniversary of her death, her ghost, with her head in her lap, has been seen in a phantom coach pulled by headless horses and driven by a headless coachman in the vicinity of her birthplace in Kent.

There is no doubt that all horses are extremely sensitive to atmosphere and that they have an amazing 'sixth sense'. (The five senses are sight, hearing, smell, taste and touch). The sixth sense shows itself in many different ways.

A horse has the ability to sense danger before it happens, though to his rider everything appears to be normal. Scientists might say that the reason could be reaction to air pressure, or an acute sense of smell – but those who know about horses put it down to the sixth sense. How otherwise could a horse tell, for example, that a bridge which looks perfectly sound is about to collapse, or (when at a gallop) that there is a bog 20 metres ahead?

In the Middle Ages people thought that their horses could be stolen by witches in the night and 'hag-ridden' (hag is another name for witch) to meetings, or covens. If after dawn a horse was found in its stable sweating and exhausted it was reckoned that it had been hag-ridden during the night.

Herefordshire folk had an unusual way of protecting their horses from hags. On May Day they would prop birch tree branches, decorated with red and white ribbons, against their stable doors. They thought that not only would this prevent the horses from being hag-ridden but it would also stop fairies from tying knots in their manes.

The livelihood and survival of gypsies (that is the true Romany gypsies) has throughout the centuries depended on their horses. Many superstitions that we still observe today have their origins in gypsy legends. Probably the most popular one is that it is lucky to hang a horseshoe on your door. This comes from a German gypsy story, as follows:

There were once four demons called Unhappiness, Badluck, Badhealth, and Death. One day a young gypsy chief was attacked by Badluck. The chief galloped away as fast as he could, but on the way his horse cast one of his shoes. Fortunately for him, the shoe flew through the air, struck Badluck, and killed him. The gypsy dismounted and picked up the shoe. When he reached home he propped the shoe up outside the door of his caravan.

The other three demons, hearing about Badluck's death, came storming into the gypsy camp, determined to kill the young chief. But when they reached his caravan they were all suddenly halted in their tracks by a mysterious force. Terrified, they all galloped off – having realised that the chief's horse still had three more shoes to cast!

So this is why a horseshoe at your door will save you from unhappiness, bad luck, bad health and death.

Winter Ride

Deciduous trees have now lost their leaves. Animals hibernate. Birds flock together. Rivers swell. Snow has fallen.

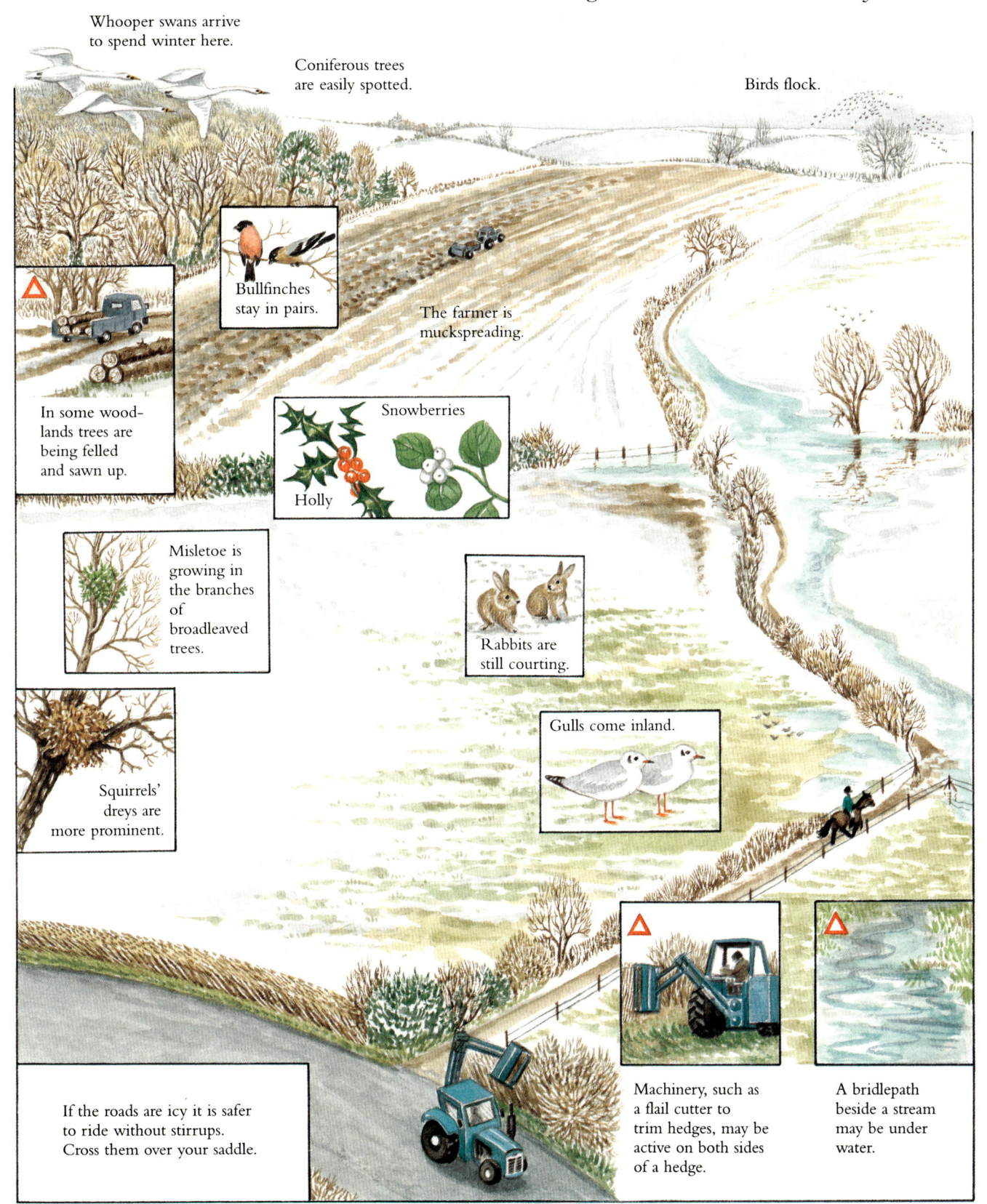

Whooper swans arrive to spend winter here.

Coniferous trees are easily spotted.

Birds flock.

Bullfinches stay in pairs.

The farmer is muckspreading.

In some woodlands trees are being felled and sawn up.

Snowberries

Holly

Misletoe is growing in the branches of broadleaved trees.

Rabbits are still courting.

Squirrels' dreys are more prominent.

Gulls come inland.

If the roads are icy it is safer to ride without stirrups. Cross them over your saddle.

Machinery, such as a flail cutter to trim hedges, may be active on both sides of a hedge.

A bridlepath beside a stream may be under water.

Faithful Friends

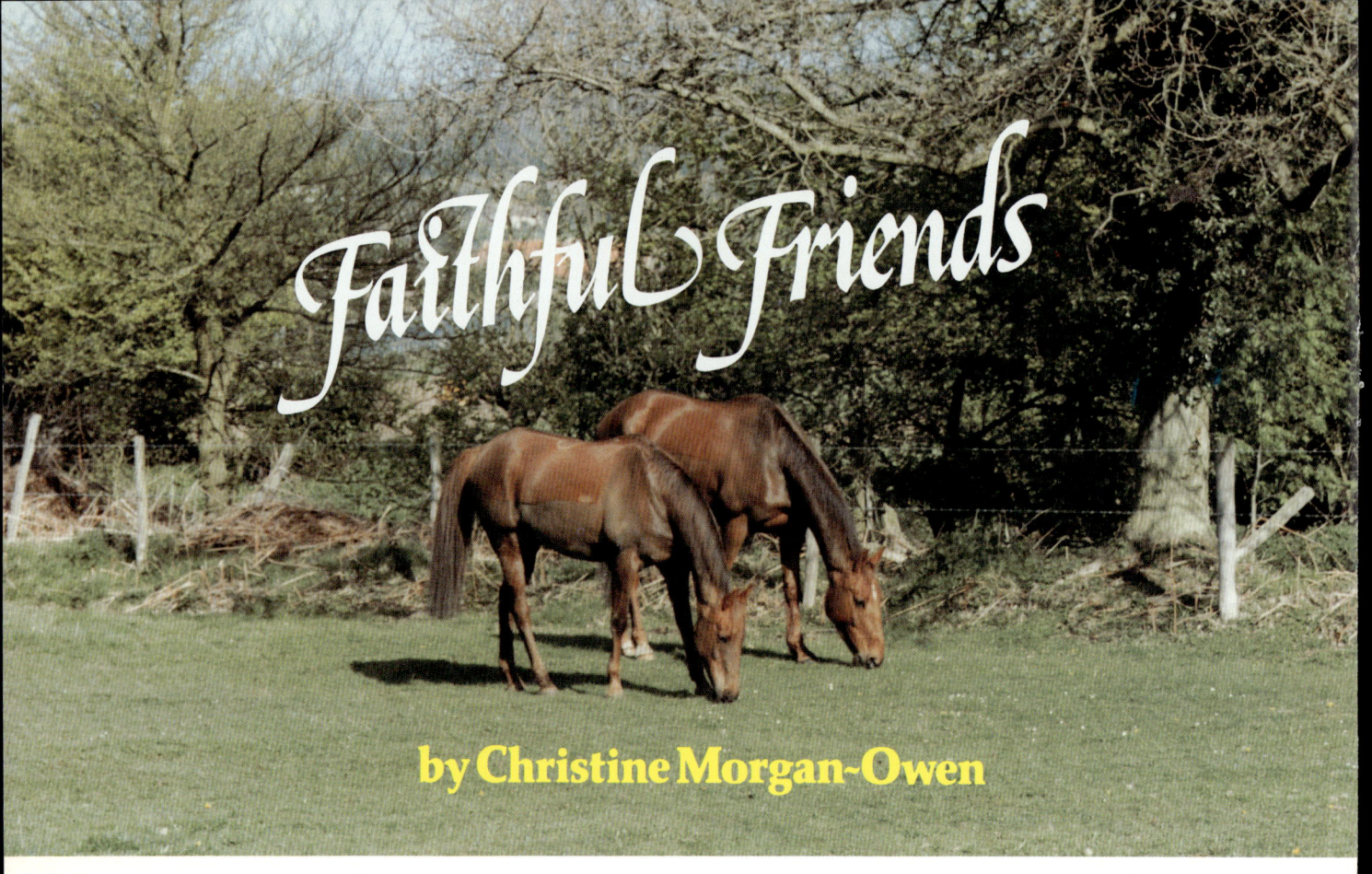

by Christine Morgan-Owen

Horses are basically nervous and sensitive animals who in the distant past roamed wild and free in large herds. Although over the centuries most of them have been tamed, domesticated, and dominated by man, their basic instincts – which govern the way they think and act – are exactly the same as those that they needed for survival in the wild. Nowadays horses are often kept in what, for them, is a completely unnatural environment – even sometimes in solitary confinement in stables, away from the company of their own kind. In order to help them to live happily and trustingly in the surroundings that we provide for them we must therefore learn to understand their true instincts.

Once a human has been totally accepted by a horse, an unspoken understanding exists between them. It is based not only on trust, but also on the horse's respect for the human. If any of these ingredients is missing, or if you were to act in a hasty or thoughtless way, the relationship and the trust that has been built up will be destroyed, perhaps for ever. There is nothing more thrilling to an owner than when her horse greets her with a shrill whinny of recognition – even after a prolonged separation. This may be followed by an obvious expression of pleasure in the re-union, the horse nuzzling around and demonstrating his delight at being re-united with his friend. Once a horse has learned to trust his human friend he will respond to quite unusual demands with surprising calmness and confidence. There have been many instances in history of the faithfulness of a horse in remaining by the side of his injured master.

The herd instinct is very noticeable when a group of horses is turned out together in a field. They will quite quickly work out amongst themselves a very definite 'pecking order' (who is dominant and who gives way to whom). This order applies to all those in the group, from the leader to the lowest member of the herd. Once this order is established, peace will normally reign in the field, because the more timid animals will keep out of the way of their superiors. When a new horse is introduced into the field the whole herd will often 'gang up' on the unfortunate intruder and try to drive him away.

If you study a group of horses living out at grass together you will usually find that the same two horses will graze close to each other and share the task of swishing away flies, nose to tail, or 'grooming' each other's necks. Such friends often go in for 'horse play' which if it is aimed at humans is no fun at all, since there is much nipping and squealing – and often rearing and bucking as well!

Horses *need* friends, and when they are not living naturally with their own kind they have to make do with whatever friends their human masters can provide. Two horses stabled in the same yard, or turned out together, can become

Harry the Horse peers at his friends the Marans cockerels.

extremely attached to each other. From the owner's point of view the disadvantage of this state of affairs is that sometimes when one horse is taken away – perhaps to go to a show or out for a ride – the partner will become quite frantic. Or often, when the two friends are taken together to a show where there are other, strange, horses about, their desire to remain together over-rules all their training and concentration on the job in hand. They may well call ceaselessly to each other, disturbing all around them and not giving the performance that their riders have come to expect.

If two horse friends have to be parted or sold to separate homes, much distress may result for both of them. They may well pine and refuse to eat properly for a considerable time, until they form new friendships. In fact, some pairs are so close to each other that it has been known for one horse to react to its partner's death or injury with out-of-the-ordinary behaviour – even though they are many miles apart. Whenever two friends are reunited, there is no mistaking their overwhelming joy, expressed in noisy greeting.

Horses can suffer acutely from loneliness, boredom, and often anxiety, if denied the company of their own kind. This is particularly likely to happen if they live most of their lives in a stable. It is hardly surprising if some of them develop strange habits which then become 'stable vices', such as weaving, box-walking, or crib-biting. To relieve their horses' boredom, some owners will give them a toy to play with, such as a car-tyre or a rubber ball suspended from the ceiling. But the best solution may well be a companion – even of a different species – who will bring comfort to the lonely sufferer.

A famous racehorse called Remittance Man, once a constant 'box-walker', now shares his quarters with a sheep called Nobby, who accompanies him to races and who has a calming effect on his highly-strung friend. Other horses have found companionship with a goat or a stable cat. Some have even allowed a trusted hen to sit upon their back. One of my foals had a goat as companion, and the two were the best of friends until the foal decided that it was fun to bite and pull the goat's ears, causing quite serious injury. Eventually they had to be parted, to live in adjoining paddocks.

A donkey can make a satisfactory companion for a lonely horse at grass and can have a calming effect, as donkeys are not so fidgety or liable to gallop about. They do, however, have one disadvantage: they tend to suffer from lung-worm, a nasty parasite which can spread to the horses sharing the donkey's pasture. Owners keeping donkeys and horses together must follow a routine of dosing them all for lung-worm (as well as guarding against the more common equine parasites.)

Most horses tolerate dogs fairly well, and once they get used to them running around are unlikely to kick out – unless molested by a dog that they do not recognise. However, meeting a motionless, crouching dog (e.g. a sheep dog) while out riding is quite another matter. It will make a horse extremely wary – a hark-back, no

Ebony (pony) and Agussi (cat) are obviously very good friends.

Making for the gate in the usual pecking order: Wally chases Humpy. Humpy chases Zephy.

doubt, to the days when wild cats or wolves would leap upon a horse's back to bring it down and kill it. Once the dog moves and the horse realises that it is a mere dog, the fear is usually removed.

Occasionally a horse will choose a particular dog as its friend. My springer spaniel, Honey, became firm friends with Bronwen, my Welsh cob. When out hacking, Bronwen kept a careful watch on Honey wherever she went, and became very anxious whenever Honey disappeared from sight. Once, when Honey was threatened by another dog, Bronwen's behaviour became decidedly unruly. She bucked and kicked and tried to dive to the rescue. A horse may attack a loose dog threatening the group in its field – by galloping at it and trying to trample it underfoot. So if your dog accompanies you into a field full of strange horses, be careful!

Racehorse trainers know that their horses will be at their best if they are contented and happy in their home, and if they feel secure in the friendship of the human who looks after them. When choosing a stable-lad to look after a particular horse they will try to ensure that they are suitable for each other in temperament. The lad, or lass, must command that horse's special needs and habits. Once trust and friendship are established, the horse will follow wherever his lad leads him, without fear or anxiety.

Some people encourage their horses to learn tricks, such as snatching food from a pocket or from under a hat: or even pawing the ground or standing on their hind legs. Such tricks can quickly get out of hand, and are definitely NOT recommended.

A final word of warning: when several horses are loose in a field, do not make the mistake of feeding titbits to your special pal. In fact, go easy on the feeding of tit-bits at any time, except perhaps for the occasional reward; it is not necessary once friendship has been established. Loose horses (yes, even your friend) can cause a great deal of trouble in their jealousy of one another, and you could end up in the middle of a kicking match.

The author in pre-crash-hat days on her mare The Red Queen, followed by Samba.

ABOVE and BEYOND
THE ENCYCLOPEDIA OF AVIATION and SPACE SCIENCES

VOLUME 12
SPACEFLIGHT PRINCIPLES – TRACK

ABOVE and BEYOND

THE ENCYCLOPEDIA OF AVIATION and SPACE SCIENCES

NEW HORIZONS PUBLISHERS, INC.
CHICAGO

COVER PHOTO:
The British/French supersonic transport, the Concorde, which will carry about 130 passengers at Mach 2.2.
British Aircraft Corp.

First Edition
©1968, New Horizons Publishers, Inc.
Library of Congress Catalog Card Number 68–14013
Published simultaneously in Canada
Printed in the United States of America

Printed by Kingsport Press, Inc., Kingsport, Tennessee
Typesetting by American Typesetting Company, Chicago
Color separations and preparatory by Schawk Graphics, Inc.
Litho Color Separators, Chicago

Spaceflight principles

Spaceflight involves ascent from and descent to the surface of a celestial body (a planet or moon), and transfer from one orbit to another (space navigation). To successfully accomplish a spaceflight mission, three basic requirements must be met: (a) the velocity changes (maneuvers) and flight times or mission durations involved must be known; (b) the propulsive energy to match the mission's energy requirements must be available; and (c) the technology for building a mission-worthy spacecraft must be available. The latter includes structural, propulsion, and guidance systems, and also payload.

dards, however, they are high and the distances are large. Therefore, it is most fortunate that space is an almost perfect vacuum. Otherwise, spacecraft could not possibly attain the high velocities required to reach other planets without intolerably long flight times. Even if long flight times were acceptable—and if space contained a sufficient density of oxygen for the operation of airbreathing engines—enormous quantities of fuel and the need for continuous propulsion for long periods would far outweigh the savings in oxidized weight which the spacecraft must carry.

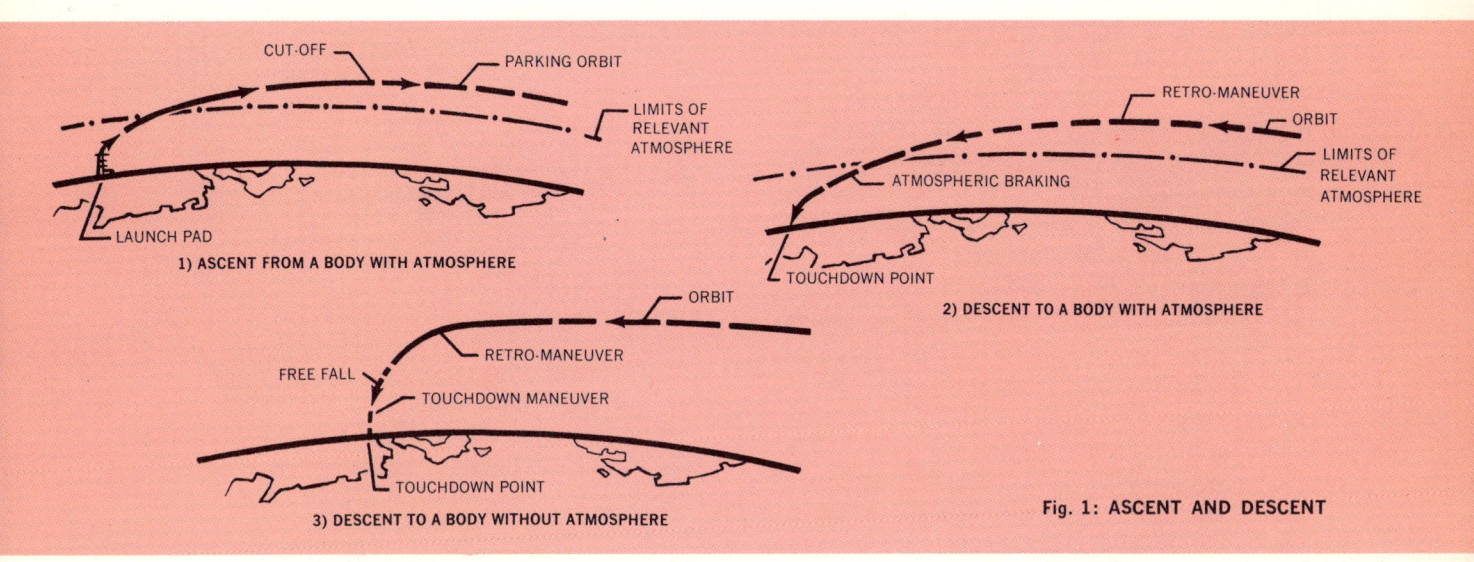

Fig. 1: ASCENT AND DESCENT

Case 1) shows the horizontal tilt of a powered ascent orbit. The rate of trajectory deflection is governed by the height of the atmosphere to assure position of the parking orbit in a region of near vacuum. Ascent from a body without atmosphere is not subject to this constraint so that the parking orbit can be established very close to the surface at a corresponding reduction in gravitational losses. Case 2) shows descent accomplished primarily by atmospheric braking, preceded by only a small retro-maneuver for deorbiting and atmospheric entry. In descending to an airless body, Case 3), a considerably larger retro-maneuver is required to compensate for the lack of atmospheric braking. This is followed by free fall with a subsequent touchdown retro-maneuver to reduce free fall speed to a low enough value for the spacecraft structure to absorb the remaining touchdown shock.

Energy Requirements

Earth is one of the smaller planets with a thin, but not too tenuous, atmosphere. All planets (*see*) and most moons (*see*) revolve in the same direction about the sun (*see*). Planet orbits and the orbits of the more important moons are more or less nearly circular. The orbits of most planets lie very nearly in the same plane as the Earth's orbit (*ecliptic*).

Because of these facts, the energy requirements for spaceflight in general and for interplanetary flight in particular are about the lowest possible under the given gravitational conditions. By terrestrial stan-

Ascent and Descent (*Fig. 1*)

Large rocket-powered vehicles are accelerated gradually. To ascend vertically from a surface, their thrust must be larger than their weight.

During ascent, *losses* occur. The term *loss* defines that portion of available propulsive energy which must be used to overcome adverse forces, primarily drag (*see*) and gravity (*see*), rather than that portion used to accelerate the vehicle. Energy loss due to gravitational pull is the greater of the two adverse forces. To minimize drag losses, the vehicle accelerates slowly in the lower, denser atmosphere. Then it tilts from a vertical toward horizontal flight direc-

Spaceflight principles

tion to minimize energy losses due to gravity.

Ascending from the Earth into a circular orbit at 100 nautical miles (n. mi.) altitude (circular velocity about 25,600 ft/sec) involves a combined drag and gravity loss of some 3,400 ft/sec. The *ideal velocity* required is therefore about 29,000 ft/sec. This figure applies to launchings in northern or southern directions. When launching from Cape Kennedy due east, about 1,200 ft/sec (the circumferential velocity of the Earth at that point due to the Earth's rotation) can be deducted.

Space Navigation

When a space mission begins at the Earth's surface, the first step is ascent into a low-altitude (100-200 n. mi.) Earth orbit where the vehicle "parks" until it reaches the correct position for departure toward its destination. Hence the term *parking orbit*.

Subsequent navigation in space is governed by several rules, some of which are discussed here. For better understanding, a knowledge of orbits and trajectories (*see*) would be helpful.

Spaceflight Maneuvers

In a gravitational field, a change in orbital energy is best accomplished by a *tangential maneuver* (thrust direction parallel to velocity direction) at the point of highest orbital velocity (*periapsis*). It is usually more economical in terms of propellant consumption to combine maneuvers rather than carry them out separately. For example, a change in orbital velocity, such as a change in flight direction, usually should be done in one maneuver.

When transferring from the gravitational field of the Earth to that of another planet, a two-step process requires more propellants (*see*) than one maneuver. The two-step process would involve escape from the Earth's field at parabolic velocity v_p and, once in separate orbit around the sun, a second maneuver for transfer to the target planet. In the one-step process the spacecraft accelerates near the Earth to hyperbolic velocity, thus injecting the spacecraft immediately into the desired transfer orbit.

Cases (1), (2), and (3) show three different arrangements of coplanar circular and elliptic orbits. The relatively most economical transfer orbit T is shown in each case. The most economical transfer between an inner circular orbit and an outer elliptic orbit, Case (1), leads from circular orbit to apoapsis of the ellipse, or vice versa. The most economical transfer between elliptic orbit and intersecting circular orbit, Case (2), leads from apoapsis to circular orbit, or vice versa. The most economical transfer between inner elliptic and outer circular orbit, Case (3), leads from periapsis to circular orbit, or vice versa.

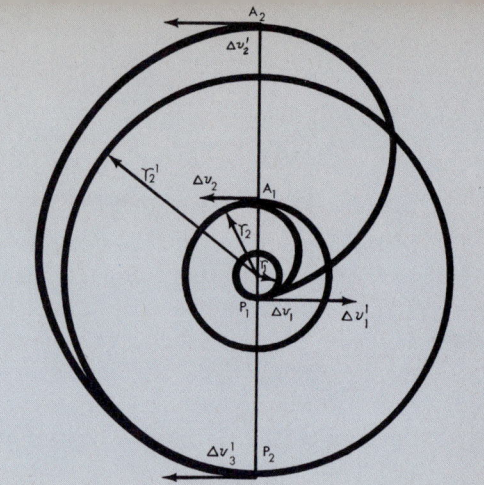

Fig. 2: METHODS OF COTANGENTIAL TRANSFER BETWEEN COPLANAR CIRCULAR ORBITS

The figure shows three circular orbits in the same plane with the radii r_1, r_2, r_2'. Transfer orbit from r_1 to r_2 is along a Hohmann flight path (a half-ellipse from periapsis P_1 to apoapsis A_1). If the ratio of distances between target orbit r_2 and departure orbit r_1 is greater than 15.582, then a bi-elliptic transfer requires less propellant (but takes more time). This case is shown in the transfer from r_1 to r_2'. The spacecraft "overshoots" r_2' along the first half-ellipse from periapsis P_1 to apoapsis A_2 where, through a maneuver adding speed, the spacecraft is injected into the second half-ellipse, leading to periapsis P_2. At this point the spacecraft enters the target orbit (radius r_2') by means of a decelerating maneuver.

A parking orbit, occupied for the purpose of imminent escape, should be established at the lowest feasible altitude because less propellant is saved by departing from a higher orbit than ascending into this higher orbit from the surface.

A change in orbital plane and a change in the

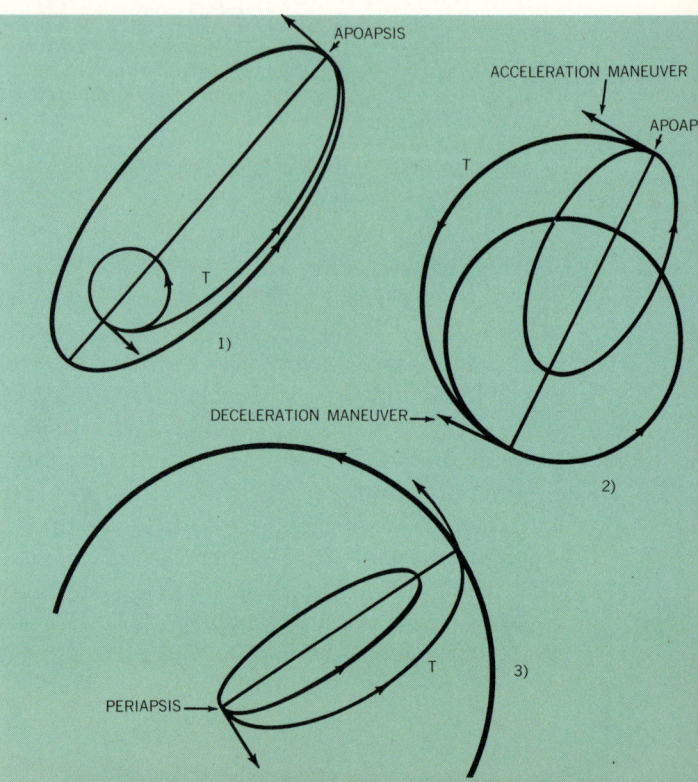

Fig. 3: ECONOMICAL METHODS OF TRANSFER BETWEEN CIRCULAR AND ELLIPTIC ORBITS

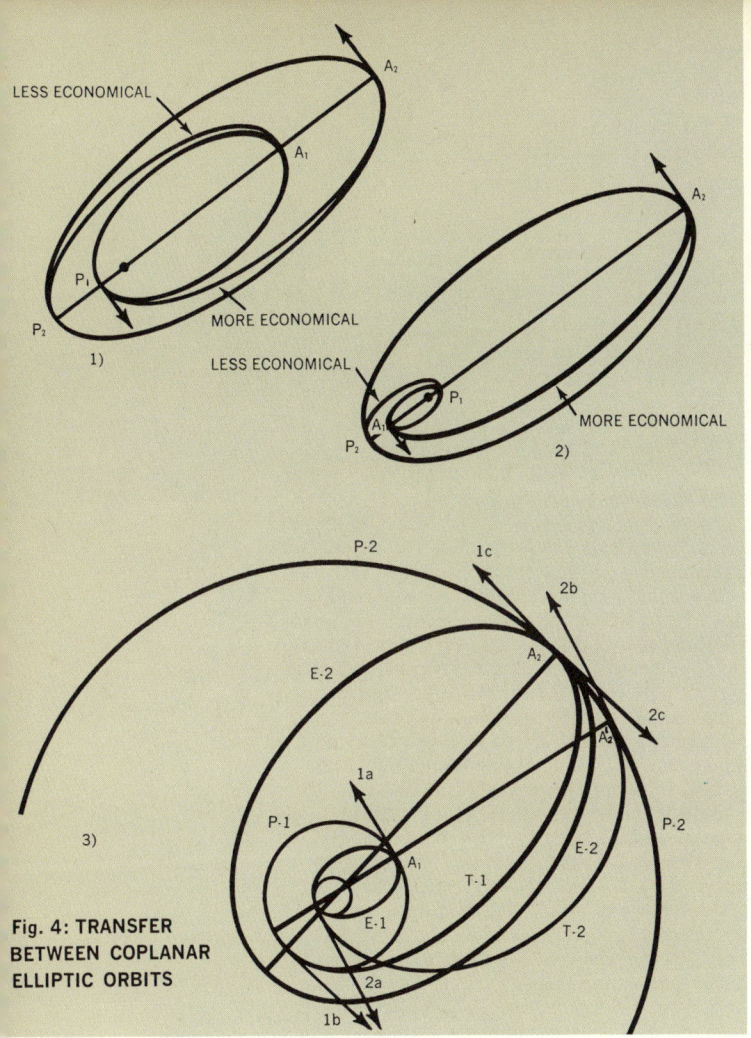

Fig. 4: TRANSFER BETWEEN COPLANAR ELLIPTIC ORBITS

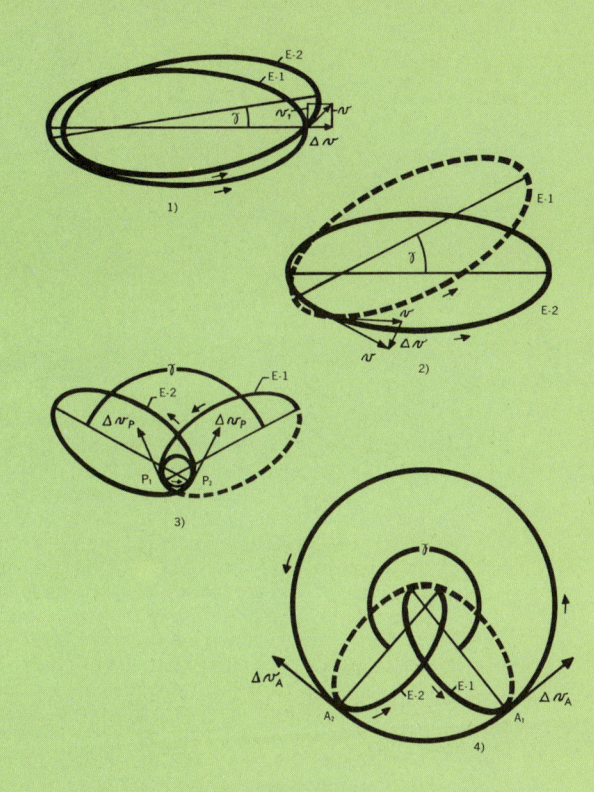

Fig. 5: METHODS OF ROTATING THE APSIDAL LINE OF AN ELLIPTIC ORBIT

Case (1) shows two elliptic orbits oriented in the same direction (their periapses and apoapses are in the same direction). In this case the least propellant-consuming transfer is between periapsis of the inner and apoapsis of the outer ellipse. Case (2) depicts two elliptic orbits which are oriented in the opposite direction. In this case the most economical transfer is between the apoapsis of the inner and the apoapsis of the outer ellipse. In Cases (1) and (2) the major axes of both ellipses coincide (coaxial ellipses). Case 3 depicts the case of transfer between two elliptic orbits which are not coaxial (E-1 and E-2). In this case the transfer is accomplished more economically by a 3-impulse maneuver than by a 2-impulse process. The two principal ways to accomplish the transfer are method 1 (impulse maneuvers 1a, 1b, and 1c) and method 2 (2a, 2b, 2c). In maneuver 1, the vehicle changes into a circular parking orbit P_1 at the apogee of E-1 (accelerating maneuver 1a) and, by accelerating maneuver 1b, enters transfer path T-1, which leads it to the apogee A_2 of ellipse E-2 where, through maneuver 1c, the vehicle enters E-2. In method 2, the vehicle is injected directly from ellipse E-1 into transfer path T-2 by maneuver 2a. It reaches apogee distance A_2' of E-2, but not at the right apogee position. Therefore, by maneuver 2b, the vehicle enters parking orbit P-2 until it reaches A_2 where, through retromaneuver 2c, it enters E-2. Comparing method 1 with method 2, the first requires more propellant, but the second is more time consuming.

A small change v' in orientation of the major axis is accomplished most economically by applying a normal impulse at the apoapsis, Case (1). The vehicle at the apoapsis has the velocity v_1. Adding an impulse maneuver at right angle to v_1 results in velocity v_2 and in a new ellipse E-2. Rotation of the major axis by a large angle can be accomplished either by a 1-impulse maneuver or by a 2-impulse maneuver. The first, shown in Case (2), represents the fastest method, but the energy requirement is high, especially if the maneuver is conducted in the vicinity of the periapsis. Two approaches to the 2-impulse maneuver are shown in Cases (3) and (4). Both require less propellant but more time than Case (1). Of the two, Case (3) is faster and requires more propellant. In Case (3) the vehicle, originally in ellipse E-1, enters a circular orbit at periapsis P_1 by means of a retro-maneuver decelerating it by the velocity Δv_p. The vehicle then follows the circular orbit to P_2 where it is accelerated by the same amount (Δv_p) into the same elliptic orbit as before except for its difference in orientation (E-2). In Case (4) the technique is the same except that the two maneuvers occur at the apoapsis. The vehicle leaves the elliptic orbit E-1 at point A_1 by accelerating and follows the circular orbit to A_2 where, by decelerating by the same amount, it enters ellipse E-2.

orientation of the major axis of the elliptic orbit should be carried out at points of lowest orbital velocity *(apoapsis)* for minimum propellant consumption. Other important rules of space navigation are illustrated in *Figures 2* through *5*.

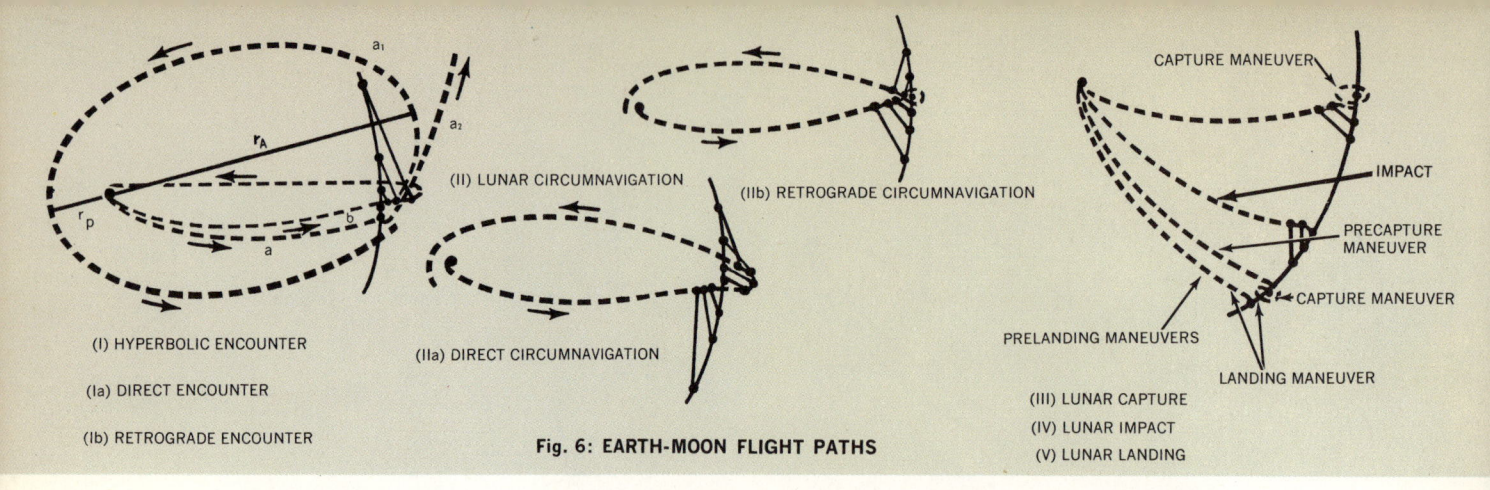

(I) HYPERBOLIC ENCOUNTER
(Ia) DIRECT ENCOUNTER
(Ib) RETROGRADE ENCOUNTER

(II) LUNAR CIRCUMNAVIGATION
(IIa) DIRECT CIRCUMNAVIGATION
(IIb) RETROGRADE CIRCUMNAVIGATION

(III) LUNAR CAPTURE
(IV) LUNAR IMPACT
(V) LUNAR LANDING

Fig. 6: EARTH-MOON FLIGHT PATHS

Based on flight missions, moon flights can be divided into five groups as shown above in the order of increasing involvement of the moon. Case 1 shows two *flyby modes* involving a direct hyperbolic encounter in which the vehicle's flight path experiences a counterclockwise rotation. The vehicle's orbital energy is thereby increased (and the moon's decreased ever so slightly) by an energy exchange with the lunar gravity field. Consequently, the vehicle's post-encounter orbit is either a far-flung ellipse about Earth (a_1), or the vehicle is thrown into an Earth escape path (a_2). In case (b), the vehicle's orbit is rotated clockwise, losing energy to the moon and resulting in a return path to Earth which is steeper than its outgoing branch. The second group, *lunar circumnavigation,* can be regarded as a modification of the hyperbolic encounter, the difference being one of degree. Therefore, direct (counterclockwise) and retrograde (clockwise) circumnavigation can be distinguished. The terms counterclockwise and clockwise refer to the observer looking at the flight path from the celestial North Pole. More generally, a counterclockwise or direct encounter with a gravity field bends the flight path *in* the direction of curvature, *adding* energy. In the clockwise or retrograde encounter, the flight path is bent *against* the direction of curvature, *losing* energy. Flight paths Ib and IIa are similar, except that IIa exposes a much greater portion of the moon's total surface, which is the primary purpose of a lunar circumnavigation. Retrograde circumnavigation results in a "figure 8" flight path. *Lunar capture* requires a capture maneuver to eliminate the vehicle's hyperbolic excess with respect to the moon, resulting in a lunar satellite orbit. *Lunar impact* represents collision with the moon, a flight path followed by early U.S.S.R. and U.S. (Ranger) probes. *Lunar landing* consists of a non-impact descent to the surface where the approach velocity is absorbed by retro-thrust as shortly as possible prior to reaching the surface (landing maneuver). Landing may be preceded by a capture maneuver (thereby increasing the choice of landing sites), or it may be direct, as in the case of the U.S. Surveyor and U.S.S.R. Luna probes.

These are but a few of the rules of space navigation. Others, pertaining to Hohmann transfers, fast transfers, and gravity assist are discussed in the entry on Interplanetary travel (*see*) where representative mission velocities and mission profiles to the planets are also shown.

Table 1 presents a survey of lunar mission velocities. Flight paths for lunar missions are shown in *Fig. 6*. Various navigational approaches to lunar landing are surveyed in *Fig. 7*.

Flight Accuracy

Besides knowledge of the velocity requirements for the maneuvers which make a particular mission possible, flight accuracy is important. The process of spacecraft guidance and navigation consists of four principal phases:

Table I: SURVEY OF IMPULSE MANEUVERS FOR LUNAR MISSIONS

Cislunar Transfer Time (hours)	72	60	48	36	24	12
Earth injection velocity (ft/sec)						
from 100 n.mi. orbit	35,950	36,020	36,250	36,700	38,300	45,300
from 150 n.mi. orbit	35,790	35,850	36,025	36,525	37,925	45,200
from 300 n.mi. orbit	35,040	35,125	35,325	35,825	37,200	45,000
Earth injection maneuver (ft/sec)						
from 150 n.mi. orbit	10,386	10,446	10,621	11,121	12,521	19,796
Lunar orbit capture maneuver (y—500,000; ft—152.5 km) (ft/sec)						
from 150 n.mi. Earth orbit	3,100	3,400	4,000	5,700	9,850	23,500
Deorbit and landing maneuver (ft/sec) (Hohmann transfer from 152.5 to 10-14 km altitude; then continuous thrust descent	←――――――――――― 7,000 ―――――――――――→					
Ascent into lunar orbit (ft/sec) (10-14 km altitude)	←――――――――――― 6,000 ―――――――――――→					
Moon injection maneuver (from 10-14 km orbit) (ft/sec)	3,300	3,550	3,900	5,700	9,900	23,500
Flyby round-trip mission duration (hrs)	138-140	....	....	....	....	....

Source: *Dr. Krafft A. Ehricke and Mrs. Betty Miller*

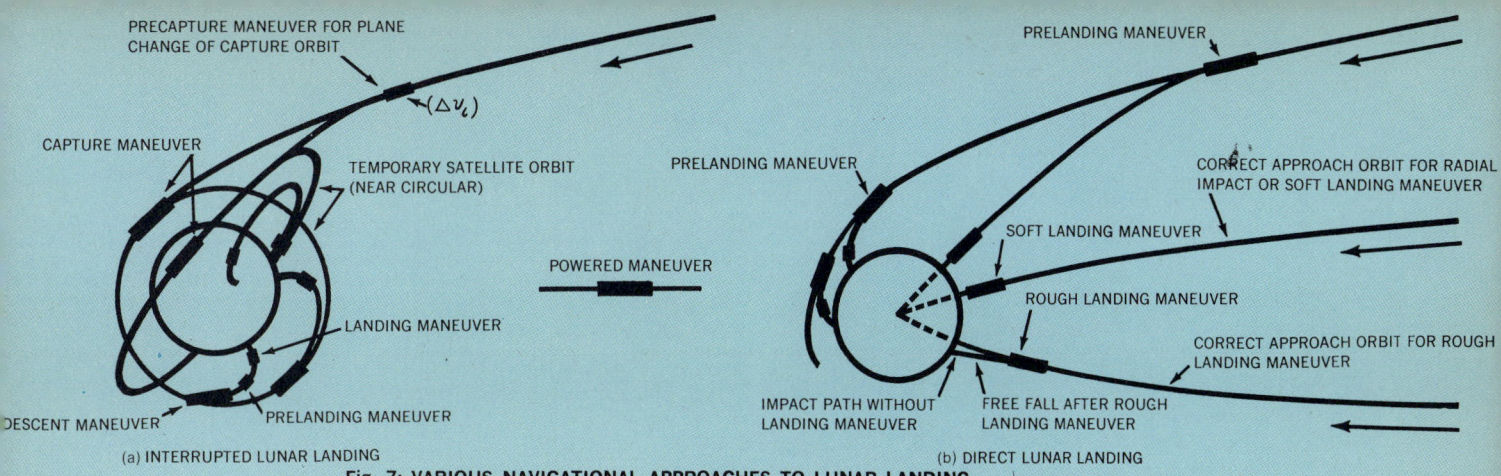

Fig. 7: VARIOUS NAVIGATIONAL APPROACHES TO LUNAR LANDING

(a) INTERRUPTED LUNAR LANDING
(b) DIRECT LUNAR LANDING

The two principal types of lunar landing are a) *interrupted lunar landing* and b) *direct lunar landing*. In type (a), the vehicle enters a lunar satellite orbit prior to landing. Depending on a precapture maneuver, the plane of the orbit can be varied as desired. This provides the greatest possible flexibility in reaching any lunar landing site. (While this type is typical for Apollo, the actual Apollo mission profile provides for an elliptic lunar capture orbit in which to park the Command and Service Modules rather than the circular orbit shown.) Type (b) represents the mission profile used for Surveyor and will eventually be used by manned spacecraft also. Direct lunar landing has a slight energy advantage and offers a greater flexibility in the choice of landing site without prelanding maneuvers on the near side of the moon. Direct landing on most parts of the lunar far side requires a prelanding maneuver.

Table 2: SURVEY OF PROPULSION SYSTEMS FOR SPACEFLIGHT

ENERGY SOURCE	PROPELLANT	SPECIFIC IMPULSE (LB THRUST PER LB/SEC PROPELLANT)[2]	THRUST ACCELERATION (IN UNITS OF EARTH GRAVITY ACCELERATION)[3]	CAN BE USED FOR ASCENT FROM WHAT CELESTIAL BODY?[4]	MAIN MISSION APPLICATIONS
Chemical Combustion. Hot combustion products are discharged, producing thrust	Oxygen-Hydrogen[1]	~450 (in space)	Any practical value desired	Earth, Moon, Mercury, Mars, moons of outer planets	Earth and Moon launch vehicles
Heat from Solid Nuclear Reactor. Hydrogen is heated in reactor and discharged, producing thrust	Hydrogen	~800 (in space)	Any practical value desired	As above	• Lunar • Venus, Mars (Starts operating in Earth parking orbit)
Heat from Solar Radiation Energy. Hydrogen is heated in solar heater and discharged, producing thrust	Hydrogen	~700-800 (in space)	10^{-3} to 10^{-4}	None	Maneuvers in low-gravity space regions not too far from sun (Earth distance or less)
Heat from Gaseous Nuclear Reactor. This reactor is much hotter than the solid nuclear reactor. Thus, hydrogen is heated to much higher temperature, yielding thrust at much higher specific impulse	Hydrogen	1,500-2,000	Any practical value desired	Earth, Moon, Mercury, Mars, moons of outer planets	• Earth-Moon shuttle transport • Venus, Mars, Jupiter
		2,500-5,000	10^{-1} to 10^{-3}	Some moons of outer planets	• Earth-Moon shuttle • Venus, Mars, Jupiter, Saturn
Heat from Solid Nuclear Reactor, Converted to an Electric Field in which to Accelerate Charged Particles to Very High Exhaust Speed (Nuclear-Electric or Ion Drive)	Electrically charged particles (ions) produced by ionizing Cesium or Mercury	5,000-20,000	$5 \cdot 10^{-3}$ to $5 \cdot 10^{-5}$	None	Interplanetary
Nuclear Explosions Behind Spacecraft. Explosions gasify propellants and drive them against specially cushioned aft-end of spacecraft, making this drive suitable for manned spacecraft (Nuclear Pulse Drive)	Metals (gasified by nuclear detonation)	2,500-10,000	Any practical value desired	Any, except where prohibited by nontechnical considerations	Interplanetary
Heat from Nuclear Fusion, such as the nuclear reaction of helium isotope He³ and heavy hydrogen (deuterium, D) to form regular helium He⁴ and protons. The resulting gas (called plasma) is 100 million degrees hot. It is mixed with cold deuterium to produce thrust (Nuclear Fusion Drive)	Deuterium	5,000-500,000	10^{-3} to 10^{-5}	None	• Earth-Moon space • Solar System • Interstellar (limited)

[1] Many other chemical propellant combinations can be used, but most yield lower specific impulse.
[2] Shown are expected lowest and highest values. In the case of the nuclear fusion drive, the highest value is obtained by exhausting the plasma directly, without first mixing it with cold deuterium.
[3] 10^{-1}, 10^{-3}, 10^{-4}, 10^{-5} are mathematical abbreviations for 1/10, 1/1000, 1/10,000, 1/100,000 respectively. Earth gravity acceleration is 32.2 ft/sec². Therefore, 10^{-3}, for example, corresponds to a thrust acceleration of 0.322 ft/sec².
[4] To be able to ascend from a celestial body, the thrust acceleration must be 15 to 30 per cent higher than the gravitational acceleration at the surface of the body (1g at Earth).

Source: *Dr. Krafft A. Ehricke and Mrs. Betty Miller*

Table 3: IDENTIFICATION OF SPACE VEHICLE SUBSYSTEMS BY THEIR PURPOSE

Spacecraft Subsystem	Purpose or Function	Corresponding Biological Subsystem	Spacecraft Subsystem	Purpose or Function	Corresponding Biological Subsystem
Propulsion	Power and locomotion	Muscle			sensors (eyes, ears, etc.) and brain
Vehicle Structures	Support and stability	Skeleton	Electric Circuitry	Internal power distribution, controls, and elimination of unnecessary or unwanted components or material	Nerves
Protection against: Atmospheric entry heating (where applicable) Solar radiation heating in space Penetration or damage by micrometeoroids in space Damage by corpuscular radiation from solar flares or in planetary radiation belts (radiation shielding) Vacuum (pressurization)	Protection of interior of spacecraft and of astronauts in manned spacecraft	Bones (Cranium, Rib Cage) Hair Skin Fat	Heat Exchanger Subsystems Hydraulic Subsystems Pneumatic Subsystems Environmental Control Subsystems Waste Elimination		Blood Circulation Heart Lung Stomach, Liver, Gallbladder, Kidneys Bowels, Urinary Tract
			Pressure Control (venting) Thermal Control Power Control Fail-Safe Provisions Attitude Control	Regulatory control, safety devices, and processes	Hormones Vitamins Transpiration Vestibulary apparatus
Information Acquisition Subsystems: sensors (sensing instrumentation for optical, infrared, ultraviolet, radar, temperature, magnetic field, acceleration vibration, pressure, etc. measurement)	Sensing and orientation	Information Acquisition Subsystems: Eyes Ears Touch (material sensitivity) Smell Taste	Information Handling Data processing (computer) Data storage (memory)	Intelligence	Brain/Memory
			Communications Antenna Transmitter/Receiver Associated electronics		Brain/Vocal Chords/ Tongue
Guidance and Navigation Equipment		Guidance Navigation Vestibulary apparatus in inner ear (orientation) Combination of	Spacecraft Operational Controls Autopilot Timer/Sequencer		Brain Control Centers

Source: *Dr. Krafft A. Ehricke and Mrs. Betty Miller*

1) Injection into a flight path as close to the desired accurate path (reference path) as possible.
2) Determination of error, such as of the difference between reference path and the path actually attained.
3) Determination of required path correction to improve accuracy.
4) Execution of path correction by means of a correction maneuver (usually small).

There are several ways in which these phases, which are repeated after every major maneuver, can be accomplished.

Propulsion

To maneuver, a spacecraft needs propulsion. A propulsion system converts basic energy to kinetic energy (*see*) of an exhaust jet. The most important basic energy forms are chemical, nuclear and solar.

The two most important intermediate energy forms in the conversion process are thermal energy (heat) and electrical energy in the case of electric propulsion, where the exhaust jet consists not of a hot gas but of high-speed, electrically charged particles. There is only one useful final energy form—the kinetic energy of the exhaust jet.

A propulsion system, therefore, converts energy. The amount of energy converted per second is defined as *power*. High power levels generally are important for propulsion, although there are exceptions, such as for correction maneuvers or very slow transfers. Therefore, energy is less important than the power which it provides. For example, solar radiation is a tremendous source of energy, but it is so thinly spread that it does not supply as much power as a jet engine or a chemical rocket engine.

For the same reason, jet power must be considered in addition to jet energy. The exhaust velocity v_e is a measure of the kinetic energy of the exhaust jet. The power of the exhaust jet is related to the momentum $m\,v_e$ where *m* is the exhaust mass. This momentum is related to the thrust *F* and thrust duration *t* by the equation: (in pounds times seconds).

$$m\,v_e = F\,t$$

A propulsion system, therefore, consists of a power source, such as chemical propellants or nuclear reactor; power conversion unit, such as combustion chamber, electric generator, etc.; thrust-producing unit, such as exhaust nozzle, electric accelerator, etc.; and auxiliary devices.

A very important propulsion system parameter is the specific impulse (I_{sp}) (*see*):

$$I_{sp}\,(\text{sec}) = \frac{F\,(\text{lb})}{w\,(\text{lb/sec})}$$

where *w* is the propellant consumption rate.

The importance of I_{sp} for spacecraft is somewhat comparable to that of gasoline mileage for automobiles. The higher the I_{sp}, the lower the propellant consumption for a mission. A survey of present and important possible future propulsion systems is given in Table 2.

Spacecraft Technology

The third of the three basic requirements mentioned in the introduction above is the availability of a spacecraft capable of carrying out the desired mission. This is a matter of research (knowledge), technology (basic technical capabilities), and engineering (specific technical solutions). Combined, their advances continuously advance spacecraft technology.

A great number of technical and scientific principles is involved in developing and building the spacecraft mechanisms involved. A spacecraft system resembles a highly developed organism. Its many subsystems can be grouped into seven categories as to their basic purpose or function. This is explained in Table 3 in which the corresponding biological subsystems are also listed.

Krafft A. Ehricke and Betty Ann Miller

See also: Energy, Guidance and control systems, Lunar bases, Navigation systems, Space propulsion systems

Spaceflight safety

The safe return of the astronauts (*see*) is the most important consideration in spacecraft design (*see*) and in planning of manned spaceflight missions Although each and every part of the spacecraft is designed and manufactured to operate as reliably as possible, allowance for the fact that parts can fail is a vital consideration in achieving safety. In general, manned spacecraft are designed so that no single failure will in itself jeopardize the crew. In fact, for many critical systems combinations of two or even more failures will not prevent a safe return.

The most common method of protection against failures is through use of backup systems and redundant components. *Backup systems* are reserve systems that can be employed when the normally used system becomes disabled. For instance, the spacecraft may have two or more transmitters. If the primary transmitter were to fail, the astronaut would switch to the backup unit.

Redundant components, which are two or more identical components, operate simultaneously to perform a single function so that a failure of one of the components will not interfere with successful performance. For instance, during descent the Apollo spacecraft deploys three main parachutes simultaneously. A safe rate of descent is achieved if only two of these function properly.

In certain cases, it is not sufficient to provide redundant or backup systems as protection against failure. Certain failures in themselves may be catastrophic. For instance, if the propellant tanks became sufficiently overpressurized they would rupture with enough energy to destroy the spacecraft. Equipment with catastrophic failure modes must be protected by the use of special safety devices. Circuit breakers, relief valves, and blow-out diaphragms are examples of devices that would cause a system to fail safely rather than catastrophically.

A significant contribution to the successful completion of the mission and safe return of the astronauts is provided by the operations personnel who man the ground stations during the missions. At the Mission Control Center (*see*) in Houston, Texas, the performance of each vital system on the craft is continuously monitored by operations engineers and system specialists. At the same time, an up-to-date status on all other aspects of the mission is maintained. This ground support becomes vital in the event of malfunctions or emergencies. An immediate assessment of the situation can be made, and various alternate corrective actions or emergency procedures can quickly be analyzed. Since the control center is so important to the safety of the mission, it is also designed with many backup and redundant features so that possible failures will not interfere with critical operations.

Rescue Capabilities

The concern that a damaged spacecraft will leave the crew stranded in orbit, awaiting certain death as critical supplies run out, has led to serious consideration of possible means of rescue. Although it is feasible to build and maintain a rescue spacecraft on stand-by for launch, its utility in comparison to its cost is doubtful. In a number of ways the rescue spacecraft would require higher performance than the spacecraft it would be called upon to aid. It would have to carry all the rescued astronauts in addition to its own crew. It would also have to be able to rendezvous rapidly into any possible orbit occupied by the stranded spacecraft. This could be accomplished only by using high-energy maneuvers. Thus far, it has proved more practical and economical to improve safety by increasing the basic reliability of the spacecraft or by incorporating additional safety devices, rather than attempting to develop rescue capabilities.

When manned orbiting space stations (*see*) become operational, the use of emergency return vehicles may be employed as another method of improving spaceflight safety. These vehicles would be carried on the space station in much the same manner as lifeboats on an ocean liner. In the event of a disaster that would make the immediate abandonment of the space station necessary or desirable, these emergency vehicles could provide a quick means of return to Earth.

Maxime A. Faget

See also: Escape systems, Recovery, Redundancy

Spaceflight simulators

A spaceflight simulator includes representation of a manned vehicle, a mathematical model of its flight characteristics and environment, visual cues, and human operators to direct and control the simulated system in real time.

Simulators are now used as the basic training technique for all astronauts (*see*). Simulators come into play in concept, design, and evaluation of guidance and control systems (*see*), and the development of crew procedures for all phases of spaceflight. Accurate and realistic representations of controls and displays, spacecraft characteristics, and real-world views are being used extensively to familiarize astronauts with procedures prior to actual flights.

Simulation Systems Components

The heart of the simulator is the exacting computation equipment, while other basic elements include visual display devices and crew compartments. Checkout and operation of simulations are facilitated by audio and visual communication links to a central control room where data are monitored and recorded. Activities in digital computer and mock-up areas can be observed through viewing windows, and monitors in the control room present closed-circuit television views of the analog computer and visual display areas, main controls and displays of the simulated vehicle, window scenes for visual cuing, and crew movements and manipulations. An entire study can be recorded on video tape for a permanent record.

Refinements gleaned from previous simulators used prior to and during the Mercury Program (*see*), Gemini (*see*), and early Apollo (*see*) flights, plus the knowledge obtained as a result of those flights, have gone into construction of the new simulation laboratory located at the North American Rockwell Corporation's Space Division in Downey, California, and connected by direct communication lines to the Mission Control Center (*see*) at NASA's Manned Spacecraft center (MSC) (*see*). In this laboratory astronauts train daily for a round trip to the moon.

Simulation experts have developed a hybrid computer system with multichannel digital-to-analog and analog-to-digital conversion available to link the computers (*see*) in the simulator or actual spacecraft with the evaluation facilities.

Inasmuch as human responses are highly complex and vary among individuals in similar situations, crew members are the most difficult element to simulate adequately. Currently, the astronauts themselves are being integrated into the simulation, and previously all test subjects have had similar mental and physical capabilities and experiences to those of the crew in the real-world system. A real-world situation is impossible to create because all the environmental factors and physiological stresses and motivations that influence men can never be completely simulated. Recent tests, however, have been as close to real as the present level of scientific research would permit.

Types of Crew Compartments

The *generalized crew compartment* is used to explore the feasibility of a concept or to analyze a potential system design wherein only the essential elements of controls and displays are required. It is constructed of plywood panels mounted on channeled-steel framing members. A variety of interchangeable window masks for a particular study can be incorporated into the basic structure. Two adjustable crew seats maintain the appropriate distance and angular relationship between the crewman and the control panel. Two hand controllers provide the ability to transmit attitude and translational commands. The crew compartment is mounted on a frame with casters to make alignment of the line of sight with the visual display presentation devices possible.

To evaluate combined systems performance or to establish optimum crew procedures, a *detailed* mock-up with all the characteristics of the actual spacecraft is used. Typical of the detailed crew compartments are the two Apollo Command Module mock-ups. The modules are fixed in the vertical launch attitude to facilitate crew movement in and between the couch positions and the lower equipment bay station. Each detailed crew compartment has active controls and displays for all guidance and control functions. The flight director attitude indicator, translational and rotational hand controllers, mode-switching panels, and the delta- and V-display are all prototype components of the stabilization and control system. Prototype or simulated elements of the guidance and navigation system, such as telescope, sextant, optics control stick, minimum-impulse controller, mark button, and coupling display units are also incorporated into the mock-up. Intercommunication headphones are provided by a 21-inch television monitor viewed through appropriate optics located in the left docking window. The scene appears to be at an infinite distance from the viewer and occupies a 40-degree field of view. The window scene is shown alternatively (with appropriate transformations) in the telescope.

The Apollo Mission Simulator, or AMS *(right)*, was installed at the Manned Spacecraft Center in January, 1968. Technicians examine the control board of the Gemini flight simulator *(left)*.

Composition of the Displays

Image generation and presentation devices provide the basis for visual displays. Precision scale models, in most instances, are viewed by a high-resolution television system operating at 1,203 lines per frame at 30 frames per second. The models provide scenes for orbital, approach, and landing flight phases, each requiring a different scale factor. If a comparatively narrow field of view is required, the scene is presented on a 21-inch television monitor. Where a wide field of view is necessary, the scene is projected by an Eidophor projector onto a 20-foot spherical segment screen. In both cases, optics are used in the window to achieve the effect of distance.

Earth-orbital scenes are presented by viewing a 72-inch-diameter model of the Earth. The model is rendered with great precision and is colored to represent the Earth at mid-August. For simulating Earth entry and approach, a flat model with a scale of 450,000 to 1 is used. This model, which represents most of the continental United States and a portion of the Pacific Ocean, is approximately 50 feet long and 20 feet wide. Flight phases in the vicinity of the moon are simulated using a 3-foot-diameter spherical model, a spherical segment with a scale factor of 40,000 to 1, and two flat models with scale factors of 1,500 to 1 and 400 to 1.

Star field scenes for navigation sightings and rotational motion cues are achieved with a gimbaled 24-inch-diameter sphere. Major constellations are readily identifiable. Views of other spacecraft for simulation of rendezvous and docking (*see*) are provided by gimbaled models. Model gimbals, optical prisms, and camera transports are activated by precise servomechanisms (*see*) that accept command signals directly from the computers.

Spaceflight simulation signals occur in a variety of forms. Many discrete signals indicate the state of various functions; many signals are generated at times differing from those at which they are to be used. Extensive interface equipment makes the signals compatible, addresses them to their proper destination, arranges them in proper sequence, and shapes and conditions them as required. Interface equipment is so specific to the particular study that it must be designed and fabricated on-site.

Technology improvements and refinements are being achieved daily to advance simulation techniques. Although the specific purpose of a spaceflight simulator is to simulate actual flight dynamics and guidance and control systems, its facilities provide the ability to analyze the dynamics of subsystems and phenomena such as space propulsion systems (*see*), life-support systems (*see*), human factors, and controls and displays.

Future Development

Optical techniques are being developed to translate data from spherical coordinates and Mercator projections to flat or spherical terrain models at any required accuracy and scale. Models can be prepared to simulate the terrain of a planet or a metropolitan skyline. Systems for providing three-dimensional scenes for simulated vehicle windows are being studied as a means of enhancing visual perception of depth.

With rapid advancement in all areas of aerospace technology, real-time simulation requirements continue to increase in complexity. To satisfy the demands, an industry has dedicated itself to further utilization of existing equipment and to the invention and discovery of new means to achieve those ends.

Len L. Simpson

See also: Cosmonauts, Environmental simulators, Flight simulators, Spaceflight training

Astronauts survey a shelter made by USAF instructors during a desert survival training course.

Spaceflight training
Preparing for a specific mission

A NASA astronaut assigned to a spaceflight mission receives more training for his specific job than a man in almost any other profession. Flight training for a ten-day mission will last six to nine months. The training includes courses on every phase of the mission, from how to fly the spacecraft to methods of surviving in the jungle if the spacecraft should land there. A man is selected to become an astronaut because his training, experience, and performance show he is highly capable. The NASA spaceflight training program is designed to insure that success.

The spaceflight training program's purpose is to teach astronauts (*see*) how to fly the spacecraft in order to best accomplish the assigned mission, and how to conduct the scientific experiments and observations scheduled for that mission. Today's training is based largely on knowledge gained during the first U.S. manned space programs, Mercury and Gemini, and also on the particular requirements of present programs.

Spaceflight training is divided into two basic programs, general training and specific mission training.

Spaceflight training

General Training

The general program was developed to train new astronauts, but astronauts who have already completed the program still take part in some portions of it to maintain their skills. General training includes classroom study of subjects such as geology and astronomy (*see*), study of spacecraft design (*see*) and development, training to live in strange conditions or emergency situations, and physical fitness. It also includes flying aircraft.

Academic Program

In the academic, or classroom, segment of general training the astronauts study geology, astronomy, computers (*see*), flight mechanics, upper atmosphere physics, meteorology (*see*), and guidance and navigation. These courses, except for guidance and navigation, are the same as those taken by high school and college science students.

Guidance and navigation deals with basic units of inertial guidance systems (*see*) and with the NASA spacecraft guidance in particular. The astronauts become familiar with their spacecraft and with the rockets that launch them.

As in most other schools, the astronaut classes take field trips from time to time. They visit the Kennedy Space Center (*see*) for briefings on launch preparations and countdown activities. At the Marshall Space Flight Center (*see*) in Alabama and at the Mississippi Test Facility, they learn about development and testing of launch vehicles (*see*). At the Manned Spacecraft Center (*see*) in Houston, Texas, where the astronauts are assigned, they study the Mission Control Center (*see*) and Recovery Operations Branch activities. Field trips also play an important role in the geology course.

Environmental and Contingency Training

Man is weightless in space. He must wear a special suit to pressurize him against the vacuum of space and to give him air to breathe. During launch into and re-entry from space he undergoes forces of acceleration many times greater than the pull of gravity he experiences on the Earth. Because these conditions of environment are not found in everyday life and often not even in aircraft flight, the astronauts get special training that tells them what to expect and how to react.

Weightless periods of about half a minute are produced in a KC-135 aircraft. The plane climbs to a high altitude, then points its nose to the ground and "falls" back toward the Earth. During this controlled fall, the astronauts are weightless. In the 30 seconds before the airplane pulls out of its dive, the astronauts practice activities such as eating and drinking, maneuvering themselves while they float, and recovering from falls and spins.

Using a technique perfected near the close of the Gemini program, the astronauts also work under water in a simulated weightless condition, or "neutral buoyancy." The tank at the Manned Spacecraft Center is large enough to take full-scale mockups of the Apollo Command and Lunar modules and to let the astronauts practice moving themselves from one spacecraft to the other. The activity familiarizes them with moving correctly in the pressurized spacesuit as well as in the weightless environment.

Contingency training teaches the students how to deal with emergencies that might arise during and after a spaceflight. The astronauts learn how to survive if their spacecraft lands in an area where rescue is not close at hand, for instance, in the jungle, the desert, or at sea.

Physical Training

The physical condition of an astronaut is very important to the success of a flight. Although he is weightless in space and can float about even inside the spacecraft, the astronaut is clothed in a heavy, pressurized protective spacesuit (*see*). Without the suit he could not survive the vacuum of space, but with it he must work hard just to move his arms or legs. More complicated tasks, such as getting out of the spacecraft to conduct an experiment, require even greater energy.

Specific Mission Training

Once a crew is assigned to a specific flight, its training concentrates on the requirements for that flight and begins six to nine months before liftoff. Some crews have had specific training of a year or more for very complex flights.

Astronaut Michael Collins experiences a condition of weightlessness during zero-gravity egress training aboard a USAF DC-135.

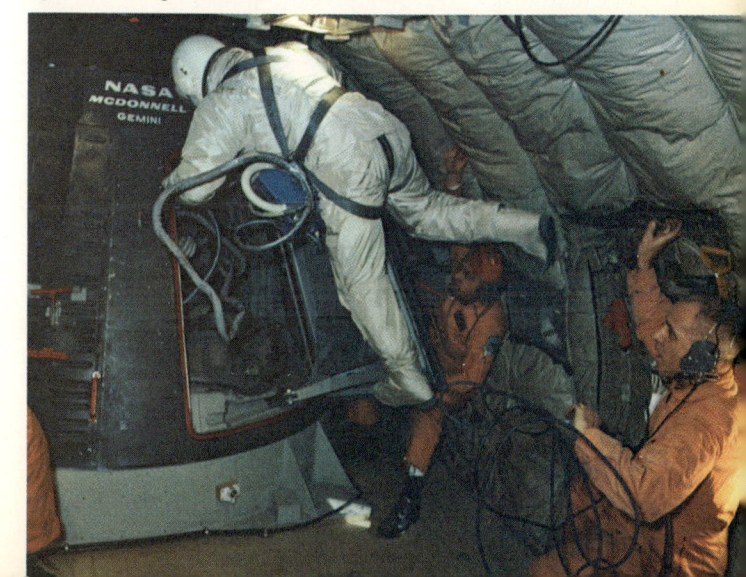

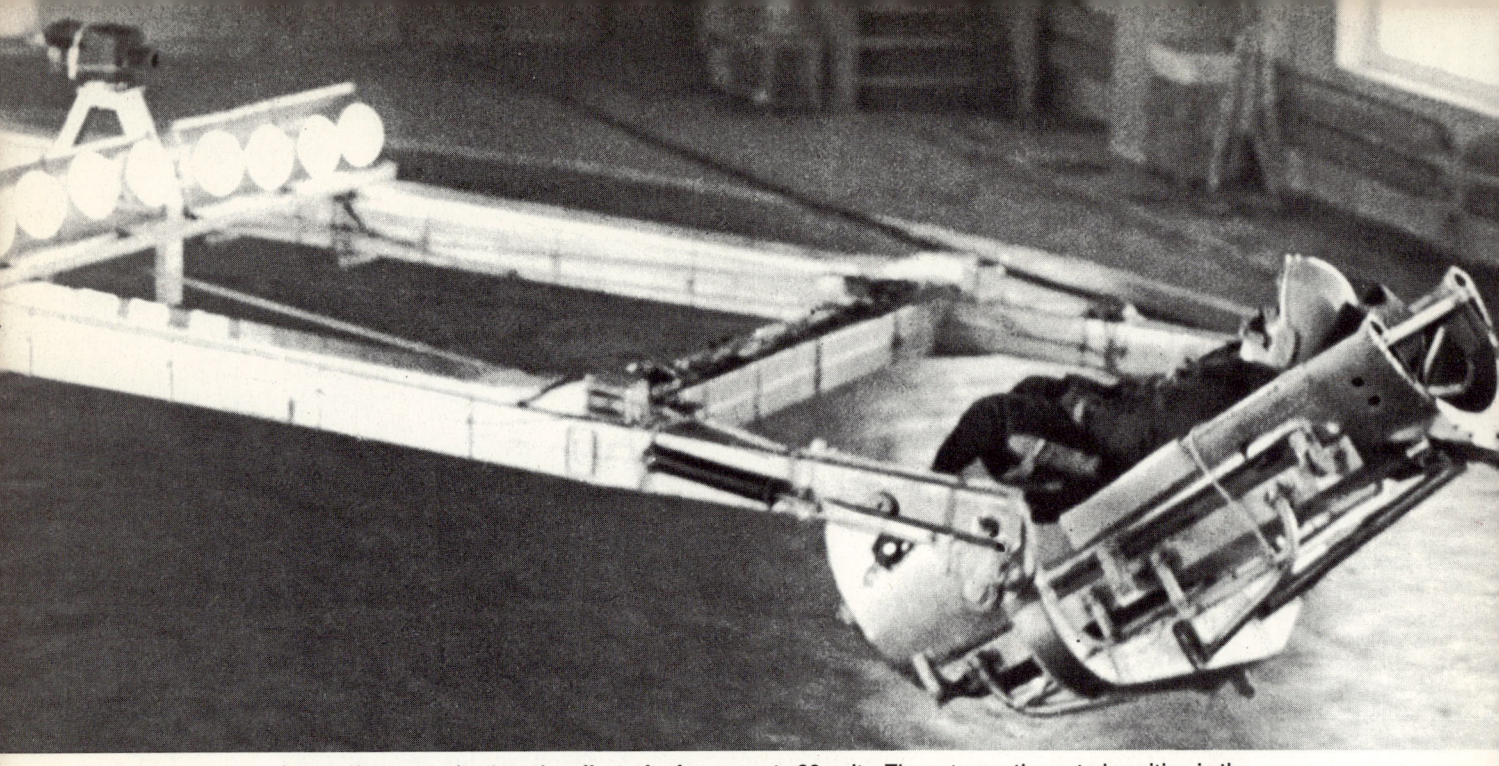

A centrifuge can simulate the effect of *g*-forces up to 30 units. The astronaut's seated position in the centrifuge is much the same as he assumes in the spaceship.

Although each astronaut in a primary or a backup crew is assigned to a definite job in the spacecraft, he also learns the more important tasks of his fellow crewmen, so that he could bring the spaceship safely back to Earth if necessary. The backup crewmen undergo exactly the same training given the primary crew so they can substitute, as a complete team or as individuals, without delaying the program. Even if the backup crew does not fly the mission for which it trained, the experience is valuable. A backup team might well become the primary crew for a later flight.

Crew training begins with briefings on the spacecraft, the launch rocket, and the guidance and navigation systems. Each system is discussed in detail. At the same time, the crewmen take part in spacecraft reviews and tests at the builder's facility or at a NASA test site. This participation lets the astronauts become familiar with the spaceship they will fly. It also gives them a chance to suggest changes in equipment, or better methods of operating the spacecraft. Because of the scope of the program, one or more astronauts are assigned to watch over specific portions of the program and to report changes and progress to the entire group.

Mission Simulators

Crews training for Apollo flights prepare for their specific duties in the Apollo Mission Simulator. Although the outside does not look anything like a spacecraft, the interior of the simulator duplicates the cabin in which the astronauts will fly. Controls are connected to displays in the Mission Control Center. Special screens in place of the spacecraft windows permit inflight scenes to be projected for viewing by the crew. Gemini astronauts who trained in similar units before flying their mission in space say the simulator gave them all the sensations of spaceflight except weightlessness (*see*). Apollo mission simulators are located at the Manned Spacecraft Center and at the Kennedy Space Center.

The mission training program consists of four phases. In the first phase, each astronaut works on the basic procedures for the mission. All members of the primary crew and the backup crew practice the major jobs at each of the different work stations in the spacecraft.

The second phase is mission task training, a series of tasks that occur at various times in the mission. Each astronaut learns to perform the tasks and to coordinate his actions with those of his teammates.

Mission training, the third phase, ties together the individual tasks in mission sequence. The crew practices doing all the mission tasks in the same order and at the same time as they occur in a real flight. To keep the training effective and the crew comfortable, relatively short "flights" of several orbits are used.

In the last few weeks before their actual flight, the astronauts progress to the fourth phase, integrated mission training. During this phase, the simulator controls are tied in with the displays in Mission Control Center and with simulated stations of the worldwide Manned Space Flight Network. These sessions give the astronauts and the flight controllers experience in working together.

Soviet Cosmonaut Boris Yegorov undergoes preflight training on an inertial wheel *(left)*. Both the cosmonaut and his backup man are drinking juice *(right)* as they prepare to board.

The mission simulator also helps to prepare the crew for possible inflight emergencies. Various malfunctions or abnormal events can be fed into the simulator by the training directors to exercise the reactions of the astronauts.

Lunar Landing Training

Because the actual landing on the moon's surface is such an important phase of the lunar exploration program, a special aircraft was built for astronaut training. It is the Lunar Landing Training Vehicle. It is similar to a helicopter, except that upward-thrusting rocket engines let it fly under conditions simulating the moon's gravity.

Only two of the three Apollo astronauts will descend to the lunar surface. Therefore, lunar landing training is given only to those two, the Commander and the Lunar Module Pilot, in the primary and the backup crew.

Two-man training also is encountered in the Lunar Module Simulator. Like the Apollo Mission Simulator, the Lunar Module trainer features the same controls and displays as the actual spacecraft. Scenes depicting the moon's surface are projected on screens in the windows. Before he has completed his sessions with the Lunar Landing Training Vehicle and the Lunar Module Simulator, an astronaut has "landed" on the moon many times.

Astronaut James Lovell occupies the command pilot seat of Gemini 12 during the final checkout of the spacecraft at the McDonnell Company's 30-foot chamber.

Docking and Other Training

Another device designed to train the astronauts in a special phase of a mission is the Translation and Docking Simulator. It teaches the techniques of maneuvering an orbiting spacecraft toward, and docking it with, another vehicle. Unlike other ground-based simulators, its controls actually move both the make-believe spaceship and its docking target vehicle. Relative velocity and motions—angular, up

Astronauts Cooper and Conrad practice the water egress exercise in preparation for the Gemini 5 mission.

and down, or side to side—between the two vehicles are simulated over a range of 100 feet to docking.

Still another phase of mission training involves postlanding procedures, the things each astronaut must do to keep himself and the spacecraft safely afloat while awaiting recovery (*see*) from a landing on the ocean. The procedures include postlanding activity inside the spacecraft, methods of exiting the ship and boarding life rafts, and helicopter pickup. The last phase of this training is conducted in the Gulf of Mexico off the Texas coast.

The crew also trains in celestial observation. Because stars and constellations are important to celestial navigation (*see*), the astronauts visit planetariums such as Morehead at Chapel Hill, North Carolina, for a general review of the celestial sphere. They specifically study the star patterns that will be visible during the mission for which they are training.

Flight Experience

Although all of his work for nearly a year is designed to insure the success of a given mission, the astronaut's training does not end with his flight. His experience in that flight is important to future mission training programs. It helps to determine what phases of training should be emphasized or perhaps minimized.

Future flights to which the astronaut may be assigned could have many requirements different from the mission he has completed. His training will begin anew. —J. W. Kroehnke

See also: Apollo, Gemini, Manned Orbiting Laboratory, Manned spaceflight, Mercury program

The POGO one-man flying device is evaluated for possible use on the moon by astronauts who must learn to use it and compensate for the restraints imposed by pressurized spacesuits.

Space garbage

On any given day, an average of more than 1,200 pieces of space-age flotsam and jetsam orbit the Earth. Included are invaluable relics, such as Sputnik I and Explorer I; interesting derelicts, such as rocket hulks and old weather satellites; and just plain trash, such as jagged chunks of metal and other scrap.

Many of these items are numbered and tracked regularly by NORAD (North American Air Defense Command) (*see*), which counts space-watching as one of its many duties. Generally, only items at least 30 inches in size are tracked, but smaller items such as early satellites are naturally included.

The majority of today's space garbage comes from rocket stages which have exploded in space, or have broken apart from other stresses. One of the first was a U.S.S.R. rocket being used in an attempt to send a satellite on an interplanetary mission. It blew up over Africa when a reignition was tried, with more than 500 identifiable pieces going into orbit. The pieces gradually re-entered the Earth's atmosphere and burned. No trace of the rocket remains today.

The worst case of space littering came about from the West Ford project. On May 10, 1963, a canister containing 400 million small needles was opened 2,000 miles above the Earth. Each needle was just 0.7 inch long and 0.001 inch in diameter. The purpose of the experiment was to try to bounce radio signals from the needles instead of using jammable communications satellites (*see*).

For several weeks, the needles stayed in a dense cloud. Then they fanned out, eventually forming a ring completely around the Earth, stretching from pole to pole. As time passed, the needles spread so far apart that experiments stopped. Orbital lifetime estimates from one year to several centuries were made for the needles. Eventually, the tiny pieces of copper were lost from radar screens.

Several items were added to the garbage list during the Gemini program. The late astronaut Edward H. White II (*see*) lost one glove during his space walk. Other astronauts lost small canisters of film, a camera, and a flight plan. Some of them even opened their spacecraft to dump accumulated waste paper into the orbital refuse pile.

Up until the late 1960's there had been no known collisions between manned spacecraft and space garbage, and only one between two satellites. Astronauts occasionally reported seeing large unidentifiable items several miles in the distance, but none came close enough to be considered dangerous.

Many times, however, large chunks have survived fierce re-entry heat to reach the Earth's surface. Pieces of rockets and other debris have crashed in Africa, South America, and Arizona. In 1967, a metal sphere smashed to the ground in Mexico near a small village. NASA scientists examining photos of the object say it may have come from a Gemini adapter section.

Jim Schefter

See also: International aviation and space agreements, Space law

Space law

Many years before the launching of Sputnik I, scholars were considering and writing about the legal problems of outer space. However, not until 1958 did the United Nations General Assembly establish a Committee, one of whose tasks was to study legal problems associated with space exploration. In 1959, the Committee expressed a developing rule of law that outer space is "freely available for exploration and use by all in accordance with existing or future international law or agreements." When the U.S.S.R. made an unmanned landing on the moon, both the Soviet Union and the United States stated that they ruled out any claims of national sovereignty to the lunar surface.

Both of these principles were embodied in a General Assembly resolution adopted in December, 1961, which also included the statement that "International law, including the Charter of the United Nations, applies to outer space and celestial bodies."

In 1963, a more formal document, entitled "Declaration of Legal Principles Governing the Activities of States in the Exploration and Use of Outer Space" was adopted by the Assembly. The Declaration served as the basis for the "Treaty on Principles Governing the Activities of States in the Exploration and Use of Outer Space, Including the Moon and Other Celestial Bodies" (Outer Space Treaty). Most of the nations of the world have signed this Treaty, and it entered into force on October 10, 1967.

The Treaty states the rule of freedom of outer space and the applicability of international law in space. It prohibits the placing of weapons of mass destruction in space and prohibits military bases, testing of weapons, or military maneuvers on celestial bodies. It provides that outer space and celestial bodies shall not be subject to national appropriation by claim of sovereignty or otherwise. It obligates the signers of the Treaty to assist astronauts in distress regardless of their nationality and provides for their safe and prompt return. It contains a provision for the jurisdiction, control, and ownership of objects launched into outer space. It provides a rule of international liability for damage caused by space ob-

Space law

jects. It states obligations on the avoidance of harmful intereference and contamination in carrying out space activities. It establishes responsibility for space activities carried on by nongovernmental organizations. It guarantees free access to all areas of celestial bodies and to all stations, installations, equipment, and space vehicles on celestial bodies, and that celestial bodies may be used only for peaceful purposes.

An "Agreement on the Rescue of Astronauts, the Return of Astronauts, and the Return of Objects Launched in Outer Space" was signed April 22, 1968. This treaty, which elaborates on two Articles of the Outer Space Treaty, provides (a) for notification or public announcement when astronauts have suffered accident, are in distress, or have made an emergency or unintended landing, (b) for taking all possible steps to rescue and assist astronauts and to return them safely and promptly, and (c) for notification that space objects have returned to Earth and for taking steps to recover such objects.

New Legal Problems of the Space Age

Another legal problem concerns the question of whether or not there is, or should be, an upward limit of territorial sovereignty. Reference has been made to the Paris Convention on International Civil Aviation of 1919 and the Chicago Convention of 1944 which recognizes the sovereignty of every nation in the "air space" above its land and territorial waters, but contains no definition of "air space." Analogy to these Conventions is unfruitful in attempting to find a solution to the question of sovereignty in outer space. It is significant that no permission was ever sought in advance to launch satellites, none was expressly given, and not a single protest has been registered by any nation. If outer space is free while air space is subject to sovereignty of the underlying states, the question is, where does the air space end and where does outer space begin? Numerous suggestions have been made to locate a boundary between the two. Some are based on supposed geophysical or astronomical constants, some on the maximum heights on which craft derive their support solely from the atmosphere, and some on purely arbitrary altitudes.

Another legal problem, which is under negotiation within the U.N. Outer Space Legal Subcommittee, is the liability of launching nations for damage to property or injury to persons caused by satellites. The proposed treaty would elaborate on the general liability provision of the Outer Space Treaty. The questions being considered are: the kinds of damages or injuries to be covered; whether liability should be based on fault, or without regard to fault for some or all activities; what principles should govern depending on the place of damage or injury; whether the liability of the launching country should be unlimited in amount; what procedures should be utilized for determining liability and ensuring the payment of compensation; and where more than one country participates in a particular activity, should the liability be joint and several.

Since there is an absolute limit on the width of the radio spectrum, and frequencies must be allocated for space and terrestrial communications, the International Telecommunication Union must consider this problem and its legal effects. The prospect of direct broadcasting from satellites to home receivers also poses many legal problems to which the international community will have to direct itself.

Paul G. Dembling

See also: International aviation and space agreements, Legal implications of aerospace

Space medicine

Aerospace medicine (*see*) began with the age of flight over 60 years ago, and is now a separate specialty in affiliation with the American Board of Preventive Medicine. Space medicine refers to that portion of aerospace medicine specifically concerned with the effects of the space environment on man. Space medicine studies are concerned with such subjects as weightlessness (*see*), man's ability to withstand very high levels of gravity (*see*), and food and nutrition (*see*).

In order to facilitate obtaining information in these and other areas, much use is made of simulators (*see*) which duplicate the stresses of the space environment. In addition, every time an astronaut makes a spaceflight, data on his physiological well-being are continuously transmitted to Earth by means of sensors (*see*) and telemetry (*see*). Dr. Charles Berry, current medical director of the Apollo program, heads a team of space physicians who monitor and interpret the data.

Marsha Goldsmith

See also: Aviation medicine, Man in flight

Space power systems

The best-known type of space power system is the solar cell (*see*), which can be seen covering the surface of some satellites and covering great paddle wheels attached to others. These cells absorb radiant energy from the sun (*see*) and convert part of it into electricity (*see*). While the conversion efficiency is actually quite good, the sun's radiation has so little power that large areas of solar cells must be used. A big disadvantage of solar cells is that they do not work on the dark side of the Earth. Advantages are that they are rugged and reliable, and they do not generate any heat of their own which must be eliminated. Disposing of waste heat to keep a satellite from getting too hot is always a problem.

Conventional batteries (*see*) are also rugged and reliable, of course, but store too little electricity to be efficient as primary power sources. They are frequently used with solar cells, with the solar cells charging the batteries during daylight and then the batteries being discharged during darkness.

Fuel cells (*see*) are being developed as primary power sources and also as storage units like batteries. For the same capacity, they weigh much less than batteries.

Nuclear power systems are very attractive for space applications because the weight of fuel is essentially zero. They can thus have an extremely long life in space. This theoretical advantage is counterbalanced to some extent by the need for radiation shielding. Nevertheless, space nuclear power holds great promise, and development is being vigorously pursued.

M. C. Atkins

See also: Nuclear energy, Nuclear propulsion

Space propulsion systems

Space propulsion systems are as exotic and varied as the airless reaches of the universe in which they must operate. They include the cold-gas hand gun held by an astronaut to assist him in extravehicular activity (EVA); the hydrogen peroxide control jets of a station-keeping satellite; the attitude control system of a manned capsule; and the descent rocket engines that Apollo's Lunar Module will employ to touch down on the moon's surface.

The first space propulsion system was employed on October 4, 1957, when the U.S.S.R. Sputnik I (*see*) became the first Earth satellite. A small American satellite soon followed, and since then British, Canadian, French, Italian, and Japanese satellites, some boosted with U.S. rockets, have joined the others in space.

True exploration of space did not begin until man himself went there. Once again, the Russians were first, with the orbital flight of the late cosmonaut Yuri Gagarin (*see*) on April 12, 1961. This was followed by a suborbital flight by American astronaut Alan Shepard (*see*) and the first U.S. orbital flight by astronaut John Glenn (*see*). Since that time, both the Russians and the Americans have launched a number of manned flights.

Principles of Propulsion Systems

The space propulsion systems used in all these applications depend on the same principle, Newton's third law of motion: for each action there is an equal and opposite reaction. Space propulsion systems differ from air-breathing systems which operate in the Earth's atmosphere in that they use no outside air to produce thrust. A high-velocity jet of gases issuing from a nozzle produces the equal and opposite reaction which makes these systems function.

The rockets used in most space programs are chemical propulsion systems with liquid-propellant rockets or solid-propellant rockets. However, in the future interplanetary and perhaps interstellar voyages will require nuclear rockets, electric rockets, or other such exotic propulsion systems.

A rocket-powered space vehicle includes the following elements: rocket engine (or engines), propellants, airframe, guidance and control system (or systems), and payload. The thrust required to lift a space vehicle from the Earth must exceed the weight of the vehicle by as much as 30 to 50 per cent.

Rocket thrust develops as a reaction to the expulsion of particles at high velocity from a nozzle opening. The material expelled may be in the form of liquids, solids, gases, or even radiant energy in some of the more exotic types of rockets. When the supply of propellant is exhausted so is the engine's capability to produce thrust, just as the engine of an automobile stops when the gas tank runs dry. Even a nuclear reactor (*see*) must have a propellant to

A hydrogen-fueled Centaur is lowered into a NASA power chamber where it will undergo a series of environmental tests.

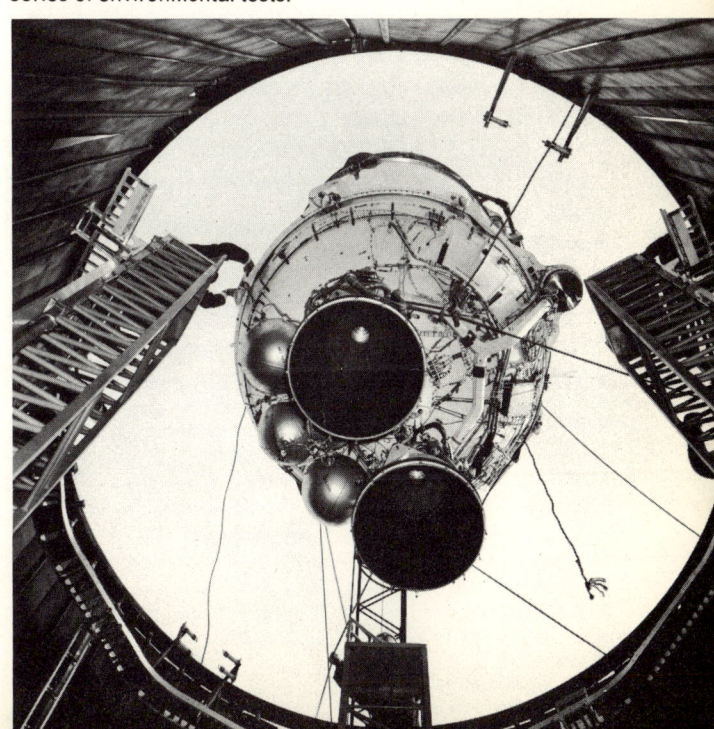

Lockheed's new liquid-solid rocket *(left)* ignites when control fluid flows over grain. After firing *(right)*, some grain is unburnt.

expel to function as a nuclear rocket.

An important index in rating a rocket engine, therefore, is specific impulse, which provides a key to the efficiency with which the engines use its propellant supply to produce thrust.

Types of Rocket Power

Solid-propellant rockets have not yet found application as initial boosters in the manned space program because of size limitations. They are used in large military missiles where instant readiness for firing overcomes other disadvantages. The fuel and oxidizer in a solid-propellant rocket are cast in a solid mass which serves also as the combustion chamber.

Liquid-propellant rockets are more complex and require flow of the separate liquid oxidizer and propellant from their individual tanks to the combustion chamber. If *hypergolic,* they ignite spontaneously as they are sprayed into the chamber. If *diergolic,* an ignitor must be used to start the process.

The Rover project (*see*) is the current U.S. program for research and development of the future nuclear rocket. In this system, a hot exhaust gas is developed by passing a working fluid such as liquid hydrogen through the heat created by the nuclear reactor. There is no combustion process involving the propellant.

Electric rockets are of three basic types: arc jet engines, ion engines, and plasma engines. An arc jet engine employs electricity to heat the propellant and exhausts it in somewhat the same manner as a chemical rocket. Ion rockets use a negative field to expel positive ions. Plasma engines employ a magnetic field to expel a neutral plasma created electrically. The electricity required by any of these engines may come from such sources as nuclear isotopes, nuclear reactors, or solar cells (*see*). All of these are advanced engines and at an early stage of development. Even more advanced are photon rockets, which would depend upon expulsion of particles of light to function as space propulsion systems.

Development of the H-1 Engine

Perhaps the best way to understand space propulsion systems is to study some of the many varying types of engines under development today.

The Saturn family of launch vehicles is initially being used in the Apollo program to place American astronauts on the moon. The H-1 rocket engine, built by Rocketdyne, a division of North American Rockwell Corp., was the first ordered into development for the Saturn rockets (*see*).

Development of this single-chamber, liquid-bipropellant engine began in September, 1958. It was designed to meet the specific requirements of operation in clusters of eight in the first stage of Saturn I, and later, in Uprated Saturn I vehicles used on the first manned Apollo launches. Clustering is a familiar technique now with rocket engines, in which more than one engine is used to provide additional thrust.

The H-1 engine was an outgrowth of engines developed for the Thor and Jupiter military missiles, as are most engines today. H-1 engines deliver a thrust of 205,000 pounds. Pounds of thrust is a more convenient standard of measurement for rocket engines than the horsepower ratings of conventional engines. Clustering the engines provided later Uprated Saturn I vehicles with a liftoff thrust of 1.64 million pounds.

Rocketdyne foresees that the H-1 engine will be used beyond the present programmed missions of the Uprated Saturn I. The company has conducted studies which suggest its application to advanced versions of the Saturn family for launching of replenishment and rescue space platforms; orbiting of space loads of 30,000 and 50,000 pounds; and launching of orbiting vehicles for practicing rendezvous at near-escape velocities.

The first Saturn vehicle employing a cluster of the 165,000-lb.-thrust H-1 engines was launched successfully on October 27, 1961. Total thrust was 1,320,000 pounds. This was the first flight of a U.S. space vehicle with thrust in the million-pound class. It is common now, but was uncommon then. It is particularly interesting that this launch came only three years after award of the initial contract. This is one of the obvious benefits which both the U.S. and the U.S.S.R. have enjoyed from development of space engines from those designed for military missiles.

The improvement in the H-1 engine, together with

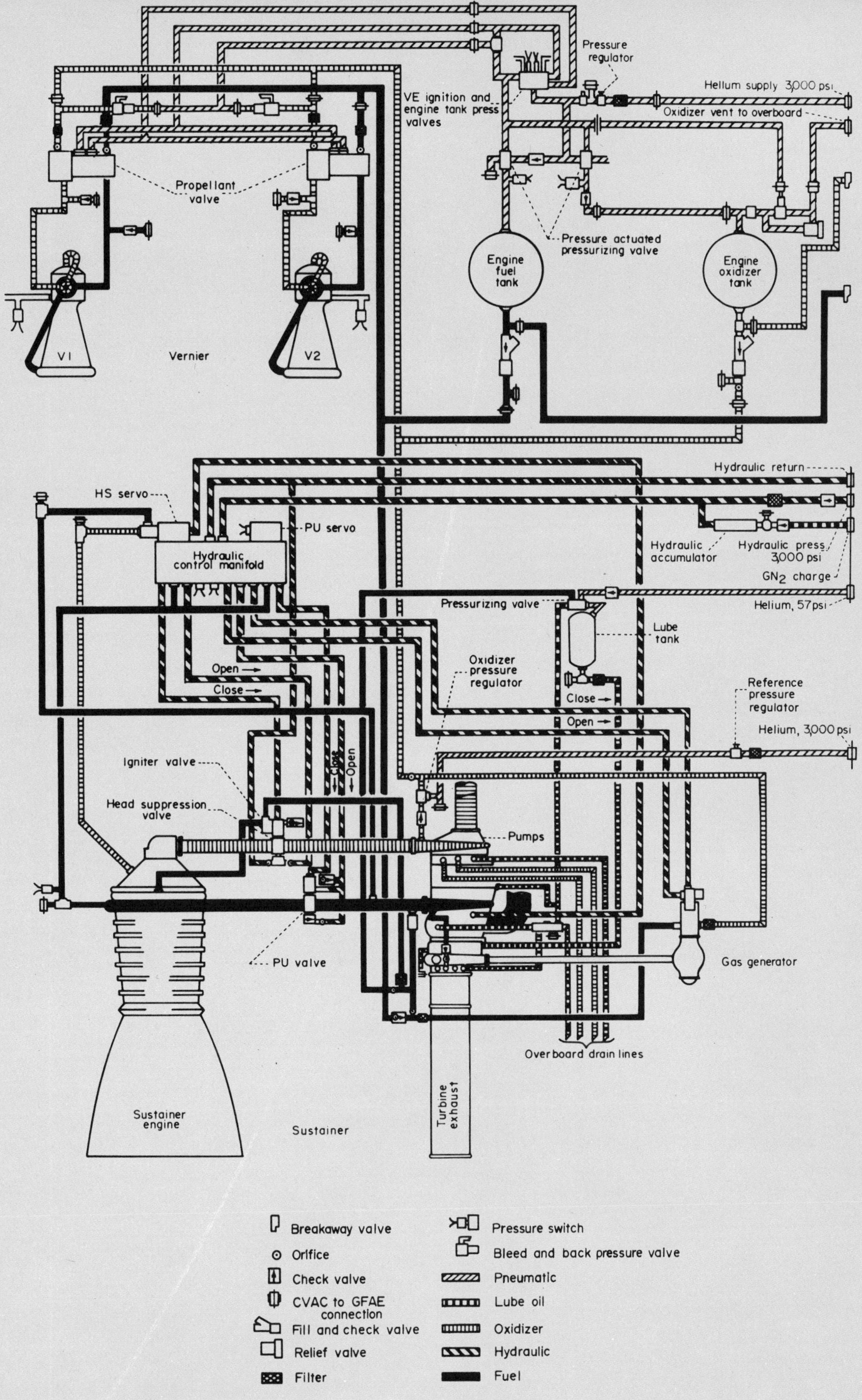
Pressure regulator
Helium supply 3,000 psi
VE ignition and engine tank press valves
Oxidizer vent to overboard
Propellant valve
Pressure actuated pressurizing valve
Engine fuel tank
Engine oxidizer tank
V1
Vernier
V2
Hydraulic return
HS servo
PU servo
Hydraulic control manifold
Hydraulic accumulator
Hydraulic press 3,000 psi
GN2 charge
Pressurizing valve
Helium, 57 psi
Lube tank
Oxidizer pressure regulator
Open
Close
Reference pressure regulator
Helium, 3,000 psi
Igniter valve
Close
Open
Head suppression valve
Pumps
PU valve
Gas generator
Overboard drain lines
Sustainer engine
Sustainer
Turbine exhaust
Breakaway valve
Orifice
Check valve
CVAC to GFAE connection
Fill and check valve
Relief valve
Filter
Pressure switch
Bleed and back pressure valve
Pneumatic
Lube oil
Oxidizer
Hydraulic
Fuel

Space propulsion systems

other improvements in the Saturn family, has provided an increase in Earth-orbit payload capability from the 11 tons of Saturn I to the 18 tons of the Uprated Saturn I vehicle. When it is realized that this has been accomplished by an engine designed for two of the nation's earliest missiles, both now long obsolete, the extraordinary development cycle with space propulsion systems can be more fully appreciated.

The J-2 Hydrogen Fuel Engine

A more exotic engine whose development cycle is worthy of study also is built by Rocketdyne. This is the J-2 hydrogen-fueled engine that will launch the first three astronauts into Earth orbit in the Apollo spacecraft program and later will fly them to the moon.

Liquid hydrogen is one of the most advanced fuels employed in the U.S. space program. It is extremely difficult to handle and presents many design disadvantages. However, it offers a greater weight-lifting capacity.

Currently, the J-2 engine develops up to 225,000 pounds of thrust at altitude and is the most powerful high-energy rocket engine currently being used in upper stages of U.S. space vehicles.

Both the Uprated Saturn I and the Saturn V launch vehicles use this high-energy engine. The J-2 is employed in a cluster of five engines in the S-II developed as the second stage of Saturn V. In that configuration, the J-2 cluster will develop a total of 1,125,000 pounds of thrust maximum. In the Uprated Saturn I, J-2 is a single second-stage engine in the S-IVB stage developed by McDonnell Douglas Co. There is a double benefit from this. The S-IVB is the third stage of the Saturn V vehicle. This engine, therefore, developed on the frontiers of propulsion technology, is one of the most important in the space program.

The J-2 was operated in flight for the first time on February 25, 1966, as it powered the S-IVB stage of the first Uprated Saturn I vehicle to be launched. Engine operation was completely successful. A new means of space propulsion was in being.

That is not the end for the J-2 engine. To meet advanced requirement for Saturn V, work continued to uprate the J-2 engine to 230,000 pound minimum thrust. The first of these uprated engines was delivered in the spring of 1966.

The Need for Smaller Systems

Not all of the activity involved in developing space propulsion systems is centered about the giant booster engines. Other propulsion systems are also

An assembly line produces the U.S.'s most powerful rocket engine, the F-1. A cluster of five F-1's compose the first stage of Saturn V.

involved in modern-day aerospace space activities.

Once the Apollo team lands the Lunar Module on the moon's surface, it must get off again for its rendezvous with the Command Module orbiting overhead. Thus, one of the most important events in the Apollo mission will be leaving the lunar surface for the return trip to Earth. That requires a space propulsion system. The task has been assigned to Bell Aerosystems, which builds the Lunar Module ascent engine. This 3,500-pound-thrust, pressure-fed rocket engine is critical. If it malfunctions, the astronauts, with limited oxygen supply, are trapped on the lunar surface. The ascent engine has to provide the thrust for a powered takeoff from the moon and insertion into an 80-mile circular lunar orbit. It must also provide the thrust for any orbit adjustments necessary for rendezvous with the Command Module overhead.

Some idea of the difficulty in designing and preparing for the Apollo missions may be gained from the fact that five Lunar Landing Training Vehicles, developed by Bell, were tested and flown at Ellington Air Force Base, Houston, Texas. Not only were astronauts trained in the piloting and operational problems of a manned lunar landing but they were

A Service Module model for Apollo shows two of the R4D 100-lb. thrust engine clusters that supply stabilization and maneuvering power.

working with cockpit controls arranged to resemble that of the Lunar Module. In strict definition, this was not a space propulsion system. Yet the whole emphasis of the design was to simulate just such systems. Primary support for the vehicle was provided by a 4,200-pounds-thrust turbofan engine. The engine counteracted five-sixths of the Earth's gravity. The remaining one-sixth gravity was comparable to the gravity of the moon. Lift for that remaining one-sixth was provided by two Bell rocket motors with a maximum of 500-pounds-thrust each. These rocket motors simulated those used for lunar landings.

Shifting a spacecraft from one position to another requires only a relatively small but important system such as the reaction controls for the Project Apollo Service Module.

The Service Module has two separate propulsion systems. The service propulsion system (SPS) is designed for major velocity changes. The reactional control system (RCS) is designed to provide thrust for programmed and emergency control maneuvers. The Marquardt Corp. provides the 16 R-4D liquid bipropellant rockets for the system. Mounted in four four-engine clusters, the R-4D rockets are designed to respond to automatic or manual control signals.

Space stations

They may be fired individually or in various combinations to carry out required maneuvers. During a typical mission, a single R-4D engine may be required to fire more than 6,250 times. It may be required to deliver 100-pounds-thrust for durations which may last as long as 10 minutes or for as short a period as 10 milliseconds. This very small rocket engine, producing only 100 pounds of thrust, is a radiation-cooled rocket using liquid hypergolic propellants: nitrogen tetrozide and pure monomethylhydrazine fuel.

Small-thrust space propulsion systems may seem minor compared to the giant boosters that generate millions of pounds of thrust to lift spacecraft off the Earth. In fact, both space propulsion systems are critical to success of the mission.

What happens tomorrow in space propulsion systems may be of even more importance than what is going on today. For example, there would have been no H-1 engine for the Saturn vehicles had there not been a military requirement for an engine for Thor and Jupiter missiles. The third firing of a 260-inch-diameter solid rocket motor, the biggest ever, was carried out in June, 1967. It was truly a remarkable achievement. Today's research and development is the heart of tomorrow's operational space propulsion systems. — William J. Coughlin

See also: Apollo, Electric propulsion, Ion propulsion, Missiles, Plasma propulsion, Rocket propulsion systems, Rockets and rocketry

Space stations

The first space stations will be large research laboratories that will be placed in orbit around the Earth some time during the 1970's. From these stations, astronauts will conduct a variety of experiments that cannot be carried out as well, if at all, from airplanes or from the ground.

The earliest space stations will use much of the equipment already developed for the Gemini and Apollo spaceflight programs. For example, construction of the first National Aeronautics and Space Administration (NASA) space station will be based on the Saturn IB launch vehicle employed in the Apollo Development Flight-Test program. During a mission in the near future, a Saturn IB will be launched so that its upper stage, the S-IVB, will be injected into an orbit around the Earth. Another Saturn IB will carry an Apollo Command/Service Module and its crew from Earth to rendezvous with the first S-IVB and dock against it. By that time the fuel in the first S-IVB will have been consumed, and any residual gases will be automatically vented.

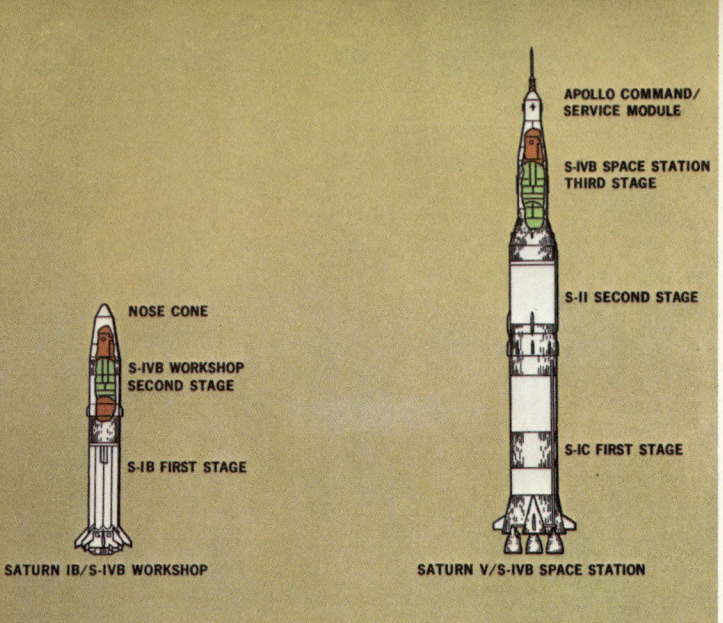

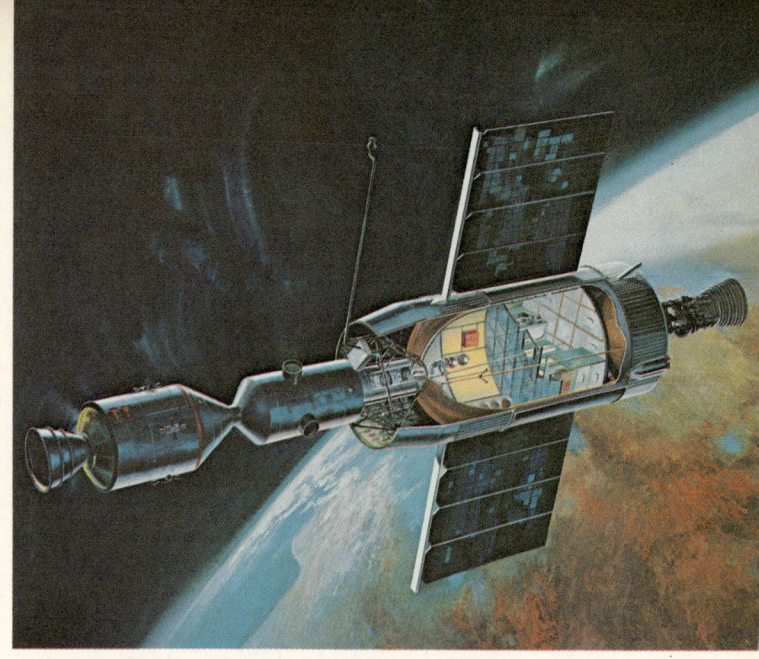

A Saturn I Workshop and Apollo Command/Service Module shown in launch configuration (*left*) are docked in space. This is where astronauts enter Workshop (*right*) to live and carry out experiments.

The astronauts will then leave the Apollo spacecraft and enter the empty S-IVB stage through a special airlock (*see*). They will carry in and install about a ton of equipment to be used for laboratory facilities and for their own living quarters.

The station, to be known as the Saturn I Workshop, will first be operated for about one month. The astronauts will then return to the Earth in the Command Module, leaving the deactivated workshop in orbit. Several months later, a second three-man crew will arrive to reactivate and operate the workshop for a two-month period. This crew will be joined by an unmanned spacecraft containing solar telescopes for scientific experiments. Still later, additional crews will also revist the workshop for extended operations.

The space station programs that follow the workshop program will be entirely different. Future stations will probably carry five to ten tons of equipment for a wider variety of research and will be able to house six to nine men for as long as a year.

Because the operations of this future space station will be more complicated than the workshop, the equipment will be more complex. Everything will be completely pre-installed and checked by specialists on the ground. In addition, because the future space stations will be heavier than the Saturn I Workshop, they will require a larger booster to put them into orbit. The giant first two stages of the Saturn V will be used.

Experiment Operations

Some of the experiments in the space stations will be done inside the station in surroundings much like those of a research laboratory on the Earth. In other experiments, sensors (*see*) will be pointed outside the station to permit the viewing or sensing of objects and conditions on the Earth, near the Earth, or in stellar space. Still another class of experiments will be installed in auxiliary spacecraft which can be separated and flown away from the mother station and operated by remote control.

Many experiments will use sensors which must be pointed at various objects, such as the sun, the horizon, a star, or the Earth. The station must therefore be oriented in different attitudes at different times. When there is no need for the station to point in a particular direction, that part of the station with the lowest drag will be pointed in the direction of flight. This is required since at an altitude of about 200 miles there are still enough air particles to cause the station to gradually lose altitude at the rate of about 10 miles every month.

The station will be oriented automatically by control-moment gyroscopes and small rocket motors which operate in three axes. The control-moment gyros are large flywheels that conserve angular momentum and rotate the station on an action-reaction principle. These devices receive their pointing-reference information from star trackers and horizon sensors. Therefore, whenever the crew injects pointing commands into the system, the attitude-control equipment turns the station accurately to the desired direction.

Aside from the many routine intercommunications between members of the crew, who are in different compartments from time to time, there will be both voice and data communications with Earth whenever the space station passes over a ground control station. During this time, experiment data and vehicle-status reports will be transmitted to the ground

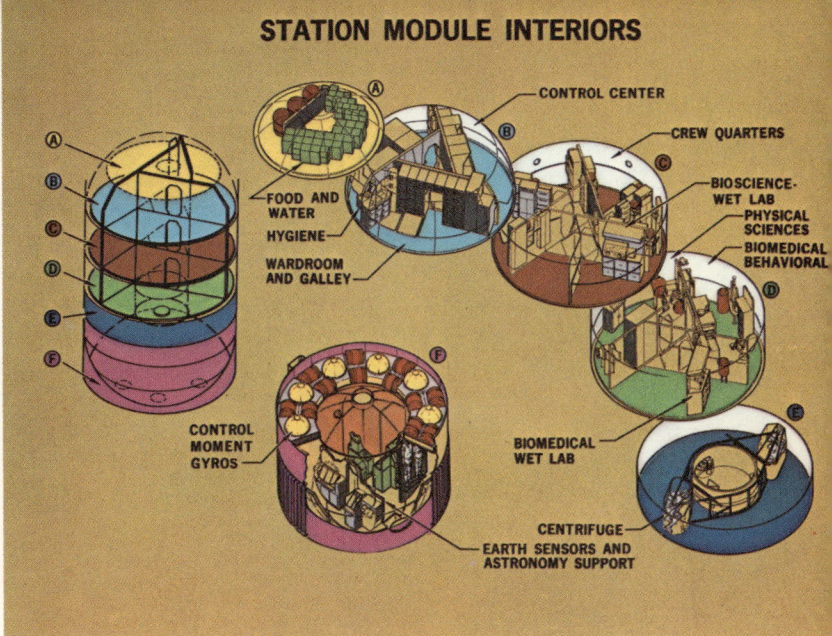

Future space stations such as the S-IVB *(left)* will contain complex systems *(right)* which will make advanced experiments on the biomedical and behavioral aspects of space life possible.

on different frequencies. Recoverable data capsules with special film, pictures, or laboratory specimens can also be ejected from the station and landed at a prescribed spot on the Earth.

The electrical power required by this type of station will average about six kilowatts. The power will be provided by solar-cell panels that have over 2,000 sq. ft. of surface area, by batteries with DC-to-AC electricity converters, and by power interconnecting equipment. As the station orbits around the Earth, the solar panels will be rotated so that they face the sun. The batteries will store the electrical energy created by the solar cells *(see)* so that it can be used when the station is on the dark side of the Earth or when it requires additional power.

Interior Design and Life-Support Facilities

In designing the interior of a typical spacecraft, the designer has to consider a number of important factors, including which equipment will be used the most, which equipment will require the use of two or more men, and which dynamic operations, such as spacecraft docking, data recovery, capsule ejection, attitude control, should be isolated from the more sensitive instruments. In the case of the design illustrated, the dynamic operations are located in front of the station, as far away as possible from the telescope and cameras, which are located in the rear.

The station will be divided into separate compartments which can be isolated. In case of an emergency, each compartment can support the entire crew if necessary. A central tunnel will be used as the main thoroughfare. The tunnel has a "fireman's pole" so that the weightless astronauts can pull themselves along.

In the cold vacuum of space, man can survive only if there is an adequate supply of oxygen and a comfortable temperature. These seemingly simple requirements involve a substantial amount of complicated equipment, both inside and outside the station. Equipment will automatically remove excess humidity, carbon dioxide, trace contaminants, and bacteria from the breathing atmosphere. Because of the nearly zero-gravity of space, warm air will not circulate as it does on the Earth. Therefore, elaborate air-circulation and mixing systems must be located in many places in the station. When the station becomes too hot, heat exchangers *(see)* in each room will absorb the heat and transport it by fluids to the outside radiators. These tubular radiators will eject the heat generated by men and machinery into the vacuum of space. When the station is too cold, electrical heaters will be used.

To live and work effectively both inside and outside the station, the crew must have a great variety of special accessories. Soft, unpressurized suits will be worn inside the station, while pressurized suits with umbilical cords *(see)* will be used for outside activities. Special body-conditioning and exercise equipment will be supplied to offset the effects of zero-gravity. Special saddle-like seats and foot restraints to secure the crewmen in required positions will also be needed.

The crew will have a recreation room that they can use during off-duty hours. Each crew member will have a sleep station with an enveloping hammock-type rig, a desk area, and a storage room for his belongings. One room will be able to be made into a sickbay, complete with medical and minor surgical equipment.

Since food variety and palatability can become

Space stations

a major influence on crew morale and performance, extremely good meals will be provided. The space diet will include meats, sea foods, dairy products, prepared dishes such as stews and fricassees, soups, desserts, and beverages. All of these can be served at the proper temperature and with the natural moisture content, original flavor, form, texture, and aroma of those foods. These dishes can be freeze-dried, water-packed, or minimum-moisture foods.

Lightweight eating and drinking containers will be used once and then thrown away. The utensils will be dry wiped after each use and stored in sterilized containers for reuse. Each man's meal will be vacuum-packed in a foil plastic wrap, which will also contain a napkin and a digestible dentifrice. The galley will have an oven, a chiller, a vacuum cleaner for loose particles, a food-preparation console with hot and cold water-dispensing devices, and storage tanks for dishwater and other waste.

The hygiene compartment will contain waste-disposal equipment and other devices that are like those found in a conventional, automated toilet. All equipment will be designed to operate in zero-gravity. For example, shaving equipment and glove-like bathing sponges will have attached devices to vacuum up the whiskers and soapsuds.

Experiments To Be Conducted

Some of the general categories of experiments being considered for the manned space stations include: biomedicine and behavior, astronomy and astrophysics, atmospheric sciences, Earth resources, bioscience, physical science, communication and navigation traffic control, advanced technology and subsystems, and manned operations and logistics.

In the biomedical and behavioral experiments, measurements will be taken to see how the space environment affects man. A number of experiments will be used to determine what preventive or therapeutic measure can be devised that will offset any bad effects of the space environment. These experiments will provide information about the effects of space on the nervous system, the heart, the bones and muscles, the blood, and the glands. Immunological and epidemiological experiments will be conducted to examine microbes in a closed environment. Behavioral experiments will help scientists to determine how a lengthy stay in orbit affects such things as man's vision, speech, and muscular reaction. These experiments will also measure how space affects man's higher mental processes, such as his vigilance, attention, memory, problem-solving ability, and speech perception.

The experiments in the fields of astronomy (*see*) and astrophysics (*see*) will augment the observations made from Earth. Telescopes mounted in the space stations will be located above the hazy and obscuring atmosphere of the Earth. Radio, gamma ray, X-ray, infrared, and ultraviolet measurements and stellar photographs will be the primary objective of these future experiments.

Earth resources experiments will augment present research work in forestry, geography, cartography, geology, hydrology, oceanography, and marine technology. From the high vantage point of a space station, man will be able to witness phenomena that he cannot observe from the ground.

In the area of bioscience, man will study a variety of animals and plants to determine the effects that weightlessness (*see*), radiation (*see*), and other stresses of the space environment have.

Experiments in the category of communication and navigation traffic control will support the rapid development of telephone communication satellites, television, rebroadcasting, and ship and aircraft traffic control. Equipment to be used will include large space-erectable antennas, lasers (*see*), radar (*see*), transmitters (*see*), receivers (*see*), and automatic navigation devices.

The physical sciences will be represented by experiments involving electromagnetic and solar radiation, particles and fields, and other physical phenomena, such as liquid behavior.

The objective of the advanced technology experiments will be to evaluate equipment and operating procedures that can be used on more advanced space stations. The experiments will investigate such systems as power, attitude control, environmental control and life support, propulsion, communications, structures, and guidance.

Man can either limit or enhance the success of these experiments depending on how well he is able to operate in the weightless condition that exists in space, both inside and outside the station. Man's activities in space are classified as IVA (Intra-Vehicular Activity) or EVA (Extra-Vehicular Activity). Experiments in the manned space operations and logistics category will aid in the development of efficient IVA and EVA procedures and equipment. The equipment includes devices for helping the weightless astronaut to move about or to remain stationary, instruments to assist him in transferring fluid and gases, devices to assist him in handling cargo, and tools to be used in fabricating and assembling various items.

Fritz Runge

See also: Apollo Applications Program, Manned Orbiting Laboratory, Space tools

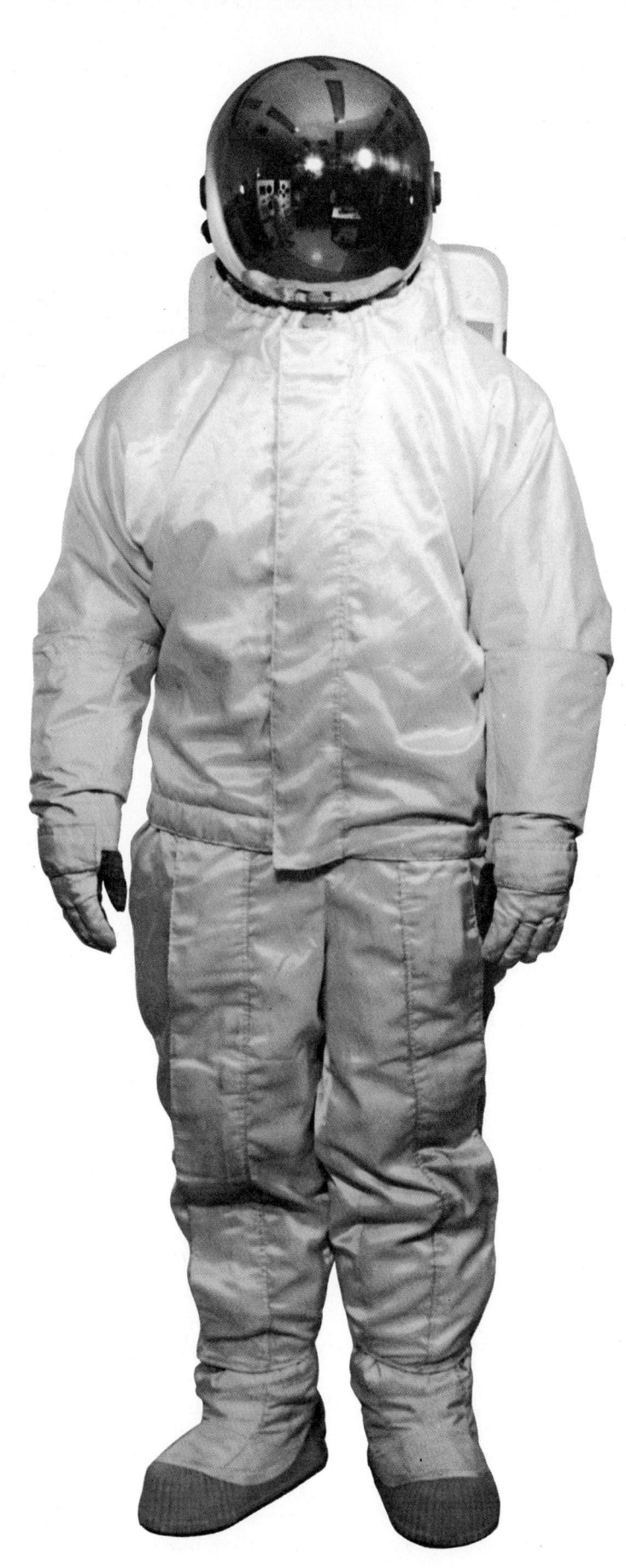

The Apollo Block II extravehicular mobility unit (EMU) with thermal meteoroid overgarment provides an artificial atmosphere, adequate mobility, and protection systems against the extreme lunar temperatures and solar light.

Spacesuits
A home away from home

During the planning and development of man's exploration of space, one of the primary considerations was the problems he would face outside his normal atmospheric environment. Early experimentation in high-altitude flying had already established the need for special protective garments in order for man to function in any meaningful way in the upper atmosphere and beyond.

As early as 1934, the first pressure suit (spacesuit) was developed for use by Wiley Post (*see*), a world-renowned aviator who was attempting to set a high-altitude record in aircraft. The suit eventually designed and built for Post resembled the type usually worn by deep-sea divers. It was of a rubberized fabric with boots and gloves attached, and was made in two pieces joined at the waist. Lack of mobility was one of its limitations. The aluminum helmet was cylindrical, with a face plate and an oxygen hose attachment.

As man began his exploration of space, mobility and comfort were the considerations immediately following basic life support. Comfort requires fitting the garment to relieve pressure points and solving the cabin was small, and the design of the craft's controls was such that mobility was not a prime requirement except for shoulder and hand movement. In short-duration flights, waste management could be achieved by proper preflight diet and the use of a urine collection device in the suit.

The suit played a primary role in putting man into space by providing reliable temperature and oxygen control. In the Mercury suit, oxygen was fed into the garment by a connector located in the torso area. Oxygen was first circulated to the extremities of the suit and then to the helmet for breathing. Exhaled waste bled off through a headpiece connector into the environmental control system (*see*) where it was reconstituted for reuse.

This temperature and oxygen control system allowed astronauts full maneuverability within the spacecraft even at temperatures as high as 100°F. Another means used to provide comfort was to tailor suits individually for each astronaut, thus eliminating unnecessary bulk and pressure points caused by folds in the material. The Mercury suits provided astronauts with emergency protection and maximum mobility as a component of the spacecraft's environmental control system.

The suit was generally made of four layers of loosely fitted material. The outer layer was a high-temperature-resistant metallic fabric. The second layer was a woven net fabric which served as a restraint layer to prevent the suit from ballooning when pressurized. The third layer was a rubberized fabric designed to make the suit airtight. The inner layer next to the astronaut's body was a smooth soft nylon designed for comfort.

The helmet of the spacesuit, attached by a special neck ring, was padded to prevent head injury. The astronaut's communications systems were built into the helmet. Gloves and custom-made boots completed the spacesuit.

Gemini Suits

In the Gemini (*see*) two-man spaceflight program, NASA faced the problem of developing a fully pressurized spacesuit that would allow a member of the crew to leave the spacecraft for varying lengths of time and to operate in a zero-gravity environment of extreme temperature variations.

The basic Gemini suit bore some similarity to that worn in the Mercury program. The Gemini suit was a multilayered garment consisting of an inner comfort liner, a gas bladder, a structural restraint layer, and an outer protective cover. To allow the suit to be more easily put on and taken off, quick disconnectors were located at the wrists for gloves, at the

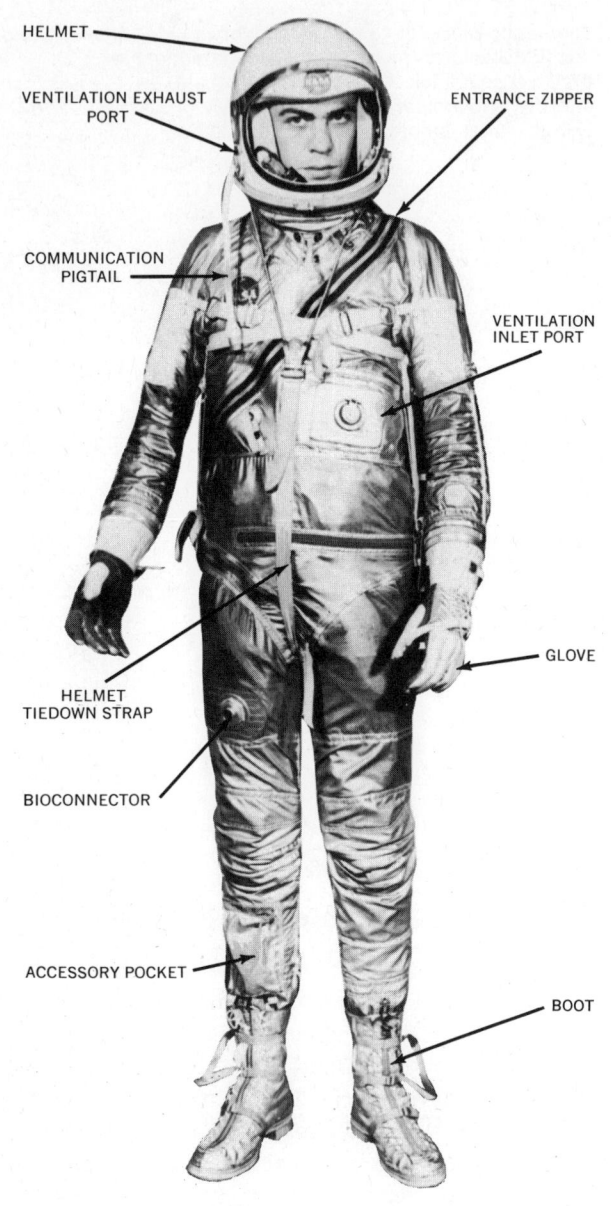

MERCURY PRESSURE SUIT

problem of waste disposal. Freedom to perform functions necessary to accomplish the mission requires mobility and must be assured in both pressurized or unpressurized conditions.

Project Mercury Spacesuits

One of the first true spacesuits was developed for the National Aeronautics and Space Administration (NASA) (*see*) Mercury program (*see*). It was designed to function like the U.S. Navy's Mark IV pressure suit which was employed in high-speed flight. This was an emergency garment worn as a backup to the craft's environmental control system. In Project Mercury, spacecraft design played a large part in the development of the suit eventually worn during missions. The interior of the spacecraft's neck for the helmet, and at the waist for ventilation-gas connections. A pressure-sealing zipper was also provided to make dressing and undressing easier. Body wastes were taken care of by a disposal system built into the suit. Oxygen was directed into the helmet area for breathing and then to the extremities for thermal (temperature) control. The basic suit was also provided with handkerchief, pencils, survival knife, scissors, neck and wrist dams (worn during recovery operations after gloves and helmet have been removed to prevent water from entering the suit), a parachute harness, and special built-in pockets on the arms and legs to hold flight books and charts.

During the Gemini 4 mission in June, 1965, it was planned that one of the crew members would leave the spacecraft to become the program's first man to walk in space. With this new requirement added to the basic mission, a slightly different suit had to be developed. A different extravehicular (EVA) outer layer was added to the basic suit as well as pressure-thermal gloves, a helmet visor with temperature control coating, and a sun visor. The EVA outer layer consisted of nylon material for micrometeoroid protection, seven layers of aluminized superinsulation, and an outer covering of high-temperature nylon cloth.

The new EVA visor was a two-lens assembly with the outer lens providing visible and infrared sun-ray protection and the inner lens providing impact protection and thermal control. The overgloves were designed for protection from conductive heat transfer in exposed sunlight. No difficulties with the spacesuit were encountered during the Gemini IV mission. In fact, it was found that the cover layer bulk could be reduced below that first considered necessary and thus make the suit more comfortable.

Another change in the Gemini spacesuit occurred in the Gemini 7 mission in December 1965. This was the *lightweight suit* designed for use within the spacecraft only. Its purpose was to provide maximum protection as well as comfort and freedom of movement. A principal consideration was reduction in the bulk of the garment itself.

This suit had a soft fabric hood which replaced the hard preshaped helmet worn previously. The hood, which was a continuation of the body of the suit, had a polycarbonate visor and a pressure-sealing zipper. The long zipper permitted removal of the hood for stowage in an area behind the astronaut's head. The lightweight suit weighed 16 pounds including a crash helmet worn under the larger soft hood. Gemini suits previously weighed approximate-

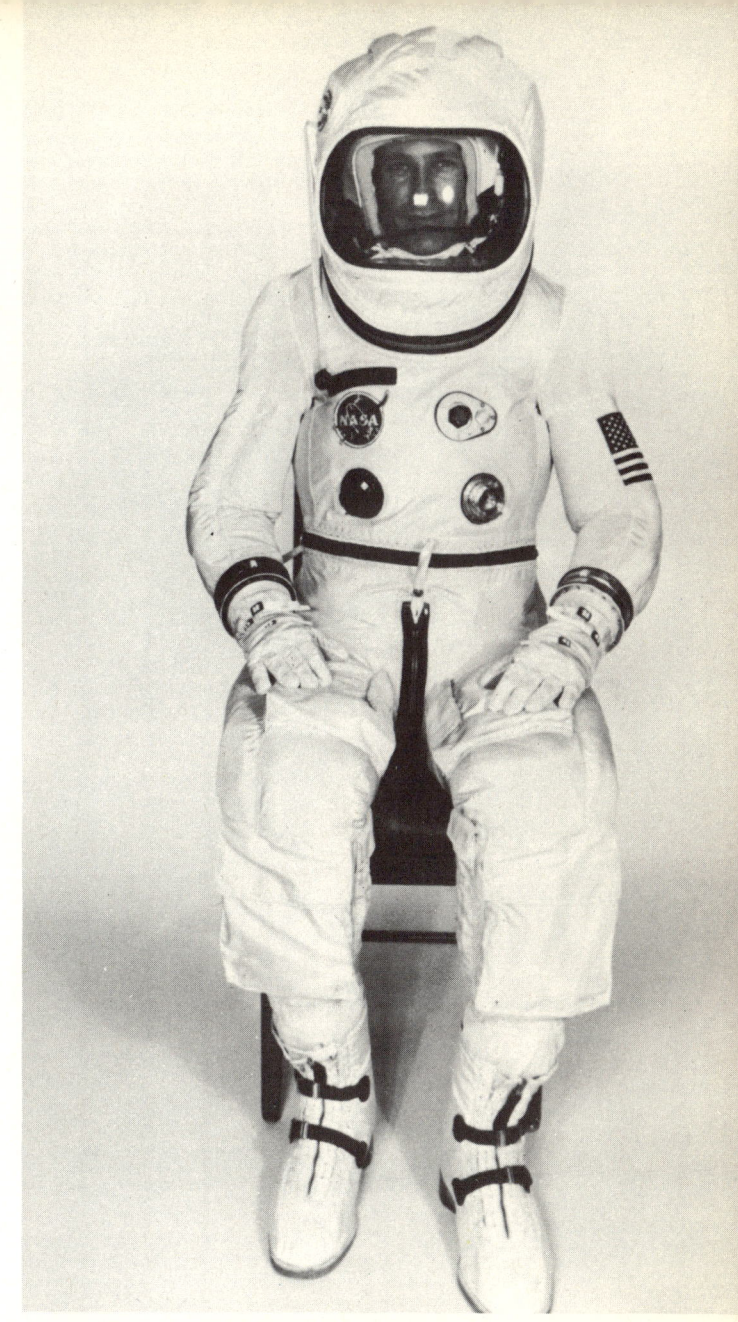

Spacesuits are constantly being improved. A lightweight suit, the Gemini G5C *(top)*, was designed for the 14-day flight of Gemini 7. It could be partially doffed or removed for added comfort. The coverlayer configuration of the extravehicular suit *(bottom)* underwent design changes between Gemini "space walks."

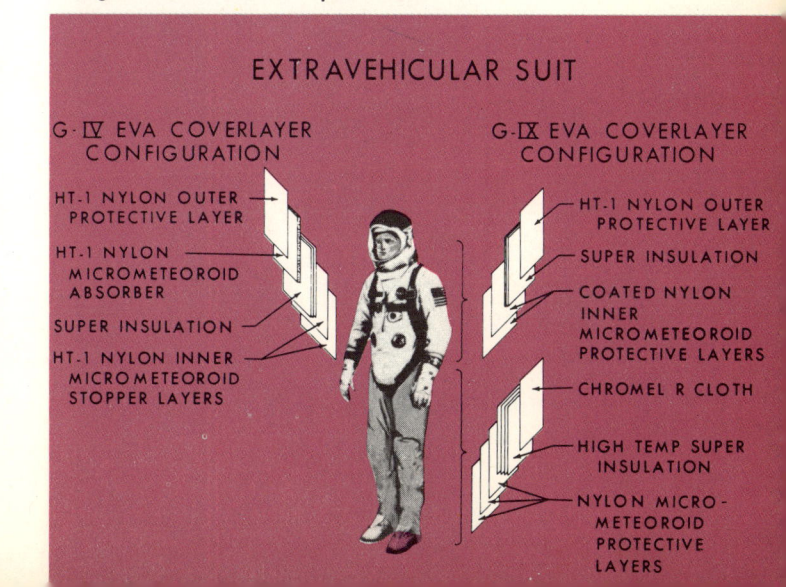

EXTRAVEHICULAR SUIT

G-IV EVA COVERLAYER CONFIGURATION
- HT-1 NYLON OUTER PROTECTIVE LAYER
- HT-1 NYLON MICROMETEOROID ABSORBER
- SUPER INSULATION
- HT-1 NYLON INNER MICROMETEOROID STOPPER LAYERS

G-IX EVA COVERLAYER CONFIGURATION
- HT-1 NYLON OUTER PROTECTIVE LAYER
- SUPER INSULATION
- COATED NYLON INNER MICROMETEOROID PROTECTIVE LAYERS
- CHROMEL R CLOTH
- HIGH TEMP SUPER INSULATION
- NYLON MICROMETEOROID PROTECTIVE LAYERS

The Gemini 4 extravehicular suit *(top)* was capable of sustaining astronauts outside the spacecraft for relatively short periods of time. For Lunar flights, the A7L Apollo pressure suit *(bottom)* was developed. It is the only personal equipment which must be designed for the entire Apollo flight and return trip.

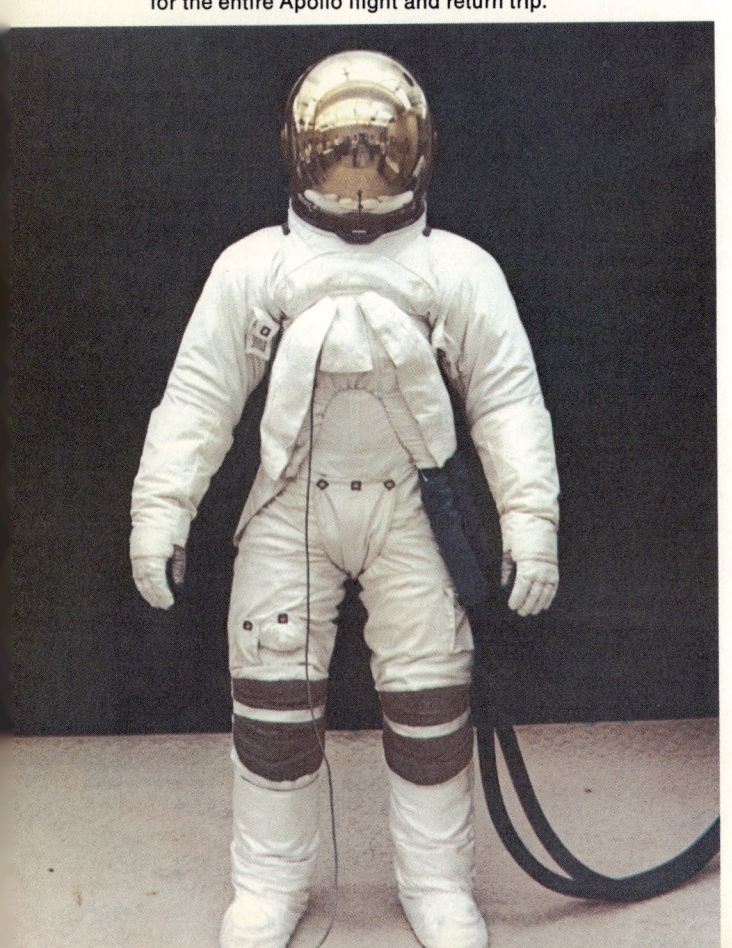

ly 23.5 pounds. The suit could be completely removed inside the spacecraft. It could also be worn with gloves and boots off and the hood unzipped at the neck and rolled back to form a head rest.

The new suit had two layers of material: the inner layer was the pressure-restraining neoprene-coated nylon bladder, and the outer layer was 6-ounce high-temperature nylon. Small sections of link net in the shoulders improved mobility. Elimination of the large metal neck ring used on previous suits to secure the helmet to the garment also reduced the weight. Ventilation was external and provided by ducts down the outside of the legs and arms of the pressure bladder at the extremities.

Because of the proved reliability of the Gemini spacecraft's environmental control system, the new suit made it possible to fly in a shirtsleeve environment (*see*). This suit proved successful in reducing bulk and in resistance to body movement. It had fewer pressure points than previous suits, and its unique design allowed easy donning and doffing within the small area of the spacecraft cabin. Donning time was about 16 minutes.

After the 14-day flight of the Gemini 7, the crew reported that they felt comfortable wearing the lightweight suit. They also reported that they perspired less and slept better after they removed the suit entirely. Elimination of the pressure garment resulted in a temperature environment that was similar to that experienced when wearing street clothes on the Earth.

Other changes in the basic Gemini suit were made during the Gemini 8 mission in March, 1966. The outer protective cover, or micrometeoroid layer, was reduced. The thermal protective fabric in the gloves was incorporated into the glove design instead of as an addition to the regular suit gloves.

The special flight requirements of the Gemini 9-A mission in June, 1966, imposed an unusual requirement on the suit. The Astronaut Maneuvering Unit (AMU) developed for use outside the spacecraft required changes in the lower portion of the spacesuit worn by the EVA astronaut. The high-temperature fire plume from the AMU's thrusters could severely damage the suit and the astronaut, so a stainless steel fabric outer covering was provided to protect the astronaut from heat erosion. A high-temperature superinsulation, used below the outer cover, consisted of alternate layers of double aluminized film and lightweight fiber glass.

In addition, further protective measures had to be taken with the helmet visor to avoid impact damage. The Plexiglas pressure visor was replaced with

Spacesuits

SPACE SUIT INSTALLED ACCESSORIES

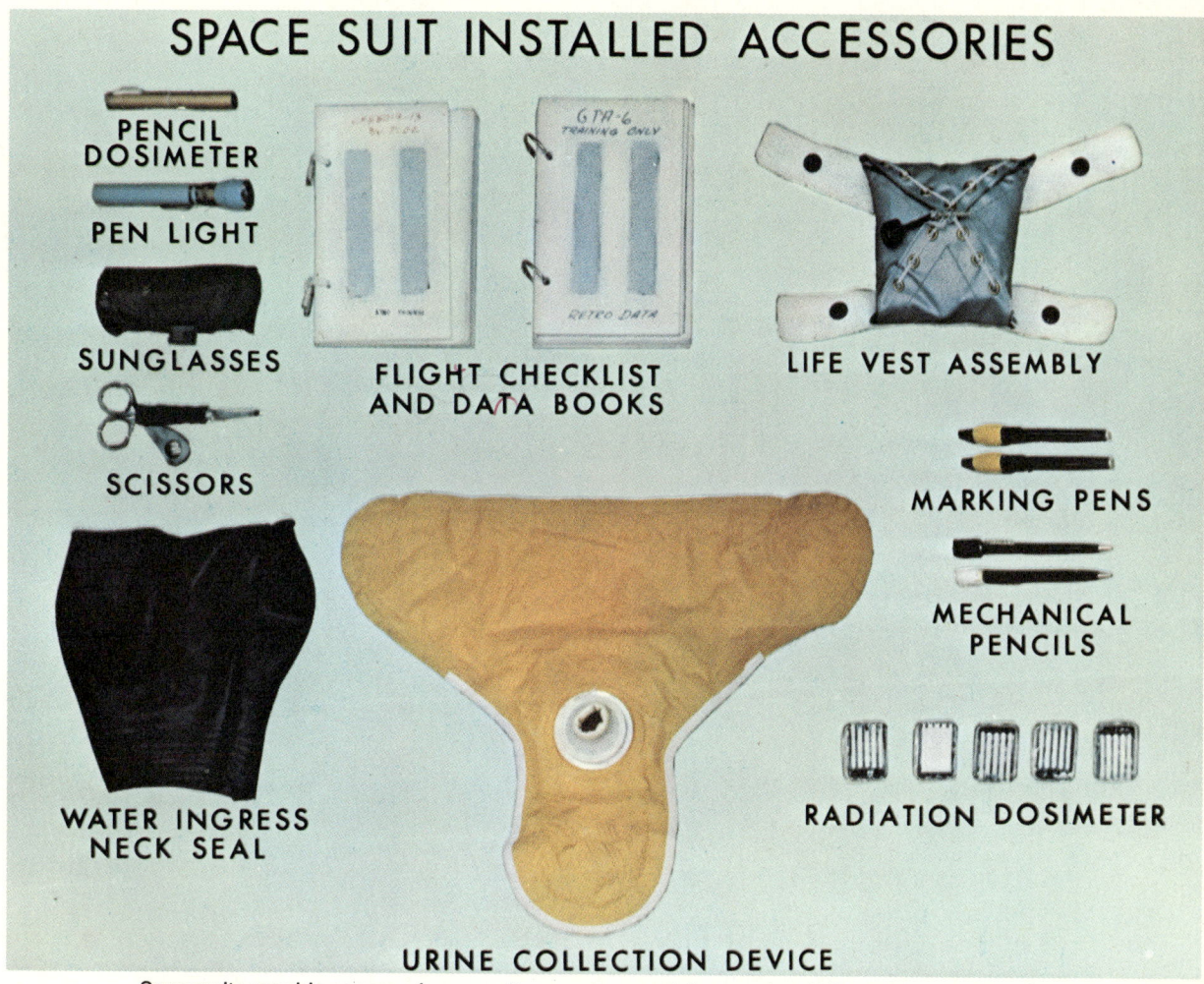

PENCIL DOSIMETER
PEN LIGHT
SUNGLASSES
FLIGHT CHECKLIST AND DATA BOOKS
LIFE VEST ASSEMBLY
SCISSORS
MARKING PENS
MECHANICAL PENCILS
WATER INGRESS NECK SEAL
RADIATION DOSIMETER
URINE COLLECTION DEVICE

Spacesuits provide accessories as well as environmental protection. Utility, record-keeping, and lifesaving items aid astronauts in conducting routine operations and meeting emergencies.

a coated polycarbonate pressure visor. This also permitted the use of a single-lens sun visor. The temperature-erosion protection modifications were not fully evaluated because of fogging of the helmet's pressure visor which occurred during EVA. The time outside the spacecraft was cut short.

Apollo Suits

The spacesuit planned for the Apollo (see) lunar missions is the only piece of equipment which must be designed to go all the way to the surface of the moon and return to Earth.

The Apollo lunar suit must provide the astronaut with positive protection against the hostile environment he will encounter on the moon's surface. It must shield him from temperatures ranging from −250° to +250° F. Micrometeoroids and the complete vacuum of the surface are additional hazards.

The Apollo spacesuit is currently still under testing and evaluation. It has gone through a long process of change and improvement to the present A7L Apollo pressure suit.

In its early stages the suit was conceived as a multigarment item. In some cases, it bore a noticeable resemblance to a suit of armor. The development of suits for the Mercury and Gemini programs provided a basis for choosing the necessary features of the Apollo suits. Better protection of the astronaut on the lunar surface necessitated some changes, and the long-duration flight required other modifications. As a result, suit designs have evolved to their current state. Several manufacturers worked from different basic concepts in designing the Apollo suit. This varied from a hard suit to a lightweight fabric suit similar to those worn during Gemini spaceflights.

Tests on the Earth determined that the work performed by the astronaut on the lunar surface would generate considerable heat. Control of body tem-

2133

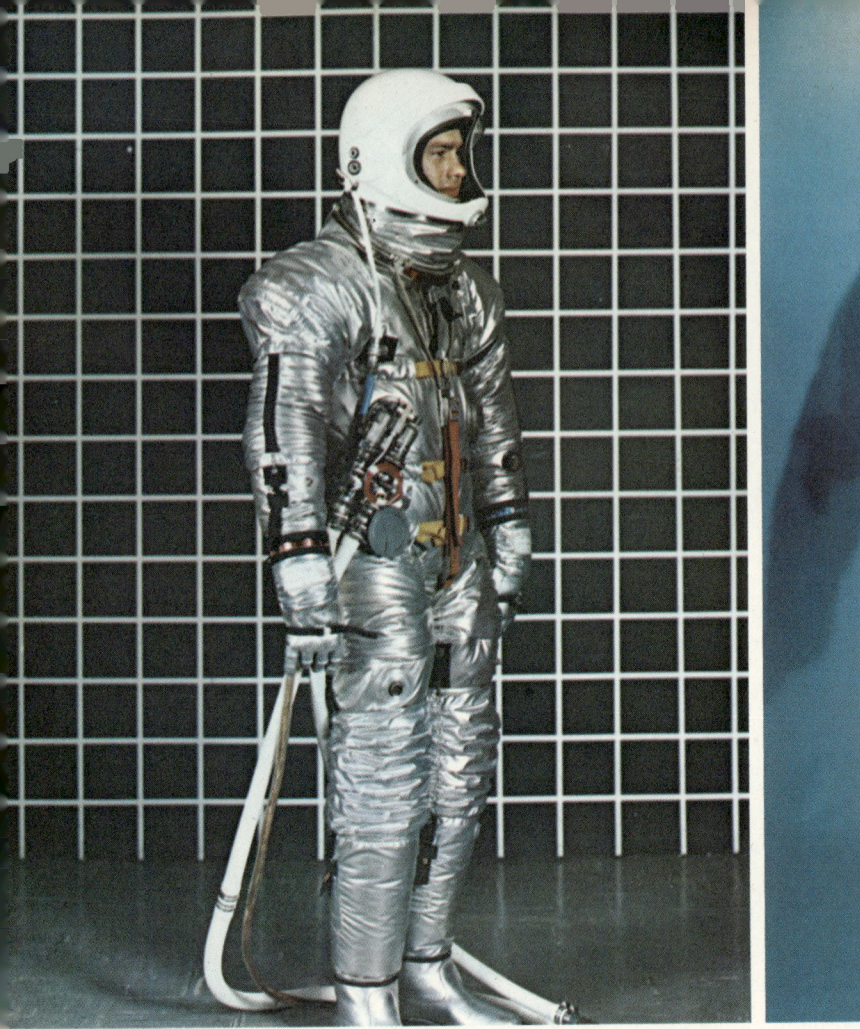

The Apollo spacesuit *(left)* for wear during lunar missions may be compared with the prototype of a "hard suit" *(right)* which is currently being evaluated for use in post-Apollo missions.

perature required development of a special undergarment. It was generally agreed that this would be a garment of several levels beginning with a water-cooled underwear layer. The second layer of the suit, the pressure garment, was the actual suit assembly. This suit was a fully pressurized unit to protect the wearer in the total-vacuum environment of the moon's surface. The pressure suit was covered by a micrometeoroid protection layer made of lightweight materials that provided as much protection from meteoroids as a thin sheet of aluminum. The astronaut's attire was completed with a thermal overgarment composed of many thin layers of superinsulation with a white synthetic fabric as an outer layer. Thermal gloves protect the hands.

A special consideration in developing a suitable garment for moon expeditions was protection of the astronaut's eyes. There is no atmosphere to disperse and reduce the power of the sun's rays as there is on the Earth. The astronaut will be exposed to visible, infrared, and ultraviolet rays. Solar reflection from the spacesuit, the Lunar Module, or equipment can produce a blinding glare outside the spacecraft.

As a solution, an adjustable visor was designed for the helmet. It is similar to a sun visor in an automobile. It can reflect 80 to 90 per cent of visible light, 60 to 80 per cent of infrared rays, and nearly all of the ultraviolet rays. An inner and outer visor arrangement prevents fogging due to temperature changes.

At one point in the development of a suit for lunar astronauts, an aluminum pressure suit was constructed. Nicknamed the "hard suit," it was officially described as a constant volume, rigid, articulated anthropomorphic protective suit.

The hard suit was considered practical for wear outside the spacecraft either on the lunar surface or eventually on other planets. The suit was fully pressurized and closely duplicated an atmospheric condition similar to that of the Earth. Because of its solid construction, normal motion of arms and legs did not crease the suit and cause pressure points. In more conventional spacesuits, when the wearer bends his torso or limbs, pressures change throughout the entire suit.

Less oxygen was required to keep the hard suit under pressure because it had no zipper and only one main opening through which the astronaut dons the suit. A single latch closes the suit and makes it airtight and leakproof.

Because of the long duration of the mission to the moon—six days' travel time round trip—the pressure suit finally chosen has several modes of dress. NASA designers decided upon a constant-wear garment for inside the spacecraft. This is a cotton suit, similar to long underwear, designed to absorb perspiration and act as a wick to allow evaporation to cool the wearer. In addition, a liquid-cooled undergarment is provided for wear under the pressure suit itself. A thermal overgarment is also provided. This is a coverall which encases the entire body with shirt, trousers, boot covers, mittens, and hood to protect the astronaut from direct rays of the sun. A meteoroid garment is provided. It is a covering garment which may be separate metallic material over the thermal garment or may be designed as part of the thermal coverall.

Final Selection

The latest design in Apollo pressure suits is designated the A7L. It is the result of changes recommended by NASA's Apollo 204 Review Board following their investigation into the fire which killed three astronauts in January, 1967. Wherever possible, flammable materials have been replaced in the redesigned suit with nonflammable or low-flammability materials. A nonflammable fiber glass cloth has been substituted for the outer layer.

The redesigned spacesuit has been changed to make it more fire resistant, more comfortable, and more mobile than its predecessor. Designers have incorporated a thermal-meteoroid protective covering to replace the cumbersome two-piece thermal meteoroid garment worn over the previous suit.

A7L Spacesuit

As in later models of the Gemini spacesuit, the A7L Apollo pressure suit has a double lock for helmet, gloves, and umbilical hose disconnects. It also has patches of metallic-fiber cloth on the elbows, knees, back, and shoulders to protect the fabric from abrasions.

The A7L suit is planned for use in all manned Apollo missions. It will be worn during prelaunch and launch phases of the flights and during re-entry. Throughout the rest of the flight, the suit will be removed, and the crew will wear unpressurized flight suits. The A7L suit will be worn for the lunar landing, exploration on the lunar surface, and rendezvous of the Lunar Module with the Command Module in lunar orbit.

The design, construction, utilization, and safety of spacesuits will undergo continuous evaluation during man's conquest of space to insure the best possible protection and serviceability.

Morris J. Haxton

See also: Astronauts, G-suit, Life-support systems, Oxygen mask, Partial pressure suit, Personal equipment, Pressure suit

Space tools

Construction in space or maintenance of orbiting hardware requires tools specially designed to function in zero gravity. Numerous studies sponsored by the National Aeronautics and Space Administration (NASA) (*see*) and by the USAF have delved into this problem, and prototype tools have been made.

The absence of gravity creates a special problem for astronauts attempting to perform mechanical space tasks. This is because of Newton's law of motion (*see*) that each action has an equal and opposite reaction. An astronaut attempting to remove a bolt from a satellite could thus find himself being turned in a circle while the bolt stayed fast. If he tried to hit something with a hammer, the reaction force could send him sailing off in the opposite direction.

As scientists delved deeper into the techniques of doing mechanical work in orbit, these problems assumed top priority. Among the solutions proposed was a series of straps, restraints, and tethers to give the astronaut leverage and hold him in place. But even then, such simple tasks as removing bolts appeared to be more difficult than on the Earth. The

A test engineer uses a Jacob's Staff for stability and wears an Apollo Extravehicular Mobility Unit which includes a life-support system.

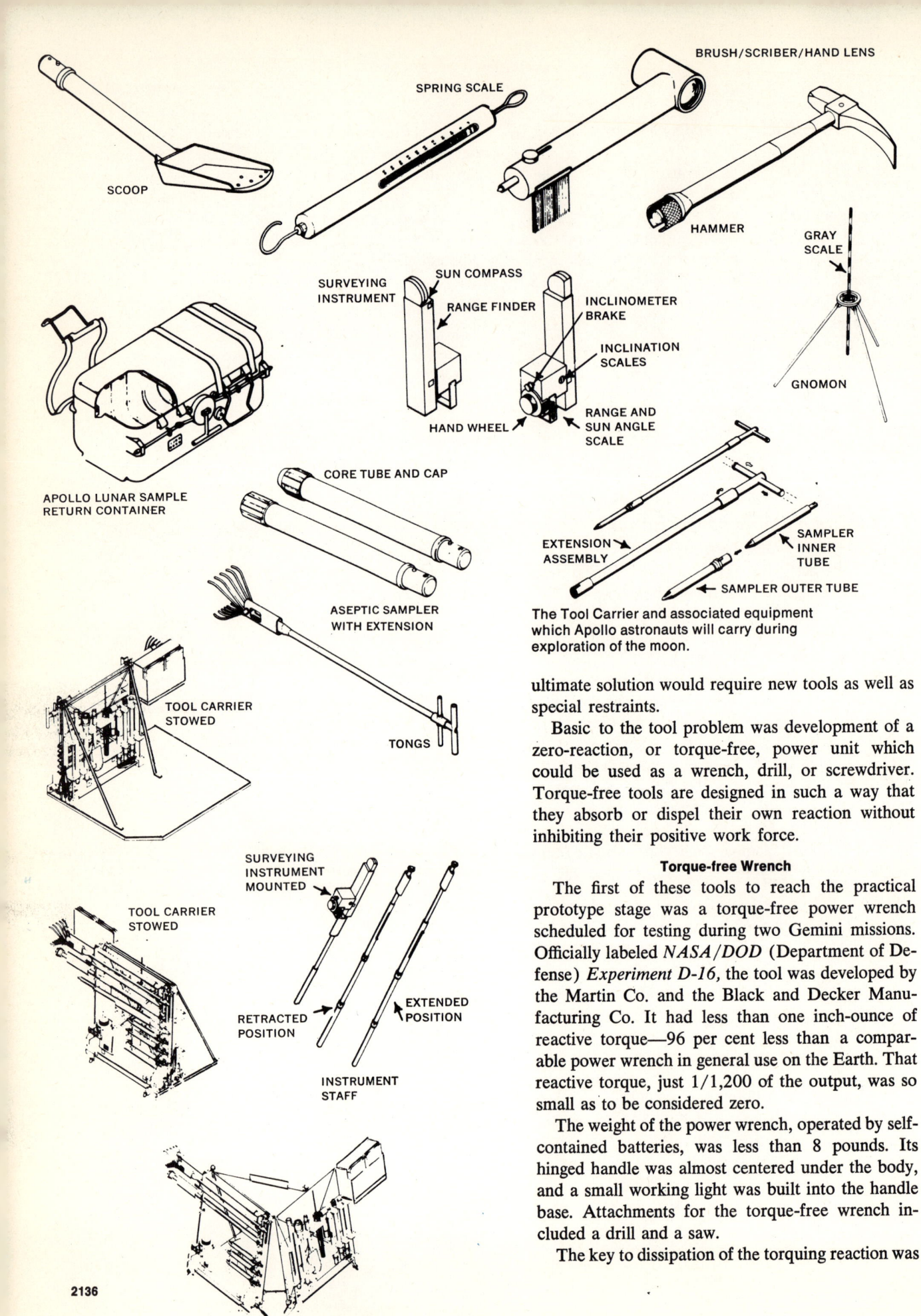

The Tool Carrier and associated equipment which Apollo astronauts will carry during exploration of the moon.

ultimate solution would require new tools as well as special restraints.

Basic to the tool problem was development of a zero-reaction, or torque-free, power unit which could be used as a wrench, drill, or screwdriver. Torque-free tools are designed in such a way that they absorb or dispel their own reaction without inhibiting their positive work force.

Torque-free Wrench

The first of these tools to reach the practical prototype stage was a torque-free power wrench scheduled for testing during two Gemini missions. Officially labeled *NASA/DOD* (Department of Defense) *Experiment D-16,* the tool was developed by the Martin Co. and the Black and Decker Manufacturing Co. It had less than one inch-ounce of reactive torque—96 per cent less than a comparable power wrench in general use on the Earth. That reactive torque, just 1/1,200 of the output, was so small as to be considered zero.

The weight of the power wrench, operated by self-contained batteries, was less than 8 pounds. Its hinged handle was almost centered under the body, and a small working light was built into the handle base. Attachments for the torque-free wrench included a drill and a saw.

The key to dissipation of the torquing reaction was

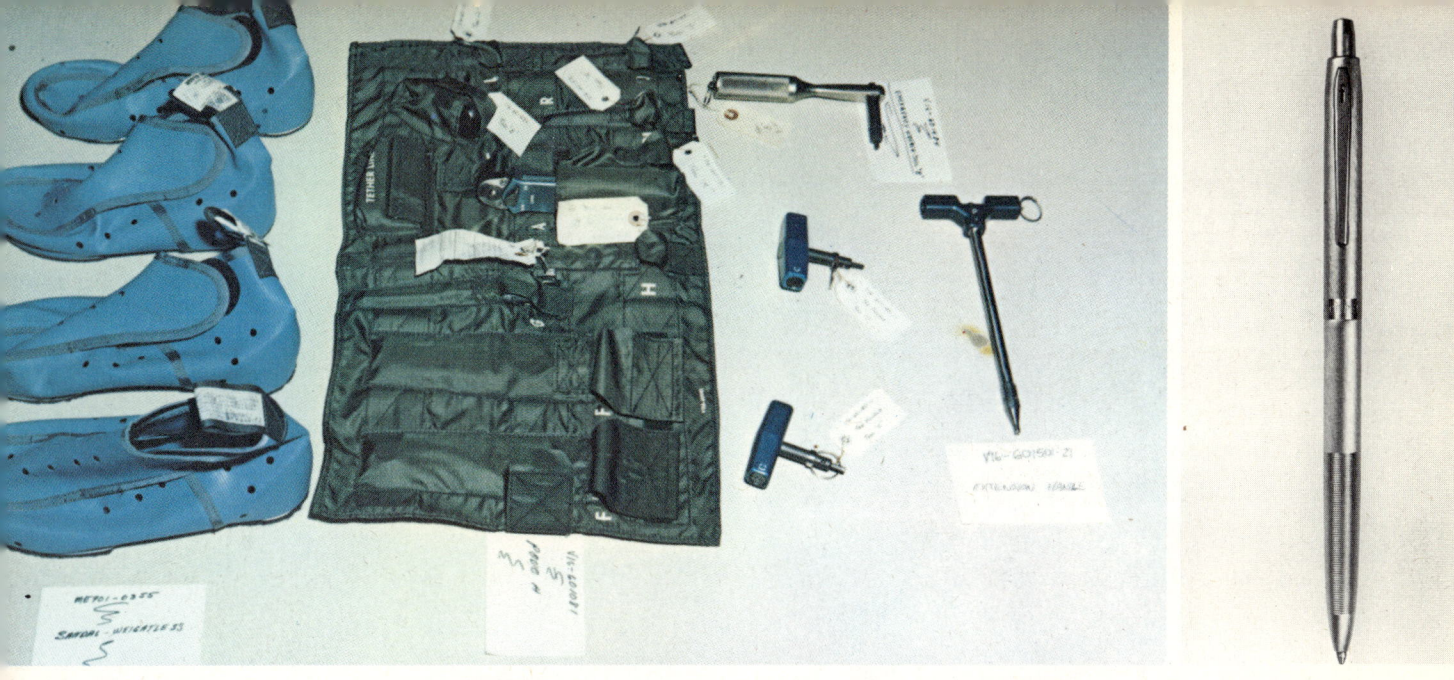

The Apollo crew equipment *(left)* and the Fisher space pen *(right)*.

a spring-loaded internal restraint system, housed in a counter-rotating assembly. When using the tool, an astronaut would be subjected only to infinitesimal torque caused by friction from bearings in the counter-rotating cylinder.

Tests on the ground and during zero-gravity aircraft runs indicated that the tool performed as planned. However, it was to become the victim of misfortune. The unit was first flown aboard Gemini 8 and was to be tried during a space walk by Astronaut David Scott *(see)*, but thruster problems forced an abort before the space walk could begin. An identical tool went into space with Gemini 11, and Astronaut Richard Gordon *(see)* was to run the tests during his space walk. Gordon succeeded in moving around outside the spacecraft and in attaching a tether connection between Gemini and an Agena rocket. Then exhaustion set in, and he was forced to end his space walk before trying out the wrench.

Similar tools are to be included in future spaceflights, particularly in the Orbital Workshop missions planned for the Apollo Applications Programs *(see)*. They are expected to be even better suited for space operations than the Gemini tool and to include additional items or attachments required for construction work.

Some Other Space Tools

Some items suggested by Martin Co. for inclusion on Gemini flights may be useful to the space worker. Among these items are electric lights which clamp onto a space helmet, metallic fingernails on space gloves for picking up small parts, a spring-driven hammer, and adhesive buttons to stick to a spacecraft for use as anchors. Even a ball-point pen with a nitrogen-pressurized sealed ink cartridge, made by Fisher Pen Co., has been tested and approved by NASA for its consistent performance in zero gravity.

One major test proposed for the USAF's Manned Orbiting Laboratory involves inflight evaluation of types of work. This includes welding, joining wires, assembling large and small components, repairing fluid systems, and others. Tools for these tasks have been designed, and some have been tested in prototype.

An electron beam welder is one example. Developed for NASA by Hamilton Standard, the unit uses a stream of electrons focused through a lens to permanently bond certain metals together under vacuum conditions. As planned, it would be able to weld stainless steel, molybdenum, titanium, and aluminum at rates up to 15 inches per minute.

Other tools under study or in various stages of design include a trigger-operated wire cutter, a device for brazing metals through heat-producing reaction of chemicals, welders employing sound waves in place of direct heat, and high-strength Velcro fasteners which could be used in erecting interior space station walls.

Most if not all of these will find their way into the orbiting tool boxes of the 1970's, as will fantastic new tools still taking form on designers' tables around the world.

—Jim Schefter

See also: Human engineering, Materials, Technological projections

Space Tracking and Data Acquisition Network,
see Tracking systems and networks

Space weather

Space is rich in a variety of phenomena which have interested physicists for centuries. It is filled with rays, energies, magnetic fields, and particles which apparently move through space in a rhythmic pattern. This pattern has given rise to the expression *space weather*. Because space weather has a relationship to Earth weather, scientists have been using satellites recently to try to understand the makeup and mechanism of space weather.

The sun (*see*), it is generally agreed, is the key space weather-maker. Moving through its 11-year active/quiet cycle, it is the scene of tremendous solar storms and giant flares of gases which leap millions of miles off the solar surface.

During these great storms the atmosphere of the Earth is bombarded with tremendous and erratic doses of ultraviolet, X-ray, and gamma rays. Electrically charged (*hot*) particles from these solar bursts shoot out across space and collide with the Earth's magnetic field. When this happens, radio transmissions are disturbed, electric power transmission lines lose "juice," and the polar skies are painted with auroras (*see*). When the sun's electromagnetic radiations strikes the Earth's lower atmosphere it produces circulation changes which in turn produce long-range climatic effects and ultimately, day to day weather movements.

The solar wind (*see*) refers to a stream of ionized particles (a neutral assemblage of protons and electrons) which spring from the sun outward. It is a plasma (*see*), a collection of charged particles dense enough to behave as a group in much the same way molecules of water behave in a fluid.

A study of solar activity and its effect on the Earth, aside from its basic scientific interest, is necessary for a fuller understanding of the space environment prior to manned flights to the moon and beyond.

E. M. Mason

See also: Atmosphere, Space, Weather

Spad

The Spad S.VII single-seat fighter of World War I was the best known but only one of a series of outstanding aircraft produced by the old *Societe pour la Production des Appareils Deperdussin* of France, from which the initials S.P.A.D. came to identify the aircraft. As early as 1912 and 1913, Spad monoplanes had swept all the speed records of those two years, including the first in excess of 100 mph.

The Deperdussin firm was taken over by the celebrated Louis Bleriot (*see*) after a financial scandal. Spads were already very popular, so Bleriot retained the initials when he changed the name to *Societe pour Aviation et ses Derives* (Society for Aviation and its Derivatives).

The S.VII was powered by a Hispano-Suiza water-cooled engine, first of 150 hp; later, more powerful 180-hp and 200-hp engines were installed. A few of the aircraft carried "motor cannons" which were guns of relatively heavy caliber mounted on the engine and fired through the propeller hub. This type of armament was to become popular in Europe in later years. However, the Spad usually carried one or two standard machine guns.

A distinctive feature of the S.VII was its two sets of interplane struts on each side of the fuselage, an unusual form of wing bracing. Also, the wings had no dihedral angle (the upward slant between the wing and the horizontal plane at the root of the wing). This was thought by some to achieve maneuverability at the expense of lateral stability, but pilots found the flat-wing plane easy to fly.

H. F. King

See also: First World War aircraft

SPAD VII
Specifications and Performance Data

Engine	150 hp Hispano-Suiza
Wingspan	25 ft. 6 in.
Length	20 ft. 1 in.
Maximum speed	120 mph
Range	200-250 miles

Spain, see European aerospace activities

Spanish Civil War

The Spanish Civil War, which broke out in July, 1936, provided a proving ground for the untested aircraft and air tactics that had been developed since World War I (see). Air support by Germany and Italy on the side of Generalissimo Francisco Franco's Nationalists was a decisive factor in the defeat of the Loyalists, aided by Russia's Air Force.

The Spanish civil struggle, which foreshadowed World War II (see), might well have ended with a quick suppression of the military revolt which began in Morocco. However, the German *Luftwaffe* (see), numbering almost 2,000 aircraft and 20,000 men, intervened modestly in August, 1936, with 40 Ju-52 transports to airlift 18,000 Fascist troops from Morocco to Spain.

By November, the German *Legion Condor* was in Spain; it consisted of *Luftwaffe* pilots flying the first fighter to enter the war, the single-seat Heinkel He-51, and other aircraft. Italy followed with the *Aviacion Legionaria,* which began to fly Italy's fighters, bombers, and reconnaissance airplanes on the Franco side. Most of the Italian fighter groups were equipped with the Fiat C.R. 32, a single-seat biplane.

The U.S.S.R. intervened on the side of the Republican forces and began sending the I-15 single-seat fighter to Spain where it was called *Chato* (Flat-nosed). Later, the advanced I-16 *Mosca* (Fly) saw service. The fastest fighter of its day, it was the first low-wing interceptor monoplane to have a retractable landing gear.

The Heinkel He-51's proved to be inferior to the Soviet aircraft in armament, speed, and maneuverability. However, early in 1937, they began to be replaced by the Messerschmitt Me-109B (see). The new, fast-climbing Me-109B fighters and the superior training of German pilots soon turned the tide against the hundreds of Soviet aircraft. The losses became so heavy that by the end of 1938, all Russian squadrons had been withdrawn.

The Savoia-Marchetti S-79 had retractable landing gear and carried about 1,000 kilos of bombs.

Development of Air Tactics

By later standards, aerial warfare was limited, but there were some valid lessons learned in Spain. The Heinkel He-111 (see), a fast medium bomber, arrived in 1938 and began to develop procedures for the unescorted daylight bombing raid. At a time when enemy air power was diminishing, the tactic was successful, but carried over to the Battle of Britain (see) in World War II, it failed. However, the German Stukas' dive-bombing of sensitive points along Loyalist rail lines proved the effectiveness of the technique, and it was used in World War II.

It soon became evident that fighters could be most effective by flying in mutually supporting elements of three or four. Attack aviation was found to be most effective when operating against troops which were changing position. Antitank weapons were developed for aircraft which employed armor piercing projectiles.

The air war was limited by the fact that Russia's production capability was unable to sustain its losses, and both sides were reluctant to heavily damage the cities. Therefore, air tactics were never fully tested. As a result, the *Luftwaffe*, although victorious, never developed an air function of its own beyond support of ground operations, a fact that later had an important bearing on World War II. —Don Radcliffe

See also: Second World War aircraft

The Heinkel He-111 was first used as a bomber in the Spanish Civil War, and after in-combat testing, was modified. Later it was built in many forms with various powerplants.

Spar

Spar, see Airplane, Wings

Spatial disorientation

When a pilot flies out of a cloud bank upside down it is because his orientation senses, visual (eye), vestibular (inner ear), and proprioceptual (impulses from muscles, tendons, and other tissues), have provided him with incorrect information and he is disoriented. Spatial disorientation can lead to other problems such as motion sickness (see) and can even lead to fatal aircraft accidents.

If vision is impaired by fog, clouds, darkness, etc., man's usual reference points, both visual and gravitational, have no means of orienting themselves during flight. Essentially man's orientation senses function better on the ground than in the environment of flight.

Training in instrument flying is the only solution. The pilot who combines his orientation senses with reliance upon his instruments will be able to fly under almost all circumstances.   Charlene A. Wrobel

See also: Man in flight

Specific gravity

Specific gravity is the ratio of weight of a specific volume of a substance to the weight of an equal volume of another substance used as a standard at a stated temperature. The usual standard for comparing solids and liquids is water at 4°C.

Specific impulse, see Launch vehicles

Spectrum, see Electromagnetism

Speed and speed records

The Federation Aeronautique Internationale (FAI) (*see*), represented in the United States by the National Aeronautic Association (NAA) (*see*), lists seven classifications for the measurement of the speed or rate of motion of an aircraft. These are: 1) speed over a 3 km course at restricted altitude; 2) speed over a 12/25 km course at nonrestricted altitude; 3) speed in a closed circuit without landing; 4) speed in a closed circuit without landing (with payload); 5) speed over a recognized course; 6) speed around the world; and 7) speed on a commercial air route.

Any new record must exceed the existing record by at least 1 per cent, and each attempt must be properly documented. The regulations for establishing speed records are as follows. (Numbers refer to above number of classification.)

1) The flight must be made over a straight course, and altitude must not exceed 100 meters. The course is flown twice in each direction, and the speed adopted is the average of the four speeds. The runs must be completed within a 30-minute period, and the aircraft may not land during the flight.

2) The same course and conditions prevail. The aircraft must fly over the course once in each direction, and the average of the two speeds is adopted.

3) Any altitude may be flown provided the turns are performed correctly, the passage over the starting and finishing points are accurately timed, and the aircraft is identified at the starting, turning, and finishing points.

4) Under closed circuit conditions a ballast pay-

25,000 MPH/ 150 MILES—22 SECONDS

18,000 MPH/ 150 MILES—30 SECONDS

4,000 MPH/ 150 MILES—2.25 MINUTES

1,200 MPH/ 150 MILES—8 MINUTES

600 MPH/ 150 MILES—15 MINUTES

140 MPH/ 150 MILES—1.1 HOURS   PERSONAL AIRCRAFT

80 MPH/ 150 MILES—1.9 HOURS   AUTO

15 MPH/ 150 MILES—2 DAYS   HORSEBACK

3 MPH/ 150 MILES—4 DAYS   WALKING

Speed and speed records

Aircraft speed records: 1920-1965

Record Holder	Country	Place	Date	Aircraft	Record (mph)
Maximum speed for piston engine land planes					
Sadi Lecointe	France	Villacoublay	1-7-20	Nieuport	171.412
Francesco Brack-Papa	Italy	Turin	5-3-20	Fiat 700	172.071
Jean Casale	France	Villacoublay	2-28-20	Spad	176.136
Bernard de Romanet	France	Buc	10-9-20	Spad	181.863
Sadi Lecointe	France	Buc	10-10-20	Nieuport	184.356
Sadi Lecointe	France	Villacoublay	10-20-20	Nieuport	187.982
Bernard de Romanet	France	Buc	11-4-20	Spad	192.010
Sadi Lecointe	France	Buc	12-12-20	Nieuport	194.575
Sadi Lecointe	France	Villesauvage	9-26-21	Nieuport	205.220
Francesco Brack-Papa	Italy	Turin	8-26-22	Fiat 700	208.565
Sadi Lecointe	France	Villesauvage	9-21-22	Nieuport	212.035
Sadi Lecointe	France	Istres	12-31-22	Nieuport	216.254
USAS Gen. William E. Mitchell	U.S.	Detroit, Michigan	10-18-22	Curtiss 375	222.969
Sadi Lecointe	France	Istres	1-15-23	Nieuport	233.013
USAS Lt. R. L. Maughan	U.S.	Dayton, O.	3-29-23	Curtiss 465	236.587
USN Lt. Harold J. Brow	U.S.	Mineola, N.Y.	11-2-23	Curtiss 500	259.115
USN Lt. A. J. Williams	U.S.	Mineola, N.Y.	11-4-23	Curtiss 500	266.583
Adj. A. Bonnet	France	Istres	12-11-24	Ferbois	278.480
James H. Doolittle	U.S.	Cleveland, O.	9-3-32	Granville Gee-Bee	294.380
James R. Wedell	U.S.	Glenview, Ill.	9-4-33	Wedell-Williams	304.980
Raymond Delmotte	France	Istres	12-25-34	Caudron C-460	314.319
Howard Hughes	U.S.	Santa Ana, Calif.	9-13-35	Hughes "Special"	352.388
Herman Wurster	Germany	Augsburg	11-11-37	BF 113 R	379.626
Fritz Wendel	Germany	Augsburg	4-26-39	—	469.220
Captain N. Wilson	England	Herne Bay	11-7-46	Gloster Meteor IV	606.255
USMC Major Marion Carl	U.S.	Muroc, Calif.	8-25-47	—	650.600
USAF Major Richard L. Johnson	U.S.	Muroc, Calif.	9-15-48	F-86	670.981
Maximum speed for jet aircraft 1.8 mile course					
USAF Major Richard L. Johnson	U.S.	Muroc, Calif.	9-15-48	F-86	679.981
USAF Capt. James S. Nash	U.S.	Salton Sea, Calif.	11-19-52	F-86 D	699.920
USN Lt. Cdr. J. B. Verdin	U.S.	Salton Sea, Calif.	10-3-53	XF-4D	753.400
USAF Lt. Huntington Hardesty	U.S.	Holman AFB, N.M.	8-28-61	F-4H-1	902.174
Maximum speed for jet aircraft 9.3 mile course					
Lt. Col. F. K. Everest	U.S.	Salton Sea, Calif.	10-29-53	YF-100A	755.149
Col. H. A. Hanes	U.S.	Palmdale, Calif.	8-20-55	F-100C	822.660
L. Peter Twiss	England	Ford-Chichester	3-10-56	Fairey Delta 2	1,132.136
G. Mollolov	U.S.S.R.	Joukovski	10-31-59	E-66	1,482.948
USAF Major J. W. Rogers	U.S.	Edwards AFB, Calif.	12-15-59	F-106A	1,525.012
USMC Lt. Col. R. W. Robinson	U.S.	Edwards AFB, Calif.	11-22-61	F-4H-1	1,605.548
G. Mossolov	U.S.S.R.	Podmoskovnoe	7-7-62	E-166	1,664.901
Col. R. Stephens	U.S.	—	5-1-65	YF-12A	2,068.865

Source: *National Aeronautic Association* (NAA)

SPACE PROBE

MERCURY SPACECRAFT

X-15

JET FIGHTER

JET AIRLINER

Most travel 60 years ago was conducted at a speed no greater than that of a horse—15 mph. Today, no two people anywhere in the world are more than 24 hours apart by air.

While the automobile raised the typical traveling speed considerably from 15 mph, it remained for the airplane to drastically reduce travel time. Even though light aircraft may fly no faster than the top speed of a typical automobile, the airplane's advantage lies in the fact that, once airborne, it can fly at a constant speed without slowing down or stopping until it reaches its destination.

In order to comprehend and appreciate the impact of speeds possible in the aerospace age, select a point 150 miles from your home and compare the time it takes to walk or drive the distance with the time required for other means of travel shown on the chart.

Speed and speed records

load is added which must be carried in compartments specifically designed for transporting the useful load of the aircraft.

5) This is the most popular category for the average private pilot. The course may be between two capitals of countries or between certain cities of international importance that are represented in the FAI. Refueling is allowed and the aircraft may land for repairs so long as the crew is not changed.

6) The minimum distance flown must be equal to the length of the Tropic of Cancer, with the start and finish at the same point. The competitor must state in advance where landings will be made. Refueling in flight is allowed and repairs may be made at landing points. The crew must remain on board the aircraft, and log book must be checked at each stop.

7) The record must be set between recognized airports on an air route used by regular air service. Time is measured between the last contact with the ground and the time contact is again resumed. The distance is that which has been officially calculated between the two airports. The record is officially listed in the name of the company owning the aircraft and in the pilot's name.

The first official speed records were made by Santos-Dumont, in 1906, when he reached a speed of 25.497 mph in Bagatelle, France. The first speed record for a jet powered aircraft was made in 1946 when Lt. John Hancock took a Lockheed P-80 to the speed of 440.928 mph. Today's absolute world speed record is held by Col. R. L. Stephens, USAF, and stands at 2070.101 mph for performance in a straight line. The record was set in 1965.

Fred A. Hufnagel, Jr.

See also: Altitude and altitude records, Distance and distance records, Endurance and endurance records

Spin

In the early days of flying, the tailspin was a common and dangerous problem. It is an uncontrolled, rotating dive earthward by the airplane, and the motion resembles a corkscrew being drilled into a bottle.

Now called simply a *spin,* it results when the aircraft is severely and fully stalled, but it actually begins when one wing stalls ahead of the other one, with the aircraft then falling off in the direction of the first wing. (This could happen, for instance, in a poorly performed steep turn.) The second wing, having more lift, ends up chasing the other one. As the plane descends, fully stalled, it rotates around its center of gravity, usually with the nose well down.

Modern lightplanes are of advanced design; they are well-balanced machines which do not spin easily. Therefore, some piloting skill is required to force one into a tailspin. Starting the maneuver at a safe altitude, a pilot first must perform a straight-ahead, power-off stall, using full back pressure. As the stalled condition is reached and the nose starts to drop, his technique is to apply sharply either left or right rudder, keeping ailerons neutral. Rotation of the aircraft then will commence either left or right.

Recovery can be achieved fairly easily with application of full rudder opposite the direction in which the plane is spinning. This slows rotation. Then, with rudder pedals neutralized, the stall itself must be broken by forward pressure on the elevator controls. With the plane still in a dive, final recovery to straight-and-level flight must be gradual until all the controls become effective again. Intentional spins, for practice purposes, are executed with power off. If a spin is accidental, with power on, then power must be chopped off quickly, for it aggravates the rotation.

Flight instructors are required to perform spins to qualify for the rating, but spin demonstration is not required for private licenses.

D. William Bennett

See also: Airplane, Maneuvers, Stall

Spinoff

The nature of aerospace missions insures the generation of new knowledge, particularly technology, in the course of conducting the research and development (R&D) leading to successful conduct of such missions. This new knowledge spans the spectrum of sciences and technology. It has potential for additional application in many industries and professions. The use of technology for a purpose other than that for which it was developed is often termed *spinoff*. This technology includes materials (*see*), devices, techniques, concepts, principles, management methods, etc.

To assure that the technology developed in its programs would be rapidly made available to industry and others for non-aerospace application, the National Aeronautics and Space Administration (NASA) (*see*) established the Technology Utilization Program in late 1962. The purpose of the program has been to increase the return on the national investment in aerospace R&D by actively encouraging additional uses for the knowledge gained.

Some examples, among hundreds possible, of spinoff are as follows:

1) Digital computer techniques developed to clarify photographs telemetered across 140 million miles

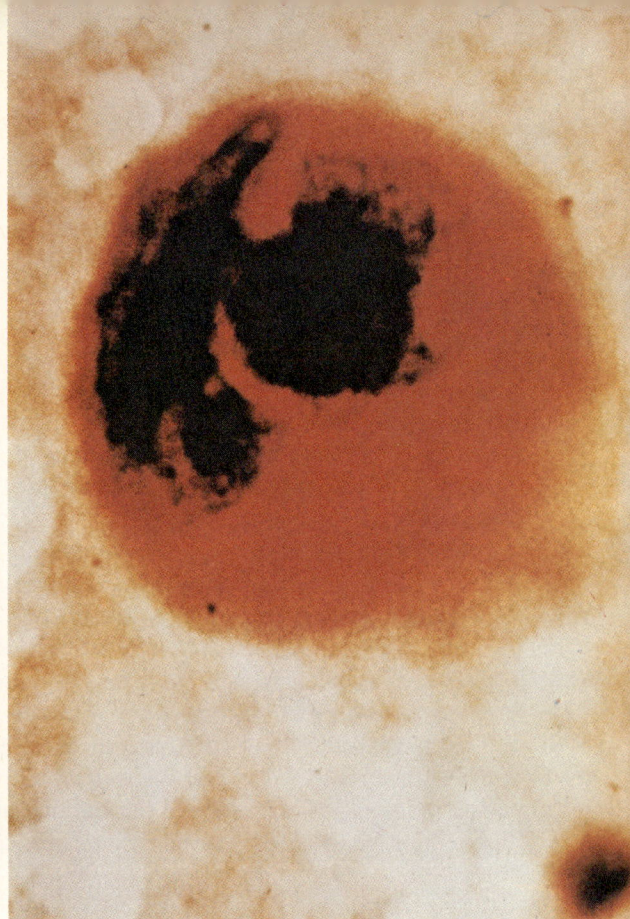

Weather satellites orbiting the Earth *(left)* have improved the Weather Bureau's accuracy in making weather forecasts, an early and major spinoff of space activity. Laser beams *(right)* are used in medicine for their capability of being focused to a very narrow beam to examine the smallest part of a biological cell through a microscope.

of space from Mars to Earth are now being used to make medical X-rays more revealing.

2) A remotely-controlled walking device conceived as a means of transport on the lunar surface has been adapted as a walking chair for crippled persons. Unlike a wheelchair, this device moves easily across a sandy beach, a gravel lane, or uneven ground, and will also climb over curbs.

3) Because it was once thought that an astronaut would be unable to manipulate controls during the high-gravity pull of liftoff, a device was developed which would enable the astronaut to maintain control by simply moving his eyes. This "sight switch" can be used to permit a paralyzed person to dial a telephone, raise and lower a hospital bed, etc.

4) A new diagnostic tool has been developed to detect and record the subtle postural reflexes, or muscle tremors, associated with such illnesses as Parkinson's disease. This diagnostic tool, a muscle accelerometer, is based on technology developed for the detection of micrometeorites in space.

6) The NASA Langley Research Center was assigned the task of learning why airplanes skid on wet runways and to seek means of preventing the hazard. The researchers found that at high speeds water was forced between the runway and the tire, literally lifting the tire from the runway so that it would ride on the surface of the water. NASA undertook a joint project with the Bureau of Public Roads to learn whether the same findings were applicable to automobiles. The answer was yes. It was then determined that accidents as a result of this effect might be avoided by grooving runways and highways. These grooves would permit the water to disperse rather than build up under the tire. Several states undertook pilot projects, grooving stretches of highway where accident frequency was great during wet and rainy conditions. As a result of grooving five stretches of highway in Los Angeles, accidents were reduced by 92 per cent.

Methods of Technology Dissemination

To transfer technology, the first step is the identification and documentation of all new inventions, innovations, improvements, and discoveries. To assure that all new technology generated in its programs is documented and made available, NASA has appointed Technology Utilization Officers at its 14 major installations. These men also administer a clause in all NASA contracts which obligates the contractor to report new technology developed dur-

Spin-off

ing contract work. The technology is then evaluated by independent research institutes under contract to NASA. Those advances deemed to have additional utility are announced to industry and others in one of several ways as follows:

1) The most common is the *Tech Brief,* a short description of a single development or invention and a brief explanation of the underlying concepts and principles. Additional informaton can be obtained.

2) The *Technological Survey* method is used when a whole area of technology has been advanced. NASA retains noted authorities to write "guidebooks" on the latest advancements, indicating where additional information may be obtained.

3) *Regional Dissemination Centers* (RDC's) have been established by NASA at universities and research institutes. Their purpose is to deliver tailored packages of knowledge based on data supplied by NASA in response to user needs. RDC's also educate industrial management in the use of externally generated knowledge by demonstration of the value of actively seeking the results of R&D performed elsewhere.

NASA also disseminates information by making *computer programs* available to industry and by forming Biomedical Application Teams whose purpose is to assist researchers in biology and medicine by a method called *Problem Abstracts.* This method identifies the barriers impeding research development and helps to break down those barriers by supplying data.

George J. Howick

See also: Man in flight, Oceanographic research, Satellites

Spirit of St. Louis

The *Spirit of St. Louis* (*Ryan NYP*) was without a doubt a most efficient airplane when viewed in terms of its intended use and actual accomplishment. It was conceived and built for one purpose only: Charles A. Lindbergh's (*see*) nonstop solo transatlantic flight. That it succeeded in serving the purpose is a well-established fact.

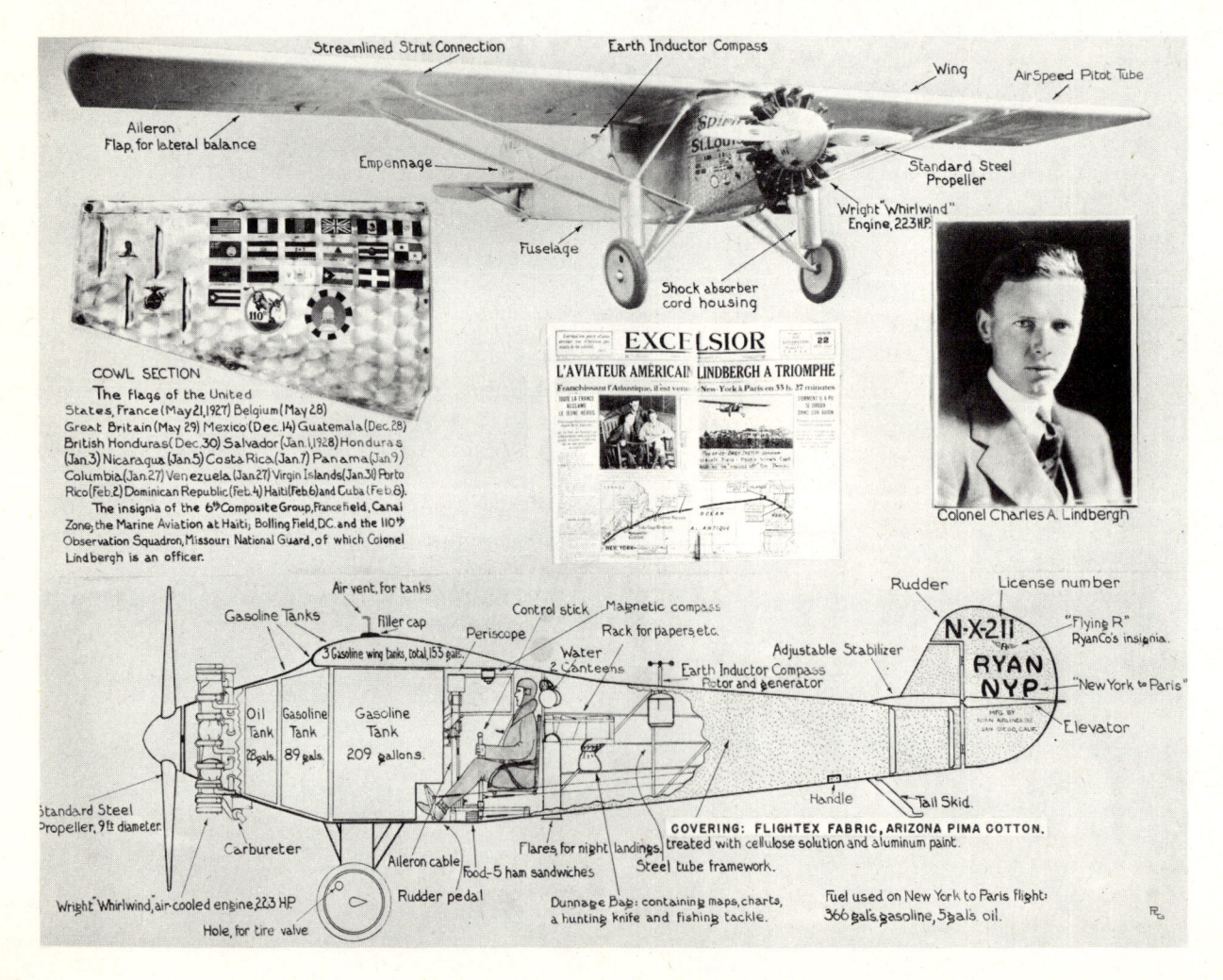

Spirit of St. Louis

Early in 1927 Lindbergh had been able to interest a group of public-spirited men in St. Louis, Missouri, to obtain the financial backing necessary to compete for the Raymond Orteig prize of $25,000, offered in 1919 for the first nonstop flight between New York and Paris, France. In February, 1927, he placed the order with Ryan Airlines in San Diego, California. Late in April the airplane was completed and test-flown by Lindbergh. He then piloted it, making only one stop at St. Louis, across the U.S., May 10-12, 1927. The flying time was 21 hours 40 minutes.

After several days of preparation and waiting for favorable weather, Lindbergh took off for Paris on the morning of May 20. A total of 33 hours 30 minutes later, on the night of May 21, he landed at Le Bourget Field near Paris. By this feat Lindbergh not only won the Orteig prize, but also enduring fame. The *Spirit of St. Louis* was returned to the U.S. aboard the USS *Memphis*, which docked at Washington, D.C., on June 11.

This airplane did not represent a technical breakthrough. It was ordinary in structure, and had a proved airfoil and a highly regarded engine. It bore only a tenuous resemblance to the Ryan M-2 monoplane which had earned its way with the airmail *(see)*. Starting with the M-2 as a point of departure, modifications were made to the wing, fuselage, and landing gear. All these design changes were made by Donald Hall, chief engineer for Ryan, under the watchful eye of the pilot.

The wing was lengthened to 46 feet, and the main fuel tank, with a capacity of 425 gallons, was placed directly under the high monoplane wing where changes in the fuel load would not change the balance of the aircraft. It would, however, obscure the pilot's forward visibility. Construction details were ordinary for the time: fabric-covered steel tube fuselage and empennage and fabric-covered wood wing. The engine was a reliable Wright J-5 with minor modifications.

In reply to often-raised questions, Lindbergh has recorded:

"A flying boat can't take off with enough fuel, a trimotor would cost too much. I'm not sure that three engines would add much safety—the plane would be overloaded with fuel anyway. There'd be three times as much chance of engine failure; and if one of them stopped over the ocean, you probably couldn't get back to land with the other two . . . we ought to give first consideration to efficiency in flight; second, to protection in a crackup; third, to pilot comfort. Extra fuel is my greatest reserve for success. I believe the chances of success are better with one pilot than with two. I'd rather have extra gasoline than an extra man. It will save 350 lbs—at least 50 gallons of fuel."

Aside from the dramatic impact of the flight, the principal contribution made by this flight was economic. It proved to a skeptical public that the airplane was indeed here to stay, and had the endurance and reliability necessary to make it a useful addition to transportation needs. It also proved that the airplane was a practical vehicle for the transportation of people and merchandise.

From July 20 to October 23, 1927, Lindbergh flew the *Spirit of St. Louis* on a tour of the U.S. Then, beginning on December 13, he flew his famous plane on a tour of Mexico and Central America.

Its final flight was on April 30, 1928, from St. Louis to Washington, D.C., where it became part of the National Aeronautical Collections, and has been on display at the National Air and Space Museum *(see)* of the Smithsonian Institution ever since.

Louis S. Casey

See also: Commercial airlines, History of aviation

Memorabilia of the *Spirit of St. Louis* and Lindbergh's flight *(left)* and the pilot's view of the instrument panel of the specially built Ryan aircraft *(below)*.

Spitfire

The Spitfire was the best British single-seat fighter of World War II with over 20,000 produced during the war years. The plane's maneuverability, speed, and rate of climb made it one of the finest fighters of the war. Designed by R. J. Mitchell, it incorporated much of the experience Mitchell gained in the design of the famous line of Supermarine racing seaplanes. With its contemporary the Hawker Hurricane (see), the Spitfire defeated the German Luftwaffe (see) during the Battle of Britain (see), and though England later turned out faster fighters, the Vickers-Supermarine Spitfire was memorably active on every battlefront.

First flown in 1936, the Spitfire entered RAF service in August, 1938, and remained in front line use throughout the war undergoing numerous modifications to keep it technically ahead of its adversaries, the German Messerschmitt Me-109 (see) and the Focke-Wulf FW-190.

Early models had an armament of eight guns in the wings outside the propeller arc. The Mark V which appeared early in 1941 had two 20mm cannon installed, and this model formed the initial equipment used in the famous fighter-sweeps over northern France. Later models added the refinement of pressurized cabins to improve conditions at high altitude, and were equipped with Merlin Rolls-Royce engines with two-stage supercharging. Beginning with the Spitfire IX, the Merlin was supplanted by another Rolls-Royce engine, the more powerful Griffon. Some versions with two-stage Griffons had a new wing designed to carry four 20mm cannon, and also had a longer and wider undercarriage and enlarged tail surfaces.

During its operational use the Spitfire's engine power was more than doubled from 1,050 hp in the Mark I, to 2,350 hp in the postwar Seafire Mark 47 (the Spitfire's naval counterpart). After the war the Spitfire was not only used by the RAF (although soon supplanted by jets) but also by numerous foreign air forces. Several examples have been retained by the RAF for display purposes, and up to 1967 it was the usual practice for a Spitfire to lead the annual flyby over London to commemorate the Battle of Britain.

Philip J. R. Moyes

See also: Second World War aircraft, World War II

Spitfire
Specifications and Performance Data:

Engine	One 1,030 hp Rolls-Royce Merlin III
Wingspan	36 ft. 10 in.
Length	29 ft. 11 in.
Gross weight	6,200 lbs.
Maximum speed	362 mph
Range	395 miles

Spoilers

Spoilers are lift control devices mounted to the top of an aircraft wing. When not in use, they lie flush with the top surface of the wing. When activated from the cockpit (see), the spoilers are forced upward against the airstream.

Spoilers are usually rectangular panels hinged at their forward edge. Jet aircraft and gliders often use spoilers to reduce lift during a landing approach, and thus increase the angle of descent. They may also be raised after touchdown to prevent the aircraft from lifting off again.

Steve Kimmell

See also: Aerodynamics, Airplane, Wings

Sport flyers gather to exhibit their airplanes and participate in contests at a typical fly-in.

Sport flying

Flying for the fun of it

In contrast to the commercial, military, and business phases of aviation, sport flying is recreational flying. Basically, it is either flying as a sport, or flying in pursuit of sport.

As a sport in itself various phases include racing, aerobatics, exhibition, soaring, and local airport hopping. Flying in pursuit of sport can also be done by a participant who is vacationing, sightseeing, hunting, or fishing.

Who Are the Sport Flyers?

Unless flying is a man's professional career, most people who fly fall into the category of sport flyers. Such people can be found in all walks of life, including average working people, professional people, clergymen, sportsmen, and even business and airline pilots who enjoy a "busman's holiday." The airplanes they fly are usually small private lightplanes, either owned outright or rented at a fixed cost per hour. For most sport flyers the easiest and eventually the most economical way to fly is to rent an airplane. However, there are limits to how far you can fly when renting an airplane by the hour, and pilots wishing to travel extensively, or fly on the spur of the moment, will usually own their own airplane.

The average working person has his job and his family to consider and for him flying is usually strictly a hobby. Furthermore, he has no reason to use the airplane in the course of his business, nor does he have adequate free time to enjoy it to any great degree. His funds are generally limited, and because he has to justify what he does spend for sport flying, he seeks the least costly means to fly. The price of airplanes is high and probably always will be due to the fact that airplanes are not produced in great numbers as are automobiles, since the demand for them is not as great. Consequently, many airplanes

A lineup of former military trainers is a popular attraction at an air show. They have special appeal for the sportsman flyer and bring back fond memories to many pilots.

are virtually handbuilt, which insures their costliness. Since they are handbuilt, an individual can also build his own airplane. Hundreds of such sport flyers have built their own airplanes, some from their own design, while still others are content to buy a set of plans of a proved design.

It takes a patient rather than a skilled person to build an airplane, as it usually requires several years of spare time to accomplish the task. When it is done the builder usually has a fine small airplane that would otherwise have cost him several thousand dollars. More likely, the type of airplane that he now has is not available on the market. Open-cockpit biplanes, or fast little two-seaters are favorites.

However, these small machines, some of which have wings which fold for towing back home, can do many things depending upon their design. They are capable of doing aerobatics, fast cross-country travel, very slow flight, racing, amphibious operation, or even the type of flying associated with helicopters and autogiros. Indeed, some of them are in the latter category. Other types of planes which engage in sport flying are sailplanes (see), restored antique airplanes, and high-powered and high-performance military fighter or trainer aircraft. Even the centuries-old hot-air balloon has a part.

As an individual's economic status rises, he desires a larger and more versatile aircraft. Professional people such as doctors and lawyers as well as businessmen form a special kind of sport flyer and will generally buy a commercially built airplane capable of carrying at least four or five people over long distances at good speed. They might also own a small sport biplane or similar craft.

Another kind of sport flyer comes from the ranks of commercial pilots, especially airline and business aircraft pilots, who have tremendous responsibilities in flying huge jets or business airplanes. It requires several people to operate such aircraft, even with all of their automatic features and electronic gear, and consequently they lack the "feel" of small aircraft. These pilots often yearn to return to the thrill and sport of less complicated flying, and they often choose small open-cockpit biplanes. They equip these ships to perform all kinds of aerobatics for the pleasure of utilizing their personal flying skill.

The term *sportsman* has always been associated with people of wealth who have the funds and the free time to do as they wish. In this sense, the flying sportsman is an individual who chooses a fast airplane, especially a former military fighter aircraft. Even though World War II is long past, many of the wartime airplanes such as the Mustangs and Bearcats still are in supply and are used for sport flying. It takes a person of means to own and fly such an airplane which requires precise maintenance and consumes tremendous amounts of fuel.

Many of these former combat aircraft are used in air racing in the "unlimited power" categories. When used in this manner they are usually modified to a great extent, resulting in far superior performance. The modification involved represents an investment of thousands of additional dollars.

There is another phase of sport flying which is the aviation counterpart of the antique automobile. Throughout the 1920's and 1930's as aviation was coming of age, there were scores of fine airplane designs and production models of a type not available

While this replica of a WW 1 Nieuport 24b is newly built by the owner from the original plans, its method of starting remains the same: it takes two men to start the airplane.

today. Many pilots appreciate the classic beauty of these older airplanes, and some for weight and power can easily outperform more modern designs. However, old aircraft present problems since parts are scarce and expensive, with supply and demand controlling the prices. In most cases, structure and engine have not been produced for several decades. Replacement parts must come from other similar craft or be custom made. The airplane structure itself can be kept in good condition, but it is another matter to forge or cast engine parts. In many instances, these old planes are kept aloft by substituting more modern engines and equipment which does not, however, limit one's enjoyment of a thrill of yesteryear.

The antique phase of sport flying again attracts a group from a higher income level because of the cost. Sometimes long searches are made to find the "right" airplane, and this often turns out to be a model badly in need of repair and often missing parts and frames. Usually another long period of research follows to acquire drawings and the needed parts. However, the sense of pride and accomplishment is great when after several years of painstaking work, the sportsman has an old airplane which is in better condition than when it left the factory new. It is also a classic, a real antique, and sure to draw attention wherever it goes and win trophies for its owner. The sport of antique airplane flying can be said to center around taking these airplanes to various aviation gatherings to show them off.

Model types go back to World War I aircraft and even earlier. Often the sport is in the hunt rather than the actual finding of a plane, and the challenge lies in the patient, persevering search for items with bits and pieces being recovered from every corner of the country. The desire for rare airplane types such as Fokkers, Sopwiths, and Nieuports leads many sportsmen into the acquisition of accurate drawings of these old airplanes in order to build exact replicas. An equal amount of work is involved in the building, and an effort is made to keep the planes as authentic as possible even if new, original engines are incorporated. These old World War I planes require different skill in flying and in maintenance, but the thrill of imagining oneself another Rickenbacker, or Von Richthofen, makes antique flying a rare sport.

How Sport Planes Are Used

Primarily, the purpose of sport flying is to show off one's plane. Just as antique and sports car buffs have their shows and rallies, sport flying also has its "fly-ins" where those of similar interests meet. The airplanes are flown in for show purposes, whereupon they are judged for many values. The aircraft are always being primped and polished, sometimes far more than they are flown. In return for the great effort and expense involved, these plane buffs are more than repaid when they win a trophy.

Breakfast flights are very popular in sport flying circles. This generally involves getting up at dawn on Sunday and flying to a distant airport for breakfast and fellowship with other pilots. After several hours visiting and comparing notes, the sportsmen head back home.

There are also navigational flights to far points which test the skill of the pilot rather than the machine. A variation of this sport is the newly popular "treasure hunt," essentially the same as a navigational flight, but it relies more on landmarks and

2149

Sport flying

other signs, especially in historical areas. These treasure hunts are extremely popular in Florida and the southwest as well as in the Bahamas.

In most cases, the sport flyer is dependent upon himself for interesting activities. A great test of skill and judgment is the "spot-landing contest," wherein the airplane must be landed on, or as near as possible to, a predetermined spot on the runway. "Flour-bombing" is a similar test in which small bags of flour are dropped onto a target. When the bomb hits, the bag bursts and the flour spills out to simulate a bomb blast.

There is also the sport of soaring (see) or gliding (see), perhaps the greatest sport in all of flying, in which the pilot is pitted against nature with a light craft that has no engine. To remain aloft, he must seek out rising columns of air to carry him to higher altitudes where he can then soar to the next column of rising air in order to repeat the operation. Sometimes such columns, or thermals (see), cannot be located quickly and the pilot easily and safely sets his craft down in any clear area. On the other hand, a sailplane or glider pilot can fly for hours by this means, and will soar for hundreds of miles. These sailplanes are usually towed aloft to a few thousand feet by another airplane, and then released.

A new sport has developed called *sky sailing,* or *parasailing.* Sky sailing is performed with a regular kite. Parasailing, or flightsailing, is accomplished with a kite with a parawing design (see). The person is towed aloft to several hundred feet, or quite often by a speedboat as the sport is often run over water.

Everyone has seen the skydiver, or parachutist. A sport that requires courage and stamina, skydiving (see) is equally rewarding to those who participate in it. It, too, has its contests of skill in landing on targets, delayed openings, free diving, and midair meeting of jumpers. This sport requires a specially fitted jump airplane which carries the divers up to their jump altitude. Skydiving clubs are usually formed to pay for the jump plane and have it available when needed. However, it is one of the few phases of sport flying where the participant is dependent on someone else for enjoyment of the sport.

Competitive Sports

Air racing (see) changes sport flying from an individual sporting activity to one similar to auto or boat racing. While most sport flying is on a personal and individual level, air racing is usually a commercially promoted and produced venture with money prizes for the winners.

It is a highly competitive sport, as well as a spectator sport, and one that depends not only on the skill of the pilot but also on the qualifications of his racing plane. In addition, it taxes the ingenuity of the pilot and his ground crew to create, modify, and improve his flying racer. Many a race is won on the ground, just as an auto race is often won in the pits.

There are two basic types of air races: the pylon race, and the cross-country race.

The *pylon race* is a race around markers, or towers, similar to those found at a race track. A very tight turn must be made around the pylons, with the race usually flown about 50 to 200 feet above the ground. The low altitude and high speed, plus the tight turns, combine to place tremendous strain on the pilot and to test his stamina and skill. It is also a great strain on the airplane, which must be in top mechanical and structural condition. The most common form of pylon racing today is with midget racers, officially known as "Formula One" racers. Small biplanes are becoming popular for this sport, and there is still some pylon racing with former military fighter planes. In these air races the engines are run wide open and at tremendous speed, and often engines are ruined, making the sport a costly gamble.

The *cross-country race* is what the name implies, and is usually flown between two distant cities. Because of the distance involved, fighter aircraft are

A form of kiting, a paraglider is about ready to leave the water for a towed flight behind the speedboat.

the main participants. While the airplane naturally has to be in the best mechanical condition, the pilot's skill in maintaining a certain speed and fuel consumption is most important. The further he can stretch his fuel, the less time he will have to spend on the ground refueling. Such races are flown at high altitudes where faster speeds are attainable, and do not offer much spectator appeal except at the starting and finishing points. They are nevertheless exciting, for the superior pilot will usually win over even a superior airplane. Official world and national records can be set in air racing, and the trophies and cash prizes are large enough to attract many pilots to this sport.

Sport flying attracts women as well as men, and the former are very active in it in all of its various forms. Each year there is a transcontinental air race for women only. Standard private airplanes with no modifications are flown, demanding great tests of skill and intelligence.

The Air Show

The *air show* is perhaps the most practical and common method of bringing sport flying to the public. It is usually a commercial venture and an admission is charged to the public.

Most air shows (*see*) follow a stock pattern with an opening of a display of skydiving. The jumpers leave smoke trails behind them while airplanes encircle them with more smoke. A touch of theater is often added when one of the jumpers displays the national flag, and the crowd is brought to its feet to the strains of the national anthem.

Aerobatic exhibitions are the main attraction of an air show. It used to be called "stunting," but that term is no longer sufficiently descriptive because aerobatics are not stunts. Aerobatics (*see*) require a great amount of training on the part of the pilot, and aerobatic "tricks" are precisely conceived, practiced, and improved. It sometimes takes many years for a pilot to master them to such a degree that he can be called a professional aerobatic pilot.

A very good airplane is a necessity for aerobatics. Most airplanes are designed for comfortable transportation and are not suitable for air show work. Therefore, many of these airplanes are specially designed and built for this purpose, or converted from former training aircraft. Either way, the air show pilot invests many thousands of dollars in these airplanes in the hopes of gaining a name in the profession.

Another act generally in a comic vein is what is known as the "flying fool," or "flying professor" act. An oddly dressed individual darts out from the crowd, climbs into an airplane nearby, and proceeds to fly it with seemingly no previous experience. He puts the airplane into many hazardous attitudes only a few feet off the ground, and necessarily is the most expert of pilots.

There are also the "static displays," which amount to an airport showroom where various new airplanes are set up for inspection by the public. This is the means used to acquaint the nonflying public with the thrill and fun of flying.

The *Pretty Purple Puddy Tat* is an open-cockpit aircraft built and flown by a woman.

Flying in Pursuit of Sport

Most pilots wish to see the world from the seat of their own airplane and at their leisure. The small commercial lightplane has a great advantage over the airliner in that it can be operated at low altitudes where even small animals can be seen on the ground, and the landscape is in its proper perspective. The modern airliner flies at an altitude which blots out most detail and the landscape is a relatively flat scene.

While there are problems connected with a lightplane, it does provide a means of traveling distances at low cost. Economically, the average model is comparable to operating a car, yet a plane can cut across hills, valley, lakes, and woods in a straight, time-saving line at better than 100 mph. The modern airplane engine is so reliable it can run continuously for months without needing repair, and long overwater flights which were once avoided now are being made daily by many kinds of small aircraft. This is the appeal of the sport, and small plane owners may travel and vacation in areas not generally accessible within the limited vacation time most people have.

Many a pilot finds his pleasure in local flying, and can be seen on weekends at local airports, or flying

A fisherman has used his small amphibian to pursue his favorite sport in an isolated area.

over the city to look at the sights. He practices take-offs and landings for hours, or will make a flying visit to a neighboring airport. He seldom goes far from home, but this is what he enjoys as his sport.

The hunter or fisherman uses the airplane mainly in pursuit of his favorite sport. The airplane opens up new vistas and hunting areas far from home that would otherwise be closed to him.

In some areas predators such as fox, wolf, and coyote are hunted and killed from the air for their bounty. The hunter lands for evidence of his game and takes off again to make a kill. If the airplane is large enough, a moose or elk can be carried home. In this type of low-level stalking in strange terrain, a hunter acquires considerable piloting skill to overcome the hazards involved.

The fisherman finds great pleasure in flying, and either buys or builds an amphibian or a lightplane which is equipped for landing on a lake or river. His seaplane brings him to a distant area in short time where he can select a good fishing spot, land close by, and fish from his plane. If fishing is poor, he can taxi to another part of the lake, or he can take off and try another lake. He can also swim from the airplane if he chooses, for not only is the seaplane an airplane, it is also a powerboat and a sailboat, or it can be paddled like a canoe. In some respects, the seaplane can go anywhere a landplane can except it obviously cannot land on the ground. However, almost every major city in the country has a lake or river, and flying a seaplane is not as restrictive as might be thought, and offers another phase in the activity of sport flying. Leo J. Kohn

See also: Business aviation, Experimental Aircraft Association, General aviation, General aviation aircraft, Homebuilt aircraft, Pleasure flying

Sputniks

The purpose of the U.S.S.R.'s Sputnik program was for man to physically project himself, his vehicle, and his instruments into space by means of rocketry. The groundwork for the Sputniks had been laid by the rocket explorations of the previous decade. Upper-atmospheric research had shown relations between many phenomena which the Sputniks were to investigate by direct exploration, making observations of the effects of weightlessness (*see*); cosmic, ultraviolet, and solar radiation; geomagnetic disturbances; the Van Allen radiation belts (*see*); radio-wave transmissions; and micrometeoroids.

The ten Sputniks in the program were a prelude to manned spaceflight. Each capsule gradually increased in size and from their data transmissions, knowledge was acquired on the nature and possible dangers to be found in the upper atmosphere.

Sputnik 1

On October 4, 1957, the U.S.S.R. successfully launched Sputnik 1, the world's first artificial Earth satellite. The spacecraft, a 23-inch aluminum sphere, carried only two radio transmitters and was powered by chemical batteries. This first and most difficult step on man's road to the stars was the outgrowth of the theoretical ideas of the Russian scientist, K. E. Tsiolkovsky (*see*). Before the first satellite, Earth's atmosphere had been studied up to an altitude of about 30 kilometers with radiosondes (*see*). Some idea of the nature of the upper and lower atmosphere had been obtained; however, the results did not cover the whole range of altitudes and were often inaccurate.

The background for Sputnik 1 was the need to know more about the geomagnetic field (*see*) at great distances from the Earth, as well as cosmic rays (*see*) and solar and stellar radiation beyond the terrestrial atmosphere. Thus, Sputnik 1 served as a measuring instrument for long-distance observations and investigations beyond the dense layers of the Earth's atmosphere. Many difficulties had to be overcome in developing instruments for such a craft. The operating temperatures for an orbiting satellite and its instrumentation were unknown. Selecting the Sputnik's orbit also presented a problem as did placement of instrumentation inside the spacecraft.

One of the main problems was to determine the limits of the upper atmosphere. Sputnik 1 performed this function by observing the changes in the parameters of its orbit which resulted from atmospheric resistance. A similar experiment was made by observing the braking of the booster rocket. An equally important experiment was the investigation of the ionosphere (*see*). This problem was solved by the observation of the propagation of radio waves emitted from the spacecraft. The nature of this propagation was also studied, resulting in data necessary to insure reliable communication with space vehicles.

The radio signals transmitted by the Sputnik were also used to send measurements to Earth. Sputnik 1 investigated temperature conditions within the capsule by utilizing sensors (*see*) which reflected temperature changes. Proper internal temperature would be necessary for the operation of instruments in subsequent experiments, and to check the efficiency of the Sputnik's thermo-regulation system.

mals could endure lengthy periods of weightlessness.

Data from Spunik 2 and similar experiments by other Sputniks on the influence of solar and cosmic radiation on a living organism aided in developing methods of protecting future cosmonauts (*see*) from the dangerous effects of solar, cosmic, and ultraviolet rays. However, an important result obtained by Sputnik 2 was the discovery of a growing intensity of flux of high-energy charged particles as the altitude of flight, and the geomagnetic latitude of the point over which the satellite was passing at a given moment, increased. It was found that this was due to the satellite entering the polar regions of the outer zone of the Van Allen radiation belt, and was the first indication of the existence of a belt of high-energy

A frame from the Soviet movie, *Ten Years of the Space Era,* shows a technician checking the first Soviet Earth-orbiting satellite, Sputnik.

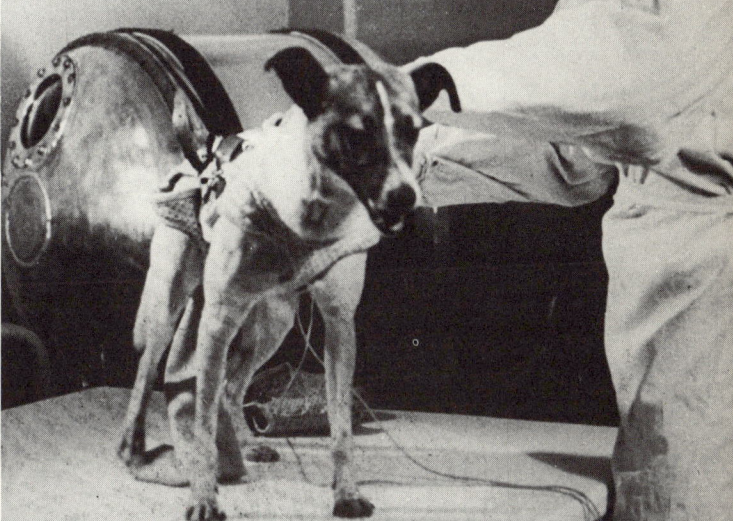

Laika, launched aboard Sputnik II on November 3, 1957, was the first animal to orbit the Earth. She remained alive in orbit for four days.

Sputniks 2 and 3

Sputnik 2 was the first of several satellites to carry dogs as passengers. It was launched November 3, 1957, and performed the first biomedical experiments in space. The satellite consisted of two spheres and a cylinder within a tubular structure, and remained attached to its launch vehicle's final stage which weighed more than five tons. Payload weight had increased to 1,120 pounds. The dog, Laika, remained alive only for a week because life-support supplies for a longer period of time had not been provided. Laika's flight was an opportunity to study her physical condition during weightlessness and her condition was recorded by instruments attached to her body and then telemetered to Earth. From this "account," U.S.S.R. scientists concluded that ani-

charged particles trapped by the geomagnetic field.

Sputnik 3, launched May 15, 1958, was the first Russian satellite to use solar cells (*see*), which made it possible to obtain scientific data over a long period of time. For nearly two years this flying laboratory recorded measurements, which showed that whenever the satellite entered the belt between 55° and 65° latitude, both North and South, there was a sharp increase in X-ray radiation, which resulted from the bombardment of the satellite casing by electrons.

Other Sputnik experiments determined the corpuscular radiation of the sun by means of photoamplifiers, detecting the presence of electrons for the first time. Their intensity was greater during the day than at night, and increased with greater altitude.

Sputnik II *(left)* with a 1,118-pound payload, also carried Laika. Sputnik III *(right)* remained in orbit for two years and used solar cell batteries as a power source.

The density of the upper atmosphere was determined by observation of the changes in the parameters of the Sputnik's orbits as a result of drag, and by registration of atmospheric pressure with ionization and magnetic manometers. Various methods were also used to study the parameters of the ionosphere by observing the propagation of radio waves emitted by the Sputnik's radio transmitter, by utilization of onboard instrumentation, and by the direct measurement of the concentration of positive electrons in the satellites' orbits.

A self-orientating magnetometer measured the Earth's magnetic field at high altitudes, and registered the full intensity of the field at distances from the Earth's surface corresponding to the altitude of the Sputniks' orbits. Instruments also registered the quantity of heavy nuclei in cosmic radiation. In addition, several sensors registered micrometeorite impacts.

Between May 15, 1960, and March 25, 1961, the U.S.S.R. launched seven super-heavy Sputniks which were unmanned tests of future manned spacecraft. The main objective of these flights was to develop spacecraft systems, study the route for a manned flight, and make further medico-biological investigations. Further physical experiments were conducted to study the registration of levels of cosmic rays and ultraviolet and X-ray radiation of the sun to determine the actual radiation danger for manned spaceflight.

A "dummy" cosmonaut was included in the May, 1960, launch. The dummy was to experience as far as possible, physical stresses which a cosmonaut would encounter, and determine if they were tolerable. Succeeding launches tested the environmental control systems, and the orientation and retro systems. Experiments with dogs and other small animals, insects, and plants continued to check the functioning of living organisms in space.

The study of cosmic rays also continued. In order to register levels of cosmic radiation and determine the lower border of the Van Allen radiation belt, the final two Sputniks carried radiation-measuring equipment. This equipment provided information on the number of charged particles in the region, and on the ionization caused by them. The capsule casing

SOVIET SPUTNIKS

Number	Launch date	Weight	Period	Perigee	Apogee	Inclination	Results	Decayed
1	10-4-57	83.6	96.17	228	947	65°	First satellite to orbit Earth; two radio transmitters	1-4-58
2	11-3-57	508.3	103.75	225	1,671	65°	First biomedic experiments; dog Laika aboard	4-14-58
3	5-15-58	1,327	105.95	226	1,881	65°	Discovered Earth's outer radiation belt	4-6-60
4	5-15-60	4,540	91.8	312	369	65°	Carried "dummy" cosmonaut to test environmental control. Broke into 8 pieces after 64 orbits	9-5-62
5	8-19-60	4,600	90.7	306	339	64°	First space vehicle to be retrieved had "dummy" cosmonaut, two dogs, and TV monitor	—
6	12-11-60	4,563	88.5	187.3	265	65°	Medical and biological experiments; recovery attempt failed	12-2-60
7	2-4-61	6,500	89.8	—	—	65°	Believed to be Venus probe abort	2-26-61
8	2-12-61	6,500	89.7	222	280	65°	Launched Venus I from parking orbit	2-25-61
9	3-9-61	4,700	88.6	183.5	248.8	64° 56'	Sputnik and dog aboard recovered after one orbit	—
10	3-25-61	4,695	88.42	178.1	247	64° 54'	Recovered after one orbit with dog Zvezdochka	—

Source: TRW Inc. Space Log

was proved to be sufficient protection from the radiation belt.

The prototypes leading to manned spaceflight had successfully performed their task. The way was paved for the first Russian manned flight which came 18 days after the last Sputnik flight when Vostok 1 was launched April 12, 1961, with cosmonaut Yuri Gagarin (*see*) who became the first man to orbit the Earth.

Helen Olian

See also: U.S.S.R. aerospace activities

SR-71, Lockheed and YF-12A

The SR-71, built by Lockheed, is the world's most advanced strategic reconnaissance aircraft (*see*). A sister ship, the YF-12A, identical in appearance and construction, is an advanced all-weather interceptor aircraft. Both are capable of Mach 3 speeds and altitudes of over 80,000 feet.

The SR-71 carries a crew of two, a pilot and Systems Reconnaissance Officer (SRO) and is equipped with a variety of advanced reconnaissance equipment. Flying at Mach 3 speeds it is capable of aerial surveys covering 60,000 to 80,000 square miles of the Earth's surface in one hour for both preattack and postattack missions. Indications are that future models may be equipped for strike missions as well as reconnaissance. The first of the SR-71 aircraft were delivered to the Strategic Air Command (SAC) (*see*) in 1965 and are currently being operated by the SAC at Beale Air Force Base, California.

The YF-12A interceptor is capable of the highest altitudes and speeds of any aircraft in the world, a fact substantiated by nine world speed and altitude records established on May 1, 1965 and certified by the National Aeronautic Association (*see*). These records include a straight course speed record of 2070.101 mph and the absolute sustained altitude record of 80,257.86 ft. The YF-12A is equipped with sensitive Doppler radar, fire control system, and an automatic navigation system. Its armament con-

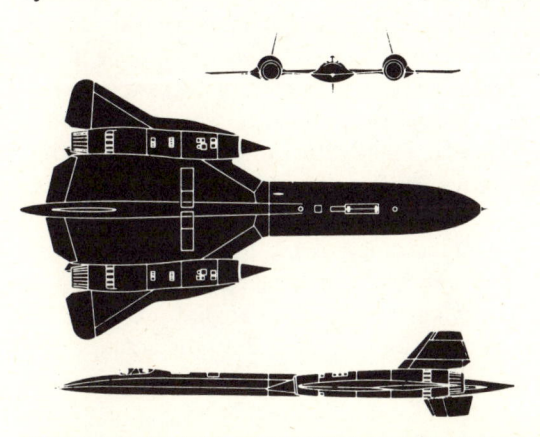

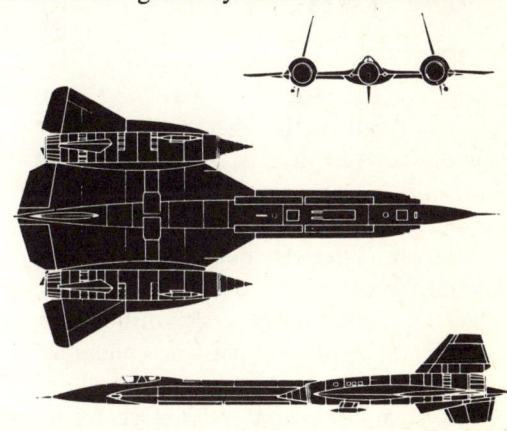

SR-71 Lockheed
Specifications and Performance Data

Engine	2 Pratt & Whitney J58 turbojets with afterburners
Wingspan	55 ft.
Length	107 ft.
Gross weight	140,000 lbs.
Maximum speed	2,000 + mph
Range	2,000 miles

YF-12A Lockheed
Specifications and Performance Data

Engine	2 Pratt & Whitney J58 turbojets with afterburners
Wingspan	52 ft.
Length	97 ft.
Gross weight	136,000 lbs.
Maximum speed	2,000 + mph
Range	3,000 miles

Stability

sists of AIM-47 air-to-air missiles (*see*). Not yet in service, it is presently undergoing test flights at Edwards Air Force Base (*see*).

With more than two years of flight devoted in large part to research, the YF-12A has provided a wealth of data for high speed flight at extreme altitudes which will be valuable in the design of America's SST. In addition to the knowledge gained from flight research, the YF-12A has been used to pioneer the machinery, fabrication, and production techniques for titanium aircraft. Both the SR-71 and the YF-12A are constructed of about 95 per cent titanium which has the strength of steel but is much lighter. Even though constructed of titanium the massive SR-71 and the YF-12A each weigh more than 100,000 lbs. Both aircraft are painted black to reduce the intense heat produced by skin friction at Mach 3.

Sanford Sasser, Jr.

See also: Fighter aircraft

Stability

Stability is the property of an object or system relating to its ability to remain as it is. A stable condition exists when there is no change in the state or condition of the device, vehicle, or system being considered.

There are three general kinds of stability: positive, neutral, and negative. *Positive stability* is present when a system or vehicle resists disturbance, or tends to return to its original position, condition, or direction if it is disturbed.

A system has *neutral stability* when a disturbance changes its performance, and it does not return to its original state, and if, when the disturbing force is removed, no further change takes place.

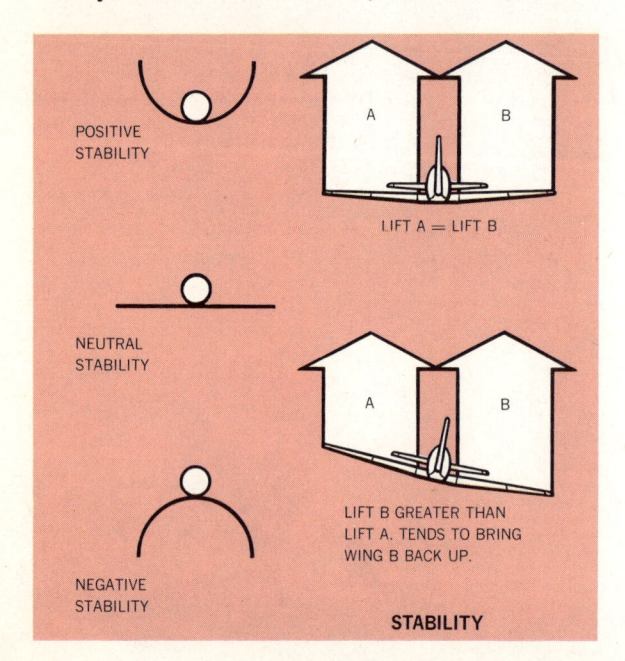

Negative stability can also be termed *instability*. A system with negative stability may not only change when outside forces are applied to it, but will continue to change after the disturbing force is removed.

Airplanes are usually designed to have positive stability. This insures that a gust or control movement will affect the attitude of the aircraft only so long as the force is acting on it, and that it will return to its original attitude and course when the forces are removed.

Some airplanes, particularly those used for aerobatics (*see*), are designed or modified to have neutral stability. This makes changing attitude easier and more rapid, and permits the execution of some maneuvers which would be difficult with a more stable aircraft.

An aircraft which had negative stability would be extremely difficult to fly straight and level. Any movement of the controls or roughness in the air would cause increasing change in attitude unless correction with the controls were made immediately. If such an aircraft were made to roll or spin, it would, without corrective action, do so with increasing speed, and could exceed its structural strength and be destroyed. Wing dihedral and fixed tail surfaces are design features which make an airplane stable in flight. The wings are set at an angle to one another so that if one wing is lifted, the other comes to a more level position, and creates a greater amount of directly vertical lift than the other, bringing the lower wing back up. This is positive stability around the roll axis. Positive pitch (*see*) and yaw (*see*) stability are provided by the vertical fin and horizontal stabilizers. These fixed tail surfaces act like the feathers of an arrow as they pass through the air and make the airplane resist forces which would turn it to the side, up, or down.

Other properties of the airplane tend to stabilize it. Forcing the nose down permits a dive in which gravity builds up the airspeed. This causes the lift of the wings to increase, and the airplane comes back to a level attitude unless the nose is held down.

Pulling the stick back reduces the airspeed and the lift, and the nose tends to drop back to a level attitude. Most modern airplanes are so stable that, properly trimmed for cruising flight, they will fly themselves perfectly well straight and level.

Helicopters (*see*) and high-speed aircraft are often equipped with electronic devices which sense unwanted movements, and automatically apply corrective control movement. Spacecraft may be stabilized by being spun. The entire vehicle then acts like a gyroscope (*see*), and retains the desired orientation. Other spacecraft stabilization systems may rely on automatic sensing of undesirable motion, and firing of control thrusters. Some space vehicles have extendable booms tipped with weights which, because of their inertia, make the spacecraft resistant to disturbance. — Steve Kimmell

See also: Aerodynamics, Airplane, Spacecraft design

Stack, John

American aeronautical engineer
Born: September 13, 1906;
Lowell, Massachusetts

John Stack was only a year out of Massachusetts Institute of Technology when, as a junior engineer with the National Advisory Committee for Aeronautics (NACA) (*see*) in 1929, he made his first significant contribution to aviation progress. It was his design of the nation's first high-speed wind tunnel that led to development of airfoils that molded the more popular airframe configurations of the 1930's and 1940's.

Over the next 12 years Stack became known throughout the aeronautical world for his brilliant work in wind tunnel design and construction and in new areas of research made possible by those tunnels. In 1942, as chief of NACA's compressibility research division, he was a leader in the move for development of research craft to explore both transonic and supersonic flight. As a result of his research with these aircraft—which included the X-1, D-558-2, X-2, X-3, X-4 and X-5—he contributed to development of the variable-sweep-wing concept.

In recent years Stack has been associated with some of the country's most vital aeronautical endeavors, including the supersonic transport (*see*), the X-15 research program (*see*), and the variable-sweep-wing F-111.

For his numerous contributions to aviation and space technology, he has twice won the Collier Trophy and was the 1962 recipient of the Wright Brothers Memorial Trophy. — Robert L. Parrish

See also: X-series aerospace vehicles

STADAN, *see* Tracking systems and networks

Stafford, Thomas P.

Astronaut
Born: September 17, 1930;
Weatherford, Oklahoma
Service: Lieutenant Colonel, USAF

Lieutenant Colonel Thomas P. Stafford was selected for the second group of astronauts in September, 1962, following five years as a fighter-interceptor pilot. He was a copilot of the Gemini 6 mission in 1965.

Stafford was graduated from the U.S. Military Academy in 1948. He later attended the USAF Aerospace Research Pilot School at Edwards AFB, California, where he served as Chief of the Performance Branch. He was responsible for the supervision and administration of flight curriculum for student test pilots and was also an instructor. He is co-author of two books on flight testing.

NASA awarded him two Exceptional Service Medals, and he has also received many honors and medals.

As command pilot of the Gemini 9 mission launched June 3, 1966, he and copilot Eugene Cernan (*see*) performed three different types of rendezvous.

Stafford is training as commander of the back-up crew for the first manned Apollo mission. He has accumulated 5,000 flying hours with over 4,000 hours in jets.

Astronaut Stafford and his wife, the former Faye L. Shoemaker, have two daughters. — Jim Schefter

See also: Apollo, Astronauts, Gemini

Staggerwing Beech

The Beech Model 17 Staggerwing was the first plane produced by the Beech Aircraft Co., and it remained in production for 15 years, from 1933 to 1948. It

Staggerwing Beech

was a single-engine biplane which carried five passengers. Its name was derived from the fact that the wings were staggered, the lower wing being placed slightly forward of the upper one.

The Model 17 was used over the years as a general aviation aircraft (*see*), finding most of its purchasers among businessmen and sportsmen. In the late 1930's, China purchased the Staggerwing for modification as a hospital transport, and during World War II (*see*) it was used by both the U.S. Army Air Corps and the Navy as a personnel and utility transport.

Various refinements were made in successive models of the airplane, including installation of retractable landing gear and the addition of a more powerful engine. As one of the early private aircraft the Staggerwing had a long and honorable career, and it contributed greatly to the growth of the Beech Aircraft Co. Claude G. Luisada

See also: Beech, Walter H.

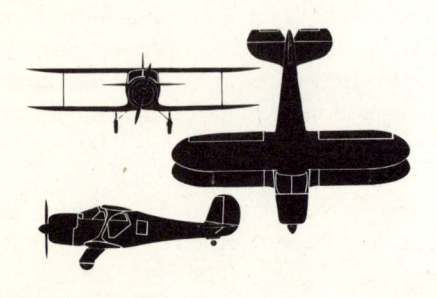

Staggerwing Beech
Specifications and Performance Data

Engine	One 285-hp to 450-hp engine, depending on model
Wingspan	32 ft.
Length	25 ft. 9 in.
Empty weight	2,800 lbs.
Cruising speed	190 mph
Range	1,400 miles

Staging, *see* Launching

Stall

A stall occurs when the smooth flow of air over and under an airplane's wings is radically disturbed. This can occur when the airspeed falls below that required to generate lift (*see*) or if the angle of attack (*see*) becomes so high that the airflow separates from the wing. Airspeed and angle of attack must be considered together to understand a stall. The higher the angle of attack, the greater the airspeed required to prevent a stall.

Pilots routinely execute *power on* and *power off* stalls in trimming in order to learn the characteristics of the aircraft in this condition. There is nothing inherently dangerous about a stall, provided it is entered at a high enough altitude to permit recovery.

To execute a power off stall the pilot closes his throttle to idle and pulls back the stick or wheel, raising the nose. As the aircraft slows down and the angle of attack increases, the controls become "loose" because the airflow around them is slowing down. More control movement is required to get the aircraft to respond. As the angle of attack increases still further, the airflow over the wing separates from the wing and becomes turbulent, causing buffeting (*see*). Sufficient lift is no longer being created to sustain the aircraft. Most aircraft will then "mush" downward, the nose dropping slowly, and the airspeed thus building up. If the stick or wheel is held back, the aircraft will continue to repeat the maneuver, stalling, nosing down, and stalling again.

Successful landing, in effect, is achieved by approaching the end of the runway at low, close-to-stall speed, and then, after leveling off, bringing the aircraft into a full or partial stall when it is slightly above the ground. D. Willliam Bennett and Steve Kimmell

See also: Maneuvers, Stall warning indicator

Stall warning indicator

Stall warning indicators are devices that cause a loud warning buzzer or horn to sound in the cockpit if an aircraft is approaching very close to its stalling speed. These indicators are extremely useful during landings when an aircraft is normally being flown at a speed just above stalling. If the pilot, through lack of attention, should allow the aircraft's speed to sink too low, the sound of the stall warning indicator will instantly remind him of the necessity for additional power and speed. Stall warning indicators work on the principle of measuring the speed of the air through the Pitot tube which feeds air to the airspeed indicator.

See also: Pitot-static system, Stall

Standard operating procedure

Standard operating procedures (SOP) generally applies to any procedure used repetitively to achieve a given task. The term probably originated in the armed forces, but today is applied extensively in many fields. In the field of aerospace, standard operating procedures are established and used in many different ways. For instance, there are SOP's for inflight emergencies, evacuation of an aircraft, starting engines, or shutting down an aircraft. Although established standard operating procedures are changed as may be required by experience, they generally are not altered radically.

Stapp, John P.

American aeromedical scientist
Born: July 11, 1910; Bahia, Brazil

U.S. Air Force Colonel John P. Stapp has been called "the fastest man on Earth" as a result of a series of human stress tolerance tests he performed as part of an Air Force research program from 1946 through 1958.

Stapp studied zoology, chemistry, and biophysics at Baylor University and the University of Texas. He was awarded a Ph.D. in biophysics after he had already enrolled in the University of Minnesota Medical School. He received his M.D. there in 1943, and the following year entered active duty with the Air Force.

After attending the Medical Field Service School, the School of Aviation Medicine, and the Industrial Medical Seminar, he was assigned to the Air Force Aeromedical Laboratory and placed on detached service as a research project officer at Edwards Air Force Base (see) in California. There he pioneered in research related to the effects of mechanical forces on living tissues. With anesthetized chimpanzees, black bears, and hogs, he investigated tolerance to crash impacts and decelerations on a special high-speed, track-mounted test sled of his own design. The purpose of these tests was to provide stress analysis data for aircraft and ground vehicle safety design, for supersonic-hypersonic aircraft ejection seat and escape capsule to tolerance limits, and for impact forces to be encountered in spaceflight.

Investigations with animals could not provide all of the information required, however, so Colonel Stapp strapped himself into the rocket-propelled sled to be fired down the test track at a velocity of 632 mph. Brought to a halt in 1.4 seconds from that speed, he sustained deceleration forces of 40 times the pressure of gravity. During his 12 years in such assignments at Edwards and Holloman Air Force Base, New Mexico, Stapp made a total of 29 sled rides, and supervised thousands of others that contributed immeasurably to aviation and aerospace medical knowledge. In subsequent assignments as chief of the Armed Forces Institute of Pathology he has continued to advance aerospace safety and knowledge. Stapp has also served as chief scientist of the Department of Transportation, National Highway Safety Bureau.

The author of more than 80 articles and papers on medical and aerospace research, Stapp has also contributed chapters to textbooks dealing with acceleration, deceleration, biodynamics of spaceflight, and related subjects. He has received some 25 special honors and awards for his achievements, and holds membership in numerous aeromedical and aerospace professional organizations.   Robert L. Parrish

See also: Aerospace medicine, Escape systems, Rocket sled

Stars

Stars, of which the sun (*see*) is the closest example, are huge spheres of gas that emit enormous amounts of light. Their masses range from about that of Jupiter (*see*) to almost 100 times that of the sun, their sizes vary from less than that of the Earth to a thousand times the solar dimensions, and their surface temperatures range from values comparable to the Earth's to tens of time hotter.

Stars with masses comparable to that of the sun rotate near their surfaces at relatively slow speeds, about 10 mph, but many more massive, hotter stars rotate at velocities of almost 1,000 mph. A few stars, particularly the stars of spectral type A, known as *peculiar A-stars,* have huge magnetic fields at their surfaces. These fields may be tens of thousands of times more intense than the magnetic field at the surface of the Earth. More typical magnetic fields are much weaker, except perhaps at small sunspot-like regions of the star's surface.

Stellar Atmospheres

Astronomers have learned much about the nature of stars by analyzing the light emitted by their outer layers, a region termed the *stellar atmosphere.* Starlight is separated into its component colors, or wavelengths, by means of a spectrograph. Chemical elements in the stellar atmosphere absorb a fraction of the star's radiation at characteristic wavelengths and cause a depression, a spectral line at the appropriate positions in the spectra.

From the positions and depths of these lines astronomers have learned the types of chemical elements present in stellar atmospheres as well as their abundance. The gases hydrogen and helium dominate the atmosphere, with heavier elements representing at most a few per cent of the stellar material. There is almost always more hydrogen than helium. From the degree of ionization of the elements, that is, the number of electrons that have been lost by the atoms, an estimate can be made of the atmospheric temperature. Study of the shapes of the lines provides information on the variation of pressure and temperature with altitude and the strength of random turbulent motions within the atmosphere.

Distance Scales

Stars have provided a means of measuring distances both within the Milky Way Galaxy (see) and to other, nearby galaxies like the Magellanic clouds and the Andromeda galaxy. The nearest stars exhibit a displacement, or parallax, with respect to the more distant stars as the Earth moves in orbit about the sun. Parallax measurements provide a distance scale for stars within several hundred light years of the Earth. Such measurements allow us to deduce the intrinsic brightness or luminosity of a star.

More distant stars will appear fainter by the inverse-square law; stars twice as far away are four times fainter. Once the intrinsic brightness of a given type of star is known, we can deduce the distance to another star of this type from its apparent brightness. To measure still larger distances, two types of stars which vary periodically in brightness, have proved useful: RR Lyrae and Cepheid variable stars. The average intrinsic luminosity of all RR Lyrae stars is about the same, while that of Cepheids depends on the period of the variation.

Herzsprung-Russell Diagram

In 1911 and 1913, respectively, Ejnar Herzsprung of Sweden and Henry Norris Russell of Princeton University developed a method which essentially graphs the intrinsic luminosities of stars versus their temperatures. Surprisingly, many stars fall along a narrow line, now termed the *main sequence,* running diagonally across the diagram. These stars, including the sun, are called *normal dwarfs.*

A number of stars have significantly higher luminosities than stars of comparable surface temperatures, which indicates that these objects are much larger. Some, the *giants,* are about 100 times larger than their main-sequence counterparts and a few, the *super-giants,* are 1,000 times bigger. Finally, a class of stars that are relatively under-luminous are called *white dwarfs*. Such stars typically have dimensions comparable to those of the Earth. As they have a mass similar to that of the sun, they are very dense. In fact, a spoonful of white dwarf would weigh several tons on the Earth.

Stellar Evolution

A star's history is primarily a function of its mass and initial chemical compositions, but its speed of rotation and the strength of its magnetic field may also significantly affect its evolution.

Stars are born from tenuous clouds of gas and dust, which initially may be a million-billion-billion times less dense than the air in the Earth's atmosphere. Stars do not usually form individually, but are created in groups called *clusters*. Initially a very massive, rarefied gas cloud is disturbed in a manner that permits gravity to gain control over random motions within the cloud. After contracting for some time, the cloud fragments and parts collapse gravitationally into smaller mass units, which are the nascent stars.

The gravitational energy generated through the collapse serves to heat the gas and lust, to decompose the latter into atoms and the gas into ions and electrons, and finally as the ultimate source of the energy radiated. For a star like the sun, the initial collapse phase occurs rapidly. Within a few hundred years, the protostar has contracted from a dimension of a few light years to a size hundreds of thousands of times smaller, and all its atoms have been ionized.

Early History

At this stage, a more orderly process of contraction takes place. For stars whose mass is comparable to that of the sun or smaller, the star becomes heated to the point at which convection begins, in an analogous manner to the bubbling of a heated kettle of water. The star continues to contract, keeping its surface temperature constant but with its interior becoming progressively hotter. Stars more massive than the sun tend to increase their surface temperatures while they contract. For these types of stars the convective bubbling is soon damped out.

While contracting, a star rotates faster and faster and some, especially the lighter stars, may eventually spin so rapidly that material is ejected from

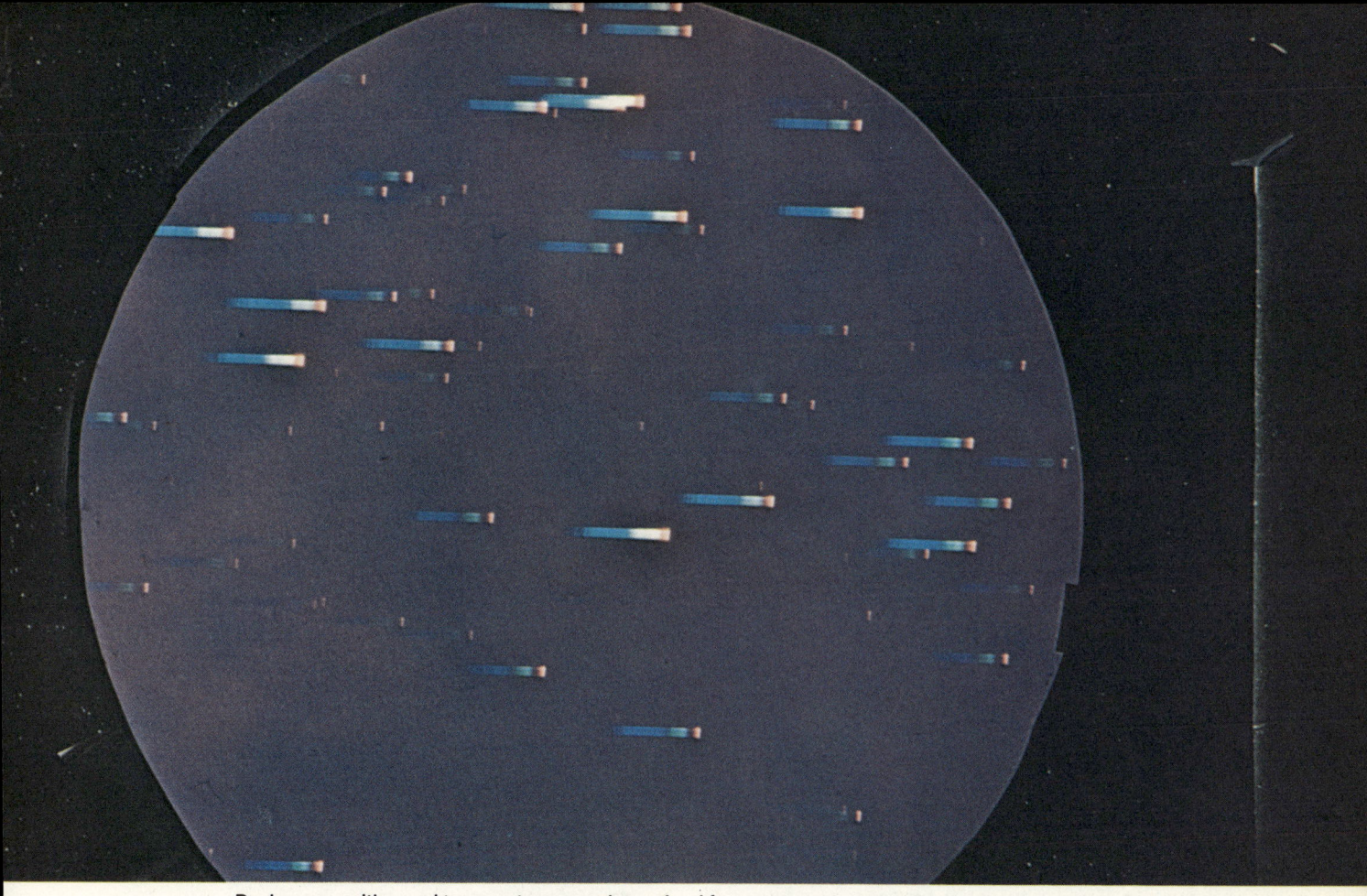

Basic composition and temperatures are determined from spectral image of the Hyades group of stars.

near their equators. This slows down the rotation and provides the material from which planets (*see*) may form. The T-Tauri stars, found in dense regions of gas and dust, such as the Orion nebula, are probably stars in the final stages of contraction. These stars show irregular variations in their brightness and rotate rapidly. Even younger, cooler stars, radiating primarily infrared light, are also found in such locations.

All but the least massive stars eventually reach sufficiently high temperatures in their interiors for nuclear processes to become the principal sources of energy. This stage begins after several million years for a star like the sun; more massive stars contract much more rapidly. The fusion of four hydrogen nuclei into a single helium necleus occurs in a several-step process and produces enough energy to stop the shrinking of the star.

The Main Sequence

The nuclear hydrogen-burning phase positions stars along the main sequence of the Herzsprung-Russell diagram. This is a relatively static and long-lasting phase (fortunately for life on the Earth). Over the last 5 billion years the sun has increased in radius by only about 4 per cent and in luminosity by 60 per cent and will remain about the same for 5 billion years.

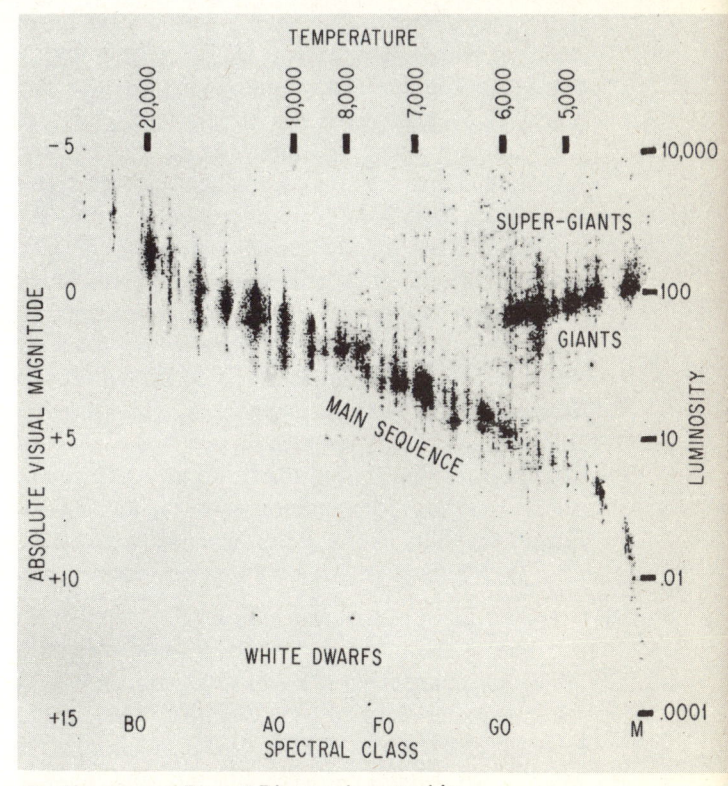

The Herzsprung-Russell Diagram is a graphic representation of Population I stars. The sun is in the main sequence at about 5600° and G2.

2161

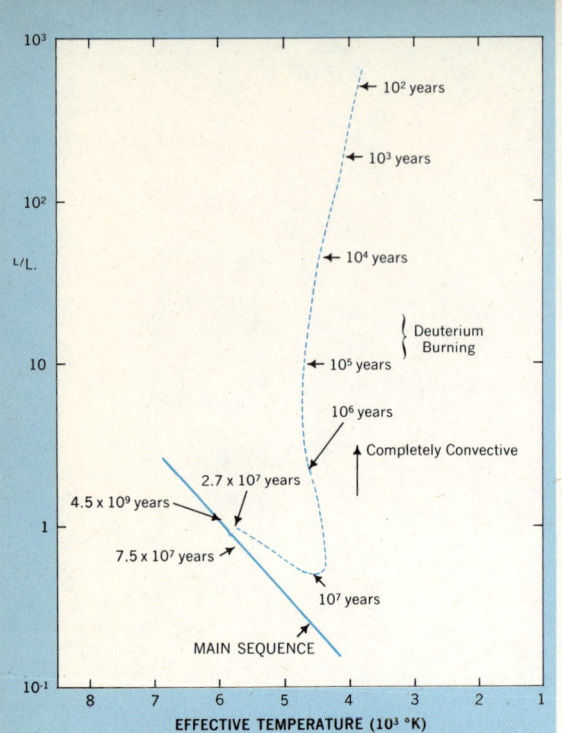

A diagram shows the theoretical history of the sun from a gaseous nebula to the present day, at 4.5 × 10⁹ years, or 4½ billion years.

Elements in a star absorb light at characteristic wavelengths in a spectrum. The sun's spectrum shows iron (Fe) prominently.

The Red Giant Phase

All the hydrogen fuel eventually becomes exhausted in the central region of the star where fusion is occurring. The central core proceeds to contract, and in so doing heats up adjacent regions and initiates fusion there. The outer envelopes of lower main-sequence stars paradoxically expand during this stage and the star eventually becomes a red giant, relatively cool and very large. Finally, the core becomes so hot that the fusion process transforming three helium nuclei into a carbon nucleus begins. But because the core is so dense the matter behaves like a solid and it initially resists expansion. All the energy of fusion goes into heating the core, which causes more fusion. All the helium is consumed in an incredibly short period of time in this runaway process. The core material is now so hot that it can expand, and it explodes outward. This stage is called the *helium flash*. An upper main-sequence star reaches the helium-flash stage much more quickly and may later become a supergiant. Subsequent evolution of the lower main-sequence stars may pass through an RR Lyrae stage at some point.

Chemical Evolution

Some of the more massive stars may undergo a whole sequence of flash stages involving the fusion of core material to heavier elements. Iron is the heaviest element that can be produced through reactions involving hydrogen, helium, and heavier nuclei since it requires, rather than produces, energy to make elements heavier than iron. However, elements as heavy as bismuth can be made in a star's interior through bombardment with a modest number of neutrons (*see*). Still heavier elements, such as uranium, require a very large number of neutrons for their manufacture.

Such conditions are probably realized only in actual explosions of stars, such as supernovae events, which may be engendered at some of the flash stages. Such major explosions release the elements produced in the interior into interstellar space. This enriches the helium and heavier-element content there and thus stars formed at later epochs. Galaxies (*see*) are believed to contain only hydrogen and helium at the time of their formation.

Dying Stars

Eventually a star is either unable to burn some of its nuclear fuel or has converted all of its central core to iron. Gravitational forces then take over again and the star collapses. Stars containing less than 1½ solar masses at this stage will collapse into the highly dense white dwarfs. These stars are so dense that they will no longer collapse, and they slowly cool by radiating heat into space.

Somewhat heavier stars weigh too much to stop contracting at this stage and will cease contraction only when they are so dense that protons and electrons have been converted into neutrons. Such *neutron stars*, in contrast to white dwarfs, have not yet been positively identified.

It has been suggested that one of these underluminous types of stars may be responsible for *pulsars*, objects which emit bursts of radio noise at very well-defined intervals of about 1 second.

Finally, very massive stars should collapse to an object of zero volume. Shortly before this occurs, the gravitational field becomes so intense that light cannot escape.

Jay M. Pasachoff and James B. Pollack

See also: Astronomy, Astrophysics, Constellations, Nova

START

START, the Spacecraft Technology and Advanced Re-entry Test Program, is a long-range USAF effort to develop a re-entry vehicle capable of pilot control from orbit to a precise landing point, as opposed to the current re-entry vehicles (*see*) which follow a trajectory over which the pilot has little or no control once the vehicle has been deorbited and committed to landing.

Although START did not begin until early 1964, the foundation was laid in a program known as ASSET (Aerothermodynamic/elastic Structural Systems Environmental Tests) (*see*) in 1961–1965. ASSET originally was begun to support the Dyna-Soar program (*see*) which later was canceled in favor of the START approach. Objectives of ASSET were to test advanced reradiative materials and to assess the accuracy and applicability of the design approach. Highly successful, ASSET increased the lifting re-entry technology base by verifying structural concepts, measuring both metallic and nonmetallic refractory materials, and investigating magnetic propagation through the re-entry ion sheath.

Six launches of ASSET vehicles were conducted from Cape Kennedy between September, 1963, and February, 1965. A modified Thor ICBM was the booster vehicle for the subscale, flatiron-shaped spacecraft flown on a re-entry trajectory down the Eastern Test Range (*see*).

Concurrent with the ASSET definition phase, the Air Force initiated a study and ground test effort to define a lifting-body configuration in the medium hypersonic lift-over-drag (L/D) range. Initiating the second phase of START, it was called PRIME (Precision Recovery Including Maneuvering Entry) (*see*) and consisted of four flight tests of a larger vehicle weighing about 800 pounds, launched down the Western Test Range (*see*) by an Atlas SLV-3 space booster. This unmanned vehicle, designated the SV-5D, was designed to maneuver at hypersonic speeds during re-entry several hundred miles across range and return to the re-entry path, arriving at a precise recovery point near Kwajalein in the Pacific. The first three flights were so successful that the fourth was canceled.

The third part of START is a project known as PILOT (Piloted Low Speed Tests) (*see*). In PILOT a manned lifting-body vehicle (*see*) designated the X-24 will be flown in a series of drop tests from a B-52 to explore the vehicle characteristics from supersonic speeds through the transonic range to landing speed in the area of 200 mph.

The final phase of START will be the design and construction of multipurpose reusable orbital vehicles. Such a spacecraft can be used to resupply orbiting space stations, ferry crews to and from the orbiting laboratories, and return data and experiments from space to scientists on the Earth.

Frank A. Burnham

State and Regional Defense Airlift, *see* National Defense Airlift Plans

Statute mile, *see* Mile

Steady state theory, *see* Astronomy, Cosmogony, Cosmology, Universe

Stearman, Lloyd

American aircraft manufacturer
Born: October 26, 1898;
Wellsford, Kansas

Lloyd Stearman, one of the leading U.S. pre-World War II light airplane producers, began his career as an architect. After military service he used his talents to design and construct aircraft.

A college student when World War I broke out, Stearman joined the Navy in 1918 and became an aircraft mechanic. He returned to architecture briefly, then joined the Laird Airplane Co. In 1923 he joined the Swallow Airplane Co. as chief engineer and was named chief engineer and director of Travel Airplane Co. two years later.

In 1925 he founded Stearman Aircraft Corp. to produce his newly designed Stearman C.1 single-bay open-cockpit biplane. In addition to designing and supervising construction, he served as test pilot for the company. The C.1 and succeeding designs led to army contracts for flight-training aircraft.

Stearman merged with Varney Airplane Co. in 1932. He also invested in the faltering Lockheed Aircraft Corp. and served as president of both companies. He served with the U.S. Department of Commerce in 1935, but the following year he became president of Stearman-Hammond Aircraft Co.

Stearman's work in airplane design and manufacturing excelled and is evidenced in the many Stearman aircraft still being flown in the U.S. and other countries for sport or agricultural uses.

Robert L. Parrish

Steels

Steel is an alloy of iron (*see*), with an atomic weight of 55.85, and small amounts of carbon. Lightweight manganese steel tubing replaced wood frames for aircraft in the early 1920's and continues to be widely used in lightplanes today.

Its greater weight put steel at a disadvantage in the military and air transport aircraft, where materials cost is subordinated to operational costs. Light metals such as aluminum (*see*), magnesium (*see*), and titanium (*see*) enjoy a considerable advantage.

Nonetheless, rising aircraft-engine temperatures in World War II, and the dawn of the supersonic era immediately following, led to a need for high-temperature metals. This in turn led to development of specialty steels for aircraft and rocket use.

The most widely used steel is *carbon steel*. It is an alloy of iron with 0.6 to 1 per cent carbon, mixed with small amounts of manganese. Residual sulfur and phosphorus are allowed to fixed maximum limits. Silicon (*see*), copper, and lead may be added for special qualities.

Aerospace service requires higher strength-for-weight-ratio steels, however. These include stainless steels, tool steels, alloy steels, the superalloys which are not true steels, and more recently, the maraging steels and vacuum-melted steels.

Designing steels to meet rising temperature requirements has also increased steel cost. A low-alloy steel may cost $800 per ton, while in stainless steels the price rises to $1,000 per ton. The superalloys may cost $2,000 per ton. By contrast, however, the lighter titanium alloys may cost $10,000 per ton.

A *stainless steel* is mainly iron, like carbon steel, but is alloyed with 15 per cent or more chromium and quantities of nickel (*see*). *Tool steels* are very tough and are of iron alloyed with manganese, silicon, carbon, nickel, chromium, molybdenum, and vanadium. As much as 18 per cent tungsten is added to many of the tool steel alloys for great toughness at high temperatures. Because of its great toughness under heat, tool steel was considered at one point for the Dyna-Soar Program (*see*) test re-entry vehicle.

Though the superalloys are often included with the stainless and maraging steels, they are not true steels. The iron matrix of a conventional steel is replaced by nickel.

Maraging Steels

The *maraging steels* are the most recent entrant in the aerospace materials market. International Nickel Co. developed these steels, though they are now available from a number of producers. An iron base is alloyed with 18 per cent nickel and lesser amounts of cobalt, molybdenum, and titanium. The maraging steels possess over 200,000 psi tensile strength (*see*) in some of their forms. Because of this great strength which holds up relatively well at high temperatures, this class of steels has a much improved strength-for-weight ratio. The maraging steels also have the added advantage that they can be formed or fabricated into a desired part while the metal is still easily workable. The completed part is then heat-treated to get a structure of great hardness and strength. The steel is distinguished by an extremely low carbon content.

A maraging steel of iron alloyed with nickel, molybdenum, cobalt, titanium, and aluminum has been formed into a 156-inch rocket motor that delivers 3,000,000 lbs. thrust. A further firing of this unit, part of the USAF large rocket motor program, is scheduled for late 1968. The maraging steel in the motor case is of unusually high strength and is rated at 390,000 psi yield strength. By contrast, standard carbon steel has a 45,000 to 55,000 psi tensile strength. A popular titanium alloy has a 126,000 psi yield strength. Commercial superalloys have yield and tensile strengths in a range from 214,000 to as low as 124,000 psi.

The last segment of a 156-inch solid fuel engine is hoisted into place. The case is made of 18 per cent nickel air-melt maraging steel.

Austenitic Steels

By the early part of World War II, aircraft designers already faced engine temperatures of over 1200°F. They responded with the high-alloy *austenitic steels* (50 per cent iron alloyed with cobalt, chromium, and nickel) and the cobalt-base alloys. As with the superalloys, the iron base of a normal steel was replaced with another metal—in this case cobalt, rather than nickel as in the superalloys. Cobalt alloys remained in use into the 1950's as cast blades for gas turbine service.

One source estimates that 40 million World War II engine supercharger blades were fashioned of cobalt alloys. The alloys were 30 to 65 per cent cobalt, only about 3 per cent iron, and as much as 25 to 30 per cent chromium.

The high-alloy austenitic steels allowed engine working temperatures to reach 1400°F. Iron content fell as low as 15 per cent in some of these alloys. Tungsten, molybdenum, and columbium were added as stabilizing agents. Aluminum or titanium were added as precipitation hardening agents.

Temperature requirements have risen steadily so that today's jet engines operate at 1900°F working temperatures, and a new generation of engines that will boost these operating temperatures well beyond the 2000° mark appears very near. Theoretically, current fuels could burn with best efficiency at 4000°F if materials were available to build an engine to operate at these working temperatures.

Stainless steel has been particularly useful in aerospace. Type 304 stainless proved able to contain the cryogenic fuels with temperatures of −450°F, yet was able to operate at 1800°F temperatures in jet engines and gas turbines. This is an iron base alloy of 2 per cent manganese, 1 per cent silicon, 18 to 20 per cent chromium, and 8 to 12 per cent nickel.

A factor that adds greatly to the potential for high-strength steels is the advent of vacuum melting techniques. Alloy and stainless steels are produced in electric arc furnaces as in standard practice. The molten steel is poured off into giant 20-ton electrodes. These are remelted under vacuum and the resulting metal outperforms conventional steels of the same alloy chemistry.

Vacuum steels are now used in helicopter armor, the F-111 tactical jet fighter, Titan IIIC, the NASA 260-inch rocket motor case, in the Minuteman missile, and in forgings for the Saturn launch complex. Use of this steel type grows at 25 to 30 per cent per year.

Keith W. Bennett

See also: Materials, Metals and metallurgy

Stewards and stewardesses

Stewards and stewardesses are an airline's most vital sales agents. In most cases they create a lasting impression of the airline which determines whether or not a passenger will become a repeat customer. The job is one of public relations using intelligence, training, and the ability to handle any flight situation.

Airlines first used stewards who doubled in such responsibilities as baggage handling. When activities became more restricted to the cabin, nurses were hired to give the passenger a feeling of assurance.

Today the steward is generally termed a *purser,* and he is especially equipped to handle ticketing and travel problems. Eastern Airlines maintains a staff of about 150, while United employs about 100 stewards.

Both men and women are used as pursers by Northwest, Pan Am, and TWA for nondomestic flights. Pan Am maintains a staff of about 500, with Northwest and TWA employing 100 to 150.

Knowledge of a foreign language and excellent health are important qualifications for a steward. Training is similar to the stewardess program, but it is more technical. Stewards, however, are not forced to retire at an early age.

Stewardesses

Boeing Air Transport hired the first stewardess in 1930, Miss Ellen Church, a nurse. She and seven other nurses without any professional airline training served passengers. As the industry grew, the

A stewardess prepares to serve a luncheon meal in the galley of a DC-9. Most food is prepared prior to being loaded on the aircraft.

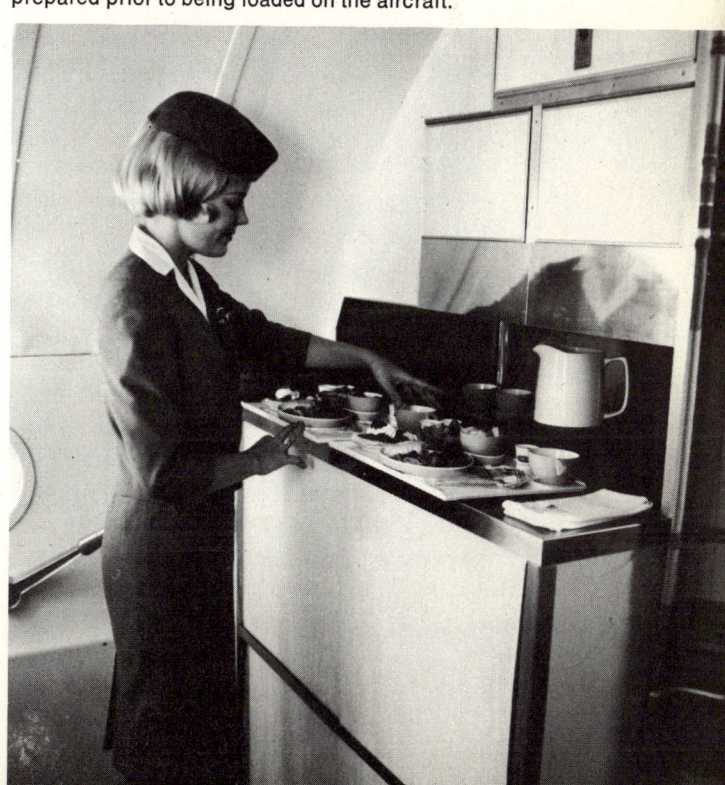

A Malaysian-Singapore Airlines hostess *(left)* in her uniform. A steward serves hors d'oeuvres and salad *(right)* to first-class passengers aboard an intercontinental flight.

training evolved into the rigorous programs of today.

Stewardesses are selected for their leadership, awareness, poise, conversational ability, and a sincere desire to be of service to others. They must meet the physical qualifications and education set by the airline of their choice. Preference is given to girls with a college education, particularly nursing or language majors.

Training programs average from four to seven weeks. The girls live and study in modern, college-like surroundings with classes during the day and studying every night. Courses include flight principles, airplane nomenclature, airport codes, location of all equipment, food service, company history and policies, public speaking, psychology, appearance, and most important, emergency procedures.

Trainees study the various aircraft interiors to learn the location and operation of all passenger service items. In addition to the classroom lectures, slides, and movies, they walk through each aircraft and operate all of the cabin equipment.

The course also provides an extensive study of beverage and meal service and the philosophy of gracious serving. Trainees practice serving in airplane mock-ups and take flights to observe experienced stewardesses.

Professional supervisors instruct the girls in hair care and styling, skin care, makeup, diet and exercise, and uniform appearance. Instruction is accompanied by application sessions, interviews, and daily instructor observations.

Prospective stewardesses learn how to handle on-board emergencies including the use, identification, and operation of all emergency equipment such as life vests, oxygen and oxygen masks, escape ropes, and exits on all types of aircraft flown by the airline. This includes procedures for fire in the air or on the ground, emergency decompression, and evacuation of an airplane on land or in water. Airplane mock-ups simulate the varied emergency situation. The trainees also receive lectures on first aid principles and learn rescue breathing and heart massage.

After a stewardess receives her wings she begins a career which averages about 30 months. The majority of stewardesses leave flying for matrimony. Other qualified stewardesses receive promotions into supervisory or instructor positions.

DiAnne Prewitt

See also: Flight

STOL aircraft, *see* V/STOL aircraft

Stout, William Bushnell

American aircraft designer
Born: March 16, 1880; Quincy, Illinois
Died: March 20, 1956; Phoenix, Arizona

William B. Stout, an intense young engineer, brought new life to aviation in America in the early 1920's with his monoplane and transport aircraft designs.

He first saw an airplane in 1910 when Glenn H. Curtiss *(see)* exhibited his *June Bug* in St. Paul, Minnesota. Long before then, however, Stout had composed some detailed and comprehensive aeronautical theories of his own. One of his earliest and firmest hypotheses was that a monoplane design was more efficient and aerodynamically stronger than the biplane concept then in vogue. In about 1911 he founded and edited *Aerial Age* magazine.

Stout learned to fly in 1914 and reportedly became an excellent pilot, but his first love was designing and building airplanes. In 1916, while employed as an engineer by Packard Motor Co., he built America's first all-metal airplane. At McCook Field, Dayton, Ohio, during World War I he served as an aerodynamicist, but had difficulty in persuading war production officials to accept his fighter plane designs, which were far ahead of his time.

He was convinced that the aerodynamic drag of biplanes reduced engine power available for lift and designed a "flying wing" and cantilever wing monoplane to prove his theories. The latter, built in 1920, proved him correct but brought little financial support for his aircraft development projects. His greatest success was the all-metal AT-2, built in 1924.

Stout sold his aircraft manufacturing company to the Ford Motor Co. in 1925, but remained active in aeronautical design and consulting until his death.

Robert L. Parrish

See also: Commercial air transports

Strafe

The word *strafe* is German for "punish" and refers to the act of firing bullets, shells or rockets at troops, roads, railways, factories, or other installations from a low-flying aircraft. The use of the word *strafe* began during World War I and was derived from the German phrase *Gott strafe England* (God punish England). However, after the word was adopted by the English, it soon came to be used exclusively for machine gun, cannon, or rocket attacks on ground targets by low-flying aircraft.

Strategic Air Command

The Strategic Air Command, commonly known as SAC, is a major command of the United States Air Force *(see)*. Headquarters of the command is located at Offut Air Force Base near Omaha, Nebraska, and the force has more than 50 bases around the world. The command has an authorized strength of more than 200,000 personnel with 27,000 officers, 151,000 enlisted men, and 22,000 civilians.

SAC is the U.S. Air Force's global nuclear strike force which operates intercontinental weapons systems, including manned bombers and intercontinental ballistic missiles *(see)*. Its peacetime mission is to "maintain a force capable of deterring Communist aggression." Its stated wartime mission is to "destroy the enemy's warmaking capability."

Within the continental United States, SAC has three numbered air forces, the 2nd, the 8th, the 15th, and a missile division, the 1st Strategic Aerospace Division. Located in Europe is the 98th Strategic Wing, while an air division, the 3rd, is located in the Far East.

SAC combat crew members for both aircraft and missiles stand alert duty around the clock, and accept their responsibilities as an integral part of their assignments. Crews live close to aircraft and missile bases. All forces are controlled from the underground command post located at Offut Air Force Base. In addition, alternate command posts are located at several other U.S. bases. In the event that the SAC underground command post and alternate command posts are lost, an airborne command post complete with communication equipment and controllers is constantly airborne over the U.S.

The EC-135 Looking Glass *(below)* serves as the base for a Strategic Air Command Airborne Command Post *(bottom)*.

Strategic Air Command

From its bases located in the western Pacific, SAC is conducting conventional bombing missions and air refueling operations in support of military operations in Vietnam. The first southeast Asia mission using conventional bombs was flown on June 18, 1965. Since that time B-52's have been flying almost daily bombing missions against the Viet Cong in South Vietnam. SAC is also in charge of the Air Force tanker force, and its KC-135's refuel U.S. fighter and reconnaissance aircraft en route to their targets in Vietnam. With the SR-71, strategic reconnaissance, both photographic and electronic, obtains information pertinent to the enemy's warmaking capability.

The command's strategic forces are composed of a mixture of weapons systems, and missiles and bombers exploit the inherent characteristics of each system. This concept of flexibility backs the U.S. national defense policy which requires a variety of options of response to all levels of military aggression. In the event of global war, the SAC force and other military elements would be employed against selected enemy targets. A single integrated operational plan for initial U.S. retaliatory strikes has been developed at SAC headquarters by the Joint Strategic Planning Staff (JSTPS). The SAC commander-in-chief directs the staff, which in turn blueprints wartime targets and selects the weapons to be used. The JSTPS is composed of Army, Navy, Air Force, and Marine personnel who are at SAC headquarters, with the staff responsible to the U.S. Joint Chiefs of Staff.

Aircraft Inventory

SAC's aircraft inventory consists of the following bombers, tankers, and reconnaissance planes:

B-52 Stratofortress: eight-jet heavy bomber with near-sonic speed. Although gradually being phased out of the bomber force, the B-52 is still the heavy-duty bomber of SAC. The newer versions are the U.S.'s first missile-carrying bombers carrying either a nuclear or conventional payload.

B-58 Hustler: supersonic bomber; flies at more than twice the speed of sound; operational since August, 1960. This delta-wing aircraft was the world's first supersonic bomber with intercontinental range. A nuclear weapon and a portion of the aircraft's fuel are carried in a slim disposable pod mounted under the fuselage.

KC-135 Stratotanker: four-jet refueling tanker with near-sonic speed; operational since 1957. It can refuel all jet aircraft in the USAF inventory at their own altitudes and airspeeds.

SR-71: 2000 mph strategic reconnaissance aircraft. One of the newest aircraft in the Air Force, this Mach 3 plane can photograph 60,000 sq. mi. of the Earth's surface in one hour.

Missile Inventory

The missile inventory consists of the following:

ADM-20 Quail: decoy missile used as a penetration aid for the B-52. Several of these air-launched missiles can be carried in the B-52 bomb bay. The missile operates at the same speed as the subsonic bomber and forms an image on the enemy radar screen which helps hide the mother aircraft.

AGM-28A and B Hound Dog: supersonic air-to-surface guided missile. Can be launched in flight from high or low altitudes. The missile is controlled by a guidance system that cannot be jammed by enemy electronics.

LGM-30A, B and F Minuteman: ICBM. Launched from hardened underground facilities, the solid-fuel Minuteman is virtually immune to enemy attack and can be knocked out only by a direct nuclear hit. The missile can be launched in 30 seconds and has a range of more than 6,000 miles.

LGM-25C Titan: liquid-fuel ICBM. Carries the largest of all ICBM payloads with a reaction time of one minute and has a range of more than 6,000 miles. Also launched from underground facilities.

Although SAC is ready to strike instantly, its motto is *Peace Is Our Profession,* and the men who are in its ranks work long hours—an average 74-hour week—to maintain peace by, paradoxically, being at all times ready for war.

Captain Ronald L. Sherman

See also: Military Airlift Command, Tactical Air Command

Stratocumulus, *see* Clouds

Stratofortress, Boeing B-52

The Boeing B-52 Stratofortress is the largest and probably the last of the big bomber aircraft (*see*) produced for the USAF Strategic Air Command (*see*). The B-52 is a lineal descendant of the B-47 medium bomber, except it is much larger, with greater bomb-carrying capacity and range. The B-52

prototype which flew in October, 1952, clearly showed the relationship to the B-47, having the same 35° wing sweepback and tandem-type cockpit canopy. All later B-52's had side-by-side cockpit arrangements.

The B-52 was built in seven models, with a total of 740 being produced. With each succeeding model improvements were made, and the last, the H model, was equipped with turbofan engines and Hound Dog air-to-surface missiles (see) carried under the wing. The B-52 wing is one huge fuel tank featuring in-flight refueling capabilities. The plane normally carries six crew members.

Until recently the B-52 had never flown against an enemy target. However, it is now being used in Vietnam (see) to drop standard bombs against jungle targets, instead of the nuclear weapons it was originally designed to deliver. Some of these aircraft are flying from a U.S. base in Guam, which means the round trip is extremely long and requires inflight refueling (see).

It is interesting to note that until recently the H model, with a gross takeoff weight in excess of 488,000 lbs., was the heaviest production aircraft flying in the world.

Claude G. Luisada

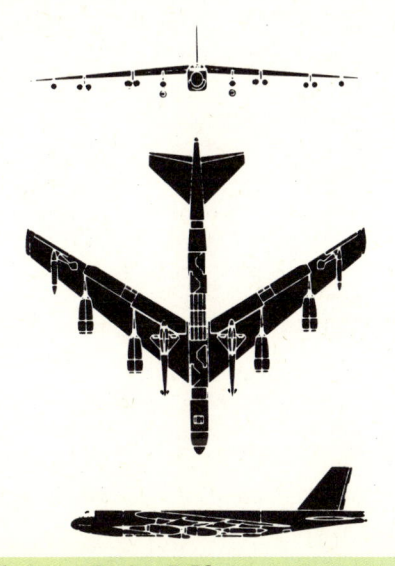

Stratojet, Boeing B-47

First flown in December, 1947, the Boeing B-47 Stratojet was the first sweptwing jet bomber capable of subsonic speeds in excess of 600 mph. It was an extremely successful design, and Boeing built a total of 2,030 for the U.S. Air Force.

The B-47 won a USAF design competition which began in 1943 for jet reconnaissance/light-bomber aircraft. Boeing considered many designs, but decided on the revolutionary sweptwing along with an aerodynamically clean fuselage. The six engines were placed beneath the wings in pods rather than buried in the fuselage or wings. By using this design, Boeing built an airplane which, despite relatively low-powered jet engines and a gross weight of over 200,000 lbs., was able to fly as fast as current jet fighters.

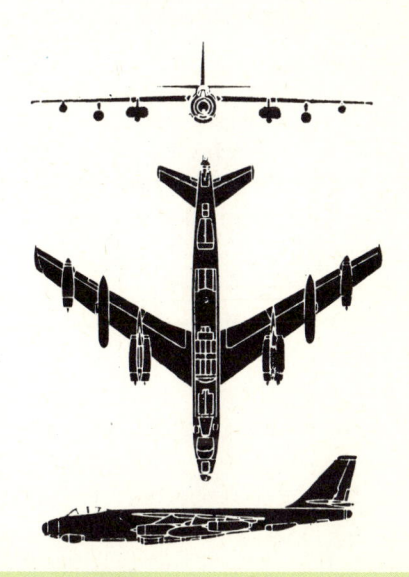

Stratofortress, Boeing B-52
Specifications and Performance Data (H model)

Engine	Eight Pratt & Whitney TF33-P-3 turbofan engines rated at 17,000-lbs. thrust
Wingspan	185 ft.
Length	157 ft. 6 in.
Gross weight	Over 488,000 lbs.
Maximum speed	Mach 0.95 (665 mph) at 20,000 ft.
Range	12,000 miles

Stratojet Boeing B-47
Specifications and Performance Data

Engine	Six General Electric J47 turbojets with 5,970-lb. static thrust
Wingspan	116 ft.
Length	109 ft. 10 in.
Gross weight	202,000 lbs.
Cruising speed	Mach 0.83 at 30,000 feet
Range	3,200 miles

Stratojet, Boeing B-47

The B-47 was slated from its inception for use by the Strategic Air Command (SAC) (*see*) as a nuclear bomber. It was in service for almost 20 years without ever being used in battle. However, as the principal nuclear weapon carrier of the 1950's, the B-47 was the single main deterrent against any major attacks against the western world.

In SAC the B-47 was also the first aircraft to utilize aerial refueling as a normal operational system. The Stratojet was also used as an overseas-based bomber. SAC wings were rotated periodically among bases in England, Spain, North Africa, Japan, and Okinawa, thus effectively setting up a ring of combat-ready B-47's around the world.

Claude G. Luisada

See also: Bomber aircraft, Refueling

Stratosphere

The stratosphere is that part of the Earth's atmosphere (*see*) that extends upward from the troposphere (*see*), from an altitude of about 6 to 31 miles and is characterized by little vertical change in temperature. There is a strong horizontal temperature gradient, however, caused by the polar jet stream between the troposphere and the stratosphere. Because of the extremely low concentration of water vapor, there are very few clouds (*see*) and no icing conditions in the stratosphere. The presence of ozone (*see*) in the upper stratosphere makes it necessary for a space vehicle to have a sealed cabin, in which atmospheric conditions close to that of the Earth are duplicated, and for astronauts to wear pressure suits (*see*).

Stratus, *see* Clouds

Streamlining

The features of an aircraft which have been designed with smooth contours to reduce air resistance are referred to as *streamlining*. The streamlining of modern aircraft is a necessary part of aerodynamic design in order to achieve a laminar flow of air over wings and fuselage and prevent the buildup of turbulence (*see*) at high speeds. The trend in streamlining supersonic aircraft is toward a delta wing design which eliminates the separate tail structure and combines wing and fuselage into smoother continuous contours. Most supersonic aircraft are also characterized by "needle nosed" fuselages which reduce shock wave effects.

See also: Aerodynamics, Airplane, Fuselage, Laminar flow, Shock waves, Supersonic transports, Wings

Stringfellow, John

British engineer and airplane designer
Born: December 6, 1799; Attercliffe, England
Died: December 13, 1883

John Stringfellow, whose name is usually linked with that of William Samuel Henson (*see*), is credited with the design and construction of two steam-powered model airplanes.

Stringfellow met Henson about 1820 in Chard where they both had set up lace factories. In 1842-43 they became partners in a venture which was to lead to the construction of the *Aerial Steam Carriage*. Although the design was patented by Henson, the project never materialized.

After some unsuccessful tests of models of the design, Henson emigrated to the U.S., and Stringfellow continued to improve the basic design. In 1848 his first model flew briefly at Chard, but was not capable of sustained flight.

In 1868 the Aeronautical Society of Great Britain held the world's first aeronautical exhibition and Stringfellow exhibited his model triplane. This model, besides winning the society's prize of £100 "for the lightest steam engine in proportion to its power," had a far-reaching effect on airplane design.

Stringfellow's contribution to aeronautics was probably limited to these two models, but his son F. J. Stringfellow carried on the family interest by building a powered model biplane in 1886, parts of which are in London's Science Museum.

For some time, doubt was cast on the originality of John Stringfellow's designs, but more recent research has shown that he was an innovator as well as a competent engineer.

F. H. Smith

See also: History of aviation

This engine, without boiler, was designed and constructed by John Stringfellow in 1843.

Strughold, Hubertus

German-American aerospace medical scientist
Born: June 15, 1898; Westtnennen, Germany

Dr. Hubertus Strughold has been one of the foremost contributors to the world's store of aviation and space medical knowledge. Since his entry into medical practice in Germany, the renowned scientist has focused his interest and talents on ways to make man's environment in aerospace safer and healthier.

Strughold completed studies at the universities of Muenster, Gottingen, Munich, and Wurzburg for a PhD in physiology before obtaining his medical degree in 1923. After several years in private practice, he joined the faculty at the University of Wurzburg as associate professor and researcher in physiology. In 1935 he went to the University of Berlin as a professor and director of the school's Aeromedical Research Institute. During ten years there he contributed regularly to the annals of aeromedical literature. From 1947 to 1949 he directed the Physiology Institute at the University of Heidelberg. Then, in 1949, Dr. Strughold was invited by the U.S. Air Force to join its Air University (*see*) at Maxwell Air Force Base, Alabama, as professor of aviation medicine.

He served for a year at the Air University before accepting the post of chief of the department of space medicine, USAF School of Aviation Medicine, Randolph Air Force Base, Texas. In 1957 he became advisor for research at the Air Force's Aerospace Medical Division, Brooks Air Force Base, Texas, and in 1962 was named Chief Scientist.

Strughold has received many honors and awards for his role in accelerating manned exploration of space, and has been a prolific producer of books, articles, and technical papers on physiology, aviation, and space medicine.   Robert L. Parrish

See also: Aerospace medicine, Aviation medicine, Man in flight, Mars

Struts

In aviation, a strut is any rigid bar, rod, or member which fastens components together, holds them apart at a specific distance, or supports a load. Ordinarily, they are built to bear either compression or tension loads. Unless preceded by a prefix such as *gear* strut, or *jury* strut, the term is most commonly applied to struts located between the fuselage and wings to support, brace, or hold the airfoil (*see*) in position under various load conditions encountered in flight and on the ground.

The *wing,* or *lift,* struts transmit lift and landing loads from the wings into the fuselage structure,

External struts are frequently used in light aircraft to give the wings rigidity.

the amount depending largely on whether the design is semicantilever or trussed. *Jury* or *auxiliary* struts are sometimes used to brace main struts. Biplanes use interplane struts between top and bottom wings.

Landing gear struts support the airplane on its wheels, skis, or floats and ordinarily include the shock absorbers. They can be either retractable or fixed.   Leslie L. Thomason

See also: Airplane, Wings

Sun

The sun is the star nearest to the Earth and the major source of our light and heat. It is a G2 dwarf, an average yellow star, which has been shining for about 5 billion years. It is located in a spiral arm of the Milky Way Galaxy, about half-way, or 30,000 light-years, from the center.

The other members of the solar system, including planets, asteroids, and comets, revolve in essentially elliptical orbits with the sun at one focus. Since the sun contains much more of the mass than the others combined, the gravitational interactions of the planets (*see*) ordinarily result in only minor perturbations of their orbits.

Sun

Astronomers can fix the *relative* positions of the planets very accurately, although the assignment of *absolute* distances is much more difficult. Modern radar (*see*) has enabled scientists to determine interplanetary distances with greatly increased precision. The mean distance from the Earth to the sun, the *astronomical unit,* is 149,598,000 kilometers (92,956,000 miles).

Early History

From antiquity, man has studied and worshiped the sun as the source of life. Calculations of the rising and setting of the sun, of the equinoxes (*see*), and of eclipses (*see*) have been carried out for thousands of years. Stonehenge, in southern England, is one of the earliest computers of solar phenomena.

Galileo (*see*), in 1610, was the first to point a telescope at the sun. He thus immediately observed sunspots and their growth and motion, although exceptional sunspot groups had previously been occasionally visible to the naked eye.

The spectrum of sunlight shows dark *Fraunhofer lines,* which result from the absorption of radiation by various chemical elements. These lines are named after the scientist who, in 1814, first analyzed the solar spectrum in detail. Fraunhofer (*see*) assigned letters to the brightest lines, and we still refer to the D-lines of neutral sodium and the H- and K-lines of ionized calcium.

Janssen discovered a bright yellow line in the chromosphere with a spectroscope during the solar eclipse of 1871. Scientists then attributed this line, which was not known to chemists at that time, to an unknown element, *helium,* from the Greek word for sun. Only later was it identified on Earth.

The sun is a laboratory in which we can study the physics of hot gases under extreme conditions of temperature and pressure. Astronomically, the sun provides the nearest example of phenomena common to many stars. For example, chromospheres, flares, and granulation undoubtedly exist on other stars, but these details can be seen directly only on the sun.

Furthermore, radiation (*see*) and emission of particles from the sun affect radio reception and cause the auroras (*see*). Ways must be found for predicting solar flare activity, in order to protect astronauts in space. Without warning, they could encounter lethal particles.

Eclipses

An *eclipse* of the sun occurs when the moon passes between the Earth and the sun, for the moon and the sun fortuitously both subtend an angle of ½° from the Earth. The moon's shadow consists of a tapering *umbra,* within which the entire disk of the sun is obscured, and a *penumbra,* wherein part of the disk is visible. A *total eclipse* occurs when the Earth passes through the umbra, and totality may last as long as seven minutes. If the tip of the umbra falls short of the Earth, the moon appears to be slightly smaller than the sun. A ring of light surrounds the moon, and this type of eclipse is thus called *annular.* An observer in the penumbra views a *partial eclipse.*

The chromosphere and corona are so faint that they are visible only in a total eclipse. These events occur only about once every year and a half in a band perhaps 50 miles wide somewhere on the Earth, so astronomers often travel to remote areas in order to observe them. Scientists have recently used jet planes to follow the speeding shadow of the moon and thus prolong the duration of totality.

Solar Telescopes and Accessories

The unsteadiness of the Earth's atmosphere, called *the seeing,* limits our perception of solar detail to about one second of arc, or 800 kilometers (km). Mounting a telescope in a tower may improve the image quality. A system of mirrors known as a *heliostat* or a *coelostat* (pronounced *see-lo-stat*) often directs sunlight into a stationary telescope.

The brightness of the sun permits the use of *spectrographs* which spread out the spectrum more than those ordinarily employed for observations of stars. Scientists take monochromatic pictures with *spectroheliographs* and *birefringent* (Lyot) filters. They show the sun in the light of a particular chemical element under particular conditions of temperature and density.

In a *coronagraph,* a metal disk artificially eclipses the photosphere so that one can observe the inner corona. A Lyot filter in the system enhances the contribution of the corona relative to the light scattered by the Earth's atmosphere. Coronagraphs can only be located at the few sites in the world with sufficiently clear skies. *Radio telescopes* show emission from flares, the chromosphere, and the corona.

New Observing Techniques

From satellites in orbit we can observe the ultraviolet light and X-rays ordinarily blocked by the Earth's atmosphere. Future observations from space will not encounter the problems of resolution (*see*) and atmospheric absorption and scattering that currently limit solar studies. The Apollo Applications Program (*see*) includes several ultraviolet and X-ray experiments.

The emission spectrum of the chromosphere of the sun can be observed an instant before the beginning and after the end of a total eclipse of the sun. The phenomenon is called a flash spectrum.

Recent work on detectors in the far infrared has led to new observations at those wavelengths. Project Stratoscope sent a telescope up in a balloon to observe in visible light. A French group has made ultraviolet observations from a balloon-borne telescope.

A current experiment employs a tank containing thousands of gallons of carbon tetrachloride deep in a mine in an attempt to detect solar neutrinos. The thick layers of the Earth shield the tank from other types of cosmic particles.

The Photosphere

The *photosphere,* the layer of the sun normally visible to the naked eye, has a temperature which decreases outward from about 6000° Kelvin before it begins to rise in the chromosphere. The gaseous layers near the surface absorb some of the radiation and produce the Fraunhofer lines. These lines correspond to most of Earth's chemical elements.

The edge or *limb* appears darker than the center of the sun. Near the center of the disk, we see inward vertically until the gas becomes opaque at the 6000°K level, when the line of sight has passed through a certain amount of material. Near the edge, we view along an oblique path, and the line of sight to that level is longer. The gas becomes opaque to us at a higher level which is cooler and hence darker.

We measure the rotation of the sun on its axis spectroscopically (with the Doppler effect) and by the apparent motion of sunspots. The rotation is not uniform, and varies from about 25 days at the equator to perhaps 35 days near the poles.

Under good seeing conditions, the surface of the sun exhibits a granular structure, with cells some 1,000 km across which live for about 15 minutes. Scientists are currently investigating whether the sun departs appreciably from the shape of a sphere.

Chromosphere

The *chromosphere* is the level of the solar atmosphere immediately above the visible surface. Its bright-line emission spectrum flashes into view for a few seconds at the instant of totality and shows lines characteristic of 15,000°K temperatures. The lines of many elements appear, including those from hydrogen, neutral and singly ionized metals, and

A 40-foot antenna, one of 96 in a large circular array in Australia *(left),* used to make high-resolution, instantaneous maps of the sun. The 150-foot solar tower *(right)* at Mount Wilson Observatory.

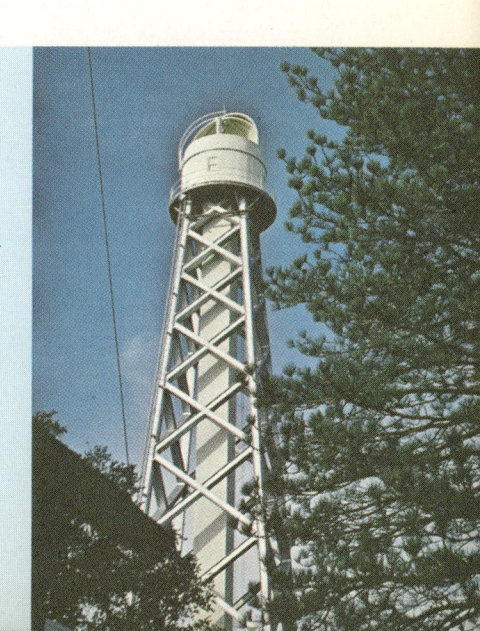

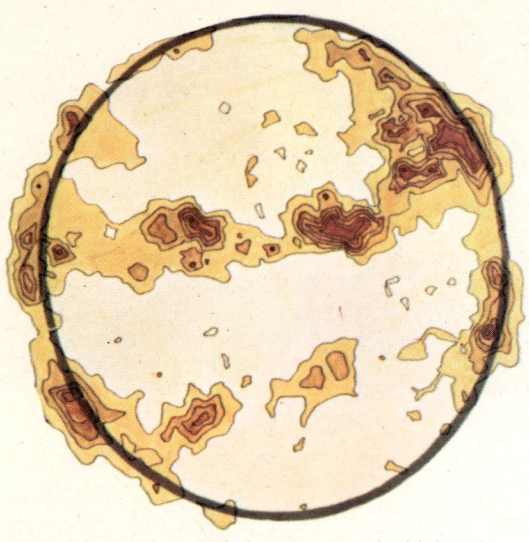

Magnesium stripped of nine electrons by high temperatures (Mg X) is evident in an ultraviolet spectroheliograph taken from OSO-IV.

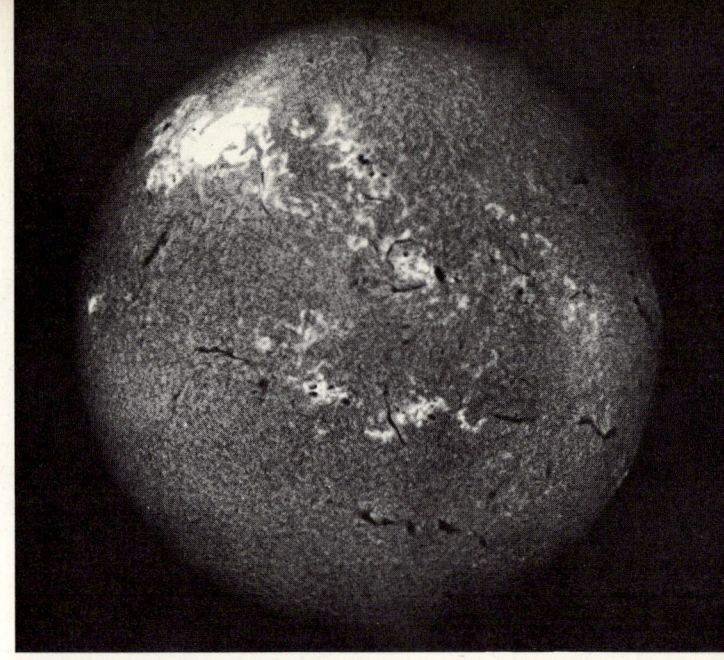

The solar disk in Hα, the first line in the Balmer series, shows the brightening of solar flares and limb darkening.

those from the rare-earth group.

The chromosphere actually consists of jets of gas called *spicules*. Magnetic fields presumably guide their forms and motions.

When we observe the sun in the light of a strong spectral line, we actually see the lower chromosphere, for the matter becomes opaque at that level. The structure shows a chromospheric network, called *supergranulation*, which corresponds to regions of higher magnetic field. Matter flows horizontally from the center to the boundary of a supergranulation cell with a typical velocity of ½ km per second. Small regions of the lower chromosphere and photosphere show vertical oscillations with periods of about five minutes. Above active regions, prominences may jet explosively outward or cascade gracefully to the solar surface.

Corona

The *corona* is the pearly white solar halo most visible during a total solar eclipse. The total brightness of this gaseous envelope is only one-millionth that of the photosphere, about half that of the full moon. The corona actually extends outward past the orbit of the Earth. Its temperature is very high, about 2,000,000°K, but since the density is very low, the total energy content is reasonable. The continuous outward expansion of the corona forms the *solar wind* (see).

Radiation visible from the Earth at an eclipse comes from three sources. Scattering of light from the photosphere by electrons close to the sun forms the K-corona. Scattering of photospheric light by particles between the sun and the orbit of Mercury (see) forms the Fraunhofer, or F-corona. The emission of the corona itself in spectral lines of highly ionized elements such as Fe XIV, iron stripped of 13 electrons, is sometimes called the E-corona. These lines, characteristic of the high temperatures and low densities of the corona, defied interpretation for many years. Edlen solved this mystery in 1939 when, with atomic theory, he calculated identifications.

Active Regions and Sunspots

The extent of special activity on the surface of the sun varies with a period of 11 years. The actual cycle is 22 years long, since the polarity of the magnetic field reverses every 11 years.

Sunspots are the most obvious manifestation of solar activity. A central, dark umbra is surrounded by a lighter penumbra. Spots appear either singly or in groups and represent regions of high magnetic field, typically 2,000 gauss. They appear dark in visible light because they are somewhat cooler than the surrounding photosphere, about 4000°K, although they would shine brightly if we could remove them from the sun. Spectroheliograms display active regions as *plages* or *faculae,* areas brighter than the normal photosphere, and as darker *filaments*.

Solar flares occur when the sunspot cycle approaches its maximum. A flare, which becomes visible on the disk as a sudden brightening, ejects matter into space explosively. A shock wave races over the solar surface at speeds of from 1,000 to 2,000 miles per second.

The corona displays equatorial streamers and polar tufts. The level of activity varies with the sunspot cycle.

Interior

The outer zone of the solar interior is highly convective, a phenomenon which results in the sur-

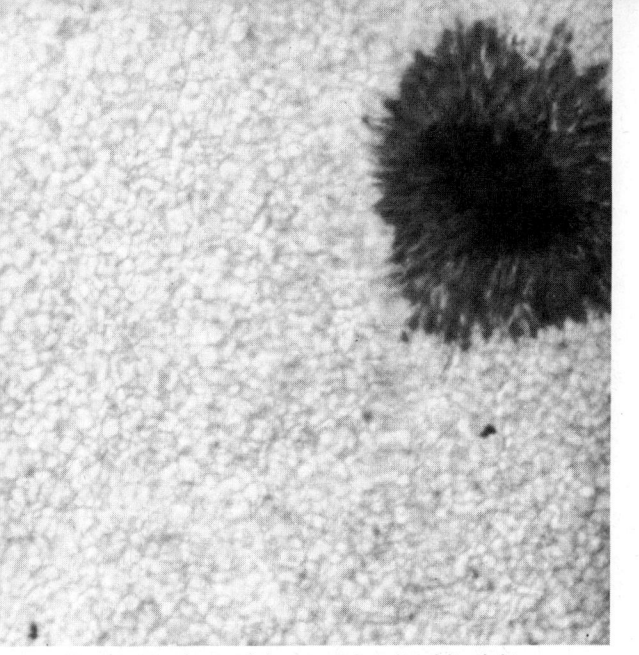

The photosphere of the sun taken in white light (without filters) shows a sunspot and granulation, bright spots about 600 miles in diameter.

face granulation. The temperature increases inward toward the center, where it reaches several millions of degrees.

Fusion processes, such as the carbon cycle, in the interior provide the solar energy. In each case a small amount of matter is converted into energy according to Einstein's equation, $E=mc^2$.

Tests of General Relativity

The sun is at the basis of some of the classical tests of Einstein's theory of general relativity because of its large mass and proximity to the Earth. Astronomers have traveled to many eclipses to see if light from stars bends when it passes near the sun. They have also studied the slight red shift of photospheric radiation by the sun's own gravitational field. Currently, scientists are bouncing radar off Mercury and Venus (see) as the planets pass near the sun to test the effect of the solar mass. Although these experiments agree generally with Einstein's theory, they are still surprisingly inaccurate.

Donald H. Menzel and Jay M. Pasachoff

See also: Moon, Relativity theory, Solar system, Stars, Van Allen radiation belts

Sunspots, see Sun

Supercharger

A supercharger is a pump or compressor which forces air or fuel-air mixtures into an internal-combustion, reciprocating engine (see). The purpose is to provide more air or fuel-air mixture than would normally be available at the prevailing atmospheric pressure. Increasing use of supercharging grows out of requirements for greater efficiency at high altitudes, providing the benefits of comfort, safety, economy of operation, and ability to fly above unfavorable winds.

The principles of supercharging involve the characteristics and relationships of mass, volume, and density of gases. Mass airflow induced into the cylinders determines the power developed. Without auxiliary means, only a given weight of air could be induced into the cylinders, depending upon the displacement and volumetric efficiency. Unsupercharged engines operate at full power only at sea level where the atmospheric pressure is 29.92 inches of mercury. Atmospheric pressure decreases at higher altitudes, causing a decrease in charge to the cylinders, manifold pressure, and brake horsepower. For example, an unsupercharged engine which develops 500 hp will produce only 225 hp at 15,000 feet.

Superchargers can be internal, gear-driven as part of the engine or separate from the engine, operating as a second-stage supercharger, such as in the *turbo-superchargers* which maintain air-intake pressure at altitudes above the effective range of internal superchargers.

The internal, gear-driven single-stage supercharger is the simplest. The air-fuel mixture enters a device known as an *impeller,* a rotating wheel with vanes which impels the air or fuel under centrifugal force. Leaving the impeller, the mixture passes through a duct or vane to the manifold or combustion chamber with its velocity reduced and static pressure increased. The mixture then enters the manifold (see) and goes on to the cylinders.

Improvements in superchargers include two-speed, single-stage systems with two impeller speeds through gear ratios and two-stage superchargers with two impellers. Trends indicate increasing use of the turbosupercharger with an exhaust-driven turbine to operate the impeller. The turbosupercharger is not an integral part of the engine but a second-stage supercharger used to maintain air-intake pressure at high altitudes.

Leslie L. Thomason

See also: Aircraft propulsion systems, Mixture control, Pressure gauges

Superfortress, Boeing B-29

The Boeing B-29 Superfortress was developed early in World War II (see) to fill the need for a precision bomber which could fly at 400 mph with a 2,000-pound bomb load at a range of more than 5,000 miles. The largest single aircraft production project of the war, the B-29 was the first aircraft ever ordered into production before a prototype had flown;

by the time the first XB-29 flew in September, 1942, over 1,600 aircraft were on order. In all, 3,970 B-29's were built.

The B-29 featured fully pressurized crew compartments for safe and comfortable flight at high altitudes and an electronically controlled, and centralized gun-firing system.

The Superfort received its baptism of fire in June, 1944, in China-based bombing raids on Bangkok, Thailand, then held by the Japanese. Soon after, B-29's bombed the Japanese home islands from these same bases. In November, 1944, more than a hundred B-29's, flying from newly won bases in the Mariana Islands, struck at Tokyo itself, the first of many bombing missions against Japan's major cities.

In March, 1945, Major General Curtis LeMay (see) devised a major change of bombing strategy. He ordered the B-29's stripped of armament and loaded with incendiary instead of high-explosive bombs. Daylight bombing was stopped, and the large bombers were sent out exclusively at night. Destruction increased, and aircraft losses dwindled. The fire raids almost literally obliterated the population and industrial centers of Japan's major cities and hastened the end of the war. In August, 1945, B-29's dropped the first and only two atomic bombs (see) ever used in wartime.

The B-29 also saw action during the Korean war (see), and in the 1950's Superforts were used as tanker aircraft (see) and for weather reconnaissance.

Claude G. Luisada

See also: Bomber aircraft, Second World War aircraft

Supernova, see Nova

Super Sabre, North American F-100

The North American F-100 Super Sabre was the first supersonic fighter produced in the U.S. and was a direct result of fighter aircraft needs of the Korean war (see). North American Aviation had produced the successful F-86 which was used extensively in Korea, but there was a need for a larger and faster fighter for use against the MiG-15's.

The F-100, first flown in May, 1953, was evolved from the F-86. However, its wings have a greater sweepback to allow easier passage through the transonic speed zone, and the engine is equipped with an afterburner (see) for use in reaching top speed more quickly and for additional bursts of speed in combat.

From the beginning, the F-100 was generally successful in accomplishing its missions. A number of models were built, and a total of 2,294 were produced. The F-100D model, produced in the largest quantities, had an air-to-air refueling system, an improved electronic automatic pilot, and a bigger armament payload with more variety, including air-to-air missiles (see).

The F-100 was never involved in combat until, as it neared the end of its useful life, a need arose for it in Vietnam. Used by units of the Tactical Air Command (see) with which it has always served,

Superfortress, Boeing B-29
Specifications and Performance Data

Engine............Four Wright R-3350 2,200-hp engines
Wingspan.........141 ft. 2 in.
Length...........99 ft.
Gross weight.....140,000 lbs.
Cruise speed.....230 mph at 20,000 ft.
Range............5,600 miles, or 3,250 miles with 2,000-lb. bomb load

the F-100 has been serving with distinction over both North and South Vietnam. Its primary function has been as a fighter-bomber.

Claude G. Luisada

See also: Fighter aircraft, Vietnam

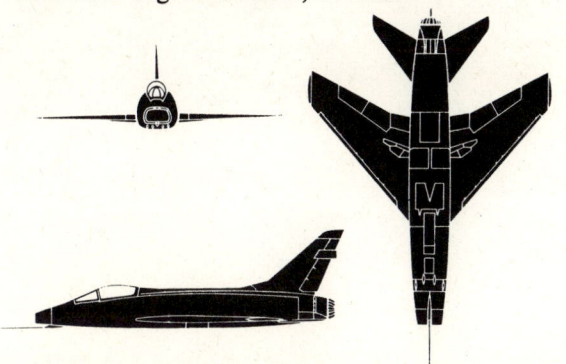

Super Sabre, North American F-100
Specifications and Performance Data

Engine	One Pratt & Whitney J57 turbojet of 10,000-lb. static thrust (16,000-lb. with afterburner)
Wingspan	38 ft. 9 in.
Length	47 ft. 1 in.
Empty weight	19,000 lbs.
Maximum speed	925 mph at 35,000 ft.
Range	1,100 miles

Supersonic flight

The speed of sound (*see*), once thought to be a limiting factor in aircraft design and performance, today is surpassed regularly by a variety of high-performance planes and rockets.

At sea level, sound travels at a speed of about 760 mph. It moves in the form of a shock wave by bumping, or agitating, air molecules along the leading edge of the wave. Its speed decreases with altitude, where the air is thinner and colder, to about 660 mph at 35,000. Regardless of the actual velocity of sound, its speed is called Mach 1, after Ernst Mach (*see*).

All moving objects send out sound waves—pressure waves in the air. As long as the object is moving slower than Mach 1, the waves remain ahead. They travel in an orderly fashion, with wide spacing.

However, when an aircraft approaches the speed of sound, these waves no longer can stay in the lead. They tend to compress, or bunch up, into a turbulent mass. At this point, buffeting (*see*) may set in. In early supersonic aircraft, the buffeting could be quite severe. It was accompanied by a tendency for the aircraft to pitch nose downward and by a degradation in control responses. Unless the plane is designed to overcome these effects, the result could be a complete loss of control.

Surpassing Sonic Speed

Captain Charles Yeager (*see*) became the first human to fly faster than sound in October 14, 1947, when he flew the experimental Bell X-1 rocket plane at 670 mph. The X-1 only slightly resembled current sleek, supersonic craft. It had the familiar tapered needle nose, but its body was fat and chunky. Its wings (*see*) extended straight out from the fuselage and did not sweep back. Designers soon discovered that sound barrier problems were greatly lessened by swept-back wings. Another answer to the problem of transonic buffeting is the delta wing. This wing is triangular in shape—an extended or expanded swept wing.

The most familiar phenomenon associated with the sound barrier and supersonis flight is the sonic boom (*see*). An explosive sound like thunder, its force may be extremely great. But the pilot of the aircraft generating the boom hears nothing. Even though he is sitting just a few feet from its point of origin, he is ahead of the noise, and since he is now traveling faster than sound, he stays ahead of it. To him, the flight is almost silent.

With the evolution of supersonic aircraft, more problems had to be conquered. Wings on supersonic planes are extremely thin and even stubby. While this is efficient for high-speed flight, it can make an aircraft hard to control or unstable at very low speeds. Most supersonic craft land at speeds above 150 knots—faster than many small planes can go at full throttle. As the maximum speed goes ever higher, so does the minimum flying speed. The best design for extremely high speeds would be a plane with no wings at all. But then it couldn't land.

One answer to this is the variable geometry aircraft, such as the F-111 or the Boeing SST. For landing, taking off, or other slow maneuvering, the wings are extended outward from the fuselage. For supersonic flight at high altitudes, the wings fold back into efficient swept positions. This gives the aircraft the best configuration.

Speeds far beyond Mach 1 have been achieved by pilots and astronauts. Only a few seconds after lift-off, a spacebound rocket exceeds the speed of sound. The X-15 rocket aircraft has topped 4,000 mph—nearly seven times the speed of the X-1—on several occasions. Fighter and interceptor craft routinely cruise between Mach 1 and Mach 2.5. So, too, will the supersonic transports (*see*) of the 1970's. The speed of sound is no longer a barrier. It is just a bump in a pleasant flight.

Jim Schefter

See also: Variable geometry, X-15 research program, X-series aerospace vehicles

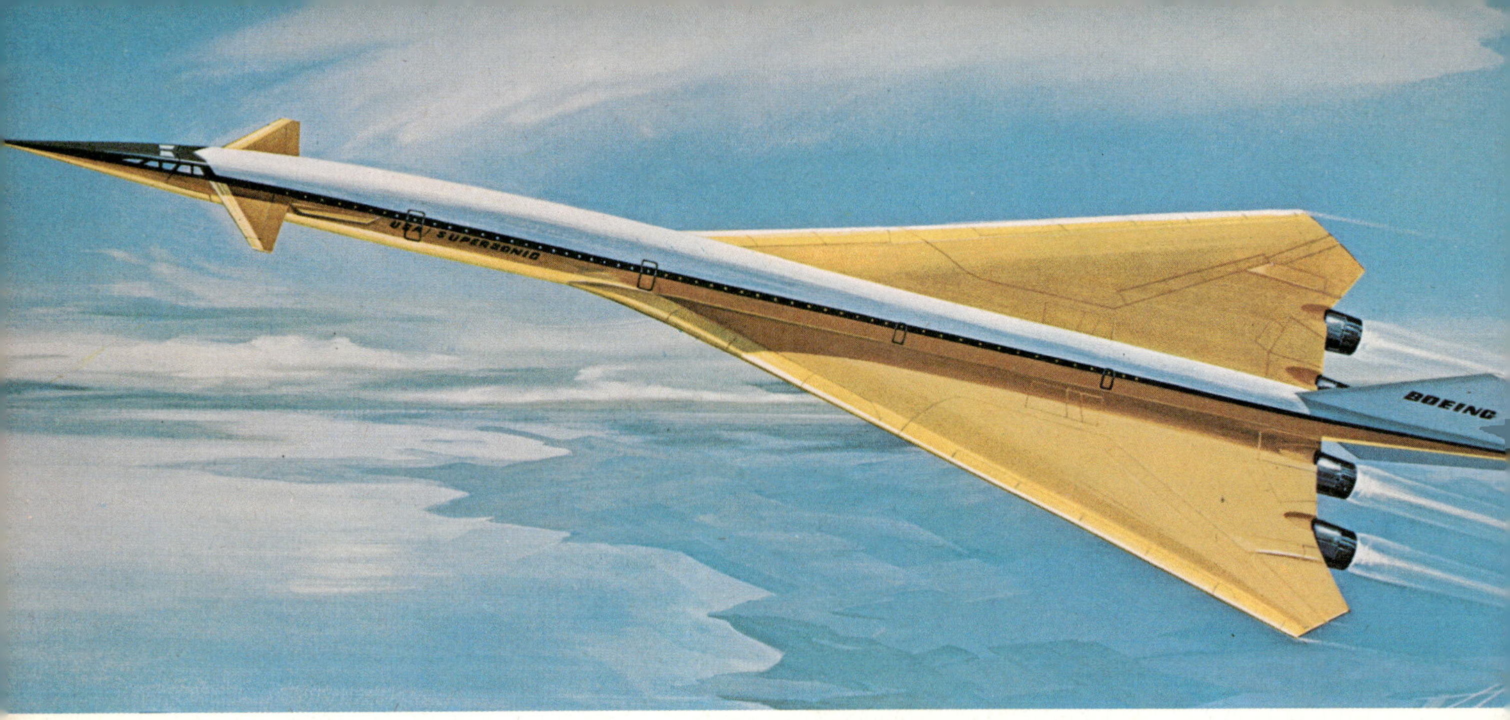
USA/ SUPERSONIC
BOEING

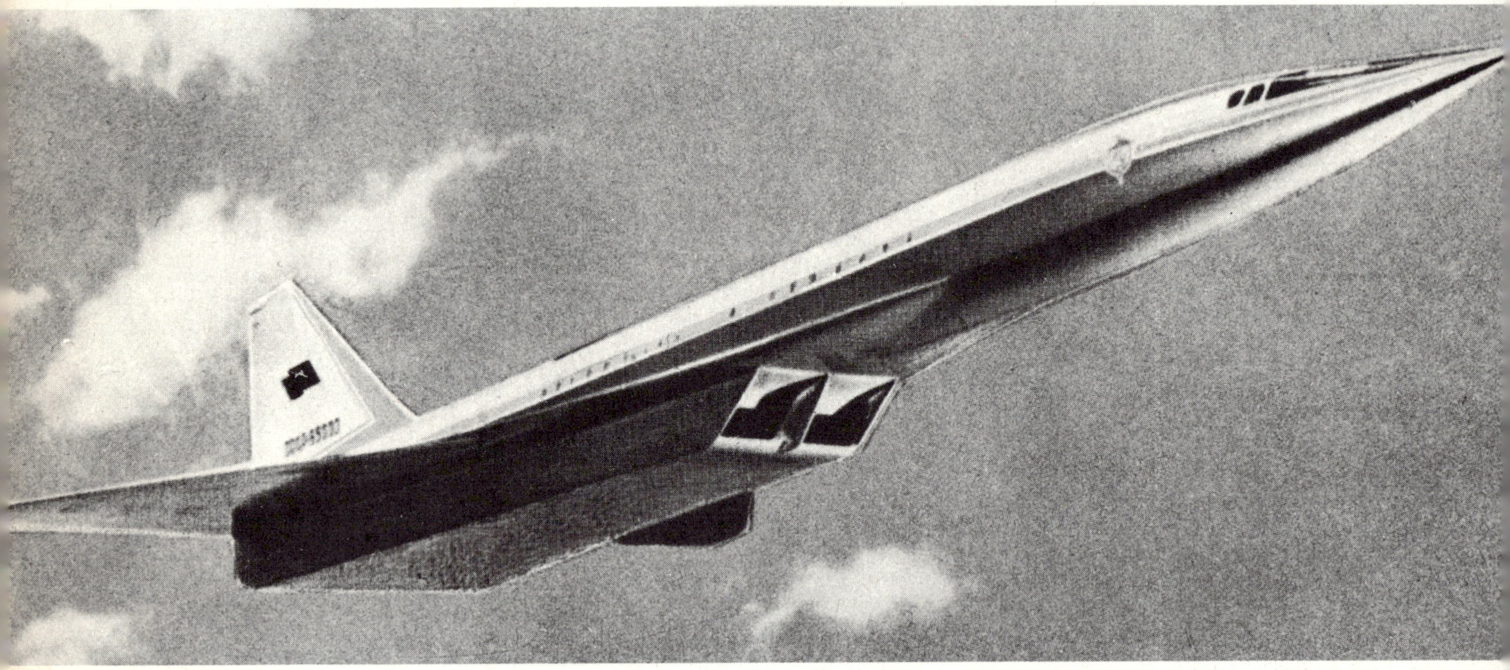

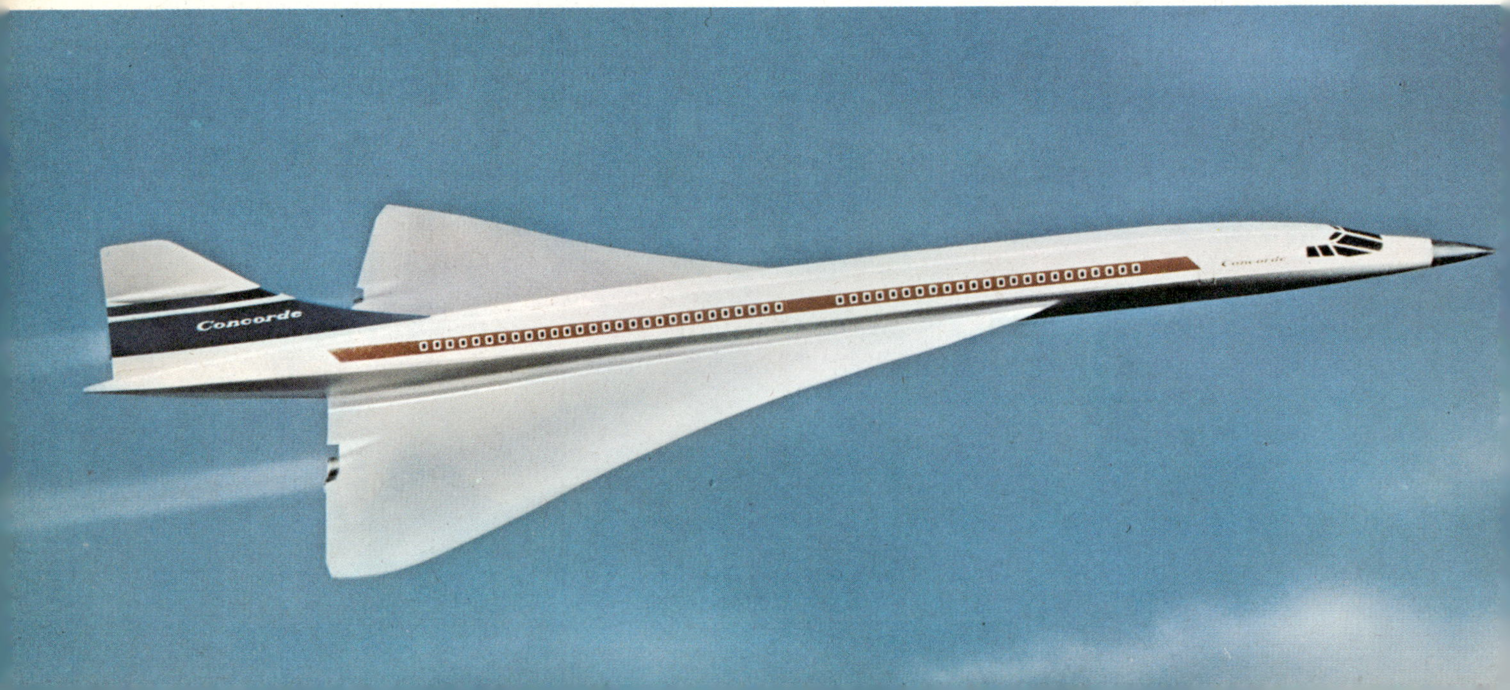
Concorde

The three supersonic transports now under development include the U. S. Boeing 2707 *(top)* with its wings in the high speed position, the Russian TU-144 *(center)*, a delta-wing model whose configuration is similar to the BAC/SUD Concorde *(bottom)*. The TU-144 and Concorde are scheduled for test flights in 1968. All three have movable nose sections to permit improved pilot visibility at slower speeds.

Supersonic transports

Commercial travel at the edge of space

Imagine it is 1978 and you are about to board your first supersonic transport (SST) for a flight to New York City from Los Angeles, California.

The departure hour, 2 a.m. Pacific daylight time, may seem inconvenient, but arrival times usually are more important than departure times in commercial aviation. It is now 5 a.m. in New York City, and when your SST lands at Kennedy International Airport, it will be shortly after 7 a.m., and you can avoid the rush-hour traffic into downtown Manhattan. (If you were flying westward, you would arrive in Los Angeles an hour before you left New York, by the clock.)

The size of the giant Boeing SST seen through the terminal windows is enough to make you catch your breath—three hundred and six feet from the needle nose to the huge tail. It is longer than a football field. That nose, by the way, is drooping now. It is hinged to provide greater visibility, in fact, than pilots had in subsonic jets. Later, as the SST shifts to supersonic flight, the nose will be raised to give the aircraft the slim, rapier profile needed for its 1,800-mph cruising speed. The Boeing SST has been in service for two years, five years behind the British-French Concorde.

When you arrive at the airport, you put your baggage in a red, wheeled bin marked with a large *A*. The bin is towed to the SST itself and lifted aboard the plane bodily. When you arrive in New York, you merely have to ride a moving sidewalk to the baggage claim area where you'll look for a red-painted area and locate your *A* bin.

The metallic voice of the airline's terminal public address system blares out, "Your attention please. Announcing the departure of flight six, nonstop supersonic service to New York."

On Board

Now it is time to board the SST. The first surprise is the width of the main door, which is twice that of the subsonic jets, wide enough for two big men to enter simultaneously. The door size is a safety factor, because it carries not one but two inflatable escape slides which can be activated in five seconds. The Boeing SST carries 300 passengers, but evacuation tests have shown that in the event of a crash landing, the passengers can leave the plane in 80 seconds using only four of the eight large exits.

The second surprise is the lighting. The cabin walls are softly illuminated in a soothing, rosy pastel that blends nicely with the brighter lighting in the cabin ceiling. It is not only relaxing and cheerful, but somehow it seems to break up the tube-like effect of the enormous fuselage.

You are traveling first class at about the same price you used to pay for a subsonic flight. When supersonic operations began, the airlines levied an SST surcharge, but the increasing number of SST's in service (more than 100 in service in 1980 and at least 500 by 1990), plus the incredible productivity of supersonics (one Boeing SST does the work of three conventional jets), and low operating costs (only slightly more than a 707 or DC-8), all have made possible the elimination of the extra charge.

The fuselage looked slim from the outside, but inside there is the same four-abreast first-class seating of the subsonic jetliners, and you can see by peeking up the aisle that the coach section has the usual six-abreast seating. It is now time for you and about 300 fellow passengers to settle back, fasten your seat belts, and await takeoff.

Above every three rows of seats is a modernistic bin where you have stored your coat and other items.

Supersonic transports

When all passengers have been seated, stewardesses walk up and down the cabin, closing up the bins, which have hinged, spring-loaded covers. The bins are another safety item. In the event of an abnormal landing or other emergency involving sudden deceleration, there are no small but lethal pieces of hand luggage free to be tossed around the cabin.

A Word From the Captain

Suspended underneath each bin is a closed circuit television screen. It flickers into life, and you are looking into the mammoth flight deck and into the face of the captain.

"Good morning, ladies and gentlemen. I'm Captain McKay, in command of your flight to New York. Our flight time to the east coast will be two hours and two minutes, and our assigned cruising altitude for supersonic flight will be 69,000 feet. The weather ahead is good, both en route and at destination. There are thunderstorms throughout the Midwest, but we will be flying approximately 20,000 feet above the weather. For those of you making your first supersonic trip, it may interest you to know that our cruising speed at 69,000 feet will be just over 1,800 miles per hour, or nearly three times the speed of sound. We'll consume on this flight more than 25,000 gallons of fuel, or enough to drive your automobile for about 35 years. If you'll look out your window, you'll notice that the wings of our Boeing SST are extended almost straight out, with less sweepback than on subsonic jets. When we climb out of the Los Angeles area and begin shifting from subsonic to transonic speeds, you will hear a slight rumbling sound something like the noise of a landing gear being raised or lowered as our wings fold back toward the fuselage. This provides us with the aerodynamic profile necessary for supersonic flight. We'll start this process at around 45,000 feet, and you'll feel an almost immediate acceleration. It's all normal, I assure you. Later, as we start our descent 400 miles out of New York, we'll be extending the wings to their approach and landing position, which enables us to land this great new airplane at speeds only slightly higher than those of the old jets. Now, I'm going to switch your TV sets back to the cabin monitor and have you meet your flight attendants. Thank you, and I hope you have a pleasant trip."

Meeting the Stewardesses

The captain's image on the screen is replaced by that of a trim, pretty stewardess. "Good morning," she says softly. "I'm Miss Kay Crumly. The other girls serving you on today's flight are Miss Pitcher, Miss Hillis, Miss Henderson, Miss Pitts, Miss Jackson, and Miss Lamb, all in the coach section, and with me in the first-class cabin will be Miss Higgs, Miss Smith, and Miss Baxter. Now, just before we leave the ramp area, we'd like you to keep your eyes on the screen. We'll be showing you a two-minute film designed to acquaint you with the various safety features of your SST—the location of the emergency exits, how to use your oxygen masks if the cabin pressure should change drastically, and other important information. We urge you to watch—the film is for your own comfort and safety. After we reach our cruising altitude, we'll be serving a hot breakfast. Now, please make sure your seat belts are fastened and all seats are in the upright position for our takeoff. Thank you, and here's our safety film."

The film has scarcely ended when the big plane moves away from the ramp and waddles toward the runway for takeoff. Inside the sound-conditioned cabin (there is three times more insulating material in the SST than in subsonic jets), you can hardly hear the mighty engines. You glance at the little pamphlet *All About the SST* in your seatback pocket and read that each engine develops 67,000 pounds of thrust (three times that of the most powerful commercial jet engine of the 1960's) and costs $1.5 million, which was the price tag for an entire DC-6 in 1950.

You feel rather than hear the engines increase power as the SST trembles before takeoff. Brakes are released. The giant begins to roll. In the early morning darkness, runway lights blur as speed builds up to 186 mph, actually a so-called *rotation speed,* and the nose wheel lifts off the ground. This speed is 5 to 10 mph less than what is required to get the largest version of the 707 airborne and requires 4,000 feet less runway roll.

You are in the air now, traveling in a titanium monster that weighs 575,000 pounds, of which nearly half is the immense fuel load. The angle of climb is slightly steeper than what you have been used to but it is not uncomfortable, contrary to what the cynics were dourly predicting a decade ago: SST passengers are not flat on their backs during takeoff or during most of the flight. The acceleration of the SST is faster, also. This aircraft has the power for more than double the climb rate of a 707, an important factor in noise abatement on the ground, because it reduces the time of exposure to noise.

At Supersonic Speeds

The captain's voice, metallic and calm, sounds through the cabin, "Ladies and gentlemen, we've reached 45,000 feet and we're about to shift gears, so to speak, to make the transition to supersonic flight. We've been climbing at only 600 miles an hour, to keep us from generating sonic booms. Now we're at an altitude at which the boom on the ground won't be any worse than a distant clap of thunder. Thank you."

A rumbling noise. You look outside, through the tiny window with a diameter of only six inches. (Although the peepholes in the SST are four times stronger than windows in ordinary jets, larger windows would weaken the structure.) The big wings are folding back, the movement generated by big steel pivots in each wing. Now you can feel the acceleration, but the feeling is momentary. Shortly, there is no sensation of speed. In fact, you are surprised when the captain announces, "Folks, we're leveling off at 69,000 feet and our groundspeed is 1,805 miles per hour."

The belt sign goes off. The flight is silk-smooth. As the pamphlet explains, turbulence at SST altitudes is rare, as is poor weather. You look outside again, and the very stars seem millions of miles closer.

The stewardesses are starting to serve breakfast from the plane's four galleys. You are sitting just across from the first-class galley and watch curiously. The stewardess presses a button on a panel in front of her. The panel opens, there is a slight grinding sound, and all of a sudden a covered food tray pops out of the panel. The stewardess lifts the tray out of the panel and places it on a compartmented gadget that looks like a cart without wheels. The grinding noise continues, and seconds later another tray appears. The stewardess explains as she loads the trays on the cart that the actual galleys of the SST are in a special compartment below the cabin floor. The button she pushed activated an ingenious series of dumbwaiter lifts that carry the food to the serving area like a revolving ferris wheel. The arrangement permits smaller but more efficient galleys, where the precious space is utilized more for service than for storage.

The cart loaded with the breakfast trays is actually a small air-cushion vehicle. The stewardess pulls a small lever, and with a little whirring sound, the cart moves down the cabin aisle effortlessly as the stewardesses hand out the trays.

At supersonic speed, you traveled 300 miles while you sipped your glass of orange juice and 1,000 miles as you ate your steaming ham and eggs. After breakfast, the fluorescent cabin wall illumination dims subtly, almost imperceptibly. On somewhat longer overseas SST flights, movies are shown, but the transcontinental schedules are too brief. For this early morning trip, the airline assumes you would prefer to sleep for awhile, hence the gradual dimming of the cabin lights.

You doze off, secure in the knowledge that the SST, even though it operates in a new and strange environment, was the most thoroughly tested airliner in aviation history. To fly safely in this environment required dramatic innovations and challenging responsibilities. The fuel, for example, actually serves as the coolant for the interior of the SST. At Mach 2.7 cruising speed, the temperature on the outside of the fuselage is well over 400°F and about 600°F on the leading edges of the sweptback wing. Every major system on the aircraft has three backup systems, the ultimate in what engineers call the art of *redundancy* (see) for safety.

Landing

"Ladies and gentlemen, we're starting our descent into the New York area."

The captain's voice arouses you from your nap. Outside, the first fingers of dawn have shoved the stars out of the sky. The SST noses down. The *Fasten Seat Belt* and *No Smoking* signs wink on throughout the cabin. In only a few minutes, there is a rumble underneath your feet as the great 16-wheel tandem landing gear is lowered. The landing gear is an incredible achievement in aeronautical balance that allows the heavy SST literally to tiptoe onto a runway that can be an inch less in thickness than was required for older jets.

You sneak one last look at the SST pamphlet, noting with mingled amusement and awe that the plane has shrunk one foot, or back to its normal length, as it approaches Kennedy. For it is a fact that the SST grows one foot when it reaches its 1,800-mph cruising speed. The changing of length is the result of the expansion and contraction of metal that occurs in the transition between subsonic and supersonic flight. At subsonic altitudes, the plane is exposed to temperatures as low as 60°F. But when the SST flies at supersonic speeds, the friction increases the temperature on the outside of the fuselage to more than 400°F, which accounts for the almost unbelievable change in fuselage length.

You are landing now. The needle nose has been lowered, giving the pilots a bird-cage kind of visibility. The great wings are flexed almost at right angles to the fuselage, providing the same low-speed handling characteristics as a conventional plane. Despite its weight and size, the SST needs only 450 feet more runway for landing than a 707.

Touchdown. Your first SST flight is over.

What you have just read was the story of an

Supersonic transports

imaginary flight that is on the verge of reality. For, basically, the details were derived from what is actually being planned for supersonic travel by thousands of engineers both in the United States and other countries. The story, of course, assumes the successful solution of all problems associated with faster-than-sound commercial flight operations. Let us now examine these problems, the solutions under way, and in particular the aircraft that will utilize those solutions.

Tupolev-144 (TU-144)

Comparatively little is known about the U.S.S.R. SST. The few statistics the Russians have made public indicate that it is roughly comparable to the British-French Concorde in looks, size, speed, range, and payload. The TU-144 is being built with an airframe of conventional aluminum, but with titanium placed strategically around the engines. The Soviet Ministry of Aviation has promised a plane capable of carrying 120 passengers in an all-tourist configuration, or 80 coach passengers plus 18 persons in first class. The ministry said in a special recording played for visitors to the Russian pavilion at Canada's Expo 67, that the galleys are designed for "outstanding cuisine and service."

The powerplants of the Russian SST are rated at 28,500 pounds of thrust per engine, sufficient thrust to give the plane a cruising speed of about 1,550 miles an hour. The range, 4,000 miles with a full payload, is also the same as the Concorde, although the latter has slightly more powerful engines. As with both the Boeing and Concorde, the TU-144 also sports a "droop-snoot" nose for cockpit visibility in the takeoff and landing phases.

The wing area of the Russian SST is said to be 5,000 square feet compared to the 3,800 square feet for the Concorde. The TU-144's fuselage is also reported to be wide enough to accommodate six-abreast seating in at least part of it.

Some sources have described the TU-144 powerplants as fanjet engines rather than straight turbojets such as the Concorde and U.S. Boeing SST will have. The four engines, if photographs of a model represent the actual aircraft, will be clustered together underneath the wing, with two engines on each side of the fuselage centerline.

The Russian supersonic transport was to make its first test flight in November, 1967, the 50th anniversary of the Russian Revolution, which would have been a major propaganda achievement. However, presumably because of major technical difficulties, the date for the first flight was tentatively reset for mid-1968.

The TU-144 is one of the few major Russian transports that was not derived from a military version. It will probably be flown almost exclusively by the Russian state airline, *Aeroflot*.

The Concorde

Barring unforeseen technological difficulties, the Concorde will be the first supersonic transport to carry passengers in actual airline service.

The Concorde is designed and built jointly by the British Aircraft Corp. (BAC) and Sud Aviation of France at a development cost of $1.4 billion. One prototype was constructed in Britain and another in France. The French aircraft is scheduled to make its first test flight in 1968.

The two prototypes, slightly smaller and lighter than what will be the production Concorde, are destined for the most ruthless, rigid test program devised to date for a transport aircraft. The two SST's, plus four regular production models, will be put through 4,000 test flying hours before the first passengers are carried in May, 1971. The test period is at least double the normal test period for subsonic jets.

Sixteen airlines, including seven United States carriers, have ordered a total of 74 Concordes at a cost of nearly $20 million per aircraft, about the same price tag as Boeing's huge jumbo jet, the 747. Originally, BAC and Sud Aviation (BAC-Sud) hoped to sell their SST for a relatively modest cost of $10 million, but development costs and considerable design changes necessitated the higher price. However, for that $20 million, the airlines are buying a plane that will be twice as productive as the jetliners of the 1960's. The Concorde will seat 132 passengers in an all-coach configuration, but its great speed of 1,450 mph makes it literally the equivalent of a 300-passenger subsonic jet: a Concorde can complete a round-trip transatlantic flight in the time a 707 or DC-8 makes a one-way crossing.

The Concorde, in effect, brings any two points in the world within 12 hours travel time of each other. Its passengers will be the first commercial travelers to see the Earth's curvature, to beat the sun when flying westward, and to move at more than twice the speed of sound. They will ride in a rather confined cabin markedly narrower than present jets —the fuselage width just behind the cockpit is not much wider than a DC-3—but the very narrowness means that Concorde coach passengers will have the four-abreast seating now limited to first class customers. In fact, some airlines may not have two-class service in the Concorde because the seating must be almost identical throughout the slim fuselage.

It is hoped that the Concorde's small size com-

The SST cockpit *(above)* is similar to that of the present-day jet airliner but has more avionics. Distances covered by an SST and a subsonic aircraft in a given time *(below)*.

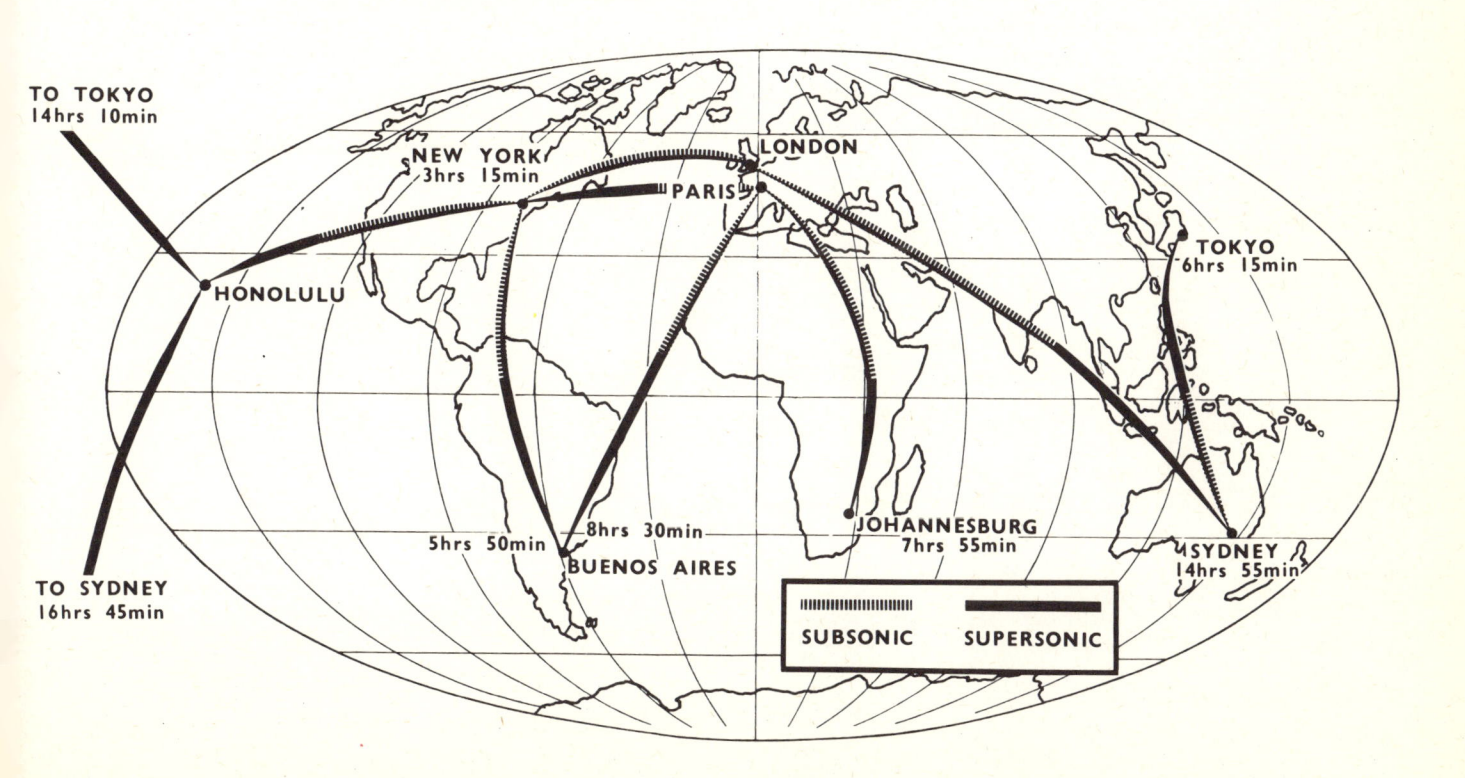

TO TOKYO
14hrs 10min

NEW YORK
3hrs 15min

LONDON

PARIS

TOKYO
6hrs 15min

HONOLULU

5hrs 50min 8hrs 30min
BUENOS AIRES

JOHANNESBURG
7hrs 55min

SYDNEY
14hrs 55min

TO SYDNEY
16hrs 45min

SUBSONIC SUPERSONIC

The Concorde 001, the world's first supersonic transport, was formally rolled out at Sud Aviation's Toulouse factory in southern France on December 11, 1967.

pared to the mammoth Boeing SST (the Concorde actually is nearly 42 feet longer than the largest Boeing 707) will reduce the sonic boom (*see*) menace to something that people on the ground can live with. The Concorde's designers believe the aircraft will not generate booms of any great magnitude, and it may well be that the Concorde will be the SST permitted to fly overland routes, while the Boeing could be limited to overseas operations.

Speed Mach 2

The limited passenger capacity and the Mach 1-2 cruising speed make the Concorde complementary to rather than competitive with the larger and faster American SST. The British-French plane will dominate the North Atlantic routes starting in 1971, but when the giant Boeing supersonic transport makes its appearance, the Concorde undoubtedly will be shifted to short routes and routes of less traffic density. Some aviation economists predict the Concorde will become the primary transcontinental SST in the United States, while the Boeing SST will fly long-haul intercontinental routes.

BAC-Sud carefully considered all aspects of restricting their SST to speeds of Mach 2.2. The principal reason for the restriction was to avoid the expense of using titanium in the airframe. Above Mach 2.2, the strongest of aluminum alloys are weakened by the enormous heat, but up to 1,450 mph the alloy being used on the Concorde actually has the same strength and metallurgic durability as titanium. If the Concorde were built of titanium, BAC-Sud would have had an airplane capable of achieving Mach 2.7 speeds, but one that would have been more expensive to build, buy, and operate—and also one that could not have been flying passengers by 1971. The titanium SST requires new manufacturing techniques and extended testing, both of which would have delayed the Concorde long enough for it to be dominated by the Boeing version.

At any rate, the 1,450-mph cruising speed of the Concorde brings Australasia and the Far East as close to the U.S. as Europe is now. Also, on a trip

The final configuration of the delta-wing Concorde is a compromise incorporating high and low speed flight characteristics.

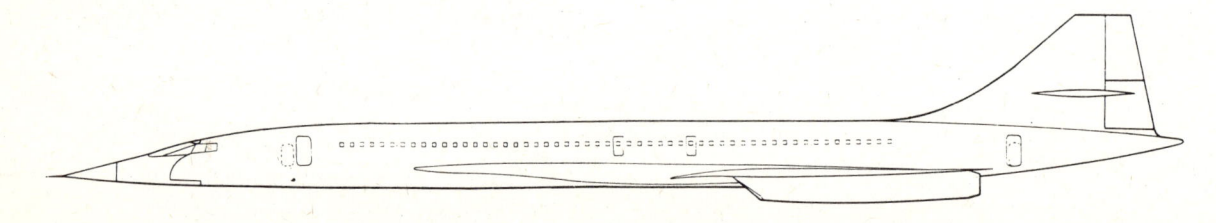

A possible interior configuration of the BAC/SUD Concorde is studied in a mock-up.

under 3,500 statute miles, a Mach 2.2 SST would be only 20 to 25 minutes flying time behind a Mach 2.7 plane.

The Delta-Wing

The Concorde is a delta-wing SST, as are most supersonic military fighters. The delta design provides many advantages, the most important of which is its extremely good aerodynamic efficiency at high speeds. The large surface area of the delta-wing also results in what aeronautical engineers term a *ground effect cushion*, which means the wing produces a cushion of air beneath it while landing. Stalling a delta-wing aircraft during the landing phase is virtually impossible. The design also provides more immunity from the effects of a severe crosswind than other designs, and the Concorde therefore should have low-speed stability superior to that of present jets.

The Concorde is flown with conventional yoke and rudder pedals, but the control movements are converted into electrical signals that actuate hydraul-

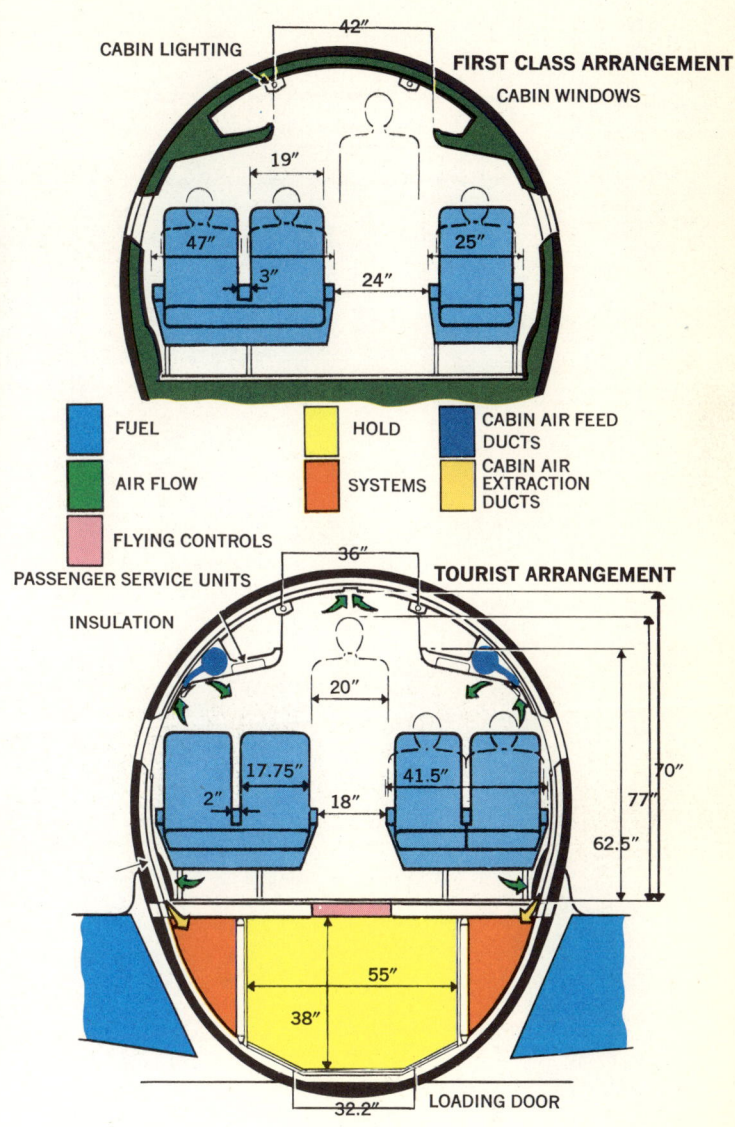

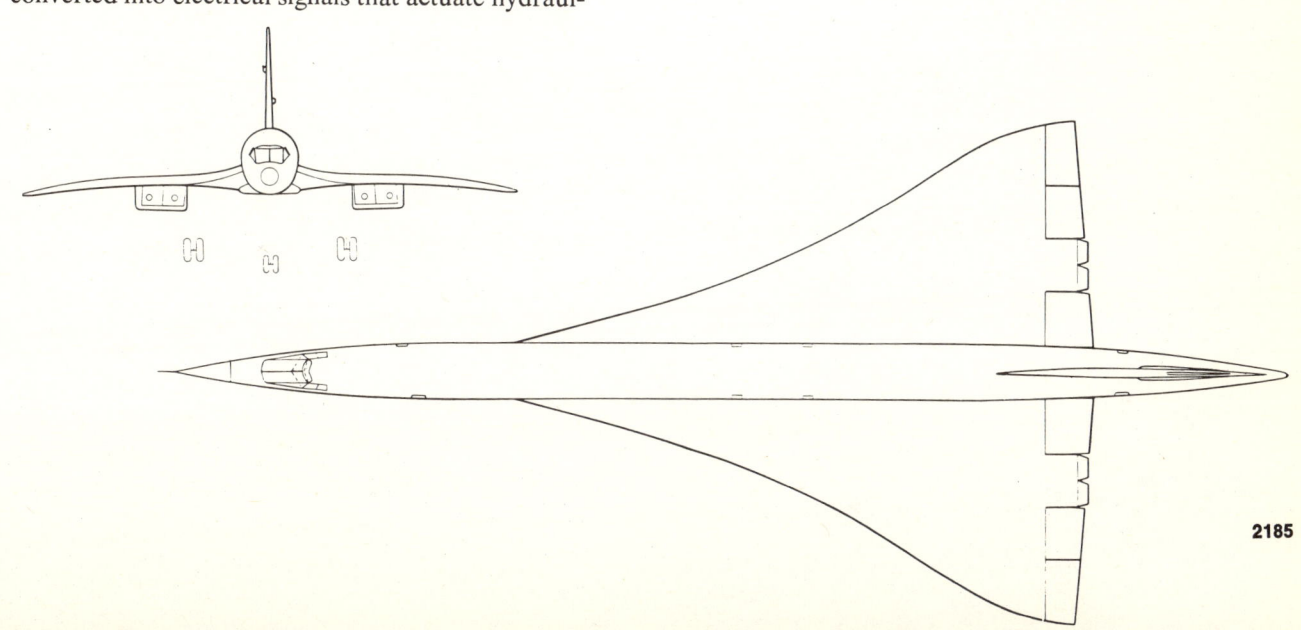

CONCORDE PRODUCTION AIRCRAFT

- GALLEY
- COATS
- BAGGAGE
- T TOILET
- EMERGENCY EQUIPMENT
- ⇨ EMERGENCY EXITS

OVERALL LENGTH	193 FT.
CABIN LENGTH	129 FT.
NO. OF PASSENGERS	132 at 34 in. PITCH
PAYLOAD	28,000 LB.
TAKE-OFF WEIGHT	367,000 LB.

1. Fuselage nose
2. Forward fuselage
3. Intermediate fuselage
4. Forward wing
5. Center wing
6. Center wing
7. Center wing
8. Center wing
9. Center wing
10. Outer wing
11. Elevons
12. Rear fuselage
13. Nacelles
14. Nozzle
15. Fin
16. Rudder
17. Landing gear main
18. Landing gear nose

One of the major concerns in the design and construction of a supersonic transport is the high temperatures resulting from aerodynamic heating. Some portions of the aircraft will be subject to greater temperatures than others.

SKIN EQUILIBRIUM TEMPERATURES   TOP SURFACE
CRUISE MACH 2.2 AT 60,000 FT. I.S.A.
NOSE TEMPERATURE
153°C

LEADING EDGE   130°C

123°C — 10
120°C
119°C — 30
118°C
117°C — 50
70
90

DISTANCE FROM LEADING EDGE IN FEET

125°C   122°C   119°C   117°C   116°C

DISTANCE FROM NOSE IN FEET

0   25   50   100   150   191'1"   FEET

ically powered units hooked to the control surfaces. A two-section rudder is used for controlling yaw, while pitch and roll maneuvers are handled by six *elevons* located in the trailing edge of the wings. Actually, the elevons do the combined work of conventional wing ailerons and the elevators in the horizontal tail stabilizers. The Concorde has no horizontal stabilizers in the tail section, because the immense delta wing enables their elimination. The delta wing also eliminates the usual devices for low-speed control such as spoilers, flaps, and lift dampers. In effect, the delta wing itself is a combination of ailerons, elevators, flaps, and spoilers all rolled into one neat and efficient package.

One disadvantage of the delta wing is that the nose of the airplane must be pitched up more sharply while landing. This characteristic will be the chief difficulty for pilots to make the transition to Concorde operations, but the "droop-nose" still permits forward visibility in such proportions that the exaggerated nose-up attitude should not present too serious a problem. Certainly, the techniques of landing delta-wing aircraft have been mastered by thousands of military pilots.

Like the Boeing SST, the Concorde will utilize its fuel to help cool the cabin. But the Concorde also will require constant monitoring of fuel flow and consumption because, unlike the Boeing, it maintains proper trim by shifting the fuel load. In other words, as the fuel supply diminishes, the vital center of gravity, which must remain constant in an SST to maintain stability at supersonic speed, could shift and cause severe pitch up or pitch down. The Concorde compensates for the threatened shift in the center of gravity by a complex pumping system that constantly transfers fuel from one tank to another in the precise required proportions. For example, fuel is moved rearward during supersonic flight and pumped forward for subsonic flight. The Boeing achieves the same delicate balance between center of gravity and center of lift without complicated plumbing.

The Powerplants

The Concorde will be powered by four Bristol Siddeley/SNECMA Olympus 593 engines, mounted in paired nacelles under the wings. Their thrust in the final production model will be around 37,000 pounds, twice that of current jets. The engines, however, will not be any noisier, because of a unique system of retractable silencers that are lowered into exhausts during takeoff and landing. In contrast, today's jet engines have fixed silencers which reduce performance slightly. Noise will be further reduced

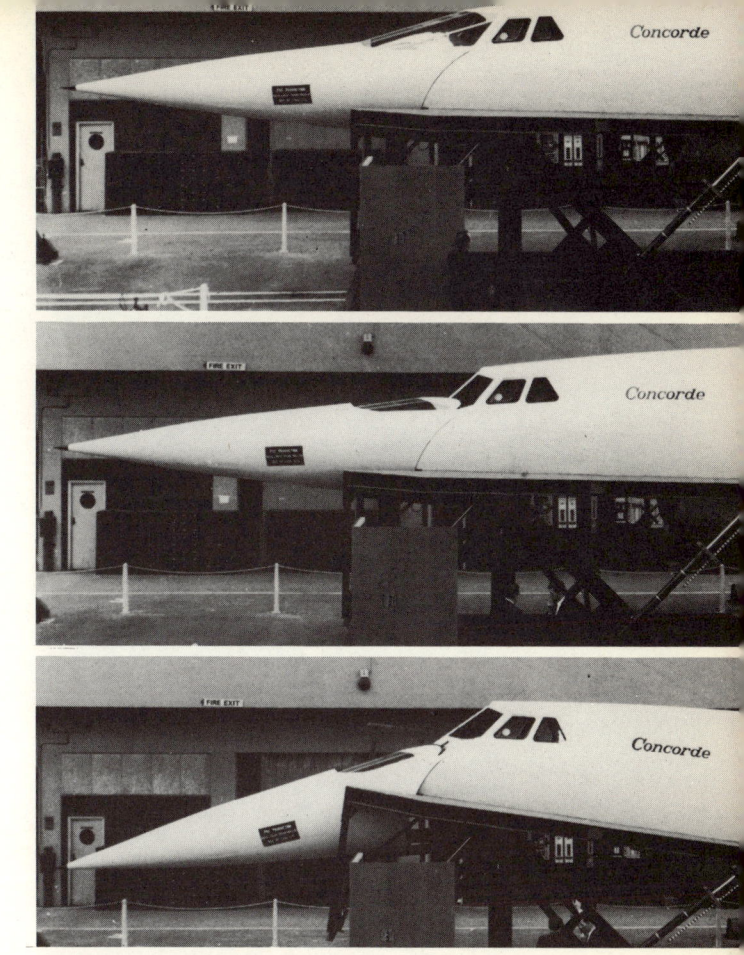

The Concorde droop nose system in supersonic flight position *(top)*, subsonic *(center)*, and positioned for landing *(bottom)*.

The basic structural material for the Concorde is a high-strength aluminum alloy.

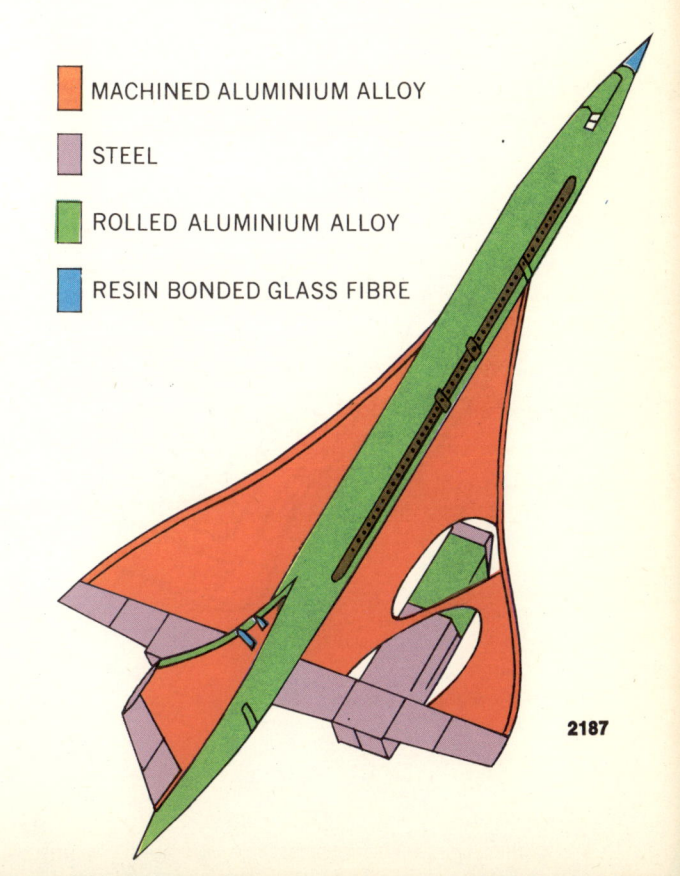

■ MACHINED ALUMINIUM ALLOY
■ STEEL
■ ROLLED ALUMINIUM ALLOY
■ RESIN BONDED GLASS FIBRE

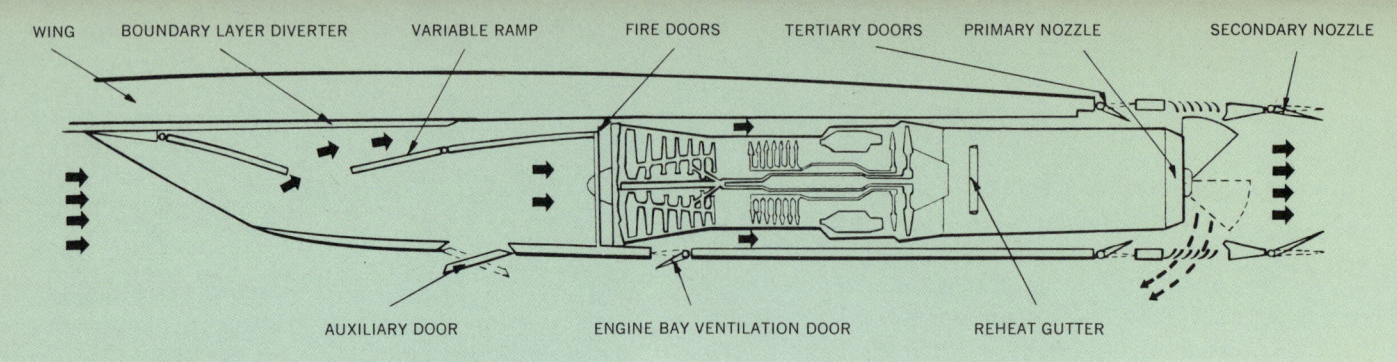

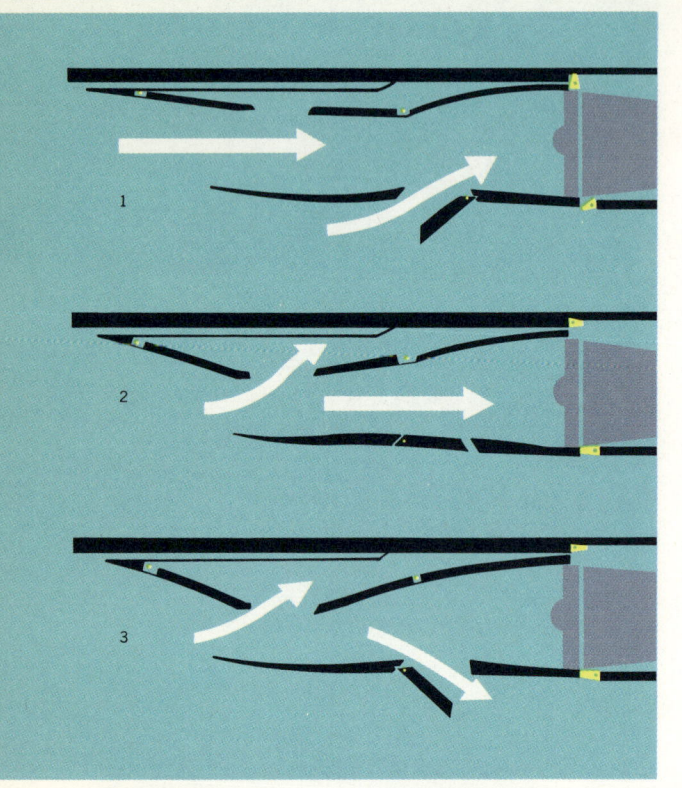

Diagram labels (top): WING, BOUNDARY LAYER DIVERTER, VARIABLE RAMP, FIRE DOORS, TERTIARY DOORS, PRIMARY NOZZLE, SECONDARY NOZZLE, AUXILIARY DOOR, ENGINE BAY VENTILATION DOOR, REHEAT GUTTER

The huge engines that will power the supersonic transports require a complex system of air inlet and exhaust ducts.

by mounting the engines in pairs instead of having separate pods for each.

The Olympus engine is a straight turbojet, with lower drag and less weight than the usual fanjet engines on today's turbine-powered transports. The General Electric engine that will power the Boeing SST also will be a turbojet rather than a turbofan. The drag and weight factors more than compensate for the better fuel consumption of the turbofan. The Concorde engines will also feature a variable geometry intake with its own automatic control system and a variable exhaust nozzle, a combination which assures the maximum power output during every speed range.

The Concorde will probably be flown by a three-man crew, although some airlines may add a fourth man to the cockpit. The electronic navigation system will be the most modern available. This highly regarded inertial system can be coupled directly to the autopilot and provides a constant flow of automat-

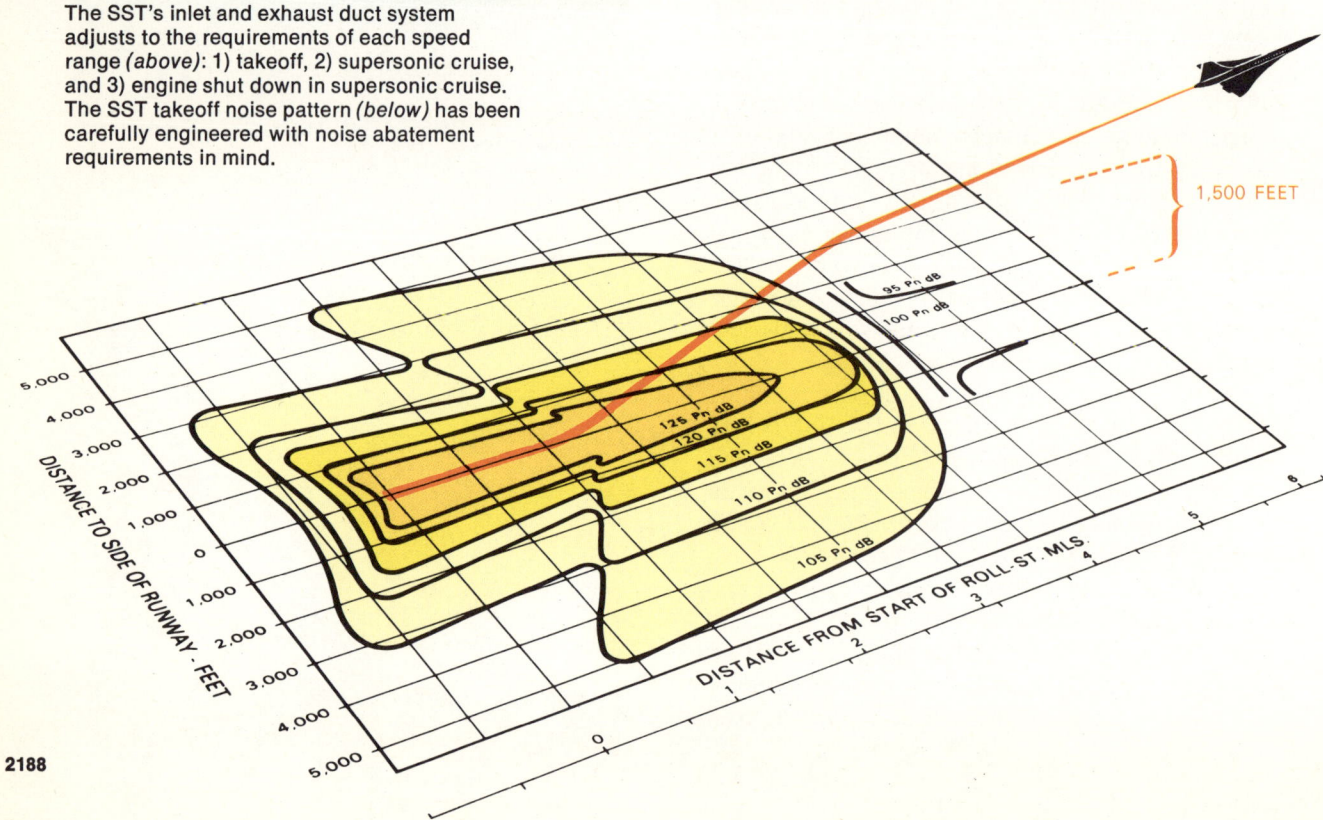

The SST's inlet and exhaust duct system adjusts to the requirements of each speed range *(above)*: 1) takeoff, 2) supersonic cruise, and 3) engine shut down in supersonic cruise. The SST takeoff noise pattern *(below)* has been carefully engineered with noise abatement requirements in mind.

ically computed data on position, wind drift, track deviations, and time of arrival. Many Concordes also will be equipped with an ingenious moving map display which gives the crew a visual indication of aircraft position in relation to the Earth below.

Changes in Design

The BAC-Sud product has undergone numerous changes since its inception. Empty operating weight, for example, has been increased from an original 142,000 pounds to 162,000 pounds, and the SST fully loaded for takeoff will gross 376,000 pounds, about the same as today's "stretched" jets. BAC and Sud at first envisioned an SST with a total passenger capacity of only 104. This was increased to 124 and later to 132. The baggage department in the initial design called for only 500 cubic feet of space, which the prospective airline purchasers protested as wholly inadequate. BAC-Sud upped this space to nearly 900 cubic feet by utilizing the entire rear fuselage as baggage area.

The wing area also was increased and a more positive wingtip twist was added that will improve low-speed handling and climb performance. Another outwardly minor but important modification was the installation of a 4-foot-long *strake,* or plank on the forward fuselage near the cockpit, to provide better low-altitude control characteristics.

The Concorde will be an impressive achievement that will revolutionize air travel. A passenger flying the Concorde across the Atlantic in 1971 will spend almost 80 per cent of his journey between 54,000 and 62,000 feet—about 11 miles high. The average London–New York flight now takes more than seven hours, and the Concorde will do it in three hours 20 minutes. The Concorde in reality shrinks the world by 50 per cent.

While the Concorde is primarily a British-French project, more than 40 American aerospace companies are supplying components that range from special nuts and bolts to intricate electronic equipment. There is wholehearted desire on the part of the U.S. aviation authorities for the Concorde to be an outstanding success and not merely because U.S. airlines will be operating the Concorde. It is generally agreed that U.S. SST program and supersonic travel in general would be dealt a severe setback in public confidence and support if the Concorde should develop serious safety or operating problems.

SUPERSONIC TRANSPORT COMPARISON

	U.S. Boeing SST	Anglo-French BAC/Sud Aviation CONCORDE	U.S.S.R. Tupolev TU-144
Characteristics			
Estimated date of flight test	Early 1970's	1968	1968
Estimated date of service	1976	1971	1973
Primary construction material	titanium	aluminum	aluminum and titanium
Wing design	variable-sweep	delta wing	delta wing
Number in flight crew	4	3-4	3-4
Specifications			
Overall length	318 ft.	193 ft.	180 ft. (est.)
Wingspan	174 ft.	83 ft. 1½ in.	78 ft. (est.)
Height, tail	45 ft.	....	44 ft. (est.)
Maximum takeoff weight	675,000 lbs.	376,000 lbs.	286,000 lbs.
Maximum payload	72,000 lbs.	28,000 lbs.	....
Number of passengers	up to 310	132 tourist	100-121 tourist
Number and type of engines	4 General Electric turbofans	4 Bristol Siddely or SNECMA turbofans with afterburners	4 turbofans with afterburners
Combined thrust	268,000 lbs.	148,000 lbs.	114,000 lbs.
Performance			
Cruise speed	Mach 2.7 1800 mph	Mach 2.2 1450 mph	Mach 2.35 1550 mph
Cruise altitude	69,000 ft.	52,000-62,000 ft.	about 65,000 ft.
Range	over 4,500 miles	....	over 4,000 miles

Supersonic transports

The United States Supersonic Transport

Originally, the gigantic Boeing SST was to be designated the 733 and then the 2707, an appropriate contraction of the plane's Mach 2.7 capability and the proud 707 that is the world's most successful large jetliner. But as yet the official name or numerical designation for the Boeing SST is undecided. Whatever the name, the Boeing SST will be the most incredible, productive, and fastest commercial transport ever built. Many of its details were described in the imaginary supersonic flight across the United States. As of February 1, 1968, more than 20 airlines had placed firm orders for 122 Boeing SST's. These orders were a remarkable display of confidence in American aeronautical integrity and ability, for at that time the U.S. supersonic transport was still a "paper airplane" that existed mostly in drawings and blueprints.

SST Competition

Boeing won the competition to build the SST airframe over Lockheed. The final decision was the careful conclusion of both airline and government experts. The verdict was not unanimous, for there was considerable support for Lockheed's double-delta design. Many aviation authorities, including Boeing and Lockheed themselves, believed that the two companies each should build a single prototype, fighting out their battle in actual test flights to prove which was the superior design.

This plan, however, would have added about $500 million in development costs to a program already costing $4 billion. The decision was therefore made to award the airframe contract to a single airframe manufacturer who would build two prototypes for testing. General Electric won the engine competition over Pratt & Whitney. The GE straight turbojet design was chosen over the Pratt & Whitney turbofan concept on the basis of lighter weight and somewhat lower price.

The Lockheed L-2000, which came so close to being the U.S. SST, had a long, needle-like fuselage curving sharply out from the center into a massive wing and engine area. There were actually two curvatures; a small sweep at the forward edge of the wing and a longer, more pronounced sweep farther back along the wing. Hence the term *double delta*.

Boeing had to make virtually last-second design changes to win the competition over the Lockheed entry. But these changes were sufficient to convince the majority of the engineering and economic experts. One of the most important factors in the decision involved the Boeing variable-sweep-wing design, which would help in noise abatement.

The double-delta wing, while it is almost stall-proof, requires faster landing and a rate of descent higher than present rates. The L-2000's landing and approach speeds would have been 20 to 30 miles an hour higher than the Boeing's. The craft would also have needed more power for takeoff. All these factors would have added to the noise, and the experts were greatly impressed with the fact that the Boeing design offered fewer noise problems. Because the variable-sweep wing gives the Boeing SST approximately the same takeoff and landing performance as present jets, it is not only quieter but transition training for pilots will be easier than it would have been for the Lockheed SST.

In range, payload, speed, and all other performance specifications, the Lockheed and Boeing contestants were almost identical. Boeing did provide greater passenger capacity. The Boeing has a capacity of 310 in an all-tourist configuration compared to Lockheed's 265, although Lockheed did claim its SST could be stretched to at least a 300-passenger aircraft.

The Boeing Supersonic Transport

Boeing had hoped to test fly its SST on December 31, 1970, but further design changes involving mostly weight reduction set back the program approximately one year. The first prototype is not likely to fly over Seattle, Washington, until late 1971 when the Concorde already will have been carrying passengers for nearly a year. This delay may mean that the U.S. SST will not go into regular service until 1976, five years after the Concorde and probably three years behind the Russian TU-144.

Nevertheless, Boeing is confident that it will furnish the airlines with the best supersonic transport, if not the first. The goal of more than 2,000 engineers now laboring is an SST that will: 1) cruise safely and comfortably at Mach 2.7, or 1,800 mph, at altitudes of up to 70,000 feet, thus shrinking the world by 60 per cent; 2) be as economical to operate as present jetliners, yet also have the productivity of three subsonic jets, making the SST the equivalent of a 600-passenger transport; 3) be able to use present runways even though it will gross 575,000 pounds on takeoff; 4) fly nonstop for well over 4,500 miles

The Lockheed contender *(above)* in the American supersonic transport design competition featured a double delta wing while the Boeing model uses the unique variable sweep-wing approach *(below)* with its wings extended for slow-speed flight.

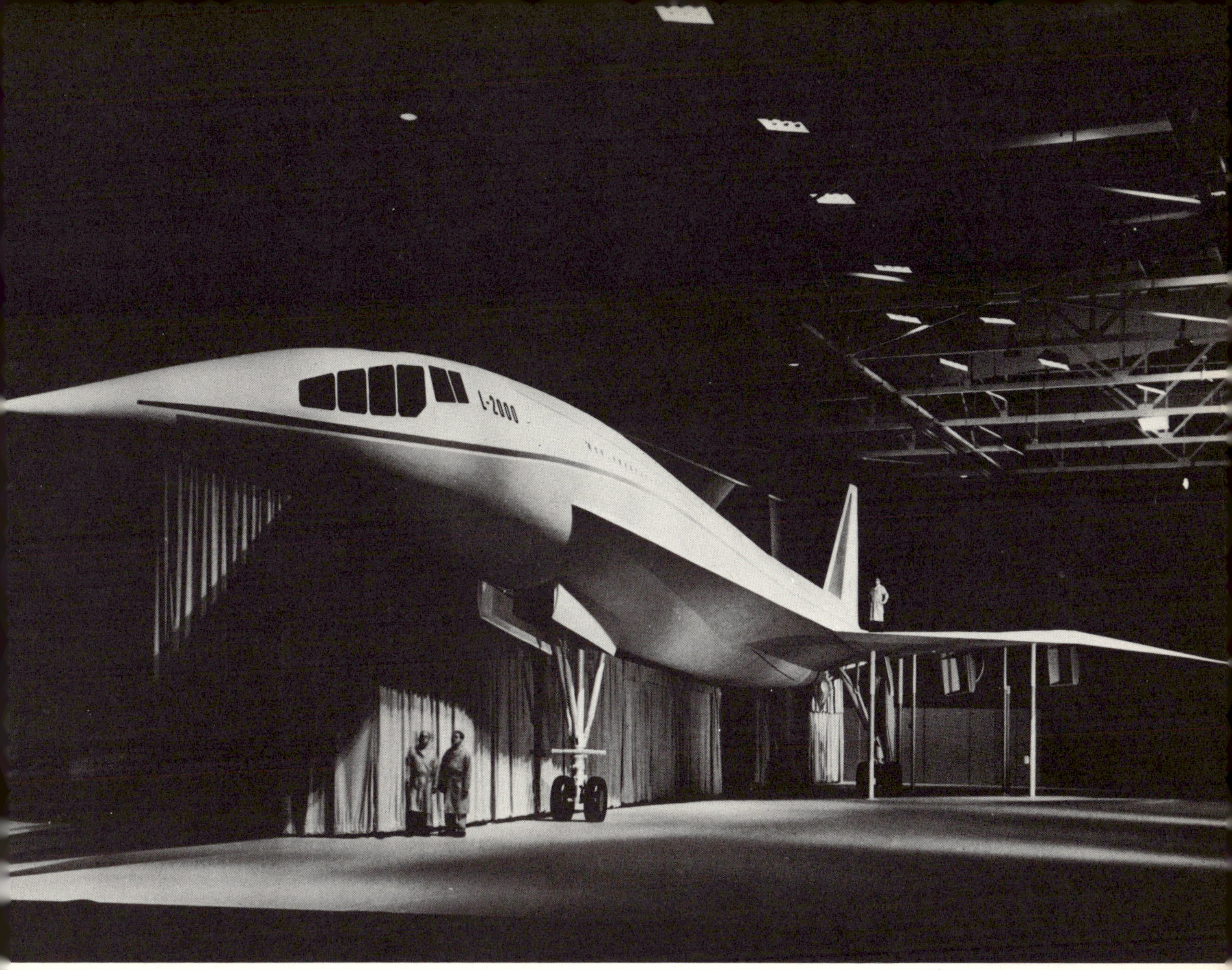
L-2000

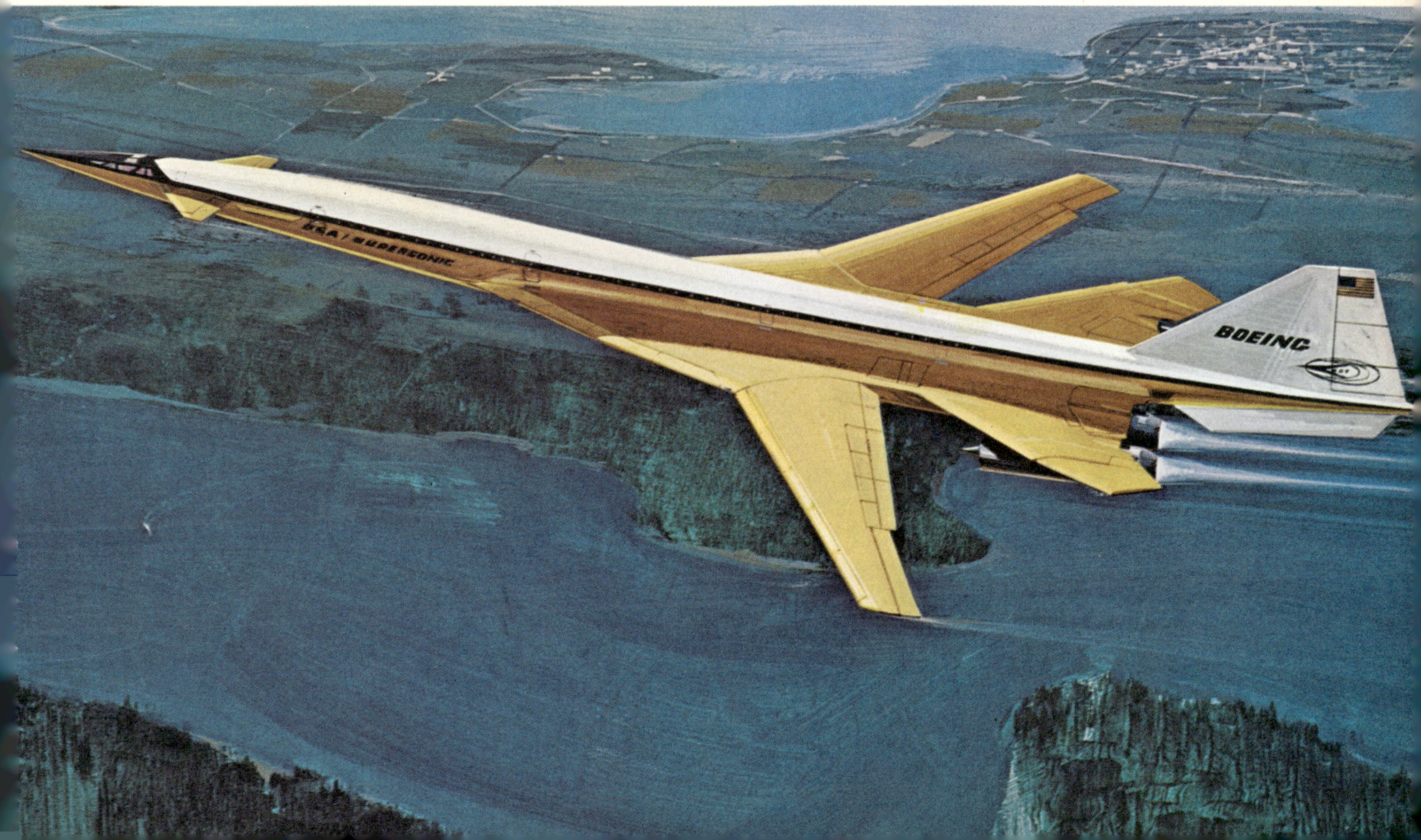
USA / SUPERSONIC
BOEING

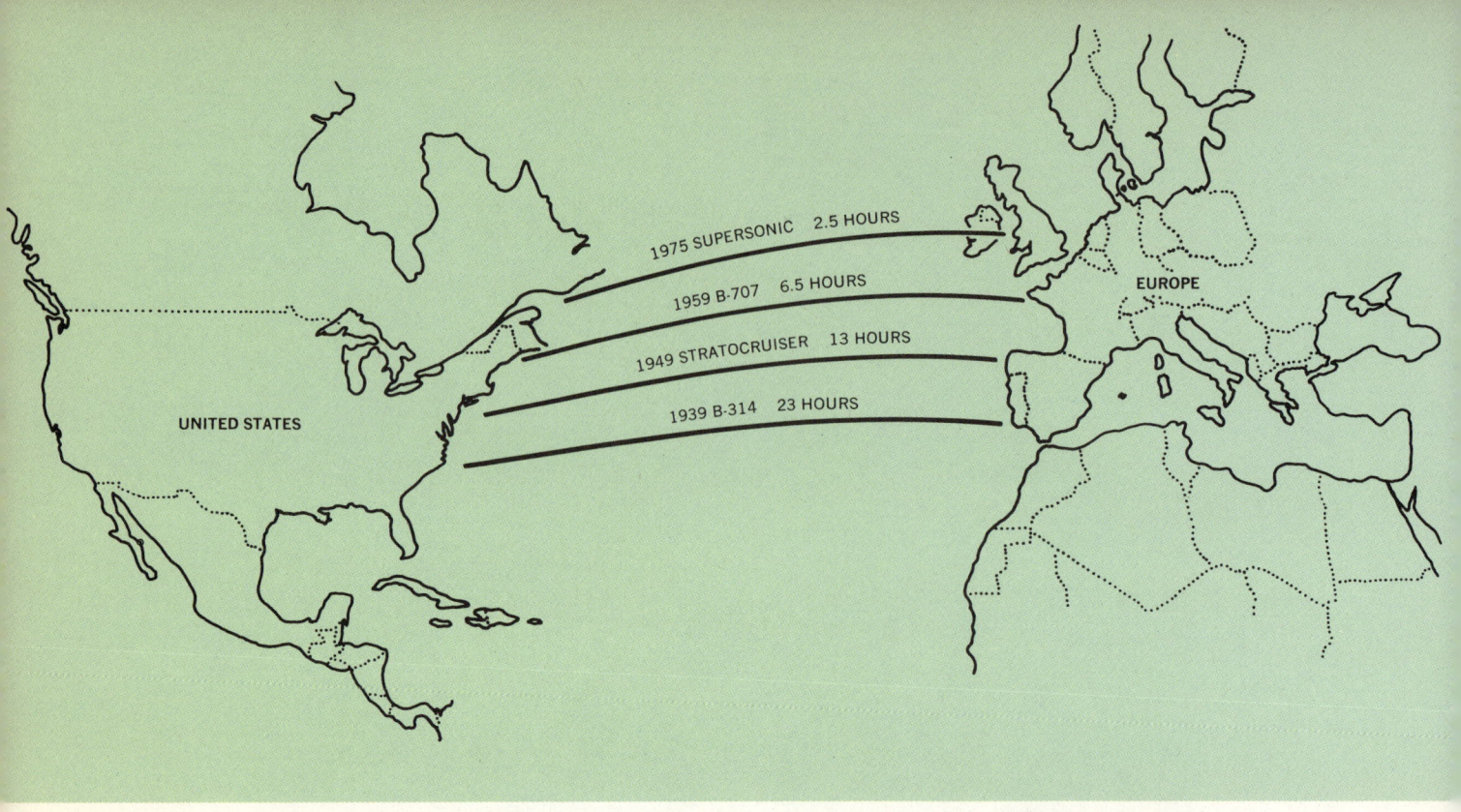

Each new generation of U.S. airliners has reduced the time required to cross the Atlantic Ocean.

with an adequate fuel reserve for delays and/or diversions; and 5) create no more noise and perhaps even less than current jets.

The impact the Mach 2.7 SST will have on air travel is best measured by a comparison of present flying time between major cities. Here are a few examples:

Route	1968 jets	Boeing SST
New York–London	6:33	2:40
Honolulu–San Francisco	4:42	2:01
San Francisco–New York	5:00	2:10
New York–Rome	8:12	3:08
New York–Paris	6:54	2:45

The Swing-wing

Probably the most interesting single feature of the Boeing SST from the standpoint of public interest and certainly from photographic interest is the swing-wing, which will give the aircraft such versatility and routine low-altitude handling. The design has been criticized, because it adds about 30,000 pounds to the weight of an already monstrous airplane. Also, some engineers have questioned its safety. "What happens," they ask, "if the swing-wing does not swing?"

The doubts and fears seem totally unfounded. The Boeing wing pivot, the heart of the variable-sweep design, is the most tested component of all. The wing is not a new concept: the F-111 interceptor-bomber has a variable-sweep wing that has given no service problems at all in several years. Boeing has sent the pivot, a 36-inch bearing made of steel and coated with a special nonwear synthetic material, through more than 30,000 cycles with no sign of wear and not a single failure. The driving mechanism for the pivot is redundant, and the pivot itself is designed to last the life of the airframe, or at least 25 years. Furthermore, wind-tunnel tests have shown that the Boeing can be landed safely even if the pivot were to fail. Although the landing speed would be fast, up to 35 miles an hour faster than with the wings extended, the speed would be fairly close to that proposed for the L-2000.

Boeing has extended the length of its prototype by 12 feet added to the rear of the fuselage to provide reduced drag as well as increased passenger and cargo capacity. Another major modification from the original design is the installation of small canards, literally two small wings, positioned just behind the flight deck. Each canard is 12 feet long with a total surface area of 266 square feet, which is sufficient to furnish significant improvement in longitudinal control at all speeds. The longer fuselage and the canards are also expected to reduce sonic boom noise by an estimated five per cent. The cargo capacity is as high as 8,000 pounds, about a ton less than the 707 is capable of carrying along with a full load of passengers.

The titanium construction of the Boeing SST promises maximum structural strength plus resistance to heat and metal fatigue. The inboard wing fuel tanks will be lined with a new plastic that makes the tanks virtually rupture-proof, thus drastically

MISSION PROFILE

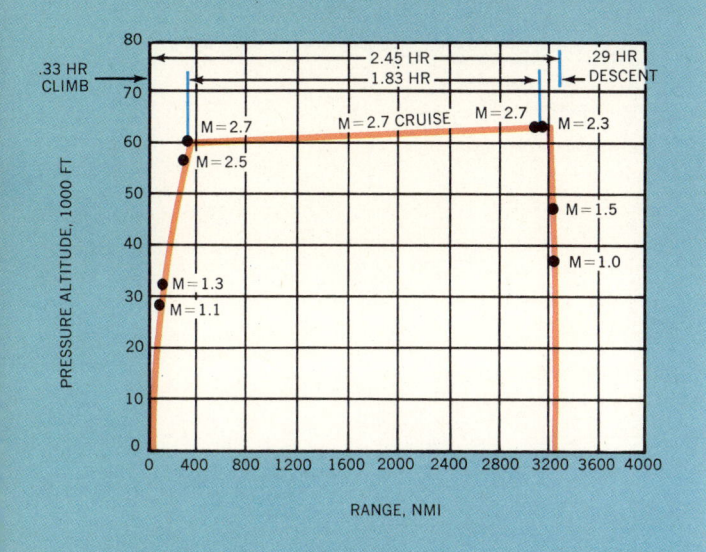

The operating characteristics of the SST.

reducing the chances of a post-impact fire in the event of a crash landing. Also, the fuel tanks are located so that constant transfer will not be necessary to maintain trim.

The original prototype of the 707, known as the Dash-80, first flew in 1954 and still is being used as a test airplane almost daily. Yet the accumulated test flight time on the Dash-80 in over a 14-year period is only 2,200 hours. Each prototype of the Boeing SST will be tested at least 1,500 hours for a total of 3,000 hours, an impressive indication that Boeing, the federal government, and the airlines are determined that the SST will have passed every conceivable safety test before it is allowed to carry a single passenger.

Why a United States SST?

There has been much criticism of the U.S. supersonic transport program from the standpoint of economic justification. No one denies that the $4 billion in development, test, and preproduction costs is a whopping price to pay to give the traveling public a faster means of flying. "Why," the critics ask, "shouldn't U.S. airlines just stick to the Concorde which will be available five years sooner, will cost about $15 million less per airplane, and can be built out of conventional aluminum more easily and less expensively?"

One answer is the consequences of the United States defaulting the entire SST market to the Concorde. It has been estimated that surrender of all actual and potential SST sales would increase the

Supersonic transports

balance of payments deficit of the U.S. by $5.8 billion and be a blow to the U.S. economy. Just the prime contractors of the United States supersonic transport program will pour $110 billion into the economy and create, conservatively speaking, up to 50,000 new jobs. Subcontracting plans for the SST involve companies in 46 states, another $30 billion, and another 100,000 new jobs.

A sizable percentage of the $4 billion in development costs is coming from the federal government. SST opponents have objected strongly to the idea of U.S. taxpayers subsidizing a commercial airliner. Supporters argue in rebuttal that the government will be paid back through a system of royalties derived from the payments the airlines make to Boeing. The government will get back its $1.3 billion investment from the sale of the first 300 SST's, and the minimum market is estimated at 500.

One market analysis calculated that 500 supersonic transports plus spare parts and flight training simulators would cost the airlines more than $25 billion by the end of 1988. But the same analysts also calculated that by 1988, those 500 aircraft will have netted the airlines $36.7 billion. Boeing claims that an airline can make a yearly profit of $6 million per SST over the first 15 years of its operation, and a larger net after that. The most conservative economic forecasts on the profitability of the SST's are based on a six per cent growth in airline traffic annually. Most industry observers expect at least a 10 per cent annual growth rate.

Optimism about SST prospects depends, of course, on the technological success of the Concorde and Boeing. If either or both planes generate intolerable sonic booms and their operations are thus limited to overseas flights, the market for the SST would be correspondingly limited. Data collected by the Federal Aviation Administration (FAA) (see), which has overall charge of the United States SST program, indicate that a restricted market would require about 800 supersonic transports: 500 Boeings and 300 Concordes. This number is still a sizable fleet, sufficient to make money for the manufacturers and return initial investments to the governments that have backed their respective SST projects. If the SST can operate over continental areas, the total market in the free world has been set as high as 1,800 planes, the size of the entire U.S. commercial airline fleet in 1967.

Why a Faster Plane?

There is little doubt that people will have no objections to paying higher fares for the swiftness of supersonic travel. Every public opinion survey

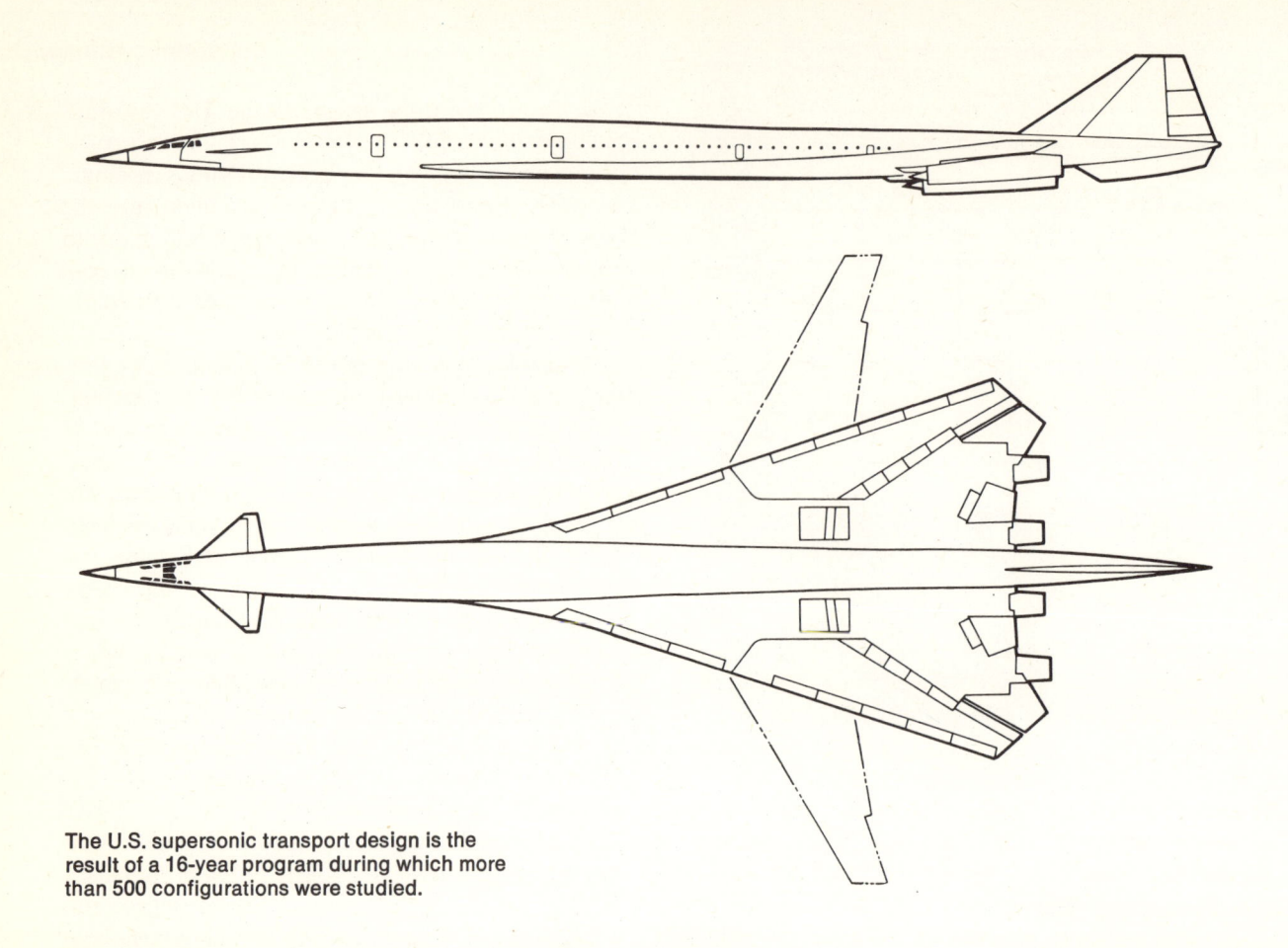

The U.S. supersonic transport design is the result of a 16-year program during which more than 500 configurations were studied.

The Boeing 2707 supersonic transport will be powered by four GE4 turbojet engines. Each will be mounted in an individual pod and each engine produces a thrust of about 67,000 pounds. The cruising speed will be about 1,800 mph.

In a full scale mock-up of the interior of the Boeing 2707, engineers evaluated design and function to provide the maximum comfort and convenience for passengers and crew. Test passengers participated in the evaluation.

made prior to the U.S. decision to build an SST showed that passengers were willing to pay up to 25 per cent more in SST fares, and one survey showed that $50 was an acceptable premium. The desire for swifter transportation has been an axiom of the airline industry from its very start. Not so long ago, pessimists doubted whether anyone would pay a $10 surcharge for subsonic jet travel. They flatly predicted that when the novelty wore off, most passengers would return to the slower but less expensive propeller planes. They did not. In fact, the early jets soon dominated every route over which they were competitive with piston-engine and propjet aircraft.

Public preference has been shown for aircraft with even a small speed advantage. In the mid-1930's, the DC-3 made the Boeing 247 obsolete almost overnight, even though the Douglas transport was only 25 miles an hour faster. Passengers flocked from the DC-4 to the speedier, pressurized DC-6 and Constellation in the post-World War II years. Propjets, such as the Viscount and Electra, had consistently higher loads than piston-engine aircraft in competing schedules. In fact, one reason often cited for an SST surcharge is that the extra fare will be needed to protect the older jets from total obsolescence. Some airline officials feel only a drastic fare differential would prompt a passenger to take a long subsonic flight. By 1985 supersonic transports are expected to carry half of the western world's passenger-seat-mile total, which would amount to about 75 per cent of long-haul traffic.

The Sonic Boom

It has been apparent from the start of supersonic transport planning that the biggest obstacle to faster-than-sound commercial air travel is not the imagined or real dangers of flying nearly 2,000 mph at 70,000 feet, but rather the phenomenon known as the *sonic boom* (see).

Few doubt that a safe supersonic airliner can be built, but there is considerable doubt about a by-product of supersonic flight and what can be done to overcome it. The boom is simply a strong pressure wave created by an airplane as it breaks the sound barrier and then moves beyond it. The wave forms two cones of turbulent air, one at the nose and the other at the tail. The resulting waves speeding toward the ground are known as *overpressures*.

The overpressures range in volume and force, creating disturbances heard as a mild, distant clap of thunder or the shattering bang of a cannon. Also, the intensity of the overpressures is often unpredictable. In the sonic boom tests conducted by the FAA over Oklahoma City, Oklahoma, several years ago (residents were subjected to sonic booms of varying degrees of overpressures for 26 weeks), scientists found that the waves varied according to atmospheric conditions, temperature, terrain, and other factors. As a result, a boom that should be tolerable to people on the ground has on a few occasions mushroomed into an intolerable blast.

The chief reason the FAA rejected the original Boeing and Lockheed SST designs was not, as widely reported, insufficient range and performance. Rather, it was the inability of either plane to keep overpressures at permissible levels, in other words, low enough to preclude possible emotional or physical damage. The determining factor is the altitude at which a large, heavy aircraft breaks Mach 1, the speed of sound. Both early SST planes would have reached Mach 1 at an altitude of about 25,000 to 35,000 feet, levels at which overpressures exceed the tolerable limits set by the FAA.

It is hoped that the forthcoming Boeing SST will be able to climb faster than the original design, fast enough so that Mach 1 will be attained at 45,000 feet or higher. This theoretically will reduce the boom waves to tolerable levels, although there is not very much agreement as to what constitutes a tolerable sonic boom. Undoubtedly, many persons will insist any boom is intolerable just as many persons will never stop denouncing the noise of jets.

The 1964 tests in Oklahoma City were designed to determine what overpressures were tolerable and how much, if any, physical damage was created by the overpressures. At best, the tests were inconclusive. Much additional research is being done on the boom phenomenon, not only to find ways to lessen the overpressures but to learn whether they can definitely cause as much damage as some persons claim.

Objections to the Boom

The Citizens League Against the Sonic Boom, an organization in the foreground of SST critics, is trying to ban any supersonic flights over land areas and even to block construction of any supersonic transport. The league has made serious charges, some of them grossly exaggerated or unfounded but some of them admittedly unanswerable until further knowledge about the boom is obtainable. Many answers, naturally, will not be available until the Concorde and Boeing SST actually fly.

The League contends that the boom path of 50 miles wide and 2,000 miles long for a single SST would jolt more than 20 million persons on one flight. One League advertisement declares that, "In

Supersonic transports

about five minutes time, a single SST could boom everyone on Long Island—all 5,000,000 people, all animals, all schools, all hospitals."

These startling statistics, however, are based on the unrealistic supposition that the transcontinental SST will be flying over heavily populated areas. There is no reason to believe that supersonic flight paths cannot be planned to avoid such areas. It should be understood that an SST will not create a boom within a radius of from 100 to 150 miles of an airport, because it will be climbing or descending at subsonic speeds. All available evidence indicates that overpressures created by a plane as large as the Boeing SST flying at altitudes of from 45,000 to 70,000 feet would not reach more than 1.5 pounds per square foot. There is no instance where an overpressure of this magnitude has hurt anything, from an eardrum to a greenhouse.

There is conflicting data on the damage booms can cause to houses and other structures. During and after the Oklahoma City tests, more than 4,000 damage claims were submitted. The majority of the claims were denied, however, and the FAA is fighting a number of still unresolved cases in the belief that some citizens are attempting to collect for damages incurred long before the tests.

In a recent ten-year period, some 34,000 claims totaling $19.1 million for sonic boom damage were filed against the Air Force. About 12,000 claims involving $1.2 million were paid. But military supersonic flights frequently take place at relatively low altitudes, and these figures are not necessarily indicative of what will happen when the SST starts operating. More recent sonic boom tests at the White Sands Missile Range in New Mexico showed that it would take an overpressure of 5 pounds per square foot to damage any structure or its contents. The FAA will not certificate any SST that produces a boom of such force.

Even the most optimistic SST supporter admits that the sonic boom will be inevitable in the age of supersonic travel. Science presumably cannot eliminate the phenomenon any more than it can repeal the law of gravity. This fact does not mean, however, that the boom cannot be kept under control or that the SST itself must inevitably generate intolerable overpressures.

Hope for Lessening the Boom

There is even a mild hope that the SST sonic boom may be made less intense than that produced by conventional jets. Two scientists have conducted wind tunnel experiments in which the sonic boom of a miniature SST was actually prevented from developing by projecting an electric field ahead of the plane.

A subsonic plane creates a kind of pressure wave moving at the speed of sound, one that parts the air ahead so it flows smoothly around the aircraft. Supersonic flight produces the same wave, but the aircraft moves faster than the wave itself, which causes the air molecules to pile up violently into the shock wave of a boom. Wind tunnel tests showed that electrical charges fired ahead of the supersonic plane in effect created an artificial wave moving faster than the aircraft. So long as the SST did not catch up with and pass its own waves, little or no sonic boom developed.

The obvious drawback to this method of prevention would be the necessity for the extremely powerful and perhaps heavy equipment capable of producing sufficient electrical force. Further experiments in this area are being planned. Even if overpressures produced by SST's prove to be acceptable, some adjustment on the part of human beings will be necessary. Most normal persons react unfavorably to unfamiliar noises, and many of the complaints about ordinary jet noise stem simply from the unfamiliarity of and not the intensity of the noise. When jets were introduced to National Airport, Washington, D.C., citizens filed angry protests against the FAA decision to allow jets. Yet FAA tests showed that planes such as the Boeing 727 and DC-9 produced noise that by every standard of scientific measurement was of less intensity than that of older Constellations and DC-6's. The jets merely produced a different kind of noise.

Currently, there is no evidence that SST flights will result in damage to health, life, and property. It also should be noted that in every sonic boom test conducted to date, the complaints came from a minority of those exposed to the booms. This is not to disparage the seriousness of the sonic boom problem. It could be the Achilles' heel of the supersonic age, but in all probability the boom problem along with the other technological battles will be solved or proved less serious than feared.

Supersonic Safety

SST detractors have made a number of allegations claiming that supersonic flight will take innocent, trusting passengers into uncharted and potentially dangerous areas.

It is true that SST will be invading an environment hitherto never experienced by commercial transports, but to say that the environment cannot be conquered is to libel the dedication and skill of thousands of aeronautical engineers and scientists who say super-

Supersonic transports

sonic flight can be as safe and in some ways even safer than subsonic flight. It should be noted with emphasis that many of the statements now being uttered about the "dubious" safety of the SST are almost identical to the gloomy predictions made about subsonic jets in the 1950's: too big, too complicated, unable to fit into traffic patterns, exposed to unknown and even mysterious dangers.

The subsonics, although they had their growing pains, have turned in a fantastic performance in terms of safety as well as economy. The jet accident rate steadily diminished in the first ten years of jetliner operations. There is little reason for pessimism toward the SST, without discounting the problems that must be overcome before passengers can fly at supersonic speed with the same confidence they now display toward conventional aircraft.

The flight test hours for both the Concorde and Boeing SST will far surpass the average test period of 1,000 hours flight time for a new subsonic jet. The principal reason for the extended test period is that all concerned with supersonic safety recognize the high stakes involved, from financial investment to the trust the public places in commercial aviation. It cannot be repeated too often that *no* SST will be allowed to carry a single paying passenger until designers, government, and airlines are convinced it is a safe plane.

Admittedly, in the past well-tested new airliners have developed unsuspected and sometimes fatal "bugs." The Martin 202, Constellation, DC-6, Comet, and Electra are unfortunate examples. The SST could possibly fall prey to a design weakness not uncovered in the massive test programs. But the scope of the tests and their duration would seem to offer insurance against this happening. And with this in mind, let us examine some of the fears expressed toward the supersonic age.

The Supersonic Environment

Claim: Passengers will be exposed to unknown hazards, for little is known about the environment in which the SST will operate.

Answer: Supersonic flight is far from new. The United States alone has accumulated more than 200,000 hours of experience with military flights surpassing the speed of sound and at least 6,000 hours in flights twice the speed of sound.

Claim: Titanium may be strong, but it is very susceptible to lightning strikes, and the Boeing SST might turn out to be nothing but a flying bomb in a thunderstorm.

Answer: Any metal aircraft is capable of attracting lightning. The SST fuel tanks, however, will have the protection of a gas that makes fuel vapors inert, thus preventing any possible ignition by lightning. To further demonstrate that the titanium SST will be safe from lightning, Boeing ran tests which exposed the metal to four times the number of strikes an SST could be expected to receive in 20 years of service.

Claim: At 70,000 feet, an SST which encounters clear air turbulence (*see*) might as well be ramming a brick wall.

Answer: The high-altitude environment of supersonic travel is not a mysterious wilderness. BAC-Sud and Boeing have been gathering data from high-altitude flights conducted by the U.S. Air Force. These flights have shown turbulence at altitudes between 40,000 and 70,000 feet is one-third less than at lower altitudes. They have also shown that what turbulence is encountered at supersonic levels offers no serious problems of stress. The aircraft used in these experimental flights included the XB-70, SR-71, B-58, and U-2 (*see*). Only the XB-70 pilots reported a rougher than normal ride, and engineers have been studying the XB-70's aerodynamic design to see if the shape of the fuselage, far different from the SST, may have contributed to turbulence discomfort.

Claim: In the thin upper atmosphere of 70,000 feet, SST crews and passengers will be exposed to cosmic radiation (*see*) that exceeds the levels deemed safe for workers in atomic plants. The more frequent exposure of pilots and stewardesses could make them unable to bear children or even result in fatal illness.

Answer: There has been a tremendous amount of research in the field of high-altitude radiation. Air sampling has been going on for years, much of it done with the famed U-2 plane. All available evidence shows that the radiation "menace" not only has been vastly overrated but is almost nonexistent. The U-2 flights revealed that in one year of supersonic flying, a Concorde or Boeing pilot would receive less than one-fifth the permissible annual dose of industrial radiation workers. The chief radiation danger would come from solar flares. However, solar flares occur only once or twice a year at most, and can be predicted far enough in advance to allow rerouting of affected SST flights. The flights could even be operated at lower altitudes for the duration of the flares. Radiation exposure was one of the dire warnings issued concerning subsonic jet travel. Early in the jet age, United Air Lines equipped two DC-8's with special radiation monitoring devices and as a control measure installed the same measuring device

Supersonic transports

at its Chicago headquarters building. It discovered there was almost as much radiation on the ground as in the air. NASA and the U.S. Air Force are currently conducting a new two-year study of upper-atmosphere radiation, the results of which will be applied to SST operations.

Claim: The slightest fuel leak on an SST at cruising altitude would result in an instantaneous and catastrophic explosion, because the fuel would come in immediate contact with the craft's outer skin already heated to as high as 600° F.

Answer: First, Boeing's plan to line the fuel tanks with a special plastic makes them leakproof, and the fuel lines themselves will be heavily insulated. Second, fuel leaking at 70,000 feet cannot ignite, no matter how high the temperature on the fuselage or wing skin. Ignition requires oxygen, and there is too little oxygen at supersonic altitudes to provide an ignition environment. Even if it were possible for fuel to catch fire at 70,000 feet, the result would be "cold ignition," which has no temperature at all.

Supersonic Metals

Claim: Very little is known about the ability of metal to withstand the heat and stresses generated in sustained supersonic operations. Inadequate knowledge makes metal fatigue a very real danger, just as inadequate knowledge caused the failure of the de-Havilland Comet (see), the world's first jetliner, that had a flight life of 1,000 hours.

Answer: The Comet was a victim of aeronautical inexperience, but it taught the priceless lesson of the necessity of making sure that failure of one part will not lead to progressive failure of others. Later models of the Comet and every jetliner built since then have incorporated this *fail-safe* creed into their design. Not only will the SST be no exception, but it will boast a fail-safe concept exceeding that of any transport of the past. The four hydraulic systems on the Boeing is just one example. As for metal fatigue, the Concorde's aluminum alloy has the strength of titanium at speeds below 1,500 mph. Titanium itself is an immensely strong metal, so strong that the severest tests have shown a titanium airframe has an almost unlimited lifespan.

Claim: To make money, the SST must be operated at greater frequency than any previous jet, which may age the airplane to the point of developing unsuspected fatigue problems.

Answer: The SST will make more flights, yes, but due to its greater speed its hours in the air will be no more than current jets. Boeing estimates that its SST will operate about 3,300 hours a year, or about 9.5 hours daily. Daily utilization of the U.S. subsonic jets ranges between 7.5 and 17 hours daily. The frequency of takeoffs and landings for the SST will be less than that of the average subsonic transport, because by its very nature, the SST will be used solely on nonstop flights.

Cabin Pressurization

Claim: If the cabin pressurization on an SST should fail at 70,000 feet, total structural collapse will result. Even the breaking of one window would cause such sudden depressurization that human blood would boil and death would come instantly to all occupants.

Answer: Complete depressurization would result in instant death, but the result would be the same in a subsonic jet flying at 40,000 feet. The SST will have the same structural safety margins as any high-flying aircraft. For example, the loss of a window at 70,000 feet would depressurize the cabin to an equivalent of 13,000 feet, and passengers would be supplied with emergency oxygen masks, just as on present jets.

It might be noted that in the first ten years of subsonic jet operations, there was not a single case of cabin window failure. The record was so good that the FAA actually considered letting the airlines eliminate their emergency oxygen masks. The cabin pressurization and air conditioning system of the SST will have at least triple redundancy (see), including standby ducting in case a primary duct should be blocked somehow. And finally, the structural integrity of the SST will be superior to that of any plane ever built. Boeing alone is putting an SST fuselage through the equivalent of 25 years of pressurization cycles to make certain there will be absolutely no possibility of fatigue failure when the aircraft enters commercial service.

Pilot Training

Claim: Handling a plane as big and fast as the SST will present new and potentially hazardous problems for pilots. Supersonic transport pilots will literally have to learn to fly all over again, which is no minor safety issue.

Answer: In a special program conducted by Lockheed, selected airline pilots have been flying supersonic military planes for several years to get the feel of Mach 2 and faster flights. The airmen's unanimous verdict was that supersonic flight will involve a few new techniques but none that cannot be learned with proper training. All agreed that pilots should have no particular difficulty in making the transition from subsonic jets to the SST, and many said there would be less difficulty than pilots experienced during their shifting from propeller planes to jets.

Traffic Pattern

Claim: It might be impossible to fit the SST into an air traffic control system already overburdened. The supersonic transport gulps fuel like a hungry dinosaur, and serious problems will arise when an SST aircraft is forced to hold over at an airport or is brought down through levels occupied by other planes if it starts running out of fuel.

Answer: The Federal Aviation Administration (FAA) for some time has been running simulated SST flights through its air traffic control system. The FAA verdict was that no special headaches arose. It may be necessary to give the SST a slightly higher approach or landing priority if fuel supply is critical, as would be done with a subsonic aircraft that has reached a critical fuel level, but not to the extent of disrupting normal traffic.

The SST will consume fuel with incredible avarice, and fuel management will be a critical problem in safe and economic operation. A subsonic jet uses about 13,000 gallons of fuel on a typical New York-London flight; the Concorde will require 18,000, and the Boeing SST, 30,000. In present jets, the fuel needed to achieve cruising speed and cruise altitude amounts to roughly 3 per cent of the gross takeoff weight. In the SST, which in climb configuration burns fuel at a rate of 200,000 pounds an hour, the figure rises sharply to 10 per cent.

Temperature may replace winds as the prime factor in SST flight planning, for every two degrees of temperature higher than anticipated could mean as much as 3,000 pounds of additional fuel consumption. The SST will be a *cold-temperature airplane,* that is, it will operate most efficiently at lower temperatures. Winds still will be an important element of flight planning, however; a 50-knot headwind on a 4,000-mile trip would require an extra 3,500 pounds of fuel, or the equivalent of 17 passengers. However, high fuel consumption was expected to be a problem in the early days of the jet age, but the problem was completely solved by careful and judicious planning; the same should be true of the supersonic age.

Robert J. Serling

See also: Commercial airlines, Commercial air transports, High-speed surface transportation, Jumbo jets, Variable geometry

Surface-to-air missiles

Surface-to-air weapons may be classified into two major groups: *antiaircraft weapons* and *antiballistic missiles* (ABM's). A close relative to the ABM, not designated as a separate category because of its limited development, is the *antisatellite missile;* these are designed to attack objects in orbit rather than those on a suborbital trajectory like the ABM.

A number of different types of missiles comprise the antiaircraft group. There is the point defense missile, which may be a very short-range weapon when the point to be defended is a ship, or an intermediate-range weapon when designed to intercept and destroy an attacking aircraft at a considerable distance from the defended point.

ABM systems necessarily carry nuclear warheads; the antiaircraft weapons of the medium-range and long-range variety may have either conventional or nuclear warheads; the short-range types used on shipboard and in the battlefield usually are equipped with high-explosive warheads.

There are two basic types of guidance systems employed by either category: command and homing. A command guidance system is one in which the missile receives course correction radio signals from an external source, usually a computer that receives data from a tracking radar. The most common types of homing systems are radar (*see*), in which the missile homes on the radar image of the target aircraft, and infrared, in which heat emanations from the target airplane, such as engine exhaust, serve as the bull's-eye. A surface-to-air missile (SAM), or ground-to-air missile (GAM), may employ both types of guidance: a command system to direct it to the general target area and a homing device which takes over for the terminal portion of the flight.

Evolution

The surface-to-air missile had its origin in World War II (*see*), when the German high command sought to develop a defensive system more effective

A model of the surface-to-air missile the *Wasserfall* was the first German missile of its type. It was developed at Peenemuende.

These Russian missiles can be launched in a group for destroying several targets simultaneously.

than antiaircraft guns against the high-flying Allied bombers.

Germany developed three types of surface-to-air missiles. The first was *Wasserfall,* 25 feet long and weighing slightly less than 4 tons. It had a range of 30 miles, at which distance it was to be capable of intercepting a bomber flying at 65,000 feet. It carried 200 pounds of explosive in its warhead section and was command guided.

Schmetterling was a smaller missile designed for use at ranges up to 10 miles. It was 13 feet long, and had a 6½-foot wingspan. A proximity fuse set off its 55-pound warhead.

Enzian, a pilotless fighter-type weapon with a 14-foot wingspan, length of 12 feet, and a weight of more than 2 tons, was designed for use against bomber formations rather than single planes. It had a range of 16 miles with an altitude capability of 48,000 feet; it was designed to carry a half-ton of explosive. None of the weapons entered operational service during the war, but all were in advanced stages of testing.

The advent of the high-altitude jet bomber in the postwar years accelerated development of the antiaircraft missile on both sides of the Iron Curtain.

In addition to the U.S. and the U.S.S.R., France and England developed antiaircraft missile systems. ABM development was initiated in the late 1950's but there was no operational deployment until 1967 when the U.S.S.R. began equipping ABM units. In the same year, the U.S. announced planned deployment of a thin ABM defense against possible Chinese ICBM threat of the 1970's.

Soviet SAM's

Less is known about Soviet SAM's than about their other types of missiles; SAM's seem to make less frequent appearances in the Moscow parades, a prime source of information about Soviet weaponry. Among the new weapons is a long-range interceptor SAM with a reported range of several hundred miles and a nuclear warhead; it carries the NATO code name *Kitchen*. Another type, first displayed in the Moscow parade of November, 1967, and not yet code-named, is a battlefield SAM—similar to the U.S. Hawk—with a battery of three missiles with launchers mounted atop a tracked armored vehicle.

In service for several years is the Guideline series. The SA-2 Guideline is more than 30 feet long, about 20 inches in diameter, and powered by both a booster and a sustainer engine. The SA-2 is the type of SAM furnished to North Vietnam by the U.S.S.R. and now deployed there against U.S. aircraft.

American observers report an improved version of the Guideline, the SA-3, which is several feet longer than the SA-2. There is no knowledge of its status or performance.

U.S. SAM's

The primary type of antiaircraft SAM in the U.S. arsenal is the Army's Nike-Hercules. Hercules, which defends major U.S. cities and important military installations, is 41 feet long, 31½ inches in diameter, and weighs 10,000 pounds at launch. It is a two-stage system which employs command guidance and carries either nuclear or conventional warheads. It has a range of 75 nautical miles and a ceiling of 150,000 feet. Its speed is listed only as supersonic (SAM speeds are generally classified information except for "supersonic" or, in the case of the ABM's, "hypersonic"). The weapon is built by Western Electric Co.

A complementary weapon operated by the USAF is the long-range interceptor Bomarc. Bomarc, a winged missile of the "pilotless fighter" variety is boosted to high speed by a 50,000-pound-thrust solid-fueled rocket; then a pair of ramjet engines (*see*) take over propulsion and accelerate the vehicle to more than Mach 2.5. Bomarc is command-guided to the target area; then its own homing system handles terminal guidance. It has a range of well over 400 nautical miles and a ceiling above 70,000 feet. Bomarc is manufactured by the Boeing Co.

For use with the field Army, the U.S. has a number of specialized SAM's. Among them are:

Hawk, which is used by the U.S. Marine Corps and five NATO (*see*) nations as well as the U.S. Army. Designed primarily for use against low-flying airplanes, Hawk is effective from treetop level to more than 50,000 feet and up to 20 miles range. It is guided by a radar homing system, and its warhead is conventional. Built by Raytheon Co., the missile is 16½ feet long, 4 feet in diameter at the widest point of its small delta wing, and weighs 1,275 pounds. Hawk is fired from a mobile launcher.

Chaparral, designed for even greater mobility to insure rapid deployment where needed, can be mounted on a variety of Army vehicles, primarily the M730 armored vehicle which has a turret mount of four missiles. The missile itself is a surface-to-air adaptation of the air-to-air Sidewinder. Built by Aeronutronic Division of Philco-Ford, it employs Sidewinder's heat-seeking homing guidance system.

The Nike-Hercules is used to intercept high-performance aircraft and has also proved successful against short-range ballistic missiles.

The Bomarc, being launched vertically, is an interceptor missile used by both the USAF Air Defense Command and the Royal Canadian Air Force.

The Hawk *(left)* is an antiaircraft missile utilizing a radar homing device. The Talos *(right)* has a long range system with both surface-to-air and surface-to-surface capabilities.

Redeye, smallest of the SAM's, is only 4 feet long, 3 inches in diameter, and 28 pounds in weight. Redeye is designed to give the individual infantryman a defensive weapon against low-flying aircraft. Carried in a back-pack, it is shoulder-fired from a bazooka tube; the gunner aims visually and an infrared heat-seeking guidance system takes over in flight. General Dynamics Corp, is manufacturer.

The three basic types of SAM's arming U.S. Navy ships are Tartar, Advanced Terrier, and Talos.

Tartar is a short-range (10 miles) weapon which arms 23 destroyers and three cruisers. A homing system guides the solid-propelled weapon. Built by General Dynamics, it is 15 feet long, 1 foot in diameter, weighs 1,500 pounds, and has a conventional warhead.

Advanced Terrier, manufactured by the same company, is the primary armament of 40 ships. A two-stage solid-fuel rocket, it has a separate booster for initial acceleration and a sustainer motor. It is 27 feet long (with booster) and weighs 2,600 pounds. It has a homing guidance system, a conventional warhead, and a range of 10 miles.

Talos is the long-range member of the Navy trio, designed for operation as much as 65 nautical miles from the launching ship. Talos has a solid-fuel booster for initial acceleration: then a 40,000-pound-thrust ramjet engine powers it to the target.

The Army's antiballistic missile, the Spartan *(right),* is used for long-range interception. The British Sea Dart *(far right),* a fully guided missile, also has surface-to-surface capabilities. The Chaparral *(opposite page),* designed for mobility, is one of the systems selected by the U.S. Army for low-altitude defense. Preparing the missile for launching takes but a matter of minutes.

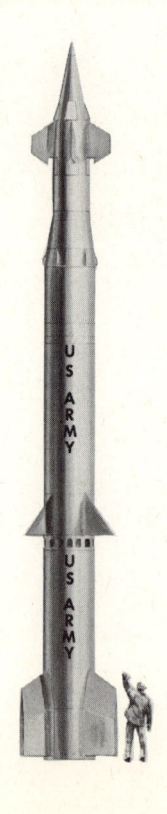

Surface-to-air missiles

Operating on seven cruisers and three destroyer escorts, it has a beam rider/radar homing type of guidance. Built by the Bendix Corp., Talos is 20 feet long, 30 inches in diameter, and weighs over 3,000 pounds.

Designed to replace both Tartar and Terrier in a standardized shipboard missile system is *Standard,* now in advanced development. Standard comes in two versions, the ER (Extended Range) and MR (Medium Range); the actual ranges have not been disclosed. The basic missile, the MR, is 15 feet long; the ER, which has a booster, is 27 feet long. Built by General Dynamics, Standard has homing guidance.

Another Navy developmental missile is the *Sea Sparrow,* also known as Point Defense Surface Missile System. Built by Raytheon Co., the weapon is 12 feet long, has a maximum diameter of 8 inches, and weighs 400 pounds; it has homing guidance.

In development for the Army is SAM-D, a field Army defense system against both aircraft and battlefield missiles, to be deployed in the 1970's. Raytheon has been named prime contractor. Few details have been released, but SAM-D is to be a single-stage, solid-fueled, highly mobile missile with radar homing guidance.

The U.S. ABM system scheduled for deployment, called *Sentinel* and managed by Western Electric Co., includes two complementary missiles backed by a variety of radars, computers (*see*), and other ground equipment. The radars track the incoming attacker and attempt to discriminate between actual warheads and decoys. Once the defensive weapon is launched, the radars track it also and provide the computer with information as to the relative paths of target and defender. Correction signals are sent automatically to the ABM.

For interception at long ranges, when the attacking missile is still in space, the Sentinel system employs the Spartan missile, built by Western Electric and McDonnell Douglas Corp. *Spartan,* an advanced development of the weapon once known as Nike-Zeus, is 50 feet long, has a diameter of 3 feet, and is 10 feet wide across the fins at the base of its lower stage. Spartan has three stages, all solid-propelled; its launch weight is approximately 25,000 pounds. It can intercept at distances up to 400 nautical miles and carries a nuclear warhead.

Attacking ICBM's that may elude the primary Spartan defenses are attacked by *Sprint,* the high-acceleration member of the team. Sprint gets off to a fast start by being "popped" out of its launch cell rather than being flown out under its own power; a gas generator under the missile ejects it like a dart from a blowgun. As soon as the missile is above ground, its own booster ignites and pushes the weapon to hypersonic speed. Sprint's rapid reaction and its ability to intercept at low altitudes (around 100,000 feet) gives the radars additional time for precise tracking and decoy discrimination.

PRIME U.S. SURFACE-TO-AIR MISSILES 1968

Name	Designation	Military Branch	Prime Contractor	Max. Length, Feet	Body Diameter, Feet	Launch Weight, Pounds	Guidance	Remarks
Bomarc B	CIM-10B	USAF	Boeing	45.0	2.92	16,000	Active homing radar	Boosted by Thiokol 50,000 lbs. thrust, M-51, spr. motor
Chaparral	MIM-72A	Army	Philco-Ford	9.5	0.42	185	Infrared	Version of Sidewinder 1C mounted on tracked vehicle
Hawk	MIM-23A	Army	Raytheon	16.8	1.2	1,275	Semiactive homing radar	Improved version being tested; will have larger warhead and different motor
Redeye	FIM-43A	Army	General-Dynamics	4.0	0.25	20	Infrared homing	Fired from bazooka launcher; USMC also uses Redeye
Talos	RIM-8G	USN	Bendix	33.0	2.5	7,000	Beam-rider semi-active homing	RGM-811 is surface-to-surface version of RIM-8G
Tartar	RIM-24B	USN	General-Dynamics	15.0	1.1	1,425	Semi-active homing	Dual-thrust rocket motor

Sprint, built by Martin Marietta Corp., is a cone-shaped weapon with two stages, both solid-propelled; it is nuclear-tipped. It is 27 feet long and 4.5 feet in diameter at its base.

In quasioperational status and advanced development are two U.S. antisatellite systems—one being developed by the Army, the other by the USAF. Two batteries are maintained at Johnston Island in the Pacific and intercepts have been made at distances described as "hundreds of miles." The Army system is based upon the Nike-Zeus, modified to include a terminal stage, while the USAF weapon is a Thor-Agena similarly modified. Most details are classified, but presumably the weapons carry nuclear warheads and are command-guided to space; both have infrared terminal guidance systems.

James J. Haggerty

See also: Air-to-air missiles, Air-to-surface missiles, Antiaircraft weapons, Launch vehicles, Missiles, Surface-to-surface missiles

Surface-to-surface missiles

The surface-to-surface missile category includes two launching areas. One is that of launching weapons at ground targets from land emplacements. The other area is the flexible-range sea-launched ballistic missiles. These missiles are usually fired from below the surface.

Surface-to-surface missiles are of three basic types: *long range ballistic missiles,* which include the intercontinental ballistic missiles (ICBM) (*see*) and the sea-launched fleet ballistic missiles; the mobile *field ballistic missile;* and the mobile, *flat trajectory antiarmor weapon.* There are, in addition to these groupings, certain surface-to-surface *special purpose missiles.*

Modern ICBM's are generally capable of traveling about 7,000 miles, and they are all inertially guided. These missiles are emplaced in underground silos (*see*)—steel-and-concrete cylinders which serve as launch pad and work stand; catwalks permit access to the various work levels. The silo also includes a battery of electronic checkout equipment for the never-ending readiness checks of the missile.

Quick reaction time is a must for the ICBM. It must be ready for launch within a minute of alert, and some ICBM's can be fired in as little as 32 seconds. Such rapid response precludes use of the boil-away type of propellants such as liquid oxygen (*see*) used in early long-range missiles. Most ICBM's are powered by solid propellants that can be stored indefinitely without service; the remainder use storable liquid propellants.

The nuclear or thermonuclear warhead that separates from the booster stages is contained in a re-entry vehicle to protect it against friction heating. Inertial guidance systems (*see*) are preprogrammed to direct the missile to a given target. Guidance is accomplished during the boost phase, and the standard re-entry vehicle is unguided. The exception is a new type of system, the maneuverable re-entry vehicle. This vehicle is capable of changing its course, then reverting to the original target trajectory. A penetration aid such as this was necessary because of the advances made in missile defense. Another advanced system, just coming into being and also maneuverable, is the MIRV (Multiple Independent Re-entry Vehicle) in which a single booster carries several warheads. These proceed independently to different impact points after separation.

The field ballistic missile, a support weapon for the advance of ground armies, is a superartillery weapon with range up to 500 miles. Within this category there are several types of missiles ranging from small, single-stage, short-range, unguided weapons carrying a high explosive charge to multi-

Surface-to-surface missiles

stage, inertially guided, nuclear-warhead missiles. They share two major requirements: ease of maintenance under field conditions, and mobility. They are moved with the army by wheeled or tracked vehicles which include a transporter, a launcher, erector, leveling system and electronic checkout, and fire control equipment. The larger weapons may require several vehicles. Practically all field ballistic missiles are solid-propelled, but there is one type in service in the U.S. that has storable, liquid propellants.

The flat trajectory antiarmor group of weapons features solid propellants for ease of handling and a variety of different guidance systems. Designed primarily for use against tanks and armored vehicles, these small weapons are also employed against troops and fortifications. Short-range weapons, they normally have conventional high-explosive warheads. Some of these weapons, like artillery rounds, are carried by the launching vehicle, such as a tank. Others are mounted on jeeps or lightweight trucks, and some are small enough to be man-handled.

An example of the special purpose weapon which does not fit into any of the basic categories is the U.S. Army battlefield missile, Davy Crockett. A short-range weapon for support of ground troops, it has a low-yield (fraction of a kiloton) nuclear warhead. It is fired from a bazooka-type launcher. Another special type is the USAF's Mace, an air-breathing weapon, boosted by a rocket, but sustained in flight for a 650-mile range by a turbojet engine. The pilotless bomber, used in tactical warfare, carries either a conventional or nuclear warhead.

Soviet Surface-To-Surface Missiles

Aside from the U.S., only the U.S.S.R. has developed a full range of all types of surface-to-surface missiles. Although the U.S.S.R. provides few details, the annual missile parades celebrating the Bolshevik Anniversary offer a general view of U.S.S.R. capability. In general, the Russians have developed several missiles in each of the three basic categories, many of them strikingly similar to their American counterparts.

The most spectacular of the Soviet weapons is the Fractional Orbital Bombardment System, an ICBM capable of bypassing U.S.-Canadian defenses in the north by flying around the opposite pole, like a suborbital spacecraft. It could, however, be detected by U.S. over-the-horizon radars scheduled for early operational deployment (U.S. observers estimated early operational status for the FOBS in 1968). The booster paraded in Red Square is a new version of the ICBM NATO code-named *Scrag*, a three-stage missile. The FOBS re-entry vehicle is about 6½ feet long and 4 feet wide. U.S. officials tended to discount the effectiveness of Scrag FOBS because the longer distance south polar route imposes penalties of reduced accuracy and payload.

Whether the Russians have deployed solid-propelled ICBM's in significant numbers is not known. One type, designated Sarage, a three-stage solid, is believed to be in production but whether they have solid fuels or storable liquids, Soviet missiles apparently have quick reaction time. In a late 1967 interview published in the U.S.S.R., Col. Gen. Vladimir F. Tolubko, deputy commander of Soviet Strategic Rocket Forces, stated that the U.S.S.R. has operational, silo-based missiles capable of launch in less than a minute, with volley capability of simultaneous launch of a number of weapons. Tolubko also claimed that the Soviets can launch ICBM's from mobile complexes.

The newest Soviet ICBM paraded in Moscow is not a solid rocket. Designated SS-9, it is a massive, multimegaton warhead weapon estimated at 120 feet long and about 7 feet wide. Termed a "city buster," it is a two-stage liquid-fueled missile with the basic stage powered by a cluster of seven engines. The weapon is being widely deployed and is in continuing production.

The Soviets have also developed the sea-launched fleet ballistic missile. On display for some time has been *Serb*, a single-stage solid-fueled sub-launched ballistic missile. It is roughly comparable in dimension to the U.S. Navy's Polaris A-3 (30 feet) though believed to have lesser range, probably about 1,000 miles. In 1967, the U.S.S.R. introduced a new sub-launched weapon about the same size as Serb but with improvements for an estimated range of 1,800 miles.

Although the U.S. has retired its Intermediate Range Ballistic Missiles (there were two with ranges of about 1,500 miles), the U.S.S.R. continues to deploy this type of weapon as a threat against attack from Western Europe. The Russians apparently have several different types, all solid-fueled and all mobile, with ranges upward of 1,000 miles. A new model displayed in 1967 was a two-stage solid.

In addition, the U.S.S.R. has several types of mobile field ballistic missiles. A typical one, displayed in 1967, is *Scud*, a 38-foot-long weapon with a reported range of 450-500 miles. One liquid-fuel type, code-named *Sandal* with a 500-mile range, may still be operational. The Russians have a variety of small antiarmor/troop missiles.

Surface-to-surface missiles

International Missile Systems

The United Kingdom attempted development of an IRBM called *Blue Streak,* but canceled the project and converted the development to a space booster. Aside from the U.S. and U.S.S.R., France is the only nation developing ballistic missiles, and France is confining that effort to the medium-range category, not ICBM's. The French have exhibited an MSBS sub-launched missile and a two-stage, land-based ballistic missile. Their major project is the *Pluton* tactical missile with a nuclear warhead, scheduled for 1969 launch.

France is a major developer of the antiarmor type of weapon, having produced several different types. Two of them, the *Entac* and *SS-11,* are in service with the U.S. Army as well as French forces.

Several other nations have produced surface-to-surface weapons, all of them in the small, nonballistic categories. Nations with their own antiarmor systems include the United Kingdom, Australia, Germany, Italy, Japan, Sweden, and Switzerland. Egypt was reportedly developing short-range battlefield missiles in the early sixties, but there has been no recent word of them.

U.S. Surface-To-Surface Missiles

The U.S. operates a wide variety of surface-to-surface weapons. They include:

Minuteman, ICBM, built by the Boeing Co. with propulsion provided by Thiokol, Aerojet-General, and Hercules Inc. Minuteman is a three-stage missile with all stages solid-fueled. Primary operational model is Minuteman II (Minuteman I being withdrawn from service). Small as ICBM's go, Minuteman II is 59.8 feet tall and weighs 70,000 pounds, but it can hurl a thermonuclear warhead more than 7,000 nautical miles. The authorized force of Minuteman ICBM's operated by the USAF is 1,000 missiles, all silo-based. Minuteman III, in advanced development, will have improved penetration aids, including a maneuverable re-entry vehicle and a multiple warhead system.

Titan II, ICBM, built by Martin Marietta Corp. and powered by Aerojet-General engines. Although a liquid-propellant missile, Titan II is still maintained by the USAF. It is silo-based and its propellants are storable and hypergolic (Aerozine-50 fuel and nitrogen tetroxide oxidizer). The nuclear-warhead missile is a two-stage weapon with 430,000 pounds of thrust in its basic stage and 100,000 pounds in the upper stage. It is 103 feet long and has a liftoff weight of 330,000 pounds. Range is 6,300 nautical miles. USAF strength is 54 missiles, three squadrons operating 18 each.

Polaris, FBM, built by Lockheed Missiles and Space Co. with Aerojet-General and Hercules Inc. supplying motors. Polaris is a two-stage, solid-propelled, submarine-launched ballistic missile built in three versions: the A-1, with a range of 1,200 nautical miles; A-2, 1,500 miles; and A-3, 2,500 miles. The A-1 has been retired from service and the planned interim mix is 28 A-3 submarines and 13 A-2 subs (each sub carries 16 missiles). Launched while the submarine is submerged, Polaris is 31 feet long and weighs about 30,000 pounds.

Poseidon, FBM, Lockheed-built with first-stage propulsion by Hercules/Thiokol and second-stage by Hercules. In advanced development, Poseidon was scheduled for first firing in the summer of 1968. The missile is essentially an advanced version of Polaris—larger and with a 500-1,000 mile range improvement. Poseidon, 34 feet tall and 6 feet wide, is able to fit into the same sub tubes as Polaris. It is described by the Navy as "eight times as effective as Polaris"; it has twice the payload and twice the accuracy of the A-3. Poseidon is planned for operational service starting in 1970; initial mix is expected to be about 50 to 60 per cent Poseidon, the rest A-3 Polaris.

Pershing, built by Martin Marietta Corp., is the longest-ranging of the U.S. field ballistic missiles. It is a two-stage missile which carries a nuclear warhead, it is 34½ feet tall, 3.3 feet in diameter, and weighs about 10,000 pounds. Both stages are solid-propelled, and the weapon has a range capability up to 400 miles. The missile is transported on a unique erector-launcher which contains its own launch pad and leveling jacks and raises the missile to firing position; three other vehicles haul the necessary ground support and firing equipment.

Sergeant, field ballistic missile, built by UNIVAC division of Sperry-Rand Corp., is a complementary weapon to Pershing and is for use at shorter ranges (about 100 miles). Inertially guided, it is 35 feet long, 31 inches in diameter, and weighs 10,000 pounds; it is a single-stage solid-propelled weapon carrying a nuclear warhead. It is transported in a manner similar to Pershing and it features utmost simplicity of operation and maintenance.

Honest John (McDonnell Douglas/Emerson Electric) and *Little John* (Emerson Electric) are a pair of short-range battlefield ballistic missiles which carry either conventional or nuclear warheads. Designed to supplement heavy artillery in airborne divisions, they are airplane and helicopter transportable. The larger of the two, Honest John is 24.8 feet long, 30 inches in diameter, and weighs 4,500

Little John *(left)* was designed to supplement heavy artillery in airborne divisions. The Lance *(right)* will eventually replace Little John. Both are capable of carrying nuclear warheads.

pounds (a later version weighs more than 5,000 pounds). Basic range is 12 miles, but the advanced version is capable of 20 miles. The 800-pound Little John has a 10-mile range.

Lance, built by LTV Aerospace Corp., is a new field ballistic missile in the short-range category, eventual replacement for Sergeant, Honest John, and Little John; it was scheduled to go into production in 1968. Nuclear-warheaded, Lance is a single-stage weapon powered by prepackaged storable liquid propellants. A division support weapon, it has a range of about 50 miles; in development is an Extended Range Lance capable of close to 100 miles. Lance features high mobility and is carried on a transporter-loader pulled by a prime mover. Other ground support equipment includes a self-propelled lightweight launcher and an electronic truck containing prefire test and fire control equipment. In addition to the Army version, the Department of Defense *(see)* was investigating the possibility of a Navy-adapted ship-to-shore ballistic missile.

Shillelagh, antiarmor missile, built by Aeronutronic Division of Philco-Ford Corp. A very small weapon, Shillelagh is handled in the field with the ease of a conventional round of artillery ammunition. Its command guidance system provides extreme accuracy against either stationary or moving targets and it has a high "first round kill" probability. The missile is standard armament on the Army's General Sheridan armored reconnaissance vehicle. It is being adapted to the M60 main battle tank and to the U.S./Federal Republic of Germany Main Battle Tank which will become operational in the seventies. Shillelagh has a small solid-propellant powerplant and it is interchangeable with conventional rounds of ammunition.

The Shillelagh *(below* and *right)* is fired from a combination gun/launcher and guided to its target by the tank gunner. The Shillelagh System includes both the guided missile and conventional ammunition fired from the 152mm gun.

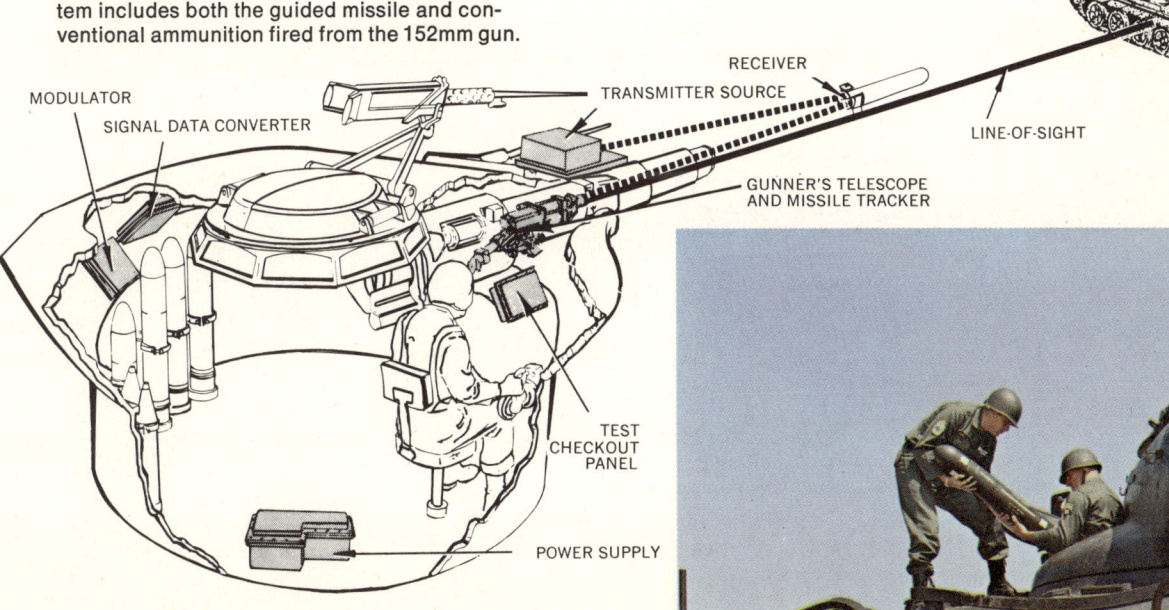

Surface-to-surface missiles

The Mace, a swept-wing missile, has a length of 44 feet. Mace can be fired from either a truck-drawn launcher or from underground bases.

TOW, a supersonic missile, gets its name from Tube-launched, Optically-tracked, Wire-guided.

TOW, antiarmor missile, built by Hughes Aircraft Co., is a 160-pound, solid-propelled weapon designed specifically for use against tanks. Although a number of short-range weapons have employed wire-guidance, TOW is the first supersonic missile to be so guided. It gets its name from the fact that it is *T*ube-launched, *O*ptically-tracked, *W*ire-guided. In firing, the gunner aligns the crosshairs of his telescopic sight on the target, fires the missile, and keeps the crosshairs aligned during flight. Signals transmitted through a two-wire link, which unreels as the missile flies, correct the weapon's course. The system eliminates the need for estimating range to the target, speed of a moving target, and angle between target course and weapon. TOW can be carried by troops and fired from a simple lightweight launcher mounted on a tripod. It can also be mounted on a variety of small Army ground vehicles. TOW was scheduled for 1968 production and service introduction and contemplated for advanced development was a modified system for firing from helicopters.

Dragon, antiarmor missile, formerly known as MAW (Medium Antitank Weapon), built by McDonnell Douglas Corp. Designed for use by the individual infantryman, Dragon is a small (27 pounds) missile, shoulder-fired from a bazooka-like launcher. It employs a guidance system similar to that of TOW; the gunner maintains sighting through a telescope and course-change signals are automatically transmitted to the missile through unreeling wires. The missile has tiny side thrusters which apply the control forces. With a maximum range of about 1,500 yards, Dragon has a warhead big enough to knock out most infantry targets; it is superior in range, accuracy, and first-round kill probability to the 90mm recoilless rifle it will replace.

James J. Haggerty

See also: Air-to-air missiles, Air-to-surface missiles, Launch vehicles, Missiles, Polaris missiles, Surface-to-air missiles

PRIME U.S. SURFACE-TO-SURFACE MISSILES 1968

Name	Designation	Military Branch	Prime Contractor	Max. Length, Feet	Body Diameter, Feet	Launch Weight, Pounds	Guidance	Remarks
Poseidon	ZUGM-73A	USN	Lockheed	34	6	60,000	Inertial	Will have double Polaris A-3 payload and twice the accuracy
Titan	LGM-25C	USAF	AFSC/SAMSO/TRW	103	10.0	330,000	Inertial	GE Mk. 6 re-entry system; underground silo launch
Lance	XMGM-52A	Army	Ling-Temco-Vought	20	1.8	3,200	Simplified inertial	Replacement for Honest John; nuclear or conventional warhead
Dragon	XM-47	Army	McDonnell-Douglas	—	—	14	Command	Medium assualt weapon was formerly called MAW and will replace 90mm recoilless rifle
Pershing	MGM-31A	Army	Martin Marietta	34.6	3.3	10,000	Inertial	Variable range nuclear warhead; 1-A version under development
Sergeant	MGM-29A	Army	Sperry Rand	34.5	2.6	10,000	Inertial	Nuclear or conventional warhead
Shillelagh	XMGM-51B	Army	Philco-Ford	3.8	0.5	60	Command/IR	An antitank missile fired by 152 mm gun/launcher

The deployed Surveyor *(left)* as it would look on the moon. Before launching, Surveyor was raised into a large space chamber *(right)* and thoroughly tested under simulated lunar conditions.

Surveyor

Preparing the way for Apollo astronauts

In 1960, the United States undertook the Surveyor program, two years after its first satellite orbited the Earth. The first satellite, Explorer I, weighed only 31 lbs. and carried one scientific experiment. Surveyor was planned to weigh more than one ton, to make a soft landing on the moon and to make complex studies of the lunar surface.

The Surveyor program was undertaken by the National Aeronautics and Space Administration (NASA) *(see)* which had been established in 1958. To launch Surveyor from Earth, NASA chose a new launch vehicle still in the design stage, the Atlas-Centaur. It was to be the first U.S. launch vehicle to use liquid hydrogen to fuel its second stage.

The technology required to design, manufacture, and test the Atlas-Centaur and Surveyor was far more advanced than any used to that time in the U.S. The six-year development effort that followed was one of the most difficult ever undertaken by NASA.

The ultimate success of Surveyor became crucial in 1961 when President John F. Kennedy declared that it was a U.S. national goal to land men on the moon and return them to Earth before the end of the decade. Before the Apollo manned lunar landing program could begin, unmanned Surveyors would have to show that a soft landing could be made on the moon and that the lunar surface was safe for man.

Surveyor

The Surveyor Team

In 1961, NASA assembled the team to accept this challenge. It selected one of its field centers, the Jet Propulsion Laboratory (*see*) in Pasadena, California, to manage the Surveyor project and another, the Lewis Research Center (*see*) in Cleveland, Ohio, to manage the Atlas-Centaur.

On March 1, 1961, NASA awarded a contract to the Hughes Aircraft Company to build seven Surveyors. Hughes selected hundreds of other companies to make the thousands of parts needed for each spacecraft. Under direction of the Lewis Center, Atlas-Centaur was built by the Convair division of General Dynamics.

The Surveyor Spacecraft

Surveyor weighed 2,200 lbs. and was awkward in appearance. It was 10 feet high, and the 3 landing legs at its base would fit inside a 14-foot circle. Its aluminum frame was triangular and weighed only 60 lbs. The three legs with their shock-absorbing feet extended from the corners of the frame. Large blocks of a crushable metal honeycomb were attached to the bottom to cushion the lunar landing.

Two flat panels were mounted on a vertical mast rising from the top of the frame. One was covered with solar cells (*see*) to convert sunlight into electricity to operate Surveyor. The other was a high-gain radio antenna which could concentrate its radio beam in a single direction. The mast and panels were movable by radio command so that the solar panel was aimed at the sun, and the high-gain antenna at receiving stations on the Earth.

Two more antennas were mounted on booms which folded out from the spacecraft like arms. These were called *omnidirectional antennas* because they could radiate radio signals in all directions. They were also used to receive Earth radio commands.

Two compartments, fastened to the sides of the frame, carried electronic equipment such as radio transmitters and receivers, batteries, and equipment

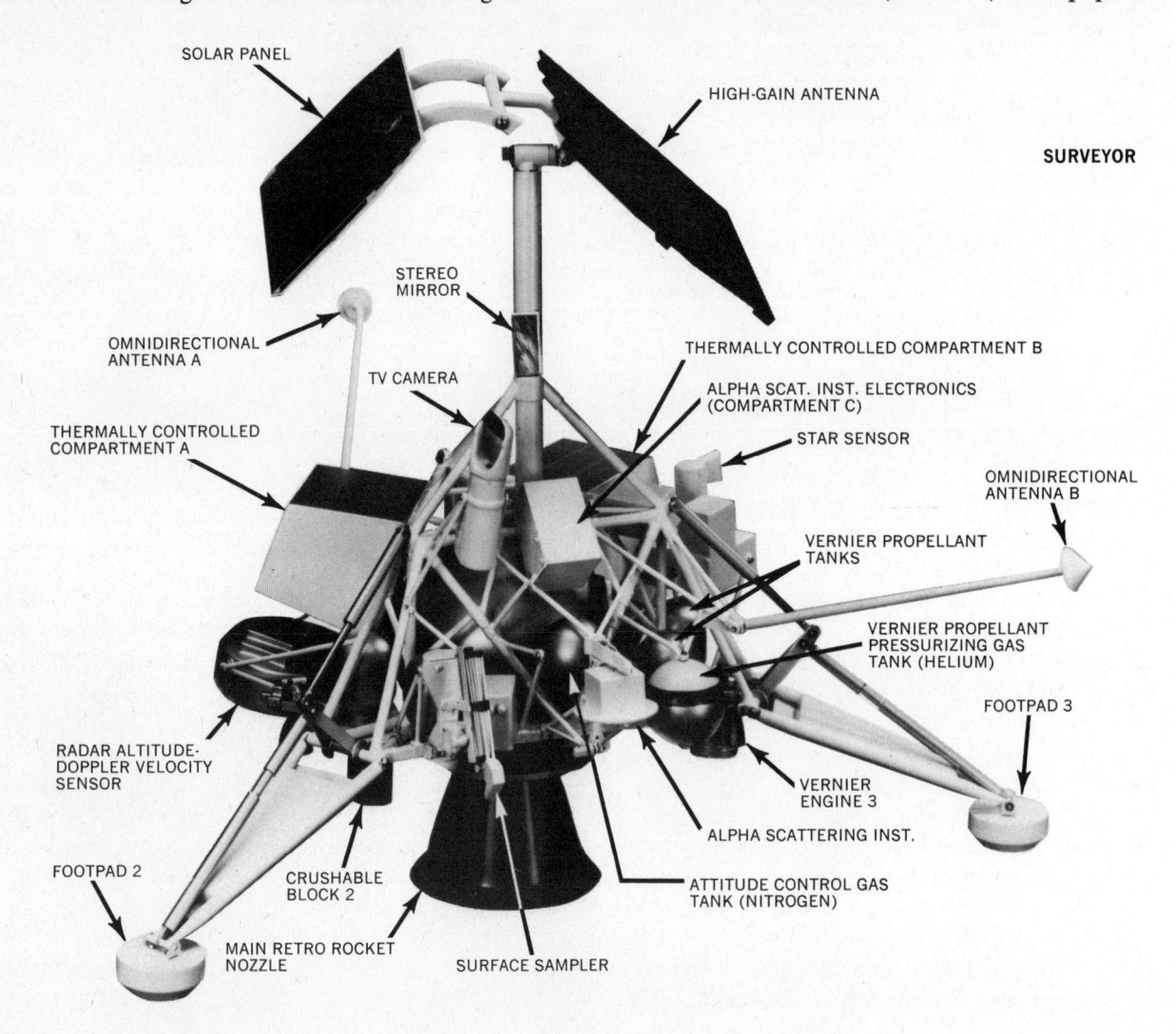

SURVEYOR

to decode radio commands from the Earth. Tiny sensors located inside Surveyor constantly measured temperatures, pressures, electric voltages, and switch positions. This stream of information, called *telemetry* (see), was radioed to Earth so engineers always knew the exact condition of the spacecraft.

Surveyor carried two kinds of rockets. A large round rocket, called the *braking* or *retrorocket* because it slowed the spacecraft for the lunar landing, was fitted inside the triangular frame. Filled with rubbery solid propellant, it made up about 60 per cent of the total spacecraft weight.

Around the retrorocket were mounted three small, liquid fuel rockets called *vernier engines*. These were used to make a trajectory change in space, called the *midcourse maneuver,* and for final descent to the moon. The chemicals burned by the engines were *hypergolic,* which means they burned on contact with each other, eliminating the need for an ignition system. The thrust of each engine could be throttled like a motor in a car so that it could fire in a range from 30 to 104 lbs. of thrust.

The most complicated system on Surveyor was called the *flight control system*. It determined Surveyor's exact orientation in space and changed the orientation when commanded by engineers on the Earth. When cruising in space, the spacecraft used sensors similar to photoelectric cells to locate the sun and the star Canopus in the Southern Hemisphere. When the sun sensor, for instance, lost sight of the sun, it ordered small nitrogen gas jets to thrust, rolling Surveyor in space until the sensor again saw the sun. During maneuvers when the sensors could not be used, gyroscopes inside the spacecraft kept track of every movement of Surveyor and ordered the gas jets to fire when a new position was desired. The gyros also were used to aim Surveyor in the desired direction to fire the vernier engines for the midcourse maneuver.

For the descent to the moon, four radars sent beams to the lunar surface to determine Surveyor's altitude above the moon and its speed of approach. They determined the time to fire the retrorocket and vernier engines in order to brake and stabilize Surveyor during the descent.

On the Earth, Surveyor weighed about 2,200 lbs. After landing on the moon it weighed only about 600 lbs. because the burned out retrorocket had been dropped and liquid rocket fuel and nitrogen for the gas jets had been used up.

Scientific Equipment

Three kinds of scientific instruments were carried to the moon by the several Surveyors. A television

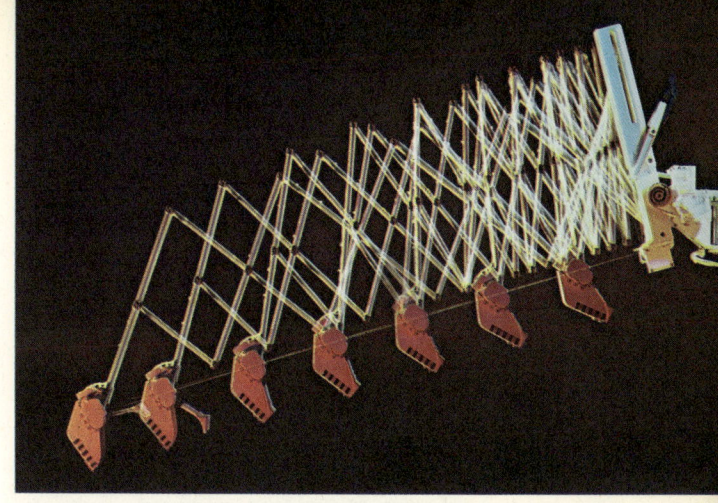

A *hand,* known as a *soil mechanics surface sampler,* was aboard Surveyor IV to scoop up soil and place it on the footpad for close-up photos.

camera, carried by all seven spacecraft, was mounted on top of the triangular frame looking straight up into a mirror which was shifted in order that pictures could be taken all around the spacecraft, and from its feet out to the horizon. Commands from the Earth aimed the camera, focused it, and adjusted it to lunar lighting conditions. The camera could radio to Earth one 600-scan line still picture every 3½ seconds. (A home TV set shows a 525-scan line picture.)

A surface sampler was flown on Surveyors III and VII, a small scoop mounted on a scissor arm that could be extended as far as 5 feet from the spacecraft. As the scoop pressed the lunar surface, or dug small trenches, the results were photographed by the TV camera, and the strain on small electric motors operating the scoop indicated the hardness of the lunar surface.

Carried on Surveyors V, VI, VII was an Alpha

Surveyor V carried the first in a series of alpha scattering instruments which study the chemical characteristics of the lunar soil.

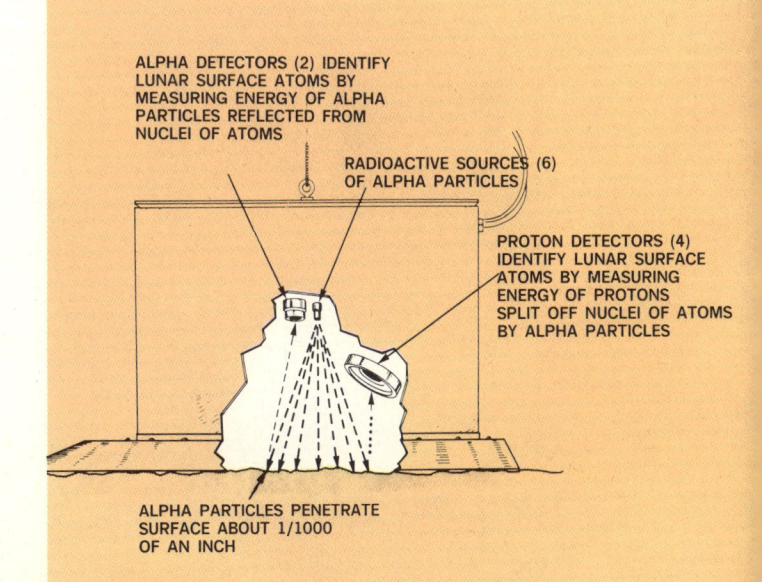

ALPHA DETECTORS (2) IDENTIFY LUNAR SURFACE ATOMS BY MEASURING ENERGY OF ALPHA PARTICLES REFLECTED FROM NUCLEI OF ATOMS

RADIOACTIVE SOURCES (6) OF ALPHA PARTICLES

PROTON DETECTORS (4) IDENTIFY LUNAR SURFACE ATOMS BY MEASURING ENERGY OF PROTONS SPLIT OFF NUCLEI OF ATOMS BY ALPHA PARTICLES

ALPHA PARTICLES PENETRATE SURFACE ABOUT 1/1000 OF AN INCH

The alpha scattering instrument *(above)* was aboard Surveyor V which landed in the eastern portion of the moon and returned photographs *(below)* and lunar soil data. The mechanism was deployed to the moon's surface by ground command.

scattering instrument to make a chemical analysis of the lunar surface. Inside a small box which was lowered to the moon was a radioactive source of Alpha particles. They were beamed at the lunar surface, and detectors in the box analyzed the particles reflected back. The nature of the reflected particles indicated that they had encountered specific elements such as oxygen, silicon, sodium, or magnesium on the lunar surface.

Getting Ready for Launch

When the Hughes Aircraft Co. began work on building seven Surveyors in 1961, it was hoped that the first could be launched in 1963. As Hughes began to assemble ground test spacecraft, an intense testing program got under way. There is no way to repair an unmanned spacecraft after it has been launched, so every part had to be perfect. Test spacecraft were vibrated, shaken, baked, and chilled to imitate conditions that Surveyors would face during flight and on the moon.

There were many test failures and each one was corrected by redesign or replacement with an improved part. The 1963 launch date slipped into 1964 and then 1965 as the work went on. The long development and testing program ended in early 1966 when the first Surveyor was shipped to Cape Kennedy, Florida, and placed on top of an Atlas-Centaur rocket, now proved after seven test launches.

A launch date of May 30 was chosen by trajectory engineers. A launch to the moon can be made only on certain days of a month when the moon is favorably positioned with the Earth in order for a lunar landing to be made near dawn of the moon's day, which lasts an equivalent of 14 days on the Earth.

At the Jet Propulsion Laboratory, a control center was manned by 300 engineers and technicians who would guide Surveyor to the moon. Three tracking stations were to be used for the mission: Goldstone, in California's Mojave desert; Johannesburg, South Africa; and Canberra, Australia. Each station was equipped with an antenna 85 feet in diameter to hear Surveyor's signals from space.

Surveyor Flight to the Moon

A final 12-hour countdown was perfect, and at 10:41 a.m. EDT, May 30, the Atlas-Centaur lifted off its pad only one second off schedule.

After burning four minutes, the Atlas first stage cut off and dropped off at an altitude of 98 miles. The nose cone surrounding Surveyor was jettisoned. The Centaur stage burned for seven minutes. At an altitude of 111 miles and 2,200 miles from Cape

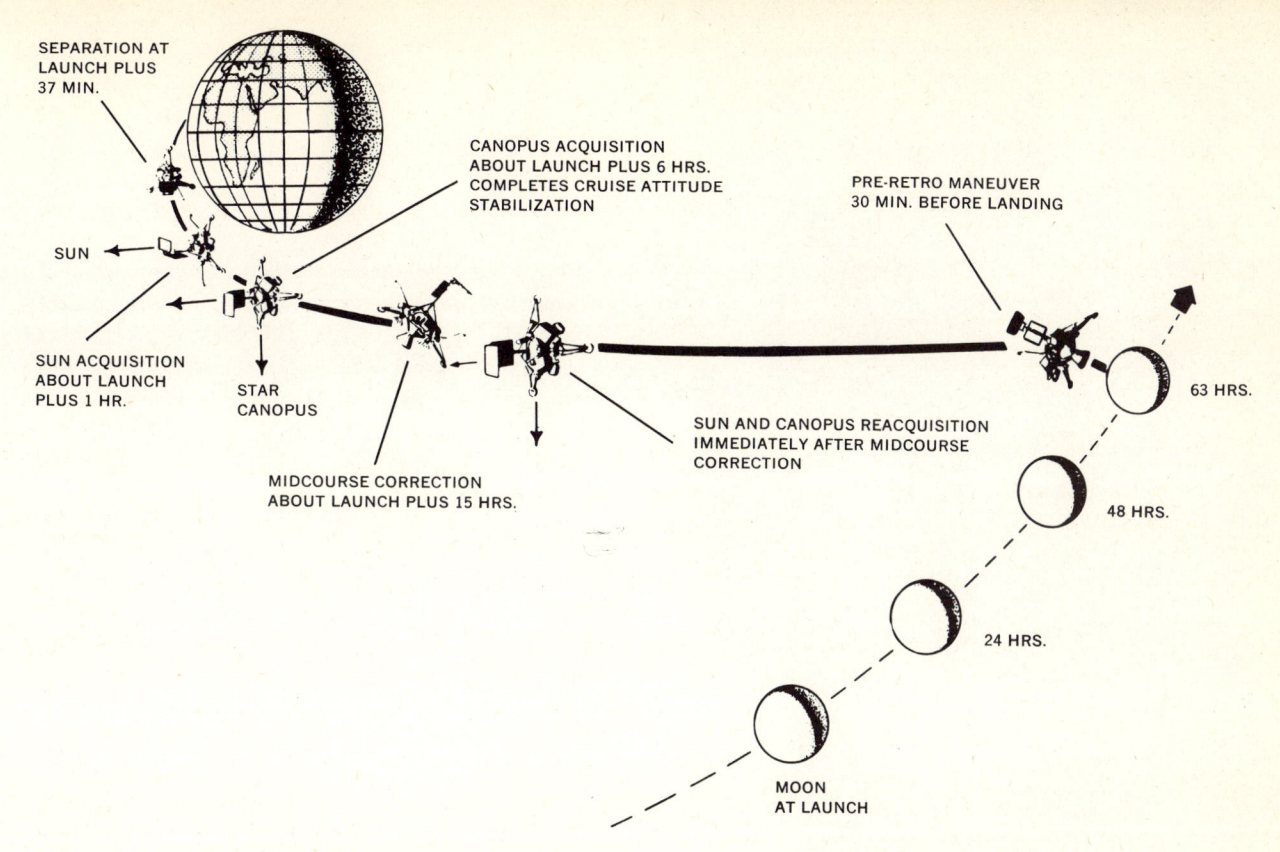

The flight profile of the Surveyor missions, five of which achieved soft landings on the moon.

Kennedy, the Centaur dropped off and Surveyor was alone, traveling at 23,500 mph.

Surveyor extended its legs and omnidirectional antennas and unlocked its solar panel. Then it rolled itself until one sensor found the sun and the other located the star Canopus. The Atlas-Centaur had been so accurate that the spacecraft was aimed within 250 miles of its target on the moon.

The midcourse maneuver occurred early next day when Surveyor stopped tracking the sun and Canopus, rolled to a position commanded from the control center, and fired its three vernier engines for 20 seconds. This changed its velocity by only 45 mph, but it aimed Surveyor at a target site in the Ocean of Storms that scientists thought would be smooth enough for a safe landing. After the maneuver, Surveyor again began tracking the sun and Canopus and the wait began for the landing attempt which would climax the 235,000 mile, 63½-hour journey to the moon.

At 1:46 a.m. EDT, June 2, the final descent began 2,000 miles and 31 minutes from the moon. The spacecraft maneuvered to aim its retrorocket in the direction of its approach to the moon. When it was 59½ miles away, the radar beams sensed the lunar surface and started an automatic sequence to time the firing of the retrorocket. At 46½ miles above the moon and traveling at 5,840 mph, the 9,000 lb.-thrust retrorocket fired for 38 seconds, slowing the spacecraft to 267 mph at 35,000 feet.

Lunar Landing

Surveyor dropped off the spent retrorocket casing while the vernier engines stabilized the spacecraft and slowed its descent. At 1,000 feet above the moon, Surveyor had slowed down to 71½ mph. Ten feet above the moon, the verniers cut off as planned and Surveyor I fell free to a soft landing on the moon at 2:17 a.m. EDT, June 2. It landed at 7½ mph with its three feet touching within 19-millionths of a second of each other and coming to rest after bouncing about four inches.

An early-morning television audience watched in homes in the United States and Europe as Surveyor began sending back to Earth a live program of lunar photography. A total of 158 pictures were relayed to Earth showing a bleak and forbidding lunar landscape in the Ocean of Storms with Surveyor's own shadow sometimes cast across it.

During the rest of the two-week-long lunar day, with the temperature rising above 200° F, Surveyor took 10,093 pictures and then was shut down for the −260° F lunar night using only enough electricity from its batteries to keep vital parts from freezing.

Surveyor I's story ended with a bonus that few of its designers expected. On July 6, with the sun again high in the sky, the spacecraft responded to an Earth command and took 899 more pictures. In early October, Surveyor again responded to an Earth command, but was unable to take any pictures. It responded again in November, and for the last time in

TERMINAL DESCENT EVENTS TO MOON'S SURFACE

CRUISE ATTITUDE

PRE-RETRO MANEUVER 30 MIN. BEFORE TOUCHDOWN ALIGNS MAIN RETRO WITH FLIGHT PATH

MAIN RETRO START BY ALTITUDE-MARKING RADAR WHICH EJECTS FROM NOZZLE, CRAFT STABILIZED BY VERNIER ENGINES AT 60-MI ALTITUDE, 5,900 MPH

MAIN RETRO BURNOUT AND EJECTION, VERNIER RETRO SYSTEM TAKEOVER AT 31,000 FT, 267 MPH

VERNIER ENGINES SHUTOFF AT 10 FT, 2.8 MPH

TOUCHDOWN AT 7.5 MPH

NOTE: ALTITUDES, VELOCITIES, AND TIMES ARE APPROXIMATE

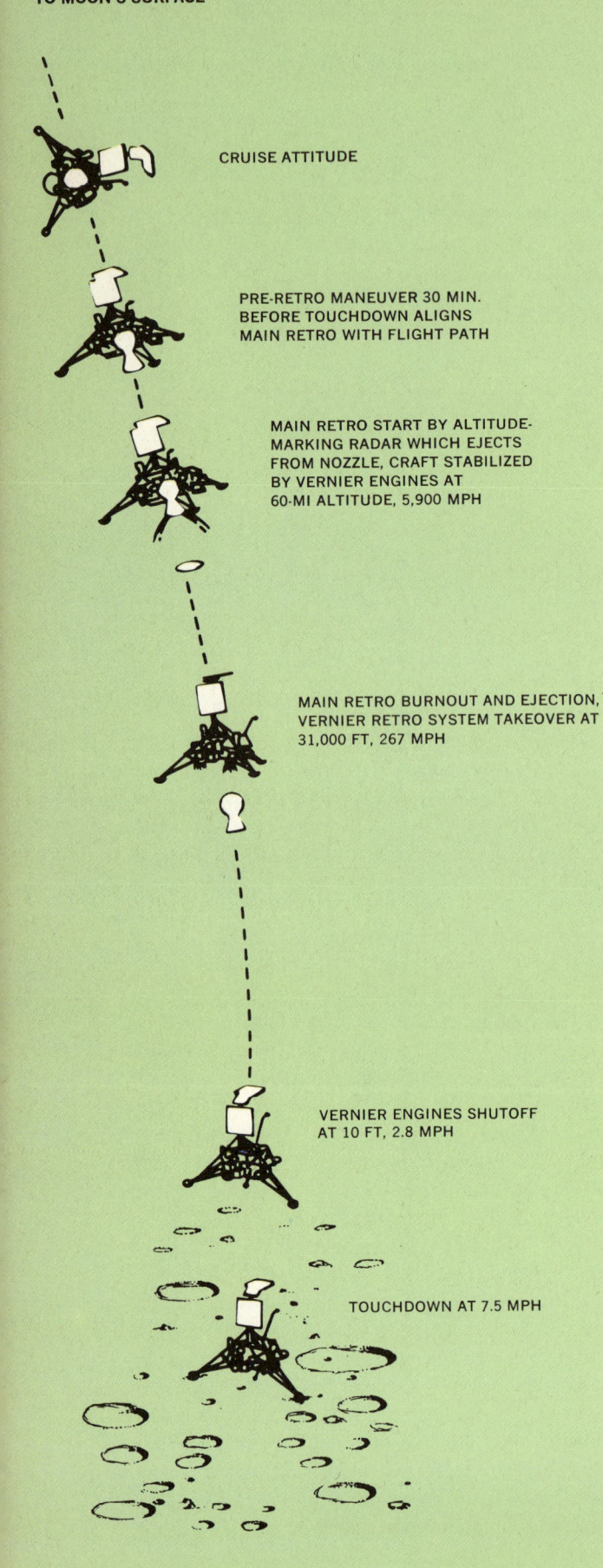

December after 220 days on the lunar surface.

Surveyor II

Encouraged by their success the Surveyor team pressed forward to the next mission, and quickly met failure. On September 20, 1966, Surveyor II was launched, but when the midcourse maneuver was attempted, only two of the three vernier engines fired. The vehicle lost stabilization, began tumbling, and impacted on the moon two days later.

Surveyor III

Although no specific cause for the Surveyor II failure was found, changes were made in the vernier engines on Surveyor III which was launched on April 17, 1967. It carried a surface sampler as well as a television camera.

Surveyor III conducted its midcourse maneuver without a flaw, but its lunar landing was full of surprises. Instead of cutting off about 10 feet above the lunar surface as planned, the vernier engines continued to fire at landing. The spacecraft rebounded off the moon to land 66 feet away, bounced again to land 36 feet away, and after the verniers were shut off by ground command, came to rest on the slope of a crater that was 650 feet in diameter. Surveyor III took 6,315 pictures and its soil sampler made pressure tests, dug small trenches, and picked up several rock-like objects.

Surveyor IV

Surveyor IV was another disappointment. Launched on July 14, 1967, it performed well until its telemetry signal abruptly stopped during the firing of the retrorocket just three minutes before landing on the moon. The dead spacecraft impacted on the moon, but no specific cause was ever found.

Surveyor V

Surveyor V had two new missions: to attempt a landing in the eastern half of the moon in the Sea of Tranquility, and to carry the Alpha scattering instrument to make a chemical analysis of the lunar surface. Surveyor V started a routine flight in September 8, 1967, when near-disaster struck. Only a heroic around-the-clock effort by hundreds of scientists and engineers saved the mission.

After the midcourse maneuver, it was discovered that pressurized helium used to force fuel into the vernier engines was leaking. However, rapid calculations gave hope that if the landing sequence was shortened, the verniers could be fired long enough to achieve a soft landing, even though a highly unusual one. The new landing sequence was put into effect on September 10.

Retrorocket ignition was commanded at 35 miles above the moon instead of 47 miles. Burnout came at 4,400 feet instead of 35,000 feet so there was just enough time to drop the retrorocket casing. The verniers continued burning down to the usual cutoff at 10 feet and Surveyor V dropped to the moon's surface at 8 mph.

Surveyor V's performance on the moon was outstanding. Its new Alpha scattering instrument worked well, and 18,073 pictures were taken during the first lunar day. In October, it responded to command and took 1,048 pictures, but by December it was too weak for further photography.

Surveyor VI

On November 7, 1967, Surveyor VI was launched toward the Central Bay in the middle of the moon and landed safely two days later in what engineers called a *textbook mission,* for it had been accomplished completely according to plan.

After taking 30,065 pictures and studying the lunar surface with the scattering instrument, Surveyor VI made space history. On November 17, its vernier engines were fired for 2½ seconds and the spacecraft rose 10 feet into the air and landed 8 feet away. For the first time, a manmade spacecraft had lifted off under rocket power from another celestial body.

Surveyor VII

Surveyors now had landed along the moon's equator in the east, central, and west. Apollo manned lunar landing officials were satisfied that man could land in the area where Apollo would be aimed. So the Surveyor VII mission became a scientific one: it would attempt to land away from the smooth lunar *maria,* or "seas," and try the rougher highlands near the crater Tycho in the southern part of the moon. It would carry both a soil sampler and an Alpha scattering device as well as a TV camera.

The final Surveyor was launched on January 7, 1968, and landed safely near Tycho 66½ hours later. When the Alpha scattering box got stuck while being lowered to the moon, the soil sampler reached over and gently forced it to the surface. In addition to taking 21,038 lunar pictures, the TV camera made history. On January 20, two laser beams were aimed at Surveyor's landing site from Arizona and California. A picture of the Earth taken by the camera showed two tiny specks of light on the Earth's surface, the first pictures taken from the moon of manmade light on Earth.

Surveyor VII came weakly alive on its second lunar day. But on February 20, 1968, the last signal was received and 21 months of active exploration of the moon by Surveyor spacecraft was over.

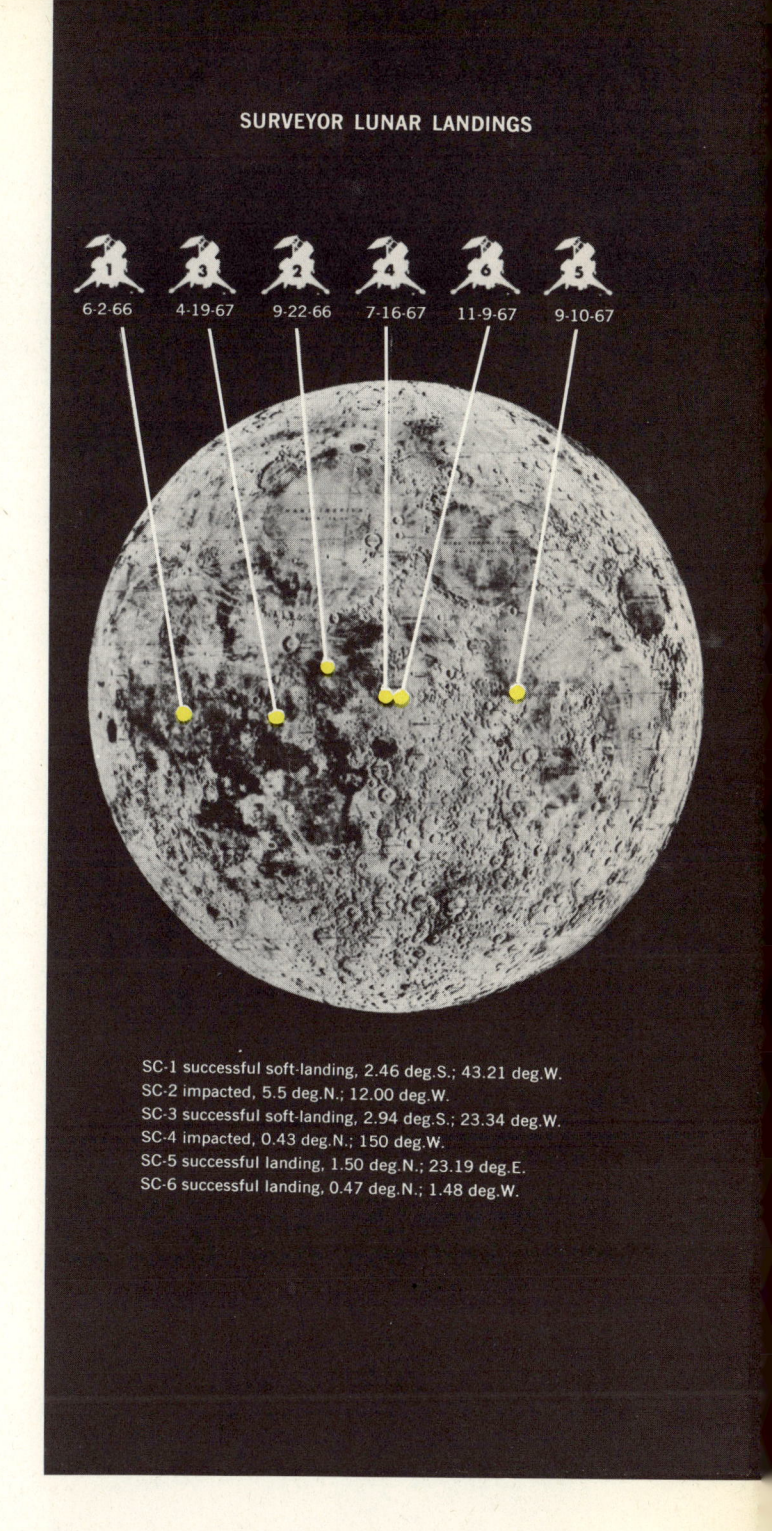

SURVEYOR LUNAR LANDINGS

Mission	Date
1	6-2-66
3	4-19-67
2	9-22-66
4	7-16-67
6	11-9-67
5	9-10-67

SC-1 successful soft-landing, 2.46 deg.S.; 43.21 deg.W.
SC-2 impacted, 5.5 deg.N.; 12.00 deg.W.
SC-3 successful soft-landing, 2.94 deg.S.; 23.34 deg.W.
SC-4 impacted, 0.43 deg.N.; 150 deg.W.
SC-5 successful landing, 1.50 deg.N.; 23.19 deg.E.
SC-6 successful landing, 0.47 deg.N.; 1.48 deg.W.

The Moon as Seen by Surveyors

The five Surveyors that soft landed on the moon took 87,689 pictures and gathered many hours of soil sampler and Alpha scattering information. Scientists will study this information for years but already they know much about the moon from Surveyors.

Astronauts can land and walk on the moon but

Surveyor

No.	Launch Date	Landing Date	Landing site Latitude	Longitude	Scientific equipment	TV pictures	Remarks
I	5-30-66	6-2-66	2.4°S	43.3°W	TV camera	11,150	Successfully landed on moon
II	9-20-66	9-23-66	4°N	11°W	TV camera	0	Mission failed at midcourse maneuver
III	4-17-67	4-19-67	2.9°S	23.1°W	TV camera, soil sampler	6,315	Landed with three rebounds
IV	7-14-67	7-17-67	0.5°S	1.6°W	TV camera, soil sampler	0	Mission failed during descent to moon
V	9-8-67	9-11-67	1.5°N	23.2°E	TV camera, alpha scanner	19,054	Landed despite helium leak in verniers
VI	11-7-67	11-9-67	0.5°N	1.5°W	TV camera, alpha scanner	30,065	Landed in moon's central bay
VII	1-6-68	1-9-68	40.9°S	11.4°W	TV camera, alpha scanner	21,319	Photographed laser beams from Earth

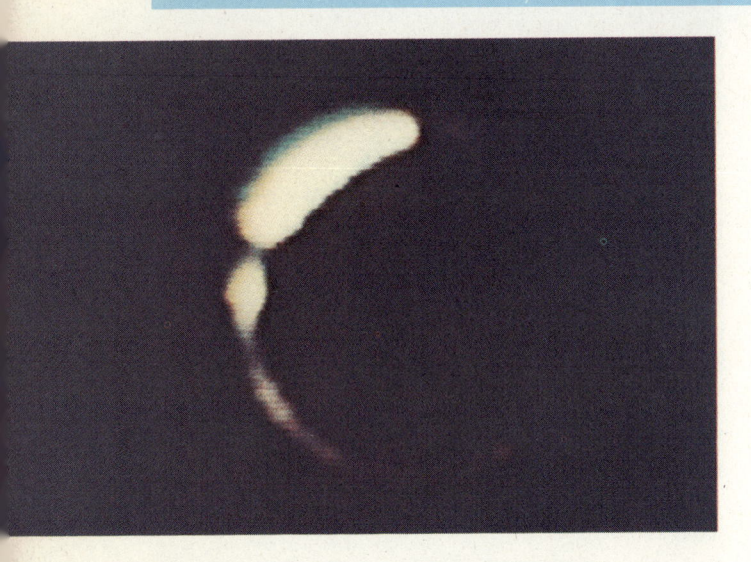

The gold tip of Surveyor III's altitude control jet is seen against the dark gray background of a sample of lunar soil *(below)* which was placed on the footpad by the surface sampler. Surveyor III also relayed photographs of the first observation of a solar eclipse by the Earth *(above)*, taken on April 24, 1967.

they will leave shallow footprints like those on a wet ocean beach. In the lunar maria, the surface is covered with particles finer than the camera's resolution of 1/50 of an inch and these particles tend to cling weakly together. There are many blocks and fragments, some of which reflect more light than the fine particles. Lunar material below the surface is darker than the material on the surface.

There is or has been activity on the surface of the moon because fragments have eroded and moved. Some of this activity results from impacts of meteors, and some from volcanic action.

The lunar maria are remarkably alike in chemistry as well as topography. The surface of the maria contains about the same proportion of oxygen, silicon, and other elements as does rock called *basalt* found on the Earth which was formed by volcanic action. In the lunar highlands, the surface material is similar but it contains less iron and reflects more light. The highlands also have more large rocks, fewer craters, and a thinner covering of fine particles than the maria.

On February 8, 1968, NASA announced that study of Surveyor and other information showed that five sites on the moon were safe for manned lunar landings. The first American astronauts to the moon will land at one of those sites.

Richard T. Mittauer

See also: Luna probes, Lunar charts, Moon

Survival and rescue

Basic survival can be defined as those actions and subsistence items required to satisfy the basic bodily needs. In a combat situation, an individual is forced to meet these basic needs while on the move and still avoid detection by the enemy. This is combat survival.

Today's aircrews must be prepared to survive in every major portion of the Earth's terrain—desert, sea, jungle, or swamp—if they are to fulfill their mission. They must be skilled at selecting and catching food, signaling rescue search planes, building

Survival and rescue

fires for warmth, or providing shelter from the blazing sun. They must be familiar also with the use of survival equipment and weapons.

Aircrews soon learn the value of fresh meat in the matter of staying alive. They are taught to consider anything that crawls, walks, swims, or flies as fair game. They learn that insects cooked until crisp have a high fat content and that to forestall death by starvation, everything from larger game including blood, intestines, and bones should be eaten.

Survival training is like insurance; it is never good until it is needed. The programs are rough; no nonsense is tolerated; but anything less would not prepare men properly for the grim task of surviving in remote areas of the land or sea. In the USAF, survival training begins early in the cadet's career. At the Air Force Academy in Colorado Springs, Colorado, the cadet's seven weeks' indoctrination is climaxed with a practical lesson in overland navigation and survival.

New cadets are taken up into the mountains where they are left in the company of upperclassmen to find their way back to the Academy. They are given certain tools for survival—a small ration box, a cake of compressed meat, and a live rabbit. By trapping squirrels, rabbits, and other small game, sampling edible plants and stewing savory insects, cadets learn from practical experience how to survive outside the comforts of home or the plush glass cage which is their dormitory. When they arrive back at the Academy tired and hungry, they are given all they can eat.

From Snow to Sea

Aircrews are sent to the Alaska Air Command where they learn to build a shelter trench from blocks cut from hard-packed snow. They are kept warm by burning candles in a tin can. This kind of shelter is soundproof, so survival experts must remember to keep a sharp eye out for rescue aircraft.

In the tropics, aircrews learn to build "parahammocks" from parachutes so they won't have to sleep on the ground where disease-bearing insects and stagnant water could cause illness. They use their chutes for clothing, shelter, ropes, and a myriad of other life-saving items, and they find that a "paratepee" with a lighted candle inside is especially visible from the air at night.

Effective signaling is vital to survival. Mirrors from survival kits or improvised from tin cans are remarkably effective in good weather. Fires are an important aid, so aircrews are taught how to start them without the aid of matches. They are shown how to conserve fuel, and they soon discover that building a fire beneath a snow-laden tree can be disastrous.

Signaling can be improvised. In grasslands, trenches can be cut; in bush country, vegetation can be cleared; and in the arctic, messages can be

Parachute sandbags will function as weights for shelters built in the desert *(below)*. As part of their training, astronauts must learn to obtain water from bamboo stems *(center)* and how to construct shelters from jungle foliage *(bottom)* during training in Panama.

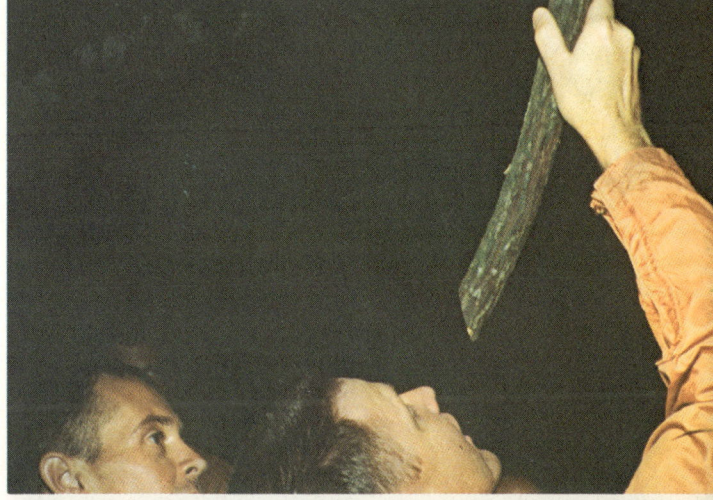

Survival and rescue

tramped in the snow. Trainees learn the use of maps and magnetic compasses.

In survival school, some specialists are taught the art of *rapelling* to descend a sheer cliff. In rapelling, a doubled climbing rope, anchored to the ground above, is passed under the climber's leg, then up and across his chest and shoulder and down his back. The friction of the rope across his body allows him to descend slowly and securely.

In sea survival, aircrews learn how to climb into life rafts and drift for half a day in the open sea. They learn to use their rafts and equipment alone with only the sun, sky, and water for company. They find that sun stills continuously provide fresh water so long as the sun shines, but when it doesn't, desalting kits properly used will also give them fresh drinking water.

Army aviators are given their basic survival insurance policy when they attend the U.S. Army Aviation School at Fort Rucker, where they spend 26 hours in the field with the Department of Tactics Survival Committee. In addition to the usual training of what to eat, how to catch it, what is safe and what isn't, and how to cope with climate, improvised survival techniques are stressed in case of dysentery, cold injury, pneumonia, malnutrition, hepatitis, heart condition, failing vision, fractures and sprains, beri-beri, burns, lice, intestinal worms, snow blindness, snake bite, and teeth and bone pains.

German Rescue Service

Successful survival, of course, is dependent upon rescue. Aerial rescue as an organized service has its origin with the German *Luftwaffe* which, even before 1939, realized that experienced pilots were of great value to the Third Reich and that a rescue organization was a tremendous morale booster. Pilots would be more daring and fight all the harder once they knew they would be rescued if they got into trouble.

To perform their rescues, the Germans depended mainly on Heinkel-59 float planes, along with fast rescue launches stationed on the European coast facing the British Isles. The Heinkel-59's, vividly marked with a red cross, carried three collapsible rubber boats, blankets, medical stores, and two-way radio communications gear. Unfortunately, the float planes, exploiting their immunity against attack, began to spy on Allied shipping. The practice was stopped only after the British protested through a neutral nation.

A unique German device was the sea rescue float, a large buoy-type float designed and equipped to maintain the life of any downed airman who might reach it. A number of these were placed in position extending almost across the English Channel. They were fitted with bunks for four men, blankets, clothing, food, water, distress signals, and lamps. Painted a vivid yellow with a red cross on either side of the central conning tower, these floats were clearly visible from a considerable distance. A 250-foot rope, attached to the float, drifted in the current to aid airmen in climbing aboard.

Periodically, these life-saving devices were checked by patrol boats, and survivors were transferred. Since Royal Air Force (RAF) (*see*) pilots in distress would head for the buoys too, both sides made the periodic checks. It became a matter of pure luck whether a survivor returned to his comrades or sat out the war in a prisoner of war camp. One can only speculate on what might have transpired if a downed German flyer had reached a buoy to find that an RAF pilot had already set up housekeeping.

The German Rescue Service also led the way in providing other survival gear which later became standard issue to Allied airmen. An inflatable dinghy was part of the regular equipment of German bomber aircraft, and in the summer of 1940, one-man dinghies were being issued to fighter pilots.

All German aircrews were provided with bags of fluorescein, a dye marker that stains a large area of water a bright green color. Bomber crews had portable radio transmitters which could be taken into a dinghy and used to call for assistance. The German Rescue Service also first employed highly visible yellow coloring for their dinghies, skull caps, and flotation jackets.

Soon, British and American airmen were equipped with similar and often improved versions of captured German survival devices. One example is the German radio transmitter which, modified and improved, became famous as the *Gibson Girl*.

U.K. and U.S. Combined Rescue Service

In August, 1940, elements of the Royal Navy and the Royal Air Force, utilizing light naval craft, RAF high-speed launches, and a few borrowed Lysander amphibians, established a formal Air/Sea Rescue for the first time in 12 months of war. By September, 1942, the U.S. Eighth Air Force and the RAF reached an agreement whereby the U.S. would participate in the already existing Air/Sea Rescue rather than attempt to establish its own. The Americans were to furnish planes and crews as best they could and at the same time step up their survival program for training crews.

A glance at the statistics shows the value of those early rescue arrangements. In 1943, only 28 per

One of the most important operations of the crew aboard the Hercules HC-130H search, rescue, and recovery aircraft *(above left)* is rescuing personnel via the Fulton skyhook recovery method *(top right)*. Special Forces units are familiarized with this recovery system as part of their training at Fort Bragg *(top left* and *center)*. Dual pickups can be made *(above right)*.

cent of Eighth Air Force crews in distress were saved. By April, 1944, the figure had risen to 43 per cent for bomber crews and 38 per cent for fighter pilots. By September, 1944, approximately 90 per cent of American aircrews forced down at sea in the European Theater of Operations were recovered. By the end of March, 1945, 1,972 American airmen had been saved by British or American rescue units in the North Sea, the English Channel, and other waters around Great Britain.

On D-Day, when thousands of airmen were participating in the Normandy Beach operation, very few were lost for lack of rescue facilities. In fact, 60 complete aircrews are known to have been picked up by Anglo-American rescue units on that one day alone.

Air Rescue Service Begins

In October, 1943, at Boca Raton, Florida, the first Emergency Rescue Squadron assembled for training. The squadron, commanded by Lieutenant Colonel Littleton J. Pardue, consisted of 52 officers and 147 enlisted men assigned to three operational flights and a headquarters section.

Equipped with nine OA-10 Catalinas, six amphibious and three boat types, three L-5's, and three B-25's to be used as administrative support aircraft, this squadron, serving in the Mediterranean, actually rescued and carried to safety 244 downed airmen. Countless survivors were rescued by high-speed surface launches directed to the airmen by the Cat's. These early rescue pioneers stood ready 24 hours a day to go to the aid of men who had been forced to ditch their aircraft.

The Air Rescue Service, now the Aerospace Rescue and Recovery Service (ARRS), was officially organized and assigned to the Military Airlift Command *(see)* in 1945. Today, their job ranges from the recovery of astronauts to the rescue of downed

In Vietnam a USAF HH-43B Huskie hovers over a downed pilot as the pararescueman lowers the jungle penetrator rescue seat to him.

airmen, even behind enemy lines, and the rescue of stranded mountain climbers. ARRS pararescuemen are qualified as parachutists, scuba divers, medical technicians, and survival experts. It is their job to parachute to the aid of downed aircrews who may be injured and in need of immediate medical attention and assistance. Pararescuemen slide down a rescue helicopter cable in Southeast Asia to look for downed pilots in the dense jungle undergrowth.

Since 1946, ARRS has rescued more than 13,000 people from probable death. It has directly aided more than 64,000 people and 65,000 aircraft.

The HC-130H Hercules, the latest addition to the ARRS fixed-wing aircraft inventory, is of special interest. With its 2,000-mile range and cruise speed of 290 knots, it is designed to carry the Fulton SKYHOOK Recovery System.

The Fulton SKYHOOK is used both for saving lives and for recovery of astronauts. It acts as a parachute-in-reverse and can be used day and night, on land and sea from the arctic to the tropics. To date, more than 108 men have been picked up, both single and dual. The first dual pick-up included Brigadier General Allison Brooks, ARRS commander.

Currently in use in Southeast Asia, the Fulton SKYHOOK Recovery System is put into operation when the HC-130H crew drops a recovery kit by parachute to the stranded personnel. The equipment is used in the order in which it comes out of the containers. The rescuee first puts on the harness which is similar to a pair of coveralls. It is attached to a liftline which is attached to a balloon. He inflates the balloon from helium modules and releases the balloon, which raises the liftline 500 feet into the air. Then the rescuee sits down with the wind at his back and waits for the plane to do the rest.

Meanwhile, the HC-130H, equipped with a yoke or wide fork horizontally mounted on its nose, flies into the line. Once caught by the skyanchor, the recovered person is gently raised to the Hercules in less than five minutes. Personnel aboard the aircraft, working from an open rear-loading ramp, drop a shepherd's hook to grab the line and attach it to a hydraulically driven winch. The rescuee is gently brought aboard. In case the stranded pilot is injured, a pararescueman will parachute to the scene, assist the pilot into the suit, and the two can be recovered simultaneously. For night pick-ups, flashing strobe lights on the line guide the pilot. In daylight, flags mark the line.

Eloise Engle

See also: Escape systems, Parachutes, Pararescue, Recovery, Rescue and recovery service

Survival kits

A great deal of care, study, and planning have gone into kits which make survival following the loss of an aircraft possible in all parts of the world. Survival kits are carried in aircraft flying over large bodies of water, over hostile territory, or in uninhabited areas where a forced landing or ejection might occur. Anticipating the unexpected, such as midair explosion or fire aboard the aircraft, advance preparation for emergency landing (*see*) or ejection can prevent fatalities and increase chances of survival for the pilot and passengers. A pilot ejecting over water can prepare for his survival even before hitting the water. Attached to his parachute harness is his survival kit which contains a life raft, food, and other necessary items. His wait for aid may last hours, even days, and with the help of these items, he can survive until rescued.

Military

Survival kits for military air crews fall into two categories. The first is a small personalized kit which

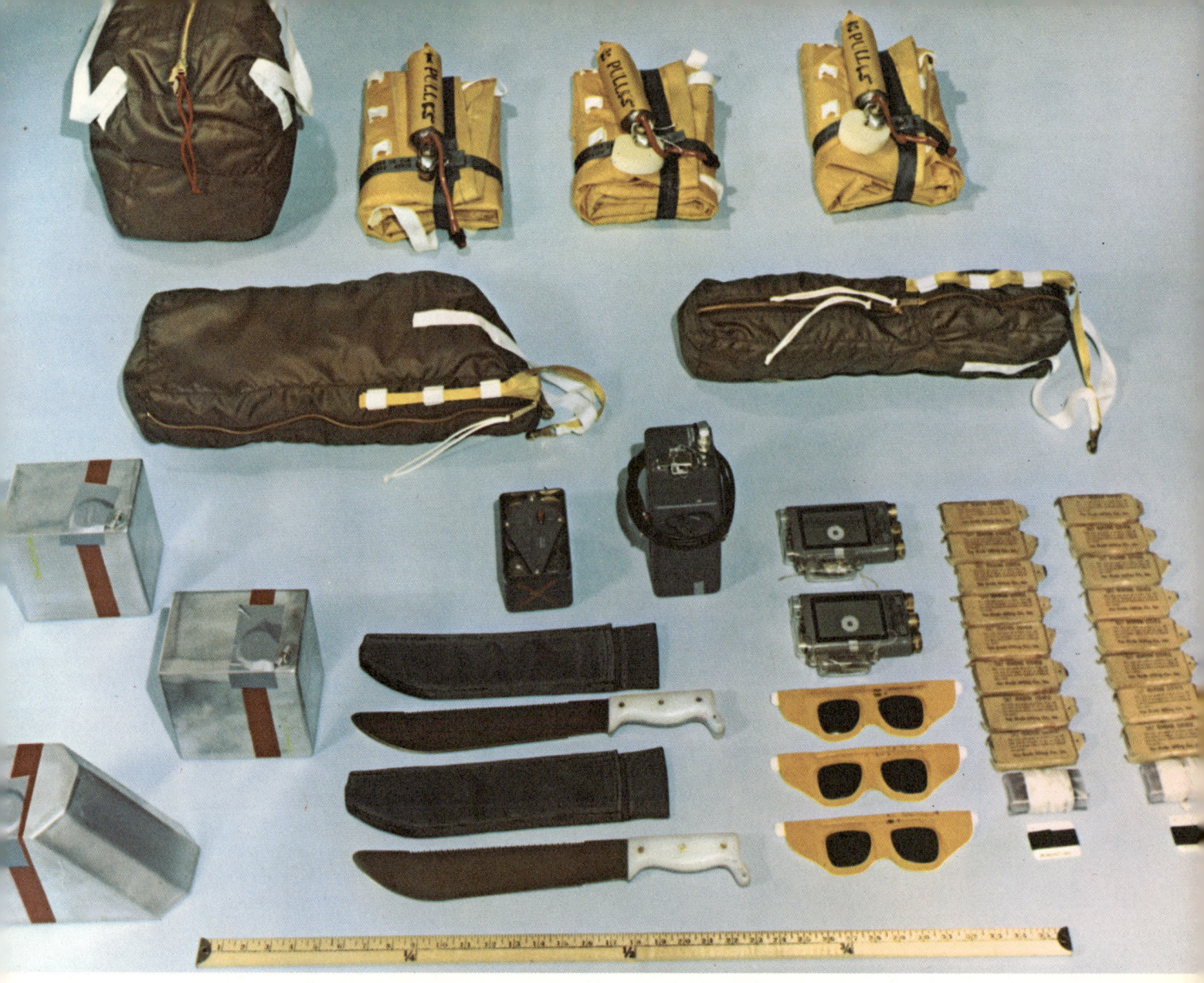

The Apollo flight kit will include survival equipment for the three astronauts.

is stowed in the pocket of the flight suit. It is 8 inches long, 4 inches wide, and 1 inch thick, and made of water-resistant material. The items, all of which are attached to the kit to avoid losing them, include first-aid materials, a survival book, concentrated food, water-purifying chemicals, matches, fish hooks, snares, and plastic bags for storing water.

The second type of survival kit is in rigid form and fitted into the seat portion of the ejection seat. Seat kits vary in size according to the cockpit configuration, but they average about 18 by 15 by 6 inches and again, everything is attached. The seat kit contains emergency oxygen, an inflatable life raft, a survival radio or beacon, a Mae West life vest, and optional equipment dependent upon climate and terrain of the flight areas.

In addition to survival kits, the following items are carried (depending on the environment): a hand gun, flare gun, survival knife, special knife designed to cut parachute lines, flotation vest and life raft, and parachutes.

U.S. Navy kits are designed more for overwater flights than are those of the U.S. Air Force.

General Aviation

According to the Federal Aviation Administration (FAA), survival kits for general aviation aircraft (*see*) are extremely important, and can be put together at very little cost from readily available off-the-shelf items. The FAA says, "A two-pound packet is home away from home . . . down is *not* out." Their suggested kit includes adhesive bandages, a roll of half-inch adhesive tape, a pack of X-acto knife blades, a tube of antiseptic ointment for burns and lacerations, aspirin, water purification tablets, ammonia inhalers, and triangle bandages. As for food, FAA suggests concentrated soup mixes, bouillion cubes (chicken and beef), dehydrated coffee and milk, sugar, salt, hard candy, and vitamin

Survival kits

capsules. The food items should be packed in heavy aluminum foil, which can be used for cooking utensils if necessary. For living off the land, FAA recommends 50 feet of high-strength fishing line and a half-dozen fish hooks. A gill net and a length of light wire from the aircraft can be used for snaring small game. A scout knife, along with a pocket whetstone, is the single most important tool. Also desirable in the general aviation survival kit are waterproof matches, compass, heat tablets, needles, safety pins, a plastic roll-up canteen, mirror for signaling, and a penlight flashlight. Important considerations are storability, lightweight, and compactness.

Space

The most elaborate survival kit ever designed traveled with the Gemini astronauts. There will undoubtedly be certain modifications on this kit for the Apollo astronauts, and for succeeding spaceflights.

The Gemini survival kit contained 14 items designed for support of the astronaut, should he land outside the recovery zone. The 23-pound kit was in two sections. The small section held a 3½-pound water container and a machete (long-bladed, swordlike knife) mounted by the astronaut's left shoulder. The main package was mounted behind the ejection seat. Both packages were attached to the astronaut's personal harness. The main package contained a life raft, which when inflated with its attached carbon dioxide bottle was 5½ feet long and 3 feet wide. The raft equipment included a sea anchor, sea dye marker, nylon sunbonnet with aluminized coating for sun protection and reflective qualities for easy spotting from the air, radio beacon, combination survival-light, sunglasses, medical kit, and desalter kit.

The combination survival-light is a new development, about the size of a paperback novel, and contains a strobe light, a flashlight, a single mirror built on the edge of the case, and a small compass. There are three cylindrical cartridges, two with batteries, a sewing kit, 14 feet of heavy nylon cord, cotton balls, and a striker for lighting fires. Also included are halazone tablets for purifying water, a whistle, and a desalter kit. The desalter kit has eight desalter briquets and a processing bag. Each briquet can desalt one pint of sea water. The medical kit contains 1cc (cubic centimeter) injection for pain; 2cc injection for motion sickness; stimulant, pain, and motion sickness tablets; antibiotics; and aspirin tablets.

USAF Aerospace Rescue and Recovery

When USAF Aerospace Rescue and Recovery Service crews fly their HC-130H rescue planes to recover downed personnel, they drop an MA-1 kit. The contents of the MA-1 kit vary according to environment, but an example can be found in a sea pick-up.

From the open ramp of the HC-130H, five containers, each about 3 by 4 feet in size, connected by 210 feet of polyethylene rope, are dropped to the stranded aircrew below. Containers 1 and 5 are each a six-man life raft which inflates on impact. Containers 2 and 4 have a radio receiving battery and cable assembly. In the center, container 3 has a food packet, water desalter kit, flares, and items for personal needs such as soap, adhesive bandages, and aspirin.

Eloise Engle

See also: Escape systems, Rescue and recovery

Sweden's aviation

Sweden's aviation is the nucleus of a strong defense organization and the heart of a vigorous commercial air service. It is the culmination of a long history of flying activity which began about 1912 when the Swedish Army and Navy acquired airplanes.

In 1925 the well-established air arms of the two services were combined to form one of the world's first independent air forces. When conditions in Europe grew unsettled, the Air Force was increased in 1936 to 12 bomber squadrons, 3 fighter squadrons, and 6 reconnaissance squadrons. Sweden remained neutral throughout World War II, but by war's end, the Air Force had grown to 21 fighter squadrons, 21 bomber (attack) squadrons, and 9 reconnaissance squadrons.

After the war, it became apparent that no small country could maintain an air force to match those of the major powers, so Sweden turned to a "total defense" concept. "First strike" has been unknown in Sweden, and the country has a history of 150 years of neutrality and impenetrability.

Sweden's Defense System

Military service is compulsory in Sweden for all males between the ages of 18 and 47. The three

Disposition of Sweden's Air Self Defense Force *(top left)* throughout the country. Many bases are built into the granite rock which underlies the country. Saab-35 Draken supersonic fighter aircraft *(top right)* used only for defense. Sweden has never initiated an air strike. A general view of Bloodhound Mk 2 surface-to-air missiles *(center)*, which became operational within the STRIL 60 electronic defense system in 1965, at their launchers at the Royal Swedish Air Force base at Barkaby, near Stockholm. Saab-37 Viggen *(bottom left)* and Saab-105 *(bottom right)*, Swedish-designed and built defense aircraft.

DISPOSITION OF AIR SELF DEFENSE FORCE

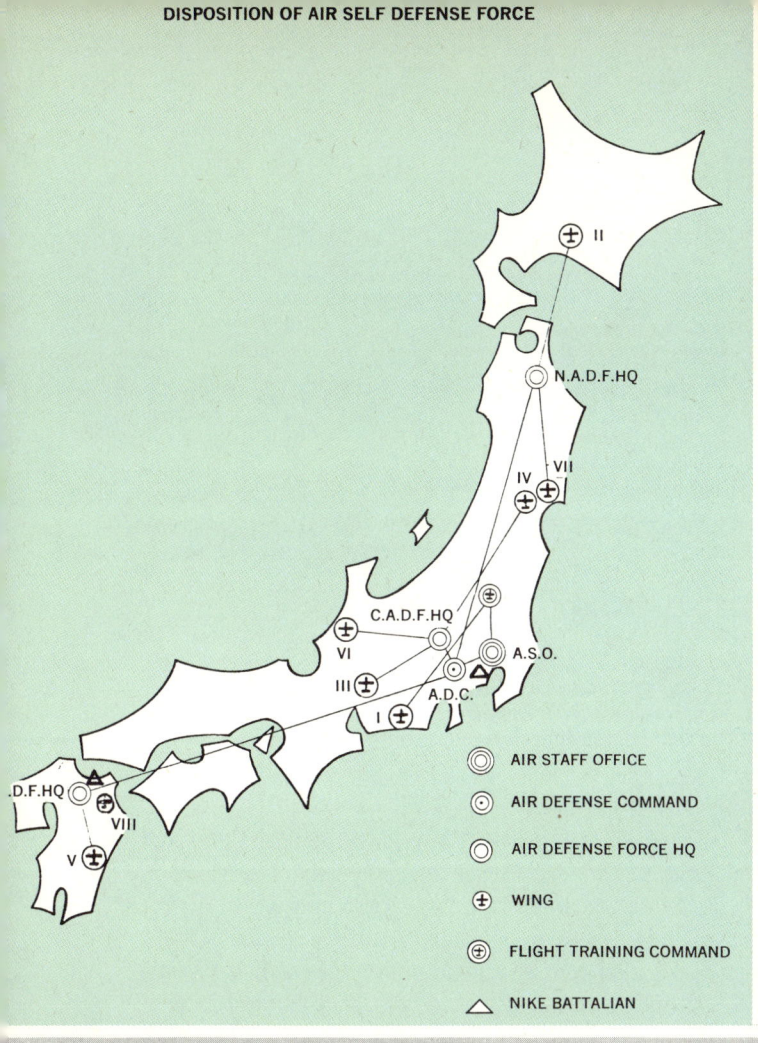

- ◎ AIR STAFF OFFICE
- ⊙ AIR DEFENSE COMMAND
- ◎ AIR DEFENSE FORCE HQ
- ⊕ WING
- ⊕ FLIGHT TRAINING COMMAND
- △ NIKE BATTALIAN

Sweden's aviation

armed services have a supreme commander under the king and a joint defense staff. Currently the Air Force is made up of 46 squadrons, including four day-fighter wings, five all-weather fighter wings, four attack wings, and five reconnaissance wings.

The "total defense" system centers around a radar and surveillance network known as STRIL/60, a highly secret system that is one of the most sophisticated and complete in the world. It includes air, sea, and land early-warning and defense alerts.

The total number of aircraft that could be used for combat is estimated to be about 1,000 to 1,200, making the Swedish Air Force one of the strongest in the world. Certain roads and highways are specially constructed and reinforced to serve as landing strips. Designated service stations throughout the country stock jet aviation fuel, and farmers who live near the improvised airstrips are trained to man antiaircraft guns to defend emergency bases. The operational center of STRIL/60 is buried in the granite rock that underlies most of Sweden, as are many of the hangars and most of the country's aircraft industry.

Sweden's Military Aircraft

Sweden's Air Force is divided into four commands, each assigned the defense of a different part of the country. It is made up mainly of Swedish-built aircraft specifically designed to carry out the defense mission.

The attack units are equipped with the SAAB 32 Lansen, which can carry a large variety of stores against all types of land and sea targets day or night and in all kinds of weather. These units are designed primarily to provide support to land and sea forces. Other fighter-interceptor units, flying the J-35 Draken for the most part, are assigned to respond to attack by air. The Draken is a modern high-performance aircraft that, with versatile armament, can deliver air and surface strikes against an enemy.

Newest aircraft contemplated in Sweden is the System 37 Viggen, built by SAAB Aircraft Co. The Viggen (Thunderbolt) is aerodynamically a revolutionary aircraft. It will fly at speeds more than twice the speed of sound and yet is able to land in less than 1,600 feet. It first flew in March, 1967, and Sweden plans to procure it in four versions: ground support, intercept, reconnaissance, and training. It is designed to replace both the Draken and Lansen aircraft, and 400 are expected to be purchased by the Swedish government eventually.

The Viggen is a single-seat aircraft, powered by an afterburning Pratt & Whitney JT8D-22 turbofan engine, which is built by the *Svenska Flygmotor AB* after extensive modification. The RM8, as it is de-

Saab 91-B Safir, with cruise speed of over 140 mph and range of 680 miles, will be used as a trainer aircraft by the Swedish Air Force.

signed, has about 14,000 pounds of thrust and will push the 16-ton Viggen up to speeds over Mach 2.

Main armament on the Viggen consists of air-to-air missiles (*see*) and air-to-surface missiles (*see*), but it also carries a wide variety of other weapons. Although the Viggen was built specifically for Sweden, other countries have expressed interest in it and, with modification, it may be sold elsewhere.

SAAB Aircraft Co., which produces the Viggen and other Swedish aircraft, is a privately owned company established in 1937 by a group of Swedish industrial companies. Initially, the company produced a number of British and German bombers and trainers under license. It first produced its own aircraft, a single-engine dive-bomber, in 1940 and went on to build several types of combat aircraft during World War II.

Now a major producer of combat aircraft, missiles, and trainers, the company produced the SAAB J29 in 1951, the first swept-wing jet fighter in Europe; the SAAB 32A Lansen, the first transonic all-weather attack aircraft to go into service in western Europe; and the SAAB 35 Draken, the first Mach 2-class fighter of Western European design in 1959-1960. In this aircraft, SAAB pioneered the double-delta wing which has been carried over in the design of the Viggen.

Commercial and General Aviation

Swedish air transportation started in early 1919 with a number of very small companies and went through five precarious years until the establishment of AB Aerotransport (ABA) in 1924. ABA, which was to become one of the parent companies of Scandinavian Airlines System (SAS), made its first passenger flight between Stockholm and Helsinki, using a Junkers F-13 on floats.

During the 1930's, it became apparent that the national airlines of Sweden, Denmark, and Norway were natural components for a large international airline. As early as 1938, meetings were held to explore the possibility of joint transatlantic air service between Scandinavia and New York. Final plans for the opening of North Atlantic service were completed by the spring of 1940, only to be cut short by the outbreak of World War II.

Despite the war, efforts to form one Scandinavian airline continued, with neutral Sweden as the focus for the negotiations. In 1942, ABA was reorganized with an international component being formed, *Svensk Interkontinental Lufttrafik AB (SILA)*. This company was then merged with the national airlines of Denmark and Norway on August 1, 1946, to form Overseas SAS. ABA continued to provide the domestic air service of Sweden until April, 1948, when it too became a part of SAS. Currently, dodestic routes are operated by SAS and *AB Linjeflyg,* which is owned jointly by SAS and a consortium of newspaper companies.

Ranked among the first ten airlines in the world in size, SAS serves over 135,000 miles of unduplicated routes linking five continents; and with its associates, it serves some 115 cities in 56 countries. As such, it has done its fair share of pioneering in the air, including the opening up of the world's first polar route system.

Sweden's large area and sparse population has contributed to the rapid growth of general aviation. Flying clubs were first formed in the early 1930's and were combined in 1937 into the Royal Aero Club of Sweden (KSAK). KSAK became officially sponsored by the government in 1943, and among other important functions it provides an organized system of fire patrol over the country's vast forest areas.

Most business aircraft are owned by the forestry companies whose airstrips in the remote parts of Sweden are also used by tourists flying into inaccessible hunting and fishing areas. Sweden's taxi-flight operators are also growing in numbers, and these companies are similar to the bush pilots in Canada and Alaska, providing an important means of communications and transportation to the more remote regions of the country.
Laurence Woods Zoeller

See also: Air forces of the world, Commercial airlines, Naval aviation worldwide

Swigert, John Leonard, Jr.

Astronaut
Born: August 30, 1931;
Denver, Colorado
Service: Civilian

John Leonard Swigert was selected for astronaut duty in April, 1966, following experience as an engineering test pilot for North American Rockwell.

He was graduated from the University of Colorado in 1953 with a B.S. degree in mechanical engineering. In 1965 he received an M.S. in aerospace science from Rensselaer Polytechnic Institute, and an M.S. in business administration in 1967 from the University of Hartford in Connecticut.

He served with the USAF from 1953-56. Upon graduating from the pilot training program at Nellis Air Force Base, Nevada, he became a fighter pilot in Japan and Korea. Swigert also served as a jet fighter pilot with the Massachusetts and Connecticut Air National Guards. He was also a research engineering test pilot for Pratt & Whitney Aircraft.

Swigert is a member of the Society of Experimental Test Pilots. He is also co-recipient of the AIAA Octave Chanute Award for 1966 for his participation in demonstrating the Rogallo wing as a feasible land landing system for returning space vehicles and astronauts.

His current assignment involves training for future manned spaceflights, and he is a member of the astronaut support crew for the first manned Apollo flight.
Jim Schefter

See also: Astronauts, Parawing

Syncom satellites, *see* Communications satellites, National Aeronautics and Space Administration, Satellites

Synergy, *see* Fuller, Buckminster; Geodesics

Synthetic materials, *see* Fabrics, Manufacturing, Materials

Systems engineering

Systems engineering is a process by which the contributing elements of a total system are designed, developed, tested, produced, and employed in accordance with an overall plan to assure the desired

Systems engineering

performance in a specified time and at an established cost. Although the term *systems engineering* is thought to apply to recently developed technology, it is more accurately a sophisticated name for a function or group of functions that have been going on for centuries in a less organized fashion than today.

The giant pyramids of Egypt, the Great Wall of China, the Roman aqueducts and roads were all built by the systems engineers of ancient times. The important difference between today's systems engineers and those of the past is that the engineers of today do not have unlimited money, manpower, and time but must operate within tight controls. The engineers of ancient times often took decades or longer to complete a project, spent as much money as was needed, and frequently used almost unlimited slave labor.

Blending of Ingredients

While there is no one "right" definition of systems engineering, it can be described as the blending of manpower, technology, time, and money as ingredients for a highly refined management and engineering technique. How much of each ingredient to use is dictated in part by the amount of time, money, manpower, and technology available. Sometimes there is a limited amount of time, as during the ballistic missile race with the U.S.S.R., when the Department of Defense (*see*) believed that in order to defend the U.S. properly, an intercontinental ballistic missile was needed in a very short time period. Sometimes there is a limited amount of money or manpower or technology available. Such single limitation is known as the *limiting factor* and the mix of the other ingredients around the limiting factor can be described by the term *tradeoffs,* which simply means that one resource is traded against another until the proper mix to get the best job done in the shortest time and with the least expenditure of money and manpower is developed. A systems engineer must be capable of understanding these necessary intermeshings with technology and be able to plan so that all these seemingly unrelated elements are blended together into a complete system.

Any system can be divided into subsystems which must be further analyzed as separate entities. If an unmanned spacecraft in its entirety is considered a complete system, then typical subsystems are: structure, communications, thermal control, propulsion, attitude control, electrical power, electrical integration, and the payload, which might be a TV weather camera, communications relay equipment, or scientific experiments.

For each subsystem there may be numerous basic design approaches which achieve the minimum requirements needed for the mission. For example, propulsion may use solid or liquid rocket engines; electrical power may be supplied by solar cells (*see*), batteries (*see*), or a nuclear generator; attitude control may employ reaction wheels or gravity gradient booms, etc.

The Optimum Approach

Within these basic approaches there may be many other design possibilities using different materials, circuits, redundancy levels, etc. When all these alternate designs are considered, the number of possible approaches becomes alarmingly large. In fact, in the eight subsystems mentioned above, if each has three basic approaches and each approach has ten different possible detailed designs, which is not a particularly large number considering the complexity of a typical spacecraft system, then the total number of possible systems designs is $(3 \times 10)^8$ or over 600 billion! The systems engineering goal is to determine which combination is optimum for the greatest return on the resources expended and maximum system effectiveness.

Modern systems engineering relies heavily upon computers (*see*) because the human mind is unable to comprehend all the interrelationships involved in a large modern system. Mathematical models of the system can be run through computers which greatly reduce the mathematical and mental dexterity required. Consider high-speed surface transportation (*see*) systems as an example. A mathematical computer program can portray and analyze alternative systems between numerous transportation points and projections may be made for the next 10 or 20 years. The computer can predict patronage of existing and proposed systems of the future on the basis of expected travel demand, cost, and service of competing transportation systems. Computer programs can also indicate the sensitivity of both new and existing systems to changes in fares, service levels, and frequency of operations, etc. The use of computers has been one of the key factors in bringing systems engineering to the high stage of refinement it enjoys today.

T. C. Irvine

See also: Aerospace industry, Cybernetics, Information systems, Manufacturing, Materials, MITRE Corporation, Production techniques, Program management, Quality control, RAND Corporation, Reliability and quality assurance, Testing

Systems for Nuclear Auxiliary Power, see Nuclear propulsion, SNAP Program

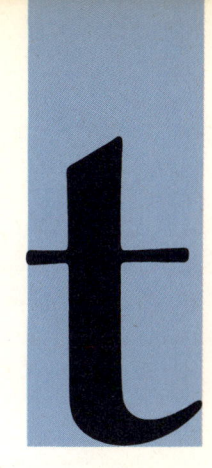

TAC, abbr., *see* Tactical Air Command

TACAN, *see* Tactical air navigation

Tachometer

One instrument which has been found in the cockpit (*see*) of airplanes almost from the beginning is the tachometer, or engine speed counter. Even prior to the invention of the airplane, various forms of it were in common use to monitor the speed of rotating shafts in machinery.

A beginning student usually flies in a plane with a minimum of instruments. Since his airplane probably has a fixed-pitch propeller, the only engine instrument to indicate power is the tachometer. By regulating the number of revolutions per minute (rpm) of the engine, the pilot can develop maximum power for takeoff, climb, and cruise.

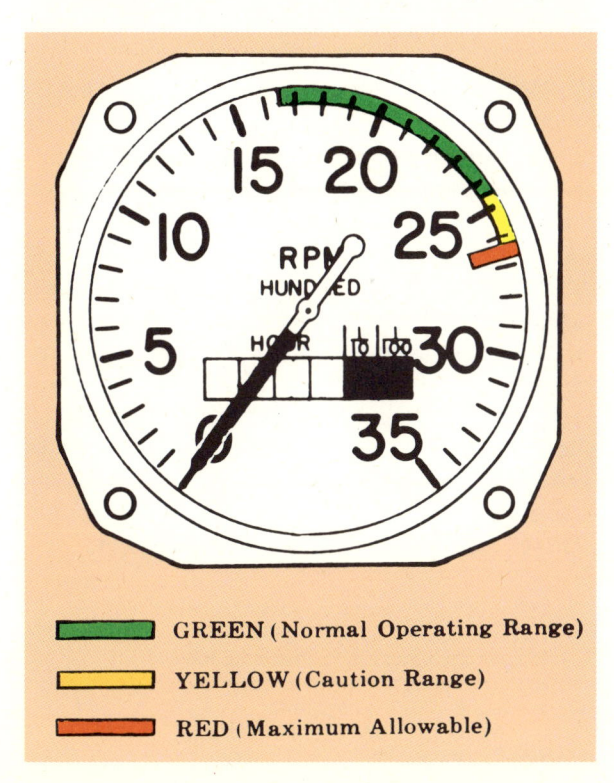

In more powerful piston engines, the tachometer is used in conjunction with the manifold pressure gauge. By adjusting one with the other, the pilot gets the power he needs and also can control fuel consumption for greatest economy.

The tachometer has less importance in gas turbine engines (*see*). The turboprop and axial-flow jet engines use other instruments to determine engine power. In turbine engines—with the exception of centrifugal flow engines—the tachometer reads in per cent of maximum rpm instead of actual rpm. The per cent figure gives pilots a basis for comparing the tachometer readings on all jet engines regardless of the actual rpm.

Either direct-drive or electrical tachometers may be used. The direct-drive is usually found on light aircraft; the electrical tachometers are used in larger single-engine and most multiengine aircraft.

The *direct-drive tachometer* works like the speedometer of a car. The engine is connected to the instrument by a cable with a small magnet at the dial end. The spinning of the magnet inside a small drum causes the drum to pull against the force of a spring and register rpm on the dial.

The *electrical tachometer* consists of a small generator connected to the engine. The instrument on the panel is actually a voltmeter, which computes the electrical charge in rpm or per cent of rpm.

John A. Eakle

See also: Aircraft propulsion systems, Engine instruments, Pressure gauges

Tactical Air Command

Tactical air power is a relatively new concept of warfare which evolved out of World War II operations. It was demonstrated then that air superiority is the first requirement for success of land operations; air power's greatest asset is its inherent flexibility; and centralized command is necessary for maximum employment of air power. In line with these concepts the Allied nations established tactical air forces composed of bomber aircraft (*see*), fighter aircraft (*see*), and reconnaissance aircraft (*see*).

With its genesis, development, and refinement in World War II, the Tactical Air Command (TAC) was officially established in 1946. By 1948, however, TAC had been taken over by the Continental Air Command (*see*) except for a command planning group of 140 military and civilian personnel. TAC was reestablished as a separate air command of the United States Air Force (*see*) during the Korean war (*see*).

Mission and Organization

The mission of TAC is to organize, train, and equip units and to prepare and execute plans for the accomplishment of tactical air operations. TAC provides a mobile, worldwide nuclear and conventional strike force, capable of operating independently or in cooperation with other air or surface forces.

TAC is both a combat and a support command. As a combat force, it provides an air component to the USAF Strike Command (*see*) prepared for rapid response to wartime emergencies. It provides professionally trained personnel, both aircrew and ground, to U.S. units overseas. In its support role, TAC provides logistical and airlift support to other air and surface forces.

With its headquarters at Langley Air Force Base, Virginia, Tactical Air Command includes the three numbered air forces, the 9th, 12th, and 19th. The 9th Air Force has assigned to it the air divisions, tactical fighter, troop carrier, and tactical reconnaissance wings and squadrons located east of the Mississippi River, while those west of the Mississippi River are assigned to the 12th Air Force. The 19th Air Force is a planning headquarters responsible for organizing combined air strike forces as packages deployable anywhere in the world.

Tactical Air Operations

A tactical air operation is the deployment of air power alone or in cooperation with ground or naval forces to achieve and sustain air superiority, interdict movement of enemy forces, seek and destroy enemy forces and their supporting installations, and provide direct assistance to ground and naval forces.

A particular tactical air operation may involve tactical fighter aircraft, assault airlift, intratheater supply airlifts, and tactical command and control. These elements may be deployed individually or in a wide variety of combinations as the battle progresses.

Training

A major part of Tactical Air Command's mission involves the training of air and ground personnel. TAC operates the Fighter Weapons School, the Air-Ground Operations School, and the Technical Missile School.

Pilots graduating from the Air Training Command Pilot Schools are well trained, but when they are assigned to TAC they must be instructed in the combat operation of their particular tactical aircraft. This postgraduate work is accomplished in the fighter or troop carrier Combat Crew Training School conducted by TAC. In addition to all of its formal schools, each TAC unit carries on specific in-unit training programs.

TAC also trains personnel for a wide variety of functions required in its overall operation, for example, in the Noncommissioned Officers Academy. Tactical Air Command also is responsible for the supervision of training and inspection of Air National Guard (*see*) and USAF Reserve units earmarked for assignment to TAC upon mobilization.

Equipment

TAC's responsibility for equipping its units includes research and development of new and improved equipment and the establishment of requirements for future equipment. The equipment list of any unit of TAC fills a thick volume. The main items, namely aircraft and weapons, are as follows: TAC employs the C-47, C-123, B-26K, P-28, A-1E, and helicopters (*see*) in its special air warfare mission. In its logistic support airlift operations, TAC employs the C-130, C-124, C-119, C-123, and C-133 transport aircraft. TAC's fighter unit aircraft include the F-84, F-100, F-105, F-104, F-5, F-4C, T-33, and F-86. The TAC reconnaissance mission is carried out with the employment of the RB-66, RF-101, RF-4C, and RF-84. Tactical Air Command units

These aircraft represent a cross section of the many air operations carried out by the Tactical Air Command. Shown are the KB-50J tanker for refueling operations; the RF-101 Voodoo and F-100 Supersabre for reconnaissance and combat operations, the RB-66 bomber and the C-123 transport.

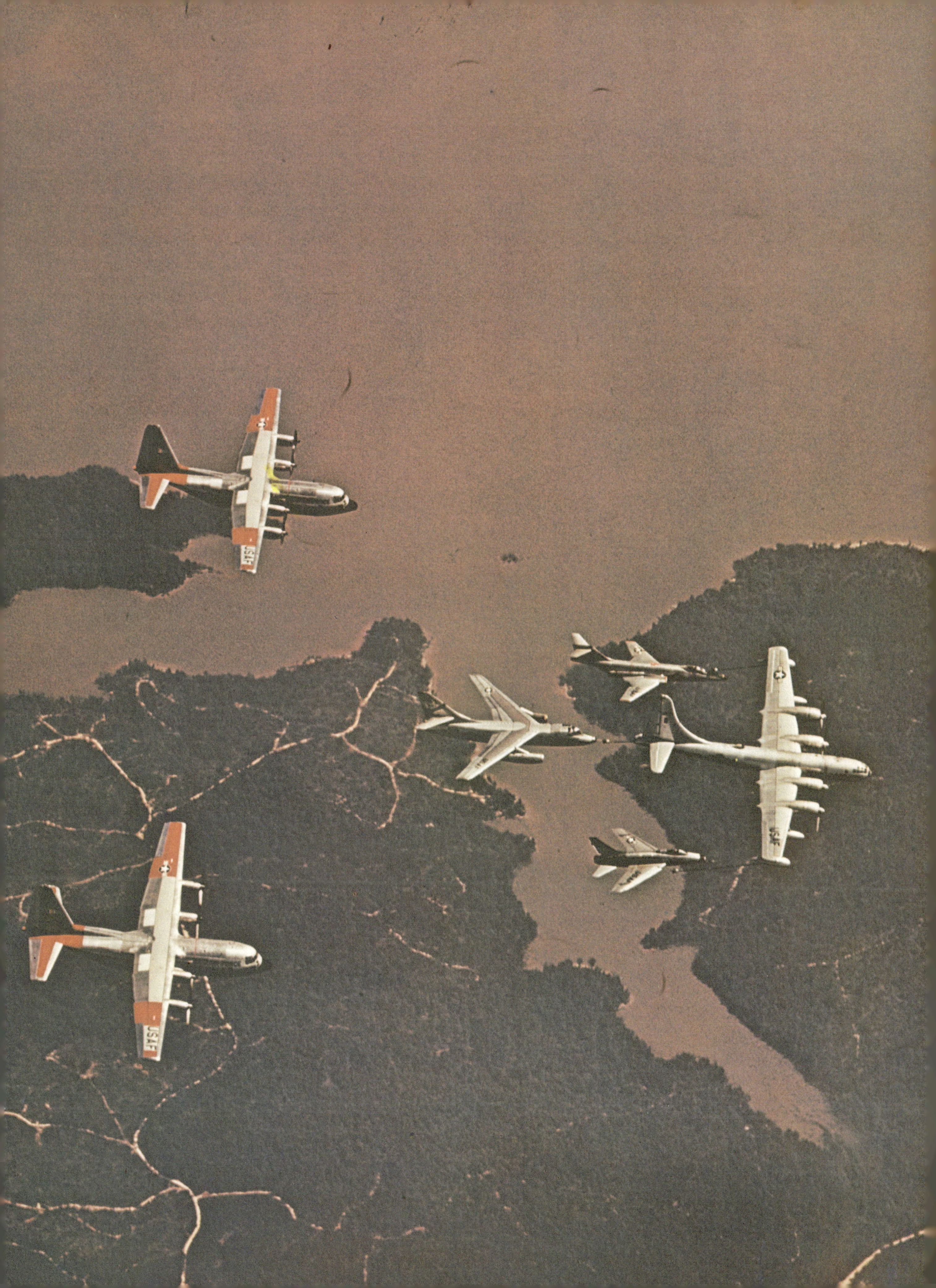
USAF

TAC'S FAMILY OF AIRCRAFT

F-104 "STARFIGHTER"

KB-50J "AERIAL TANKER"

RB-66 "DESTROYER"

F-100 "SUPERSABRE"

RF-101 "VOODOO"

C-135 "AIRBORNE COMMAND POST"

C-130 "HERCULES"

C-123 "PROVIDER"

F-105 "THUNDERCHIEF"

F-4C

The mission of the Tactical Air Command requires a wide variety of aircraft capable of covering the entire spectrum of air operations from a show of force to all-out war. TAC aircraft provide a mobile strike force which can be directed by the Airborne Command post and refueled by tankers for sustained and independent operations.

also use the F-111 (TFX) fighter.

TAC's weapons include both tactical nuclear and conventional types. The weapons systems include various types of aircraft and various combinations of weapons such as 20mm and 50-caliber guns, Incendijel, rockets, air-to-air missiles (*see*), air-to-surface missiles (*see*), and conventional bombs.

Planning

Tactical Air Command, through its 19th Air Force, prepares and maintains a wide variety of contingency plans. TAC must also develop and update policies, doctrines, and weapons systems. It maintains a library of material relating to tactical air operations, close air support of ground forces, airborne operations, special warfare operations, and joint operations with ground and naval forces.

Planning activities of Tactical Air Command are part of its role as the air component of certain unified commands, including the U.S. Strike Command (*see*), the Middle East, Africa, and Southern Asia Unified Command; and the Atlantic Command.

Howard T. Markey

See also: Military Airlift Command, Strategic Air Command

Tactical air navigation

Tactical air navigation (TACAN) was developed by the U.S. Navy to suit the particular needs of aircraft carrier and other mobile operations. The visual omni range-distance measuring equipment (VOR-DME) system was considered unwieldy for such uses. The TACAN station itself is a much smaller, more compact unit than the typical VOR station.

Since TACAN is basically a military use facility, it operates in the ultrahigh frequency (UHF) range. A total of 126 such UHF channels are provided. Aircraft equipped with TACAN receivers cannot receive VOR frequencies and vice versa, although a system of collocated transmitters is currently in use.

TACAN radial flying procedures are basically the same as those for VOR (*see*). In addition, the TACAN system provides for distance measuring in the same way as does a civilian station for distance measuring equipment (*see*).

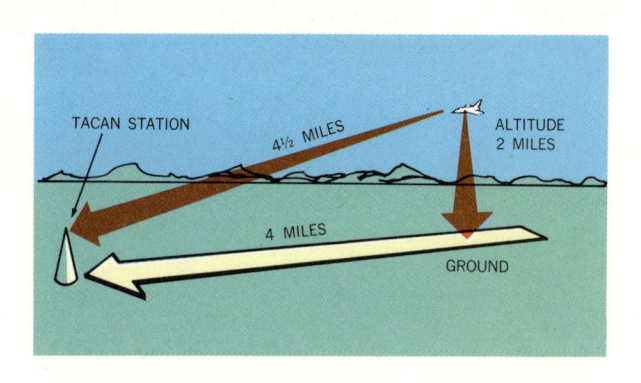

UHF reception distance is approximately the same as VHF. The TACAN distance measuring system is accurate to 0.3 miles in 100 miles. Since this distance is measured as a slant range distance, some error is inherent as the distance from the aircraft to the station is compared with the distance over the ground. To aircraft at an altitude of 50,000 feet, this slant range error is not over two miles until the airplane is 18 miles or less from the station.

Captain B.G. Baldwin

See also: Navigation techniques, VOR-TAC

Tail assembly, *see* Airplane, Empennage

Tail wind

A tail wind occurs when the airmass movement is within a 45° angle of either side of the aircraft in the same general direction of the flight path and is strong enough to noticeably increase the groundspeed. The tail wind may be *direct* or *quartering* and is the opposite of a head wind (*see*).

Takeoff and climb

Contrary to popular belief, the takeoff is the most critical portion of any flight profile except perhaps for crop dusting, low-level military operations, and other specialized aircraft uses.

Procedures Before Takeoff

After starting engine(s), the pilot taxis the airplane to what is usually called the *runup pad*. This area is used for testing the operation of piston engines and propellers (*see*) prior to takeoff. The pilot conducts the engine runup with the airplane pointed into whatever wind is blowing, so that the airflow (*see*) will provide maximum cooling for the engine. High-power operation on the ground with little or no airflow across the cylinders produces temperatures that are not good for engine reliability or long life. Jet engines (*see*) do not normally need runup because their operation can be checked on the takeoff roll.

Control-surface freedom of movement is now checked and wing flaps are extended to the takeoff position. Smaller, lighter airplanes do not require flaps for takeoff, and some of the older varieties of private airplanes still in use do not have wing flaps installed.

The Takeoff

To obtain the shortest possible takeoff roll, the runway most closely aligned with the wind is used. Since speed through the air is the only thing that makes a conventional airplane fly, a wind blowing on the nose at a velocity of 20 mph gives the plane an airspeed (*see*) of 20 mph even before the plane begins to move. If the wind is stronger, the takeoff distance on the ground will be further shortened.

After moving the aircraft into position at the end of the runway (*see*), a gradual power increase is begun. Engine power lever or throttles are slowly and gradually moved to the takeoff position. Abrupt movement could cause severe overspeeding or damaging high temperatures in the powerplants. Full power, within the limits set by the engine manufacturer, is used for takeoff.

An airplane with tricycle landing gear usually has a steerable nose wheel to control direction as it rolls down the runway. Planes equipped with conventional landing gear are also equipped with a steerable tail wheel which serves the same purpose. Pilots steer these wheels with the rudder pedals except in the case of large transport airplanes which have separate nose gear steering wheels. In either case, these wheels are used only until the rush of air flowing past the rud-

Takeoff and climb

der (*see*) makes it become a more effective directional control than the wheels (*see*).

As the plane picks up airspeed, all flight controls become effective and any deviation from a straight, wings-level takeoff path can be easily corrected by a control movement in the appropriate direction. Resistance to the application of control pressures and the airplane's reactions to these pressures are the only reliable indicators of the control developed.

An experienced pilot will fly a small, light airplane primarily by control "feel" and pressure, while a large plane is flown with reference to airspeeds.

The lightplane is lifted off the ground by a slight back pressure on the control stick (*see*) or wheel, while a large jet-powered transport is rotated, that is, the nose is lifted, again by back pressure on the wheel, to a specified angle at a definite, predetermined airspeed.

This brings the pilot and his craft, no matter what its type, to the critical point: the engine or engines are producing maximum power and are undergoing the greatest stress, and although the airplane is flying, it is at its lowest possible altitude and slowest airspeed. The pilot's two greatest safety factors are altitude and airspeed and these are precisely what he is lacking at this point. Any engine malfunction or wind gust that changes the flight path (*see*) of his plane requires prompt corrective action to insure a safe takeoff.

Climb

After the plane has reached a safe altitude and airspeed, and the landing gear and wing flaps, if present, have been retracted, the pilot reduces the engine power and speed to a value that is most commonly called *climb power*. This increases the engine's probable service life and reliability by lessening the wear and tear on its operating parts by virtue of reduced speed and temperatures.

Several operating considerations must be taken into account by the pilot while climbing his plane to the desired cruising altitude. In addition to holding his course, he must maintain a proper climb speed, usually specified by the airplane manufacturer, to promote proper engine cooling. This is of no importance to a jet pilot, since engine cooling is a function of engine speed and not of aircraft speed. However, pilots of both types of aircraft must compensate for the fact that the power output of all air-breathing engines decreases as altitude increases. This requires a change in angle of climb to maintain the desired climb speed. — Captain Robert D. Wood

See also: Cruising flight, Landing techniques, Power management

Tanker aircraft

Many advantages accrue when an aircraft is resupplied with fuel while underway at flight altitude rather than on the ground. Elimination of the time required for descending, landing, ground refueling, relaunching, and climb back to altitude is a primary and obvious advantage. Others are the increased ordnance capacity resulting from a lowered fuel load at original takeoff, the elimination of accident exposure and maintenance requirements inherent in each landing operation, and the lengthening of combat missions to insure full ordnance delivery before reaching the low-fuel level. All of these factors are particularly acute in relation to jet aircraft, the fuel consumption of which is so much greater at lower than at higher altitudes. The tanker aircraft makes all of these advantages available to military strategists and tacticians.

A tanker aircraft is necessarily large in order to carry, in addition to the fuel needed for its own flight, a sufficient quantity of "off-load" fuel to justify the cost of the operation. Even so, and while a number of fighters may be fully resupplied by a single tanker, a large bomber may empty the AR (aerial refueling) tanks of the tanker in a single refueling hook-up.

Since a combat mission takes precedence, tanker crews will deliver their "own" fuel to a fighter or bomber when necessary to insure accomplishment of the combat mission.

Therefore, the tanker carries an intercommunicating series of tanks and the piping, valves, pumps, and controls which enable the normally four-or-five-man tanker crew to transfer fuel from tank to tank, to its own engines, to the receiver aircraft, or to the atmosphere (that is, to "dump" fuel).

Equipment

The equipment carried by the tanker for transfer of fuel to receiver aircraft in flight is of two types, called the boom and probe and drogue systems.

The *boom* system includes an elongated, telescoping set of tubes pivoted below the rear of the fuselage and having control surfaces which enable the boom operator of the tanker crew to position the boom within a limited area (the *refueling envelope*) behind the tanker. The receiver aircraft has a receptacle on its wing or fuselage and, when the receiver is in position, the boom operator (*boomer*) aligns the boom and extends it into the receptacle to accomplish a hook-up. Fuel is then rapidly transferred through the boom and into the receiver aircraft's fuel tanks.

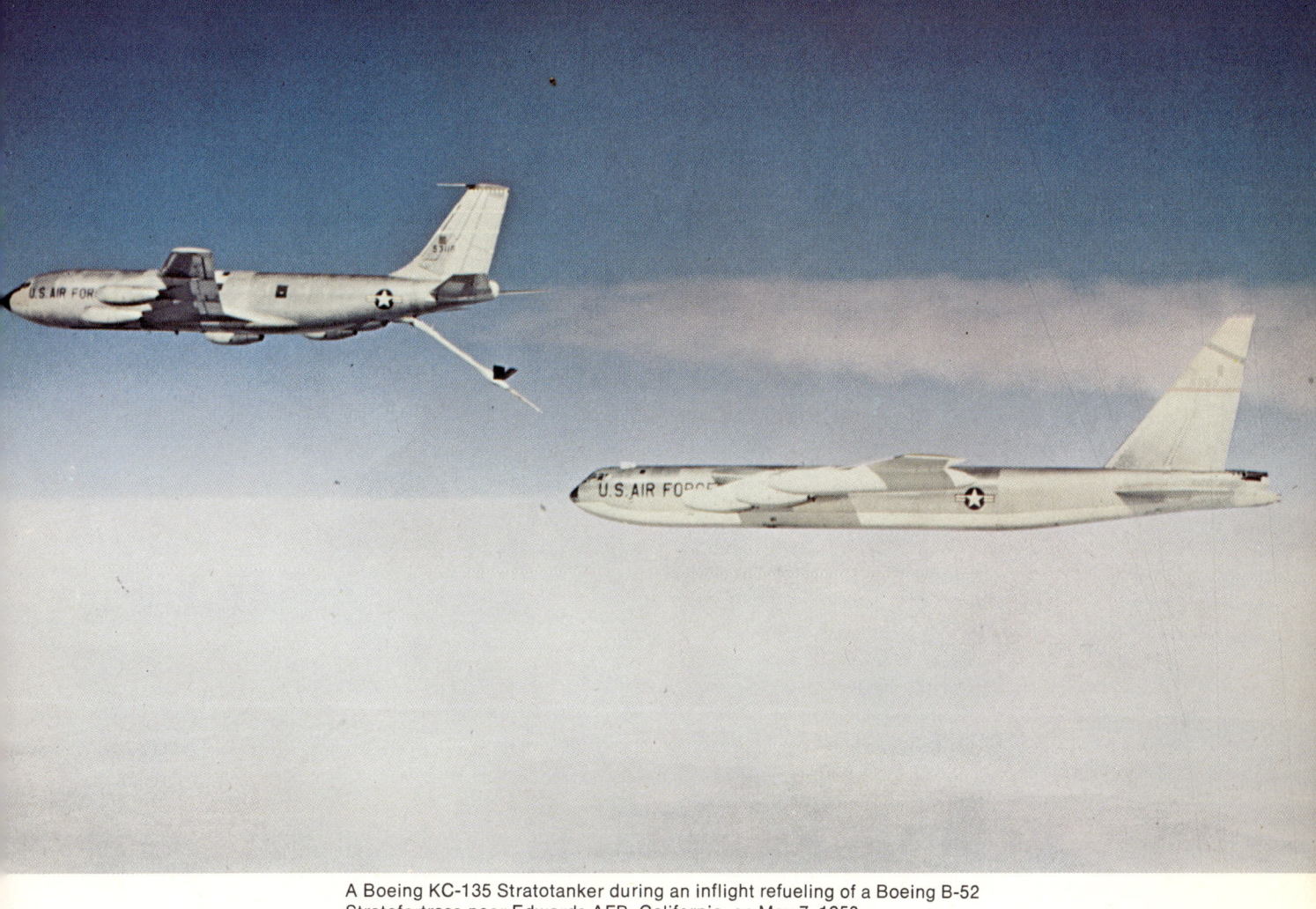

A Boeing KC-135 Stratotanker during an inflight refueling of a Boeing B-52 Stratofortress near Edwards AFB, California, on May 7, 1958.

The *probe and drogue* system comprises an elongated probe or thin tube extending forward of the wing or nose of the receiver aircraft and having a nozzle at its tip. The tanker, in this case, carries a reel of flexible hose. A *basket* or rearward-open cone is carried at the end of the hose. The tanker unreels the hose and the receiver pilot flies his probe nozzle into the basket, engaging the valve at the basket base to accomplish a hook-up and receive fuel through the hose and into its fuel tanks.

A shorter length of flexible hose, with its basket at one end, is attached to the end of the boom to enable a boom-equipped tanker to refuel a probe-equipped receiver. In this case, the fuel is transferred through the boom, the short hose, and the receiver's probe into the receiver's fuel tanks.

Thus far, current tanker aircraft have been primarily tanker versions of transport aircraft such as the modern C-135, C-141, and C-130 of the USAF. Takeoff weight limits are reached before the cabin area of these planes are filled with fuel tanks, leaving space to carry passengers and cargo in an alternate mission. As the refueling mission becomes more and more routine, it can be expected that tanker aircraft and equipment improvements will result from future research and development programs.

Howard T. Markey

See also: Refueling

Tape recording

Tape recorders are used in many ways in aviation and space science. Simple audio recorders are used to record the voices of astronauts to preserve their observations and comments for later study. Much more complex data recorders continuously monitor the readings of a large number of scientific devices, as well as the cockpit instruments of an airplane or spacecraft itself, so that the entire flight can be studied over and over for a detailed analysis of its results. Video recorders retain the electronic images from television cameras (which may be placed in hazardous or inaccessible locations) for leisurely study, either in real time (actual time) or at reduced speed rates down to still framing if desired. Large banks of digital tape recorders act as the memory units for the computers which process and analyze

Tape recording

the tremendous amounts of data collected from space voyages or aircraft tests.

Another interesting space application of tape recording is in the gathering of weather information by satellites. During the time a satellite is making a complete orbit of the Earth, pictures of cloud cover and weather conditions are being stored on tape. Then as the satellite passes over the ground control station, the tape is played back. The electronic signals derived from the tape are transmitted to the ground where they are used to generate photographs of the weather conditions around the globe.

Principles of Tape Recording

In magnetic tape recording, information is stored on the surface of a long ribbon of thin plastic tape. This thin tape has a coating on one surface which consists of tiny particles of an *oxide,* a material which can be magnetized by holding it between the poles of a magnet.

In recording, the tape is passed over the open end of a small horseshoe-shaped electromagnet, or *recording head*. Variations in the current supplied to the wire winding of this head by the recording amplifier cause variations in the strength of the magnetic field. As each tiny particle of the oxide coating passes over the recording head, the particle is magnetized with a direction and strength dependent on the current at that instant.

In playing back the recording, the tape is passed over a *playback head,* which may be the same head previously used for recording with the recording amplifier now disconnected. Each of the tiny magnetic particles on the tape emits lines of magnetic flux, just as any magnet would. As the magnetized particles pass over the recording head, the flux lines link a gap in the steel core of the head, generating a very weak voltage in the head winding. This voltage, which will vary in amplitude and polarity in

The magnetic thermoelectric recording subsystem used in Mariner stored picture data until it could be transmitted to Earth.

A diagram of a tape recorder shows the various components in the system and their functions.

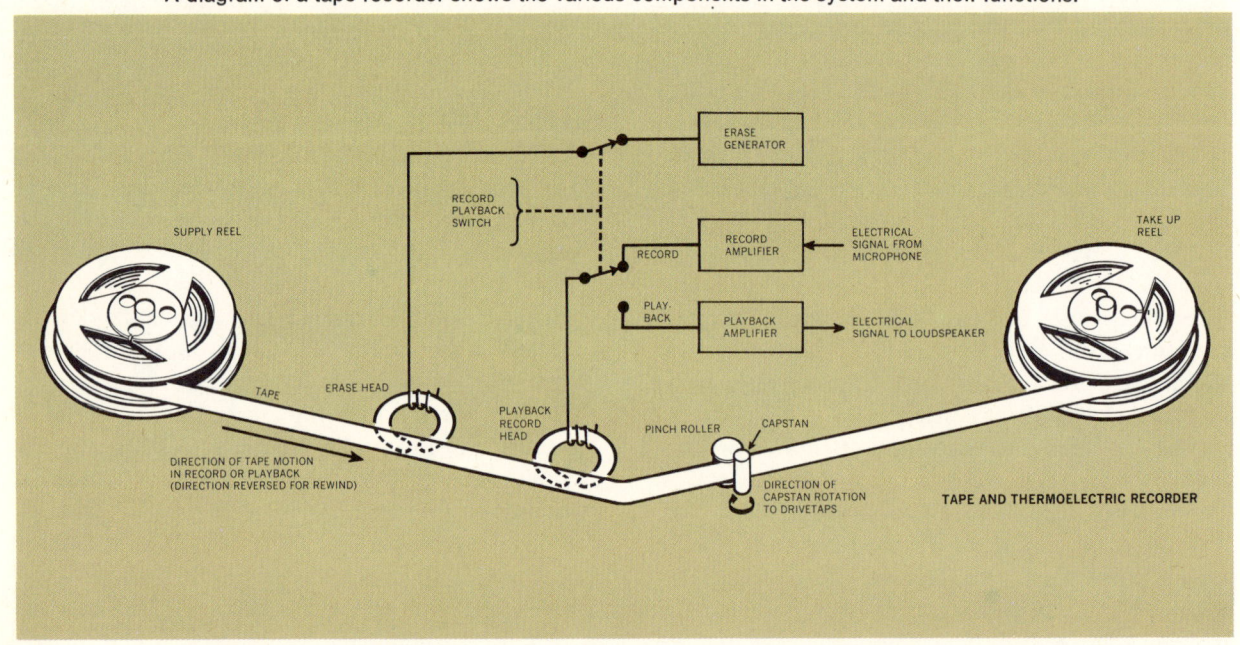

accordance with the strength and polarity of the tiny magnets on the tape, is amplified by a playback amplifier to raise it to a usable level.

Because sensing of the magnetic field of the recording causes no weakening of the recording, the recorded tape may be played back many times.

Magnetic tape is usually *erased* (cleaned of old information) by an erase head placed where the tape passes over it just before reaching the recording head. A high-frequency current from the erase circuit causes the magnetic field of the erase head to alternate at a very high rate, restoring the individual oxide particles of the tape to a magnetically neutral condition as they cross the erase head.

Because the maximum frequency of the electrical signal which can be recovered in playing back a tape recording is strongly dependent on the speed at which the tape crosses the playback head, recorders are designed for a wide range of tape speeds. Some recorders for voice and music operate at less than one inch per second, while video (television) recorders run at speeds up to 1,500 inches per second.

Basic Mechanism of a Tape Recorder

In a typical tape recorder, the tape is fed off the supply reel, past the erase head, across the record-playback head, and onto the takeup reel. The energy to move the tape at a very constant, precise rate is supplied by the *capstan,* a motor-driven wheel against which the tape is pressed by another wheel known as a *pinch roller.* The takeup reel and the supply reel (in rewind operation) may be driven by additional motors, or from the capstan motor by means of drive wheels, or by a belt and pully arrangement.

Richard F. Whiting

See also: Data acquisition and processing, Electronics, Magnets and magnetism

Taxiway, *see* Airports

Taylor, James M.

Aerospace research pilot
Born: November 27, 1930;
Stamps, Arkansas
Service: Major, USAF

Major James M. Taylor is one of the first group of aerospace research pilots assigned to the Manned Orbiting Laboratory (MOL) (*see*) program. He earned an associate of arts degree at Southern State University, Magnolia, Arkansas, in 1950, and a bachelor of science degree in electrical engineering at the University of Michigan in 1959.

Major Taylor began his Air Force career as an airman in 1951. He entered pilot training as an aviation cadet in 1952 and received his wings and commission the following year.

With over 4,200 flying hours, Major Taylor has flown the F-100, F-101, F-106, KC-135, and T-38 aircraft. Taylor has served as a fighter pilot with the USAF Air Defense Command. He was also a flight test engineer in jet bombers in jet cargo aircraft and an F-106 project officer and test pilot.

Taylor completed the Squadron Officer Course of the Air University (*see*), Maxwell Air Force Base, Alabama, in 1959. He was graduated from the Aerospace Research Pilot School, Edwards Air Force Base, California, in 1964.

MOL astronaut Taylor is married to the former Jacquelyn K. King. They have three children.

Charlene A. Wrobel

Technological projections

The present era marks the early dawn of the space age which promises to stretch over eons. This dawn represents the transition between a humanity chained to one planet and a humanity free to roam an empire whose only boundary is infinity. Because of the growing ability to quickly translate knowledge into capability, this transition may take no longer than 50 to 100 years, a very brief time by historical standards.

Space is our major source of knowledge and the only region in which we can expand virtually without limits. Our need for knowledge and understanding requires that we continue to explore space, probing the planets and going far beyond the solar system. Aerospace technological projections must therefore be related to the engineering requirements for space applications and explorations.

Space Applications

Space can be used whenever its environmental characteristics offer advantages over conditions on Earth. Space applications can be grouped into: 1) utilization of near-Earth space (geospace), 2) utilization of the moon, 3) utilization of the solar system, and 4) utilization of space regions and celestial bodies for biological and agricultural possibilities.

Geospace Applications

Geospace has many environmental characteristics such as low or zero gravity, very high and very low temperature, antiseptic conditions, and conditions

Technological projections

permitting vibration control, which can be used for a variety of applications. Table 1 surveys geospace applications and benefits to humanity, including such advanced concepts as the orbital hospital, orbital tourist facility, and geospace industries.

Communications is one of the most significant geospace applications due to the great need for information transmission. Telecasting includes transmission of television, radio, telegraph, telephone, and mail via satellites. Agricultural, weather, industrial, scientific and other information can be supplied to, or exchanged between, any two points on the Earth.

Air and sea traffic control rapidly becomes more urgent as traffic volume increases. If past growth is an example there will be seven to ten times more aircraft crossing the Atlantic in 1978, and many will be supersonic transports (*see*) traveling at 1,200 to 2,000 mph. In the 1980's and 1990's, hypersonic transports flying at 6,000 to 8,000 mph will be added. Obviously, it will become necessary to extend the existing air traffic control system over wide, densely traveled areas.

The "super-control towers" of the future will be advanced navigation satellites in synchronous orbits. A system of such satellites can serve as relay points for radio signals between users (aircraft and ships) and ground control stations.

Space meteorology has two primary objectives: 1) to provide the basis for highly reliable two- and four-week weather forecasts; and 2) to advance the understanding of global and local dynamics of Earth's weather. In turn, this understanding will form the basis for some measure of weather control through changes in land/water distribution by large-scale engineering projects, or through atmospheric changes induced from ground or orbit.

In the next five to ten years, advancements in sensor technology, especially in infrared-sensitive in-

Table 1: EARTH-ORIENTED OPPORTUNITIES AND BENEFITS RESULTING FROM GEOSPACE APPLICATIONS

Geospace Applications	Economical	Social	Entrepreneurial	Cultural
Communication • Telecasting • Traffic Control • Private Communication	• Critical information transmission	• Educational and subsidiary benefits • Improved travel safety	• Communication satellite business	• Entertainment • Improvements in recreation and leisure time
Meteorology • Weather Analysis • Weather Prediction • Weather Control	• Agriculture reduction of losses and damage due to natural stresses • Reduction of damages by air pollution	• Eventual opening of new land for settlement	• Probably only subsidiary opportunities	• Improved scheduling of recreational activities
Earth-Resources Monitoring and Identification • Agricultural • Geological and Mineral • Hydrological • Oceanic	• Food production • Forestry preservation • Discovery and exploitation of geological and mineral resources • Improved water management • Reduction of damages by water pollution	• Absorption of impact of world population increase	• Probably only subsidiary opportunities	• Improvements in living standards
Orbital Scientific Research	• Agricultural benefits from biological studies (speculative)	• Improvements in scientific education from orbit via TV classrooms	• Probably only subsidiary opportunities	• Extension and broadening of scope of scientific research
Therapeutical Application		• Development of new curative methods using low or null gravity conditions • Low or null gravity environment preferable to handicapped persons	• Probably only subsidiary opportunities	
Recreation			• Orbital hotel business	• New art forms
Manufacturing			• Special products for the Earth market • Products for the extraterrestrial market	

Source: *Dr. Krafft A. Ehricke and Mrs. Betty Miller*

struments which complement optical, observations by penetrating cloud layers to various depths, and in data processing of multispectral observations (observing various regions of the optical, infrared, and microwave spectrum simultaneously) will permit an advanced space weather observation system. This system may take over most of the work now conducted by numerous stations on land and at sea.

Identification and management of natural resources becomes increasingly urgent due to the growing world population. Observation from space and analysis of data obtained offer possibilities for discovery of previously hidden resources. A resources satellite can search thousands of square miles for sign of minerals or oil in minutes. Diseased plants can be recognized early by their different reflection characteristics in the ultraviolet and infrared. Countermeasures can then be taken before large-scale crop spoilage results.

The economic importance of food from the oceans is now self-evident. Observations by satellites will provide a more effective and economical means of scanning the oceans for seafood concentration.

New natural gas deposits, fresh water supplies, and embryonic forest fires can also be found by resources satellites. The foregoing are but a few examples of resources identification and monitoring which the applications satellites of tomorrow will perform.

Orbital Scientific Research Laboratory

Orbiting laboratories for scientific research in solar physics, astrophysics (*see*), planetology, basic physics, chemistry, and biology will make much use of the vacuum environment of space where the entire electromagnetic spectrum is available to sensors. There are no absorption bands or disturbances encountered as when looking through the atmosphere (*see*) from its bottom up. Some orbiting laboratories will also make use of space environmental characteristics.

Space utilization for therapeutic purposes: Use of the extraterrestrial environment for biological and medical research, and thus potentially for therapeutic purposes, will be based primarily on the use of low or zero gravity conditions which reduce one's weight from what it would be on the Earth.

Long-term biomedical effects of zero-gravity are still largely unknown. The level at which a new equilibrium between the body and a new environment can be established is not determined, but certain changes have been observed on astronauts or are recognized medically as possible or probable.

The use of space for therapeutic purposes can have two primary objects, curative and alleviative. Curative objectives involve cures and corrections. Alleviative objectives aim at freeing handicapped persons from their bonds by temporary or permanent transfer into low or zero gravity environments.

The first practical application of space therapy will probably take the form of a dispensary for space crews. Once proven, this approach can lead to an orbital hospital (*Fig. 1*). Its configuration would provide varying artificial gravity levels; rapid access to and egress from all hospital areas; effective isolation between areas; and extensive modularization for easy exchange, modernization, or expansion.

Recreation in Space

The space environment can also be therapeutic for basically healthy persons in need of relaxation. An orbital tourist facility (Table 2 and *Fig. 2*) would take advantage of low-gravity conditions, thereby relieving stress upon the body and particularly the heart.

Earth-orbiting, lunar, and interplanetary tourist facilities will offer an unusual spectrum of recreational activities. These can include unprecedented sight-seeing attractions, walks in space or on the surfaces of celestial bodies, three-dimensional athletics, etc.

Industry in Space

For industrial purposes, a broad range of space environmental characteristics will be used (*Fig. 3*). Manufacturing in space will be based on this and on development of more advanced and economical Earth-space transportation systems.

Products will be made for markets on Earth and in space. At first, emphasis will be on small, low-weight products of high cost and great chemo-physical sophistication because of transportation limitations. This includes microelectronic items—highly advanced solid state circuitry and highly sensitive sensors and other measuring instruments.

The second phase could be the manufacture of highly pure materials for special purposes because particulate and gaseous contamination can easily be eliminated on a scale in space which is almost unattainable and extremely costly on Earth. In this category, there is thin-film technology (conducting or magnetic coatings, solar cells, etc.) and microbial culture technologies—including some for pharmaceutical applications—which typically require extreme cleanliness.

Cryogenic temperatures in volumes shaded from sunlight permit generation of strong magnetic fields by the use of superconductive circuitry, thus minimum electric power. These fields can be used to

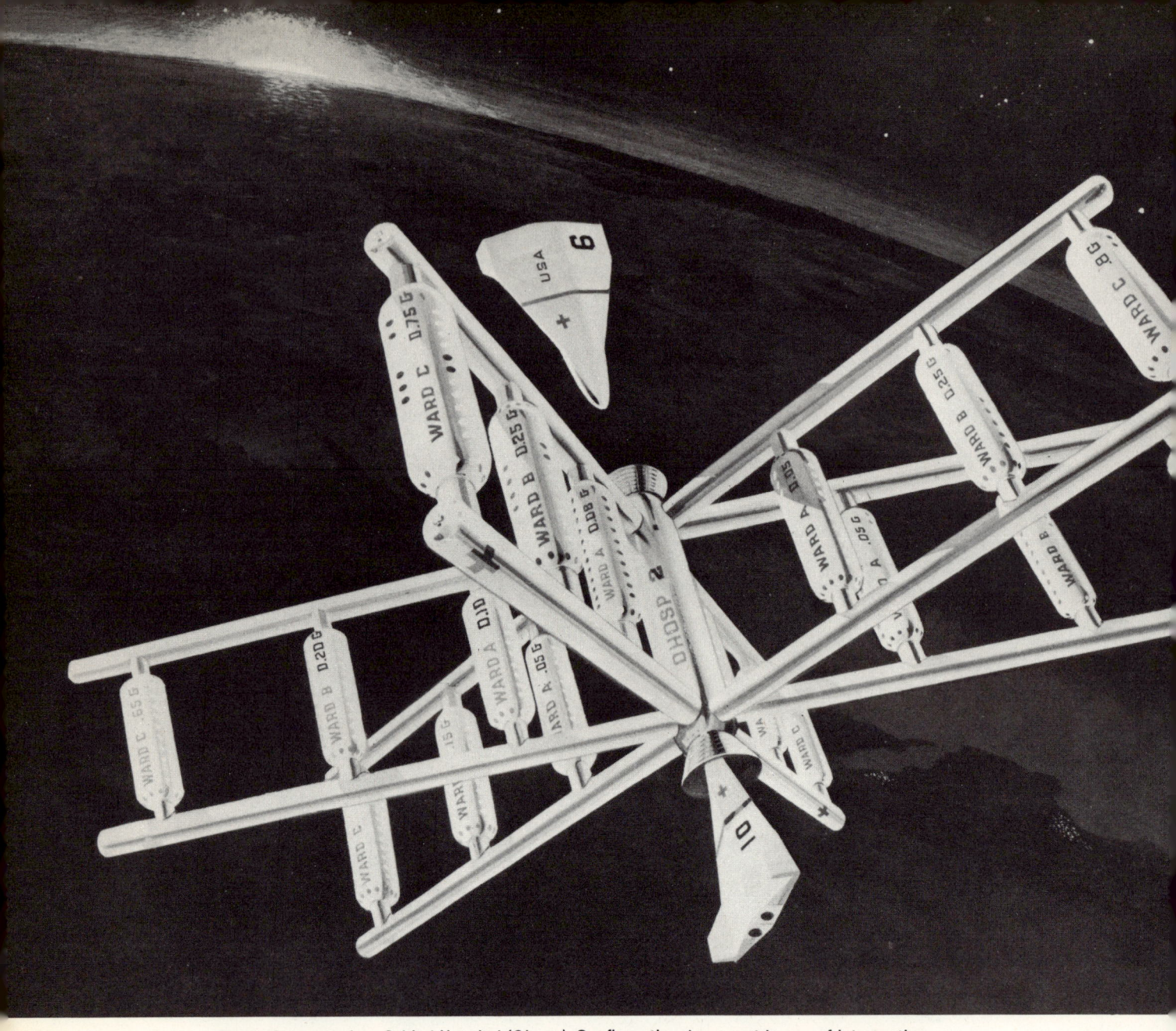

Fig. 1: Concept of an Orbital Hospital (Ohosp). Configurational concept is one of intersecting ladders with rungs representing cylindrical hospital ends. The sidepieces are passageways interconnecting the wards in such a manner that each ward is separately accessible, thereby allowing individual wards to be isolated for technical or medical reasons. Such a configuration also permits a ward to be replaced by a more advanced one without rendering the other wards inoperative. Hospital spins slowly about a hub at whose ends orbital transports can dock. Artificial *g*-level in each ward increases with distance of ward from the hub. The biomedical practicability of space therapies is not established conclusively at present.

shape and form materials on a scale which would be unacceptably costly on Earth.

The vacuum of space is important to manufacturing in that the absence of friction allows for sizable rotating equipment and rotational speeds which are virtually unattainable on Earth. In space, spin velocities can be obtained in ultra-centrifuges which produce many thousands of times Earth-gravity.

Utilization of the Moon

Like the Earth, the lunar surface has the necessary firm foundation for the establishment of very large telescopes to look and listen deep into the universe. Today's Earth telescopes can see two billion light years away, but telescopes on the moon will see at least ten billion light years into the past, the time before the sun and Earth were born.

Like space, the lunar surface permits an open view of the universe over the entire spectrum. Thus the moon combines the advantages of a celestial body with those of space, and because of its nearness to the Earth, it is a very important island between the Earth and the expanses of interplanetary space.

Fig. 2: Concept of an Ecologically Self-Sufficient Orbital Tourist Facility. Structure spins slowly about its 1,500-ft. long axis at whose ends are docking facilities for orbital transports and small excursion boats (ocher-colored disks). Large yellow spheres, about 200 ft. in diameter, are Dynaria. Red hemispherical enclosures are Other-World Rooms. Light green cylinders are hotel accommodations, each cylinder representing a 10-story building. Purple-colored disks behind each hotel row represent a theater, restaurant, casino, and a shopping center, respectively. Dark green cylinders contain hydroponic farms and animal shelters. Blue structural members are hollow and serve as interconnecting passageways.

The moon is a valuable scientific laboratory. If equipped with communications facilities operating in extremely high-frequency and even laser frequency regimes, it can link the solar system together and serve as the voice of Earth.

The moon's low gravitational pull renders departure into and return from interplanetary missions much easier than from the Earth. The moon will also serve as a training and testing ground for operations elsewhere in the solar system.

These advantages, however, cannot be realized without prior buildup of a lunar technology which turns lonely outposts into centers of production of raw materials, goods, and services. With space transportation systems which can be available in 15 to 25 years, the lunar surface and whatever raw materials it contains will be far easier to reach than the depths of Earth oceans because distance is less of a barrier than a hostile environment.

Utilization of the Solar System

The utilization of other planets (*see*), their moons, and of asteroids (*see*) and comets (*see*) is inevitable.

Technological projections

Table 2: POSSIBLE ORBITAL TOURIST FACILITY FEATURES

- Low-gravity or null-gravity Dynaria in which the vacationers can "swim", move about in three dimensions like fish in water. Air streams are circulated instead of water currents.
- Dynaria also serve as space theaters showing ballet and acrobatics under low-gravity conditions and as sports stadiums for competitive games such as three-dimensional tennis.
- Earth and Space Observation Rooms.
- Small laboratories in which guests can be shown, or can conduct themselves, interesting and entertaining experiments under low-gravity or null-gravity conditions.
- World-Rooms, large volumes simulating realistically landscapes, illumination, and thermal, atmospheric, and gravitational conditions on the surfaces of other planets or planet moons.
- Space Zoo and Botanic Exhibitions, showing animals and plants changed by generations of existence under low-gravity conditions, mutants by radiation or reared under different combinations of g-level, atmospheric pressure and composition, and temperatures.
- Video telephone service through which guests can contact friends and relatives on Earth when passing over their areas.
- Space Walks on (or without) tethers.
- Space Boats, rented for tours around the large Tourist Facility or for brief orbital excursions.

Source: *Dr. Krafft A. Ehricke and Mrs. Betty Miller*

Utilization must, however, be preceded by solar system exploration—an endeavor now in its infancy.

The most important achievements will be in the area of space biology (*see*). In large hydroponic facilities, life forms can be introduced into space. Through space experiments, it may be possible to change them into life forms capable of existing on other planets, which can potentially provide the space agricultural basis for significant extraterrestrial colonies.

Space Exploration

Exploration in space constitutes the beginning of the utilization of space. It must, therefore, continue along with the utilization of explored regions. Solar system exploration will be concerned with gathering information about 1) surface conditions on other planets, including evidence of past or present life forms; 2) planetary atmospheres; and 3) the astrophysical nature of the solar system.

Initially these missions can be accomplished by unmanned probes. Development of sensors for the probes will be of great importance. The necessary launch vehicles and upper stages are presently available for unmanned missions of the next ten years.

Advances in navigation equipment, in reliability over long-duration flight times, and in knowledge will telescope technology toward the practical feasi-

UTILIZATION OF SPACE ENVIRONMENTAL CHARACTERISTICS FOR INDUSTRIAL PURPOSES

THESE MANUFACTURING TECHNIQUES → UTILIZE THESE SPACE ENVIRONMENTAL CHARACTERISTICS → AND MAY LEAD TO THESE MATERIALS AND TECHNIQUES

			1	2	3	4	5	6	7	8	9	I	II	III	IV	V	VI
			Vacuum	Low- to null-gravity	Ultra-high gravity (thousands of g)	Cryogenic temperatures (in shade of sun and Earth)	Very-high temperatures (solar concentrator)	Noise and vibration control	Clean environment	Wide radiation spectrum	Unlimited volume	Ultra-pure materials	Ultra-precise alloys	Thin film technology	Quarantine technology	Ultra-hard or super-dense materials	Mechanical manufacturing processes (compressing, cold forming, parts assembly)
	A	Evaporation/condensation techniques	X			X	X					•	•	•			•
	B	Transportation and handling of delicate or high-precision components during manufacturing process		X								•	•	•			•
	C	Ultracentrifuge techniques	X		X							•	•	•		•	•
	D	Cryogenic techniques	X			X						•	•		•		
	E	High-temperature techniques					X					•	•				
	F	Magnetic techniques	X			X					X					•	
	G	Microbial culture techniques	X					X	X	X					•		
	H	Crystal manufacturing techniques	X	X	X			X	X	X		•	•				
	I	Techniques of joining parts (attaching, surface fusion, cold welding)	X	X	X			X	X								•

Source: *Dr. Krafft A. Ehricke and Mrs. Betty Miller*

2240

bility of manned planetary missions. Manned missions are more complex, but will yield more knowledge. They will range from planetary orbiting to landings and, ultimately, the establishment of bases. They will involve deployment of a multitude of probes, a large number of experiments, on-the-spot evaluation, and extensive exploration.

Even after manned planetary mission capability is achieved, very-long-duration automated monitors will be left in orbits or on the surfaces of planets for continued data sampling. When the technology of such monitors permits an operational life of many decades without human maintenance, monitors of this type will qualify as first-generation probes beyond the solar system.

Exploring interstellar space will be among the great challenges of the 21st century. *Fig. 4* summarizes space technological projections for the next 80 years.

Krafft A. Ehricke and Betty Ann Miller

See also: Interplanetary travel, Lunar bases, Orbits and trajectories, Space stations

Tektites, *see* Astrogeology, Moon

Telemetry

Telemetry is measurement from a distance. Although its classification as a science is more or less coincident with the advancement of electronics, its roots go far back in history. The word itself is derived from the Greek words *tele* meaning "far off," and *meter*, "to measure." Today telemetry is an important phase of space communications.

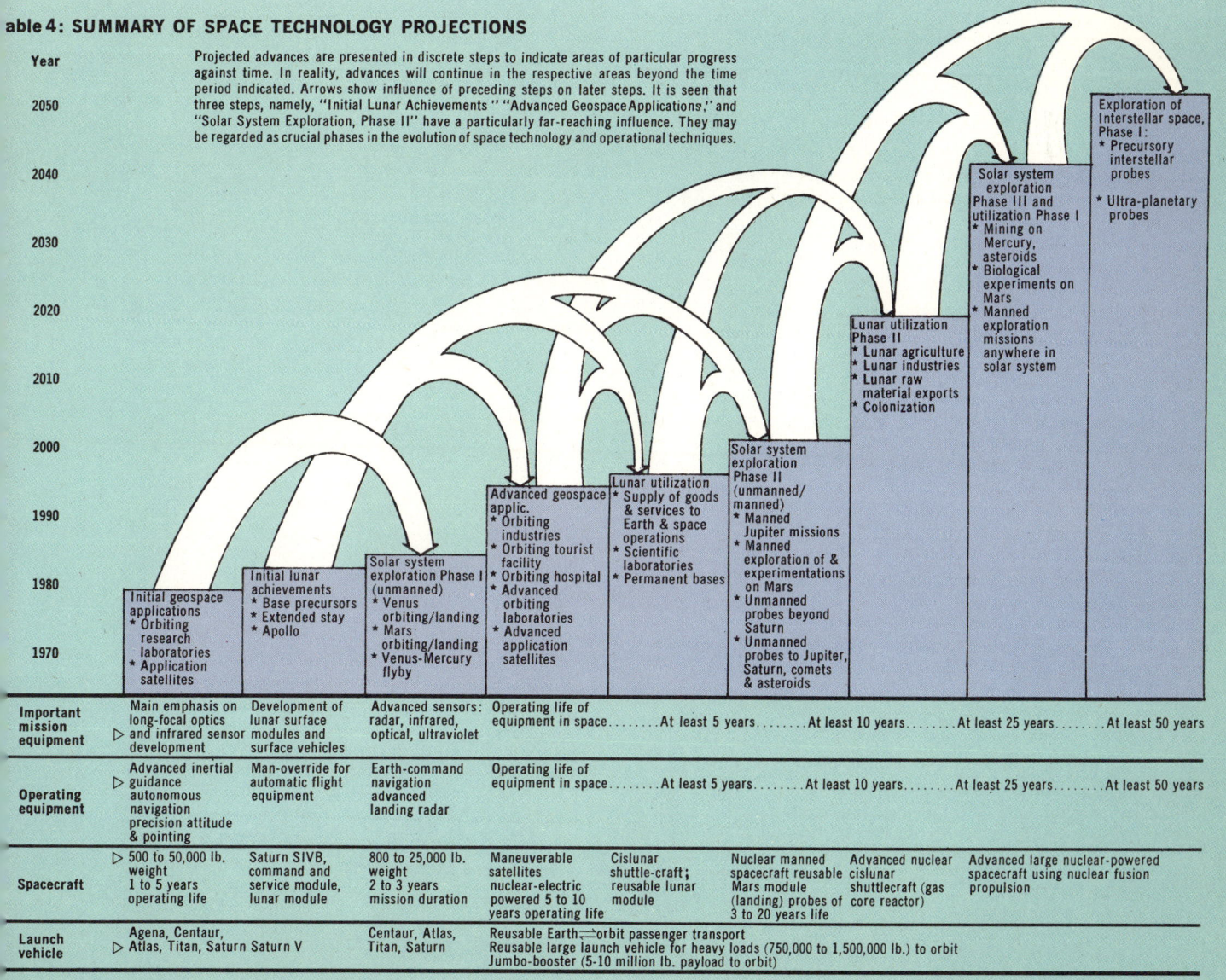

Table 4: SUMMARY OF SPACE TECHNOLOGY PROJECTIONS

Projected advances are presented in discrete steps to indicate areas of particular progress against time. In reality, advances will continue in the respective areas beyond the time period indicated. Arrows show influence of preceding steps on later steps. It is seen that three steps, namely, "Initial Lunar Achievements," "Advanced Geospace Applications," and "Solar System Exploration, Phase II" have a particularly far-reaching influence. They may be regarded as crucial phases in the evolution of space technology and operational techniques.

Year									
2050									Exploration of Interstellar space, Phase I: * Precursory interstellar probes * Ultra-planetary probes
2040								Solar system exploration Phase III and utilization Phase I * Mining on Mercury, asteroids * Biological experiments on Mars * Manned exploration missions anywhere in solar system	
2030									
2020							Lunar utilization Phase II * Lunar agriculture * Lunar industries * Lunar raw material exports * Colonization		
2010									
2000						Solar system exploration Phase II (unmanned/manned) * Manned Jupiter missions * Manned exploration of & experimentations on Mars * Unmanned probes beyond Saturn * Unmanned probes to Jupiter, Saturn, comets & asteroids			
1990					Lunar utilization * Supply of goods & services to Earth & space operations * Scientific laboratories * Permanent bases				
1980				Advanced geospace applic. * Orbiting industries * Orbiting tourist facility * Orbiting hospital * Advanced orbiting laboratories * Advanced application satellites					
1970	Initial geospace applications * Orbiting research laboratories * Application satellites	Initial lunar achievements * Base precursors * Extended stay * Apollo	Solar system exploration Phase I (unmanned) * Venus orbiting/landing * Mars orbiting/landing * Venus-Mercury flyby						

Important mission equipment	Main emphasis on long-focal optics and infrared sensor development	Development of lunar surface modules and surface vehicles	Advanced sensors: radar, infrared, optical, ultraviolet	Operating life of equipment in space....... At least 5 years....... At least 10 years....... At least 25 years....... At least 50 years
Operating equipment	Advanced inertial guidance autonomous navigation precision attitude & pointing	Man-override for automatic flight equipment	Earth-command navigation advanced landing radar	Operating life of equipment in space....... At least 5 years....... At least 10 years....... At least 25 years....... At least 50 years
Spacecraft	500 to 50,000 lb. weight 1 to 5 years operating life	Saturn SIVB, command and service module, lunar module	800 to 25,000 lb. weight 2 to 3 years mission duration	Maneuverable satellites nuclear-electric powered 5 to 10 years operating life	Cislunar shuttle-craft; reusable lunar module	Nuclear manned spacecraft reusable Mars module (landing) probes of 3 to 20 years life	Advanced nuclear cislunar shuttlecraft (gas core reactor)	Advanced large nuclear-powered spacecraft using nuclear fusion propulsion
Launch vehicle	Agena, Centaur, Atlas, Titan, Saturn Saturn V		Centaur, Atlas, Titan, Saturn	Reusable Earth⇌orbit passenger transport Reusable large launch vehicle for heavy loads (750,000 to 1,500,000 lb.) to orbit Jumbo-booster (5-10 million lb. payload to orbit)

Source: *Dr. Krafft A. Ehricke and Mrs. Betty Miller*

Telemetry

How Telemetry Works

Basically, telemetering utilizes a radio signal which contains many channels of information regarding conditions both inside and outside a spacecraft in orbit. The radio information sent from a spacecraft is picked up on the ground by a highly directional antenna and fed to a receiver (*see*). The receiver decodes the signal into separate channels of information, and the decoded signals are then sent to various recorders and other recipients.

Telemetry Standards

One key Inter-Range Instrumentation Group (IRIG) standard common to all telemetry systems is the radio frequency (rf) carrier band, presently at 2.6 to 235 megacycles (mg). Microwave transmissions (television) take place between 2,200 and 2,300 mg, using both frequency modulation (FM) and phase modulation (PM).

Multiplexing

For most telemetry applications the simultaneous transmission of a number of different data channels is necessary. Therefore, it is common to send many measurements over a single transmission link. This process is called *multiplexing*.

In the FM or FM-PM system, various methods are used to enable the rf carrier to carry more than one signal. Eighteen different channel frequencies can be applied to modulate the rf carrier and then be applied either all at once or one at a time. These 18 frequencies, called *subcarrier* frequencies, are in turn modulated by a source of information. The widths of the channels are set by IRIG standards. Basically, the lower subcarrier bands are narrower and consequently carry a smaller range of information than do higher bands.

The most commonly used multiplexing techniques are *frequency-division multiplexing* and *time-division multiplexing*. In frequency-division multiplex systems, the different measurement signals are distinguishable from one another by their frequency content; in time-division multiplex systems, by their time location.

Frequency-Division Multiplexing

The measurement signals from the transducers in a frequency-division multiplex system are used to modulate subcarrier oscillators tuned to different frequencies. The outputs of the subcarrier oscillators are then summed in voltage, and the resulting composite is used to modulate the prime transmitter. At the receiving site, the composite signal is obtained from the receiver demodulator and fed to a number of bandpass filters. The outputs of these filters are then demodulated to obtain the individual measurement signals.

All types of modulation can be used for both the subcarrier oscillators and the prime carrier. Frequency-division multiplex systems are normally designated by listing the type of modulation used for the subcarriers followed by the type of modulation used for the prime carrier.

The most commonly used frequency-division multiplex system is FM/FM. Since standard FM/FM systems can accommodate only 16 measurements, it has been usual to multiplex the higher-frequency subcarrier channels.

Time-Division Multiplex Systems

From a time-division multiplex system the signals from the transducers are fed to a commutating device which samples the channels sequentially. Thus, the output of the commutator is a series of pulses which is then passed through a device which converts it to a form suitable for modulating the transmitter. At the receiving station the process is reversed.

The modulation of the transmitter may take any form; for example AM, FM, or PM. However, the principal distinction between time-division systems lies in the form of the converter. The *analog systems* are those in which the output of the converter varies continuously in some fashion; in other words, is an analog of the input voltage to the converter. In the *digital systems*, however, the converter is capable of putting out only a discrete number of waveforms.

Analog Time-Division Systems

The primary analog time-division multiplex systems in use today are: 1) pulse-amplitude modulation (PAM); 2) pulse-duration or-width modulation (PDM or PWM); and the 3) pulse-position or-time modulation (PPM or PTM).

A PAM system is one in which the output of the commutator is used directly to modulate the prime transmitter. PAM is the simplest time-division multiplex system and PAM wavetrains are usually produced as the first step in any time-division multiplex system.

PDM is a time-division multiplex technique in which the duration of pulses is varied in proportion to the modulation signal. The pulse waveform, then, consists of a string of pulses with different widths.

PPM is similar to PDM except that, rather than using the entire duration of the pulse, only the trailing edge of the pulse is transmitted to identify the pulse width.

Telemetry

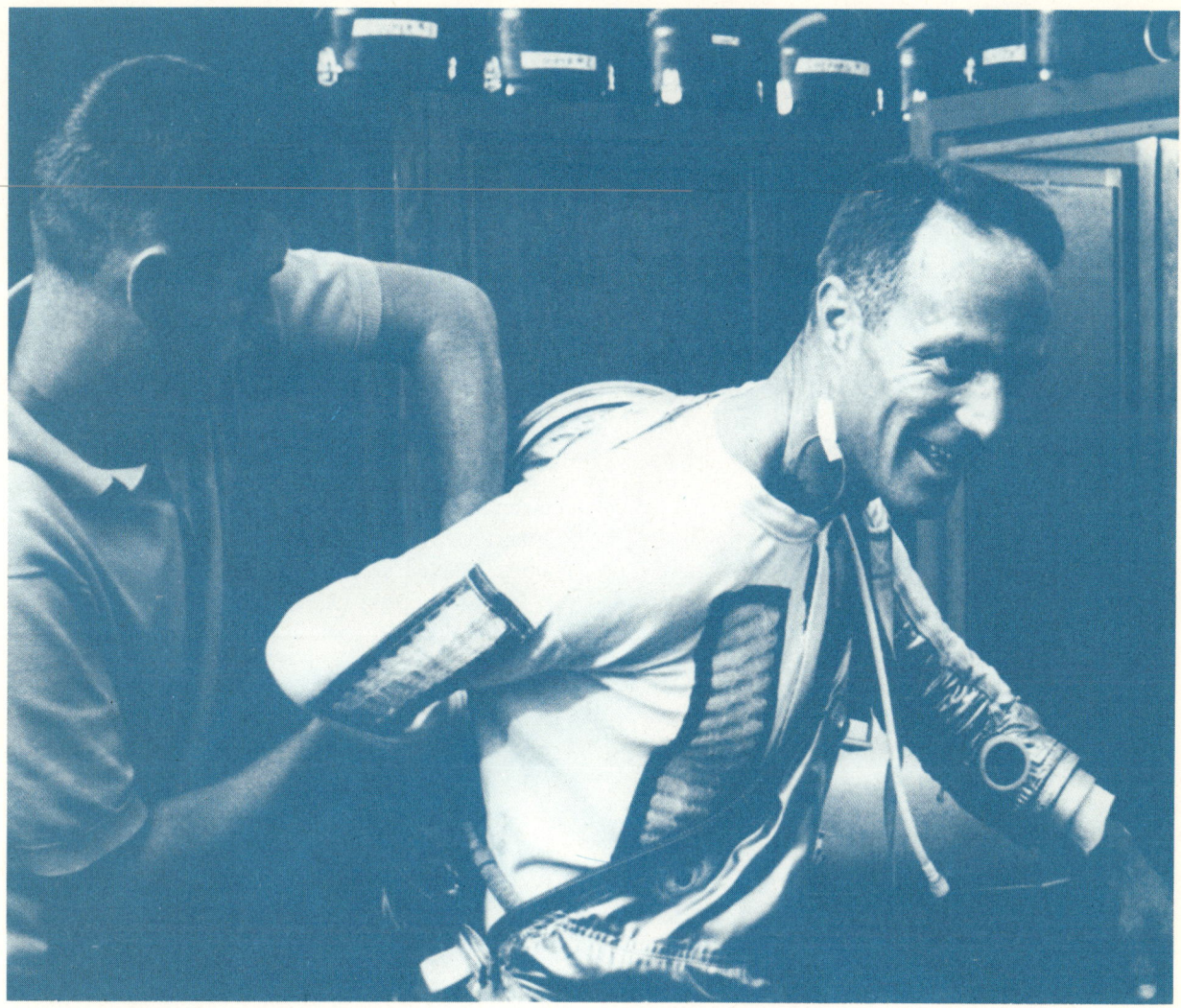

As Astronaut Carpenter suits up *(above)*, sensors are attached to his neck to measure his heartbeat during the three-orbit flight of Mercury 7. A comparison of the heartbeat rates of Schirra *(below)* during his two spaceflights as transmitted from the orbiting spacecrafts to Earth.

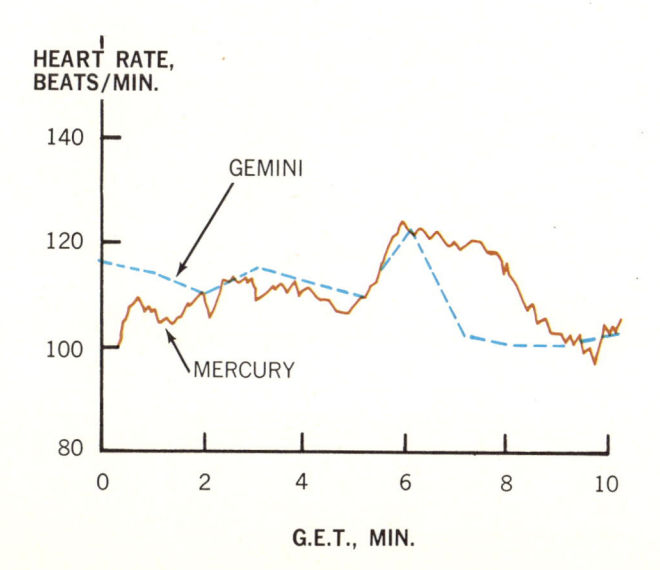

Digital Systems

The output of the converter in a digital system can take on only certain discrete forms. Each of the possible outputs of the converter can be thought of as a separate message. The converter has an output waveform assigned to each segment. This process of segmenting the input, is known as *quantizing,* and the segments themselves are referred to as *quantization* levels. The converter output is usually called a *code,* and the converter either a *coder* or *analog-to-digital converter* (A-to-D converter).

Most existing digital telemetry systems use a code which is made up of a sequence of pulses. The in-

2243

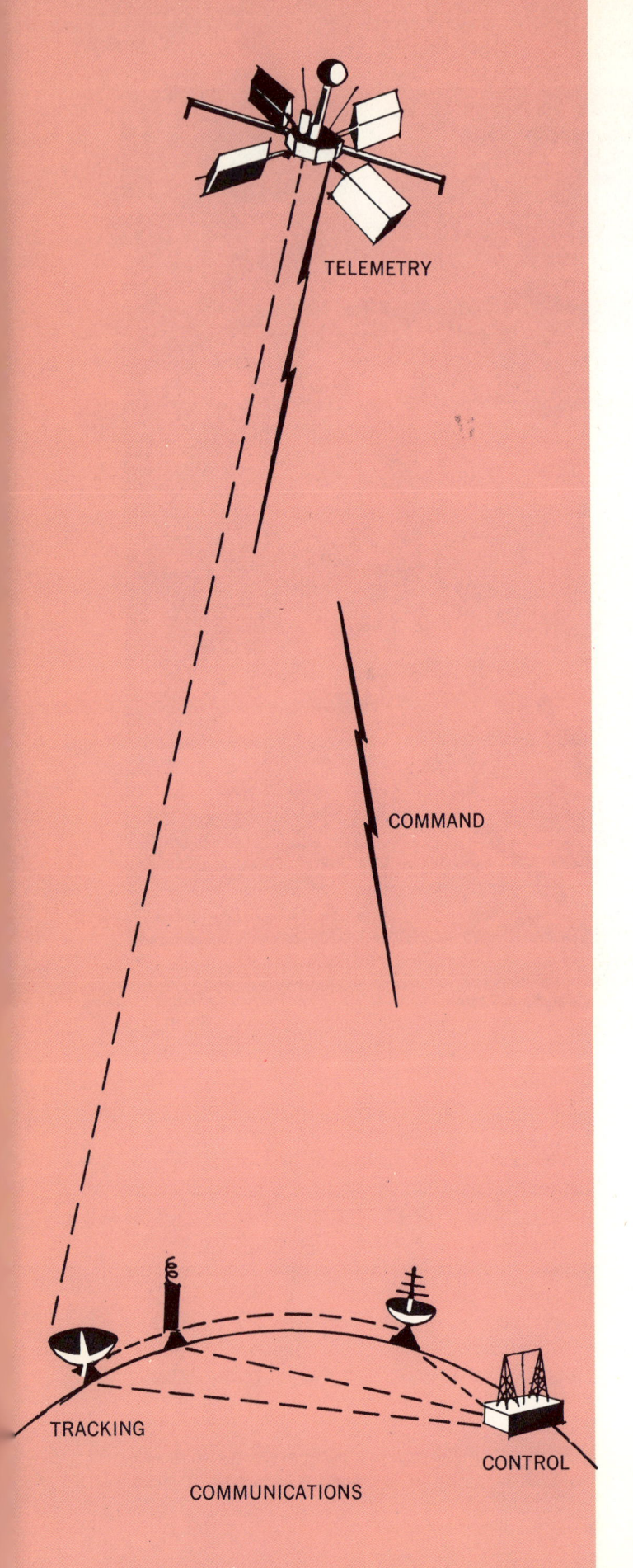

terval of time allotted for each pulse is referred to as a *bit time*. The waveform in each bit position takes on one of two possible configurations. Codes of this variety are called *two-level* codes. The weighting assigned to each is a binary number. The total value of the code can be obtained by adding up the weighting values of all bits with pulses present.

The arrangement of the code sequence in a binary transmission system is called the *format*. In general, the format is defined by the arrangement of bits in each code group representing a sample value (called a *word*), and the arrangement of these code groups with respect to one another. The bits within a particular coded word may be *information bits* (weighted binarily to represent the sample value); a *parity bit* (taking on the polarity necessary to make the total number of one bits per word either even or odd), and *synchronization* bits (normally of fixed polarity).

In the simplest cases, the information channels are sampled sequentially with fixed word length. Each word represents the code for a separate information channel, appearing sequentially in time. The sequence is repeated each time the commutator completes a cycle. This entire cycle is normally called a *frame*. It is necessary to supply timing information to designate the start of a frame.

Binary PCM systems have been used in a wide variety of missile and spacecraft applications. The compatibility of PCM systems with digital data-processing and computing facilities, and the reliability which can be achieved in digital circuits used at the remote station represent major arguments for the use of PCM. Most missile-borne PCM systems to date have utilized an FM prime carrier and hence are designated PCM/FM.

If spacecraft experiment measurements data are transmitted to Earth automatically, as upon collection of, this is called *real-time* telemetry. Usually these data are recorded on tape for eventual transmission to the ground receivers where it is recorded and fed to computers for analysis. In manned flight the need to sustain the real-time function requires that this process be instantaneous.   E. M. Mason

See also: Computers, Data acquisition and processing, Tape recording, Television

Measurements taken by sensors aboard a spacecraft are converted into electrical signals which are radioed to the receiving stations on Earth and reconverted into usable data.

The 48-inch Schmidt telescope is a hydrid camera device. The astronomer is loading a sensitized plate holder into the camera.

Telescopes and astronomical instruments

Eyes to look into space

The astronomer's most important tool, the telescope, probably was invented in Holland in 1608 by spectacle-maker Hans Lippershey. By 1610 the Italian scientist Galileo Galilei (*see*) had begun making telescopes and quickly discovered sunspots, the moon's craters, and the fact that the Milky Way is composed of innumerable faint stars.

This so-called *Galilean telescope,* with a positive lens (thickest at the center) in front, and a negative lens (thickest at the edge) for the eye to look through, has a very small field of view. Astronomers soon began using a better design, suggested by the German astronomer Johannes Kepler (*see*). The *Keplerian telescope* uses two positive lenses and, as with most telescopes which have been used by astronomers, the viewer sees things upside down.

2245

Telescopes and astronomical instruments

What Is a Telescope?

A telescope which uses only lenses is a *refracting telescope*. Most refractors have been modifications of the basic Keplerian design. Rays of light enter the front lens, or *objective,* and are bent, or refracted, and are again refracted when they meet the second lens, or *eyepiece*. The astronomer sees the celestial scene magnified, and is thus able to distinguish between two stars (*see*) which appear as one to the naked eye.

We can visualize how such a telescope works if we recognize that a positive lens can be used to project an image of a distant scene, for example, onto a sheet of paper. Suppose we take the objective lens and project such an image of a house onto a sheet

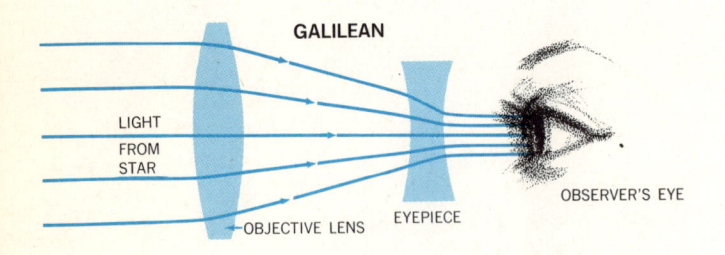

GALILEAN

of thin paper, so that we can examine the image from the *other side* of the paper. The image is upside down. (By substituting a photographic plate or film for the paper, we would have a camera.) Now, if we wish to examine this image in great detail, we can take an eyepiece lens (which is more curved than the objective) and use it as a magnifying glass, putting

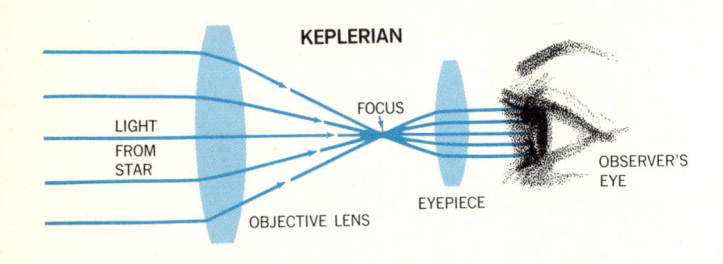

KEPLERIAN

it up against our eye so that we can approach the image to within an inch or so. We can now see the house, although upside-down, in great detail. In fact, it is magnified. While we are thus looking at the image, we can *remove* the paper. The magnified image of the house will remain visible, and we have a telescope!

The distance between a lens and the image it forms of a distant object is its *focal length*. The *magnification* (sometimes called *power*) of a telescope is found by dividing the objective focal length by the eyepiece focal length. Telescopes generally have a number of eyepieces with various focal lengths to give different magnifications.

To the modern astronomer, the telescope's ability to magnify is not its most important property. The astronomer makes use of the telescope's *light-gathering* ability. A telescope with a 1-inch objective has a diameter three times as great as the pupil of the human eye. It has an area nine times as great and enables the viewer to see stars nine times fainter. Similarly, a 6-inch telescope enables us to see stars 324 times fainter than with the eye alone. Moreover, photographic time-exposures allow light to be gathered for hours, and very faint objects become visible.

Many telescopes, particularly those owned by amateur astronomers, are used primarily with eyepieces. By using an objective with a very long focal length, and choosing an eyepiece with a short focal length, the astronomer can easily obtain a magnification of hundreds or even thousands. But the viewer who attempts to use extremely high magnifications will see only a magnified blur. The *maximum useful magnification* is about 50 for each inch of objective aperture. Thus the owner of a 6-inch telescope would almost never use as much as 300 power.

This limitation holds for all telescopes and is due to the wave nature of light. An ideal telescope with an aperture of 5 inches will allow the viewer to see detail as fine as about 1 second of arc in the sky, the angle that a dime 2⅓ miles distant would subtend. Two stars separated by 1 second of arc will be barely distinguishable as two separate stars. Similarly, a 10-inch telescope will, ideally, *resolve* an angle as small as one-half second of arc. The larger the diameter the finer the resolution (*see*). A magnification of about 50 for each inch of diameter will generally enable the viewer to see these barely resolved details. Distortions in the Earth's atmosphere (*see*) affect the resolution, and large telescopes are never able to resolve to the theoretical limit. In the future, some telescopes may be placed in space (*see*), perhaps on the moon, to avoid this problem.

As magnification is increased, the field of view is decreased. To view the whole disk of the moon at once, not more than about 100 power can be used. For observing objects such as nebulae (*see*) or tails of comets (*see*), as low a magnification as possible is desirable, because the telescope is made only for gathering light. The lowest magnification which can be used is about 3 for every inch of objective diameter, or 18 for a 6-inch telescope.

Historical Development of the Refractor

The Keplerian telescope has serious defects, the worst being *chromatic aberration*. Glass refracts light of different colors, or wavelengths, by different amounts, and this is called *dispersion*. Consequently, red light from a star focuses farther from the objective than blue light, and focusing the eyepiece on one color will result in a blur from all other colors. This problem can be minimized by using objectives of very long focal length, and some 17th century astronomers, such as Christian Huygens in Holland, built awkward telescopes over 100 feet long, although the objectives had diameters of only a few inches.

In 1729 in London, Chester Moor Hall designed an *achromatic* lens, to mitigate this defect. This was perfected some 20 years later by the London optician John Dolland. An achromat combines a positive lens of crown glass with a negative lens of flint glass. Because the refraction of the negative lens is not enough to completely counteract the opposite refraction of the positive lens, the net result is a positive lens. But because flint, for a given amount of refraction, exceeds crown in dispersive power, the negative lens can completely counteract the dispersion of the positive lens.

Eyepieces are subject to chromatic aberration, and various combinations of lenses may be used to correct this and other problems. Today many eyepieces are made of as many as four separate lenses, which provide excellent color correction as well as a wide field of view.

In the 19th century, techniques of making achromatic objectives gradually improved, along with methods of making large disks of optical-quality glass. Astronomers acquired larger and larger telescopes, including refractors of 15 inches at the Harvard College Observatory in 1847, 18½ inches in 1862 for the Chicago Astronomical Society (an instrument now at Northwestern University), and eventually 40 inches at the Yerkes Observatory of the University of Chicago in the 1890's. Each was the world's largest when it was built; the size of the Yerkes great refractor has not been surpassed. Although many of the last century's great refractors are still in use, moderate-size objectives now are generally made only for special purposes, such as wide-field cameras and coronagraphs (*see*).

The Reflecting Telescope

A reflecting telescope uses a concave mirror, rather than a lens, as an objective. The principles of operation are similar to those for a refractor. A concave mirror reflects parallel light, such as that from distant stars, to a point focus. The image may then be examined with the aid of an eyepiece, or the light may strike a photographic plate, a phototube, or the entrance slit of a spectrograph.

If the mirror is put at the bottom of a tube, starlight will be reflected back, focusing near the front. This is the *prime focus*. Very large telescopes, such as the Mount Palomar 200-inch-diameter reflector, have an "observer's cage" inside the tube for the astronomer to sit in. He can examine the image at the prime focus with an eyepiece, or expose a photographic plate there. The cage obstructs only a small part of the total light entering the tube. Since the cage obstructs light equally from all parts of the sky being viewed, the observer sees no "shadow" in the image.

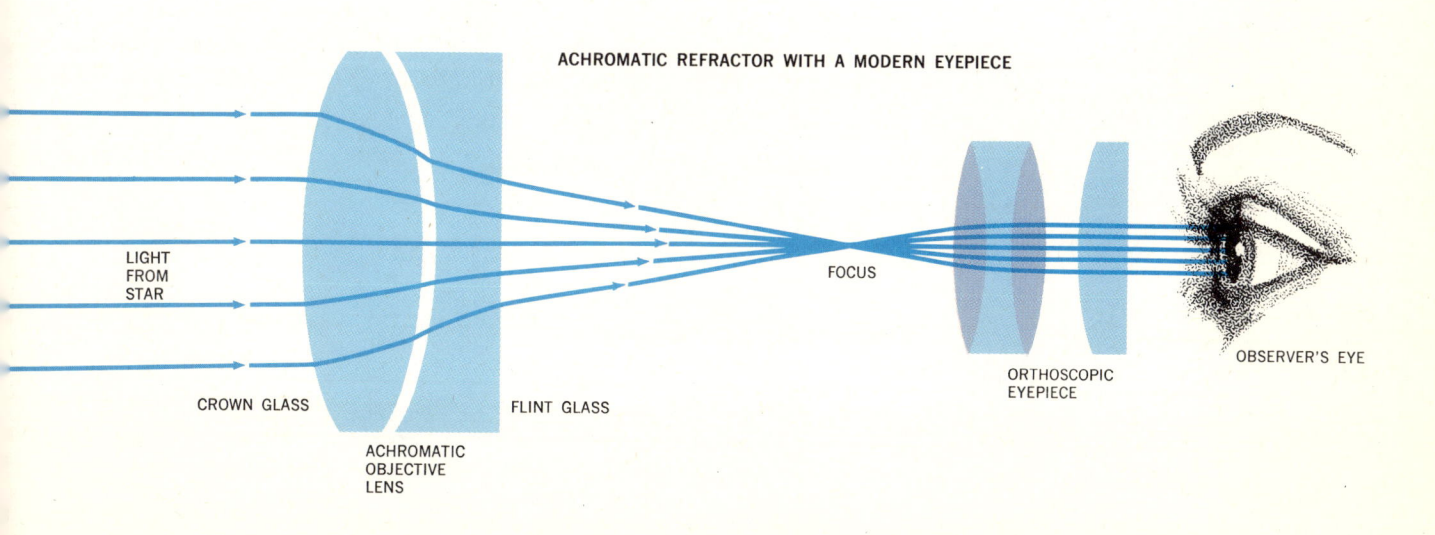

ACHROMATIC REFRACTOR WITH A MODERN EYEPIECE

REFLECTORS

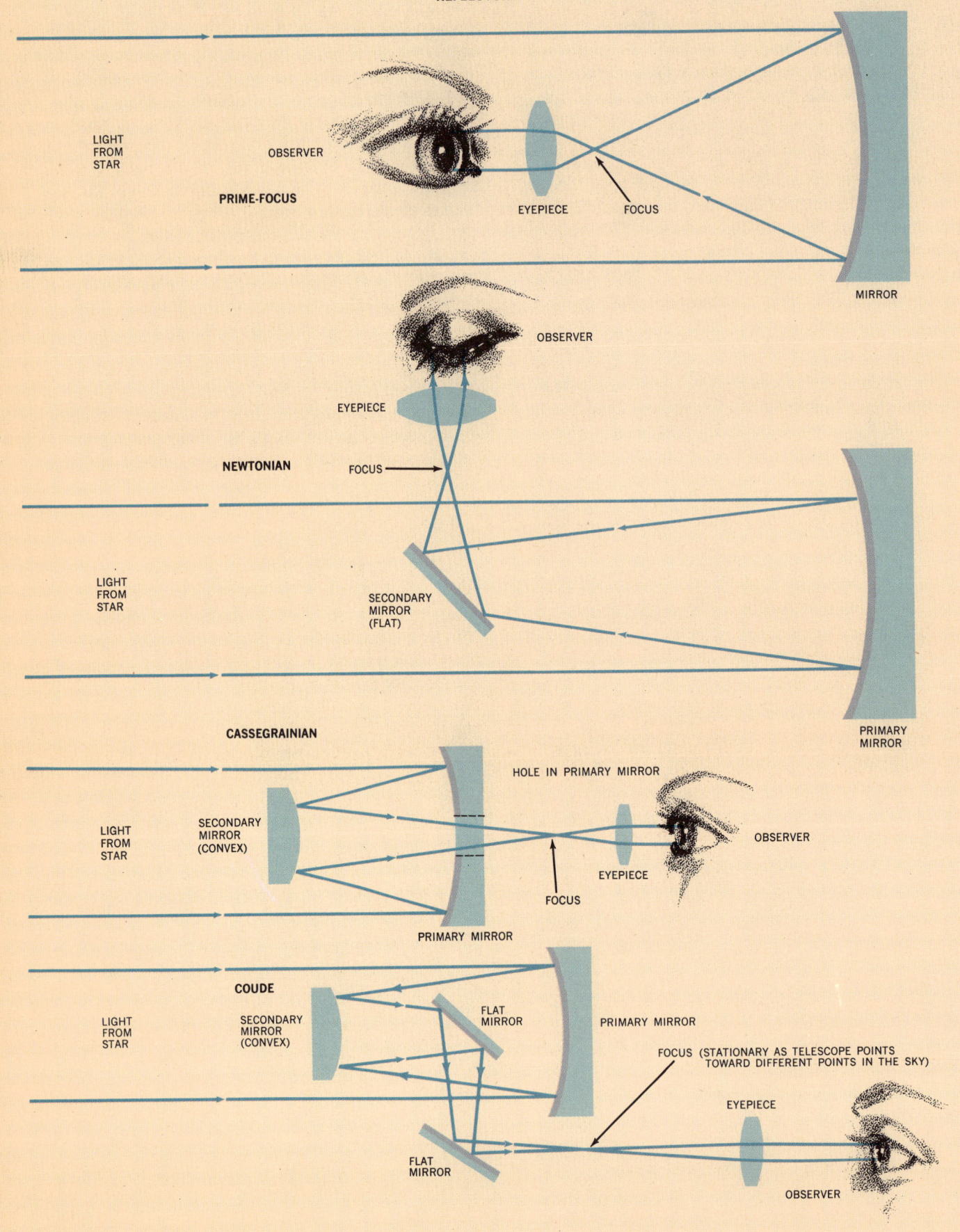

PRIME-FOCUS

LIGHT FROM STAR

OBSERVER

EYEPIECE

FOCUS

MIRROR

NEWTONIAN

OBSERVER

EYEPIECE

FOCUS

LIGHT FROM STAR

SECONDARY MIRROR (FLAT)

PRIMARY MIRROR

CASSEGRAINIAN

HOLE IN PRIMARY MIRROR

LIGHT FROM STAR

SECONDARY MIRROR (CONVEX)

OBSERVER

EYEPIECE

FOCUS

PRIMARY MIRROR

COUDE

LIGHT FROM STAR

SECONDARY MIRROR (CONVEX)

FLAT MIRROR

PRIMARY MIRROR

FOCUS (STATIONARY AS TELESCOPE POINTS TOWARD DIFFERENT POINTS IN THE SKY)

EYEPIECE

FLAT MIRROR

OBSERVER

Telescopes and astronomical instruments

For small reflectors, a small flat mirror is usually placed diagonally in the center of the tube to reflect the focus out to the side, where the image can be viewed or photographed more conveniently. Similarly, the astronomer does not see the flat mirror in the image, although it obstructs a small amount of the incoming light. This is the *Newtonian telescope,* which is the most common type of small reflector.

A curved mirror, like a lens, has a focal length. The magnification is found by dividing the objective focal length by the eyepiece focal length, as in the case of a refractor.

Another type of reflector, which is being increasingly used by astronomers, is the *Cassegrainian telescope,* named for its French designer. Before the light reflected from the concave or *primary* mirror reaches the prime focus, it is intercepted by a slightly convex mirror. This *secondary* mirror reflects the light back, through a hole in the center of the primary mirror, focusing slightly behind the primary. To calculate the magnification, or the size of an image on a photographic plane, one must use an *effective* focal length, which is typically about four times that of the primary mirror.

Large telescopes frequently include a special Cassegrainian secondary which results in an even greater effective focal length. The reflection from the secondary is not allowed to go back through the hole in the primary, but is reflected out of the tube by a flat mirror. One or more additional flat mirrors assure that the light finally focuses at a point away from the telescope tube. This focal point remains conveniently stationary as the telescope is pointed at different points in the sky. This is the *coude* focus (French for *elbowed*).

Historical Development of the Reflector

The chromatic aberration of refracting telescopes led to the development of telescopes with mirrors. A mirror has no chromatic aberration, because the law of reflection applies equally to light of all colors. The first reflecting telescope actually constructed, by Isaac Newton (*see*) in 1668, came to be called the *Newtonian* type. The curved mirror had an aperture of 1⅓ inch and a focal length of 6¼ inch, and the eyepiece used gave a magnification of about 35. Cassegrain suggested the telescope which bears his name at about this time. The design was very severely, and unjustly, criticized by Newton, and the in-

An astronomer at the Cassegrain focus of the 200-inch Hale telescope.

Telescopes and astronomical instruments

ventor never built such a reflector telescope.

The early reflectors had metal mirrors, which were difficult to make and which tarnished rapidly. At first, reflectors were hardly more than scientific toys, but by the 1720's the English scientist John Hadley had made some which compared very favorably with good refractors. Toward the end of the 18th century the great astronomer William Herschel (*see*), in England, built many reflectors, the largest having a 48-inch mirror diameter. This instrument, gigantic for its day, was 40 feet long, with both the telescope tube and the observer supported by a maze of poles, ladders, and ropes. The ultimate in metal mirror telescopes was reached in Ireland in 1845, with the 72-inch diameter reflector of William Parsons.

The giant reflectors, in spite of their light-gathering power, were inferior in resolution to the best refractors of much smaller aperture, and many astronomers felt that reflectors were inherently inferior.

In the 1850's, as reflectors were falling into disfavor, the French physicist Leon Foucault made two important contributions which were responsible for the reflector's eventual revival. First, he developed (simultaneously with Steinheil in Germany) a chemical method of depositing a highly reflecting silver coating on glass which was uniform and as thin as several millionths of an inch. The telescope maker could grind and polish the proper curve onto a disk of glass, and replace the coating when the silver tarnished.

Foucault's second innovation was a convenient method of testing mirrors in the workshop, so that defects in the shape, or *figure,* of the polished mirror can be located and measured. The defects can then be polished out so that the shape is correct to within a few millionths of an inch before silvering. In the case of a Newtonian or a prime-focus telescope, the mirror should have the shape of a paraboloid.

Foucault's technique permitted skilled opticians to produce reflecting telescopes with resolutions equal to, or better than, those of the best refractors. The Foucault test, or "knife-edge test," remains today the basic method for testing telescope mirrors.

Chemical silvering has been replaced by *aluminizing,* a process invented by John Strong in 1931. The mirror is placed in a vacuum chamber (*see*), in which aluminum (*see*) is heated until it begins to evaporate. The mirror becomes coated with a very thin, shiny, uniform layer of aluminum which has good reflectivity and lasts much longer than silver.

Interest in reflectors began to revive around the turn of the century. Photography (*see*), first used with astronomy experimentally by Harvard astron-

The 36-inch refractor at Lick Observatory was the largest of its kind when it was built in 1888 and is now second largest in the world.

omers in 1850, was becoming increasingly important. Many fascinating details of nebulae and other objects could be photographed with long exposures, as was demonstrated by a 24-inch Newtonian telescope built by George W. Ritchey at the Yerkes Observatory. Ritchey and Yerkes director George Ellery Hale realized the immense importance of gathering more light, both for direct photography and for the important new work with spectrographs. There was no hope for a refractor larger than the Yerkes 40-inch telescope because much light would be absorbed in the thick lens and the massive lens' shape would be distorted by sagging.

In 1903, Ritchey began making a 60-inch mirror for the Mt. Wilson Observatory in California. This location had more favorable atmospheric conditions than low-altitude observatories. The 60-inch telescope, finished in 1908, proved extremely successful and a 100-inch reflector was completed in 1918.

The World's Largest Telescope

Hale, who had become the director of Mt. Wilson, and other astronomers were eager for yet more light, especially for the study of distant galaxies. After

Telescopes and astronomical instruments

much deliberation it was decided to build a 200-inch-diameter reflector, and to put it on remote Mount Palomar in California. The glass would be a new material, Pyrex, a "heat-resistant" glass made by the Corning Glass Works. Thus, the 200-inch mirror would be much less affected by temperature changes, which can cause temporary irregularities in the figure of a mirror.

A successful 200-inch Pyrex disk was finally cast in December, 1934, and was allowed to cool slowly for about ten months. In March, 1936, mounted vertically on a special railway car, it began its long journey from Corning, New York, to an optical shop set up in Pasadena, California. The grinding and polishing, and then the "figuring" and testing, lasted until 1947! In October, 1947, the priceless disk was carried by truck to the telescope mounting awaiting it on Mount Palomar. Final testing was done with light from a star, using a modification of Foucault's test, and the mirror was completed on the mountain by polishing away an excess layer of glass, 20-millionths of an inch thick, near the edge. The mirror was then aluminized. George Ellery Hale had died in 1938, and the completed instrument was named the Hale Telescope and dedicated in 1948.

The 200-inch mirror has the unusually small focal ratio (ratio of focal length to diameter) of 3.3, which is useful for the photography of diffuse objects at the prime focus. It is interesting that for the world's largest telescope, weighing some 500 tons, the only essential optical surface is a thin layer of aluminum, weighing about an ounce.

The useful field of view is very limited at the prime focus of a short focal ratio paraboloid, and a Ross correcting lens is usually inserted in front of the photographic plate at the prime focus, to make the star images sharp nearer the edge of the photographic plate.

The Hale Telescope also can be used, with a convex secondary mirror, at its Cassegrainian focus; and with another convex mirror and several flat mirrors, at its coude focus.

The Cassegrain platform is occupied by one of the two operators of the Hale telescope.

Telescopes and astronomical instruments

Mountings

Although the heart of a telescope is its lenses and mirrors, they are useless unless they are held accurately in position, and can be pointed toward various points in the sky. These optical parts are usually held in a tube, although the giant reflectors usually have open, or *skeleton,* tubes. The tube is held on a *mounting* which can be turned on two perpendicular axes. Except for very small amateur telescopes, these are *equatorial* mountings, with one axis of rotation directed toward the celestial pole (near the North Star)—in other words, parallel to the Earth's axis of rotation. A *clock drive* turns the entire telescope smoothly once around this axis in about 23 hours and 56 minutes, to compensate for the Earth's rotation. The telescope will remain pointing at any star as it moves across the sky from east to west during the night.

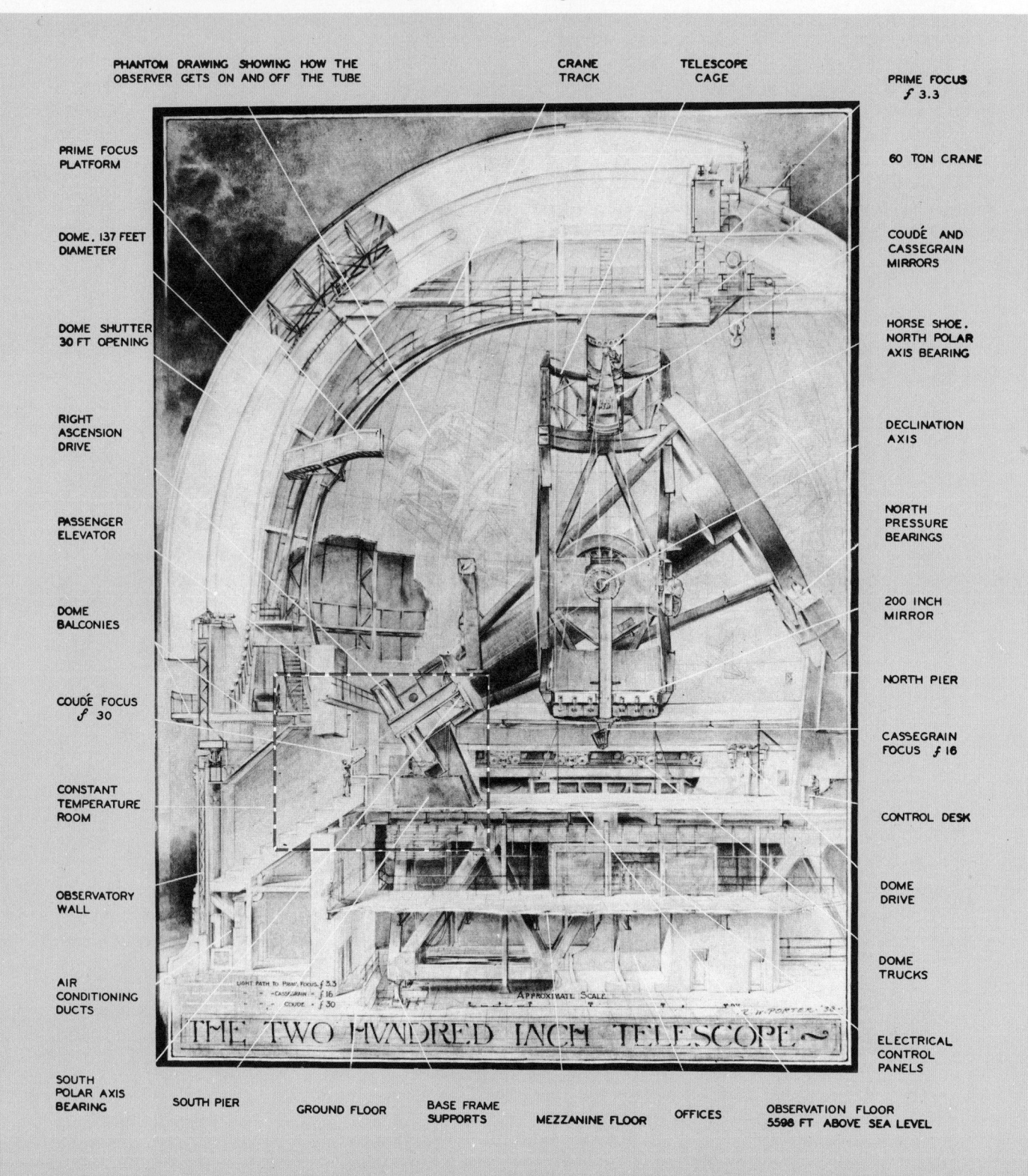

THE TWO HUNDRED INCH TELESCOPE

PHANTOM DRAWING SHOWING HOW THE OBSERVER GETS ON AND OFF THE TUBE
CRANE TRACK
TELESCOPE CAGE
PRIME FOCUS f 3.3
PRIME FOCUS PLATFORM
60 TON CRANE
DOME. 137 FEET DIAMETER
COUDÉ AND CASSEGRAIN MIRRORS
DOME SHUTTER 30 FT OPENING
HORSE SHOE. NORTH POLAR AXIS BEARING
RIGHT ASCENSION DRIVE
DECLINATION AXIS
PASSENGER ELEVATOR
NORTH PRESSURE BEARINGS
DOME BALCONIES
200 INCH MIRROR
COUDÉ FOCUS f 30
NORTH PIER
CASSEGRAIN FOCUS f 16
CONSTANT TEMPERATURE ROOM
CONTROL DESK
OBSERVATORY WALL
DOME DRIVE
DOME TRUCKS
AIR CONDITIONING DUCTS
ELECTRICAL CONTROL PANELS
SOUTH POLAR AXIS BEARING
SOUTH PIER
GROUND FLOOR
BASE FRAME SUPPORTS
MEZZANINE FLOOR
OFFICES
OBSERVATION FLOOR 5598 FT ABOVE SEA LEVEL

The most common type of mounting is the *German*, used on all the large refractors, as well as most small reflectors. The giant reflectors use various other designs, such as the unusual "horseshoe" mounting of the 200-inch telescope.

The Schmidt Telescope

For some wide-angle photography, astronomers want a large-diameter telescope with the shortest possible focal length. A focal ratio of 2 or less is frequently desired, but a paraboloidal mirror of this focal ratio would produce good images only within a small fraction of an inch of the center of the photograph, due to an aberration called *coma*. Bernhard Schmidt solved this in 1930 by using a *spherical mirror*. This results in severe *spherical aberration* which, however, affects images equally all over the field of view. He corrected this defect with a properly shaped thin glass *corrector plate* at the front of the

HYBRID TELESCOPES

A 15-inch refractor telescope and mount at the Harvard College Observatory.

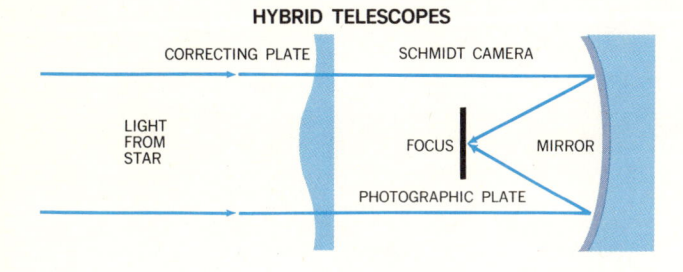

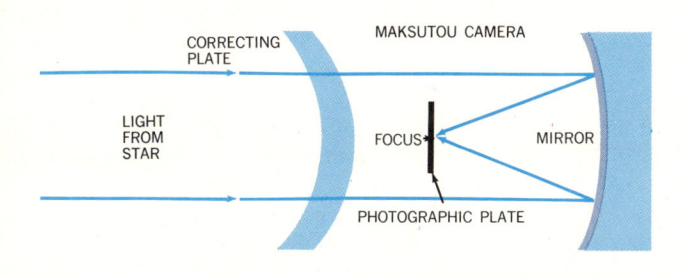

tube. Because there is usually no way provided to look through such telescopes, they are often called *Schmidt cameras*. They have been made with apertures ranging from a few inches to 48 inches for the large Schmidt on Mount Palomar. Another sort of telescope using a corrector plate is the *Baker-Nunn Camera*. A worldwide network of these has been established in order to accurately track artificial Earth satellites (*see*).

New Telescopes

Many large and medium-sized telescopes are being designed or built today. Several special-purpose telescopes have been completed in recent years, such as the world's largest solar telescope at the Kitt Peak National Observatory in Arizona, with a 60-inch mirror. California's Lick Observatory completed their 120-inch reflector, with a prime-focus cage and Cassegrainian and coude facilities, in the late 1950's. Kitt Peak is building a 158-inch reflector. The U.S.S.R. is building a 236-inch reflector.

A vast expansion of facilities is underway to observe the sky of the southern hemisphere from which important objects like the center of the Milky Way Galaxy (*see*) and the large and small Magellanic clouds are visible. Several countries are considering building large telescopes in South America. Plans for a 158-inch reflector for the Inter-American Observatory (affiliated with Kitt Peak) on Cerro Tololo in Chile are well under way. Western European astronomers will have a 144-inch reflecting telescope at the European Southern Observatory, also in Chile.

Among recent improvements for telescopes are the development of new low-expansion materials for mirrors, such as fused quartz and still more recently, ceramic materials. The traditional combination of paraboloidal primary mirror and hyperboloidal secondary for Cassegrainian telescopes is now often

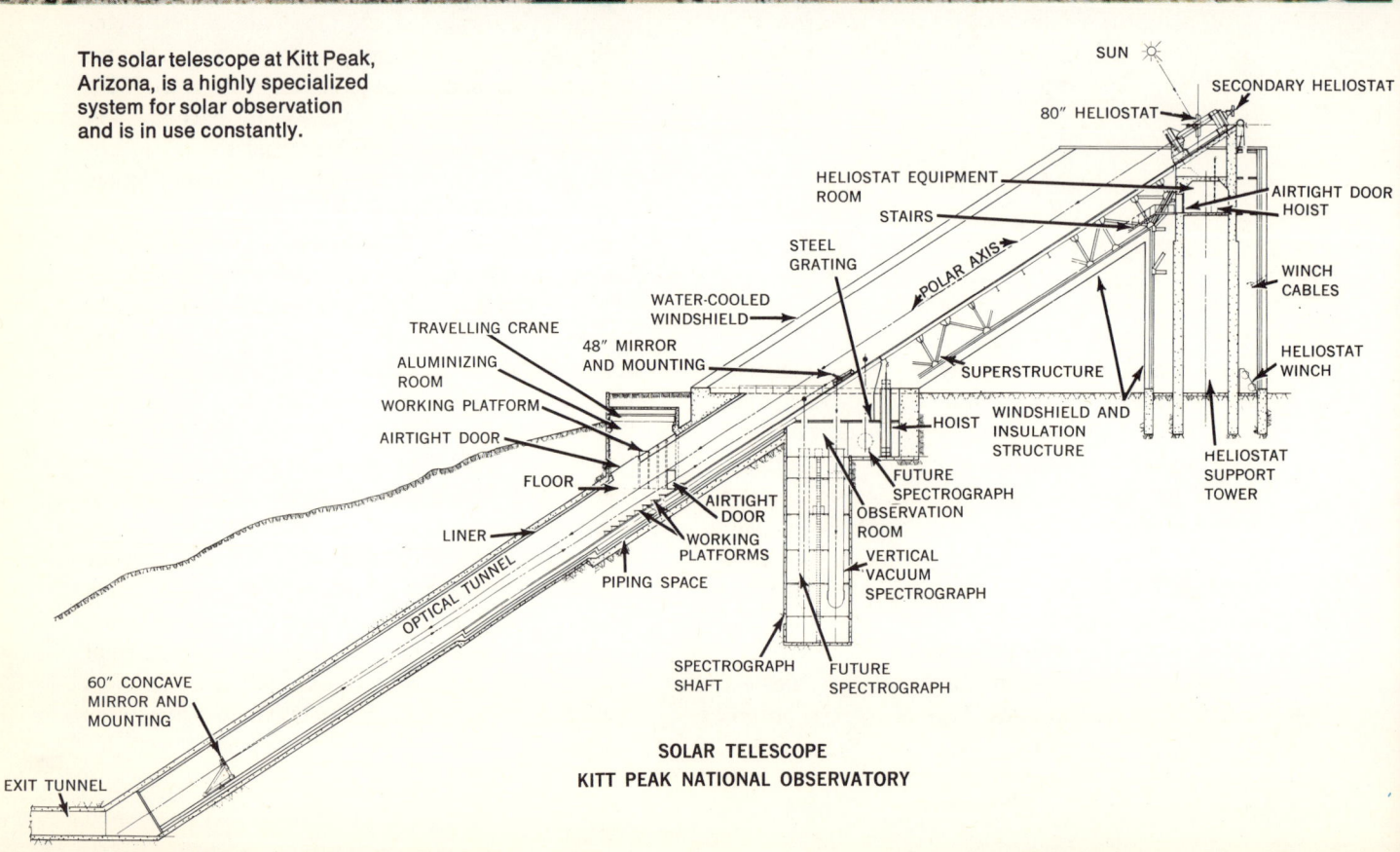

The solar telescope at Kitt Peak, Arizona, is a highly specialized system for solar observation and is in use constantly.

**SOLAR TELESCOPE
KITT PEAK NATIONAL OBSERVATORY**

Telescopes and astronomical instruments

The spectroscope breaks the light from a star into its component colors with either a prism or a grating.

Prism Spectroscope

Grating Spectroscope

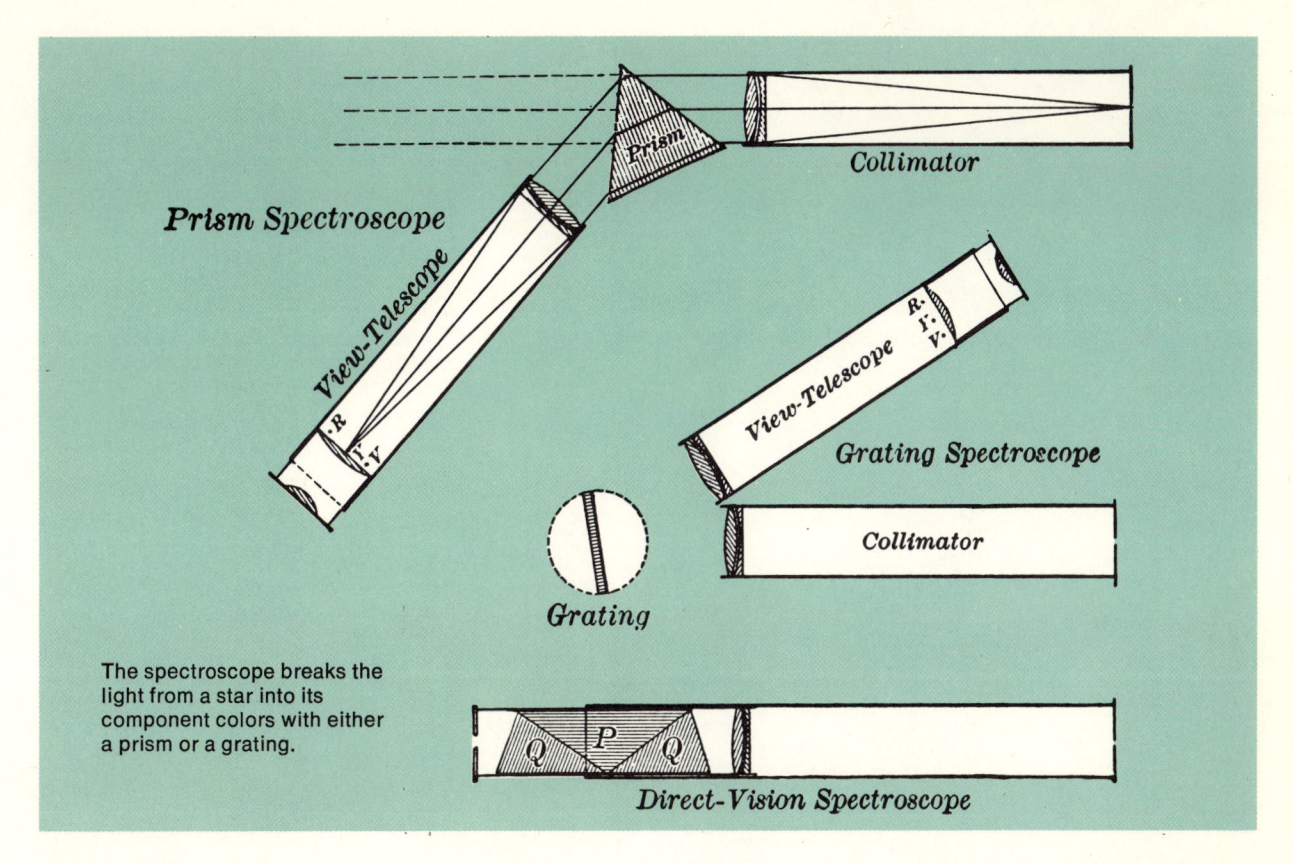

Direct-Vision Spectroscope

replaced with other curve combinations, computed to produce superior images over a wide field of view. Also, new prime-focus corrector lenses to improve image quality are being designed. Some observatories are experimenting with modern types of metal mirrors (to be vacuum-coated with aluminum for use) which may have certain advantages over glass mirrors.

Spectroscopic Instruments

In the 17th century it was found that a glass prism disperses sunlight into its component colors. About 1800, in Germany, Joseph Fraunhofer (*see*) allowed sunlight to shine through a narrow slit, and then viewed this slit through a prism, using a small telescope to magnify the effect. One would expect an image of the slit to be seen for each color, or wavelength, resulting in a continuous rainbow, or *spectrum* (*see*), extending from violet to red. However, the slit image was dark at certain points in the spectrum. These dark lines, or *Fraunhofer lines,* are now known to be caused by absorption at specific wavelengths by various elements in the sun's gaseous atmosphere. A device such as Fraunhofer's is called a *spectroscope*.

By mounting spectroscopes onto telescopes so as to focus light onto the slit, 19th century astronomers studied the dark-line spectra of stars. They observed nebulae, many of which show *bright*-line spectra, which are due to glowing gases. Chemical elements can be identified from their characteristic lines. The spectograph is created by replacing the small viewing telescope with a camera. Time exposures allow fainter spectra to be observed, and also to be preserved for future study. The spectrograms reveal temperature, composition, velocity toward or away from Earth, and much more. Most modern spectrographs use a diffraction grating rather than a prism to disperse the light.

Another way of photographing spectra is to use an *objective prism,* a large, small-angle prism placed in front of a wide-field photographic telescope of perhaps 10 or 20 inches aperture. Each star in the field will be photographed as a small spectrum.

Photoelectric Instruments

Today, much telescopic observation is done with electronic light-detectors, particularly the photomultiplier tube, which is even more sensitive to light than the photographic plate. Such a device, when used with various colored filters to measure the brightness of stars and other objects, is called a *photoelectric photometer*. The *photoelectric spectrometer* is used to measure the intensity of light through the spectrum, using a prism or diffraction grating. Another photoelectric device is the *image*

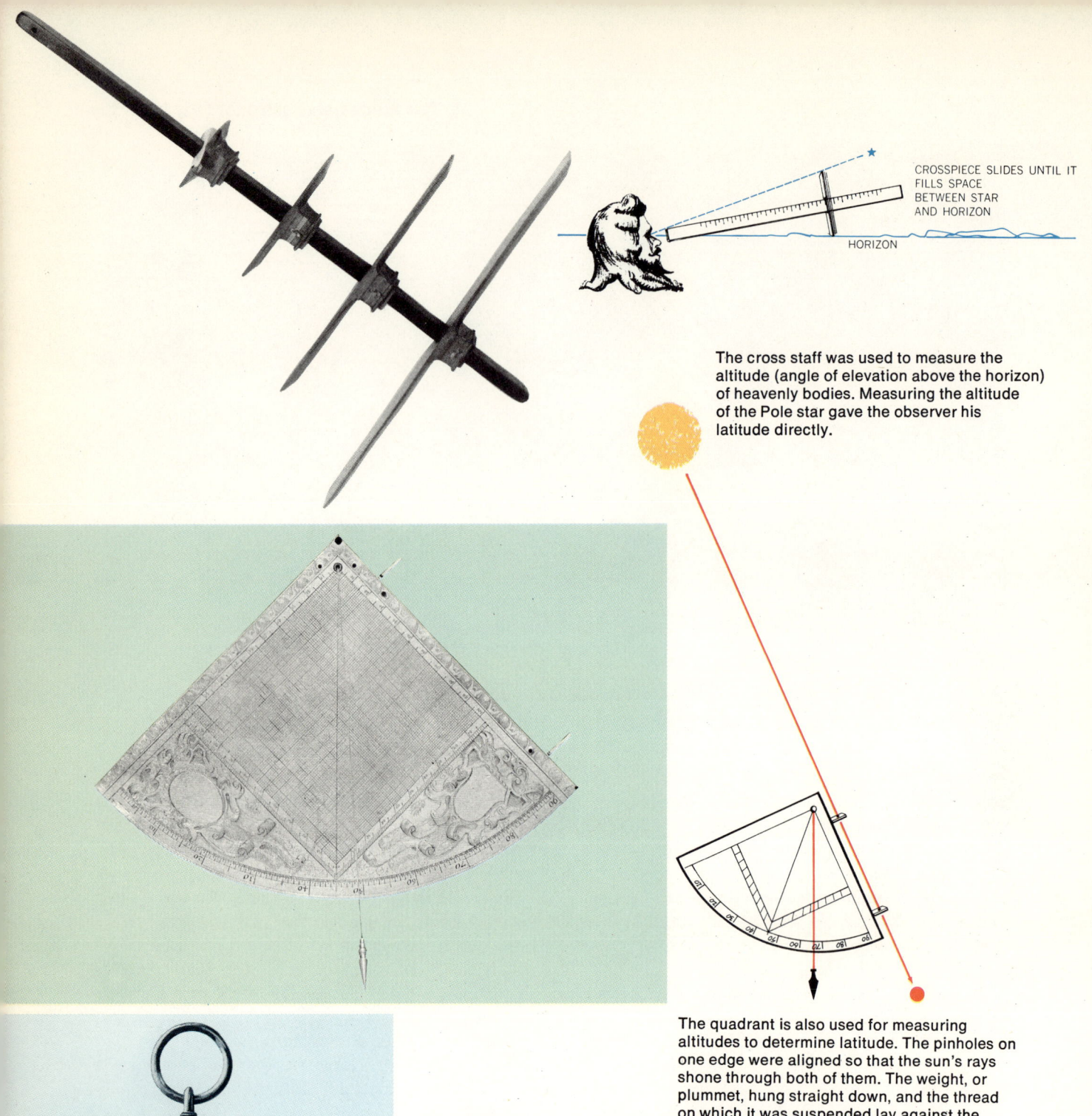

CROSSPIECE SLIDES UNTIL IT
FILLS SPACE
BETWEEN STAR
AND HORIZON
HORIZON

The cross staff was used to measure the altitude (angle of elevation above the horizon) of heavenly bodies. Measuring the altitude of the Pole star gave the observer his latitude directly.

The quadrant is also used for measuring altitudes to determine latitude. The pinholes on one edge were aligned so that the sun's rays shone through both of them. The weight, or plummet, hung straight down, and the thread on which it was suspended lay against the angle scale marking the altitude.

The astrolabe, one of the most important of the early astronomical instruments, was used to determine the bearings and altitudes of the fixed stars at a given time and date. Conversely, if the bearing and altitude of a fixed star was known, setting that information on the astrolabe gave the time and date. The rim carries the time scales, while the back plate is engraved with scales showing bearings and altitudes. The open-work plate has the fixed stars located at the points of the ornamental designs. The sighting bar, which has two slips or pinholes, was used for altitude measurement and was convenient for altitudes above 50°.

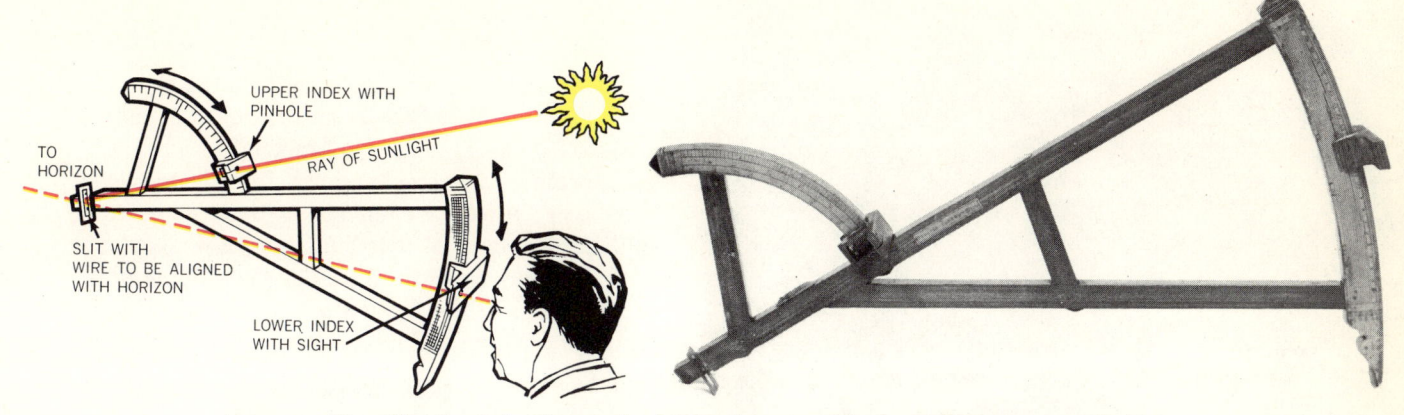

Because of the difficulty of simultaneously sighting the sun and horizon with the cross staff which required the observer to blink and shift his gaze, and to permit observation by means of cast shadows instead of looking directly at the sun, the backstaff or Davis Quadrant was developed. The observer adjusts both upper and lower index until, by sighting through the lower index, he can see the horizon and the sun's ray which has passed through the upper index and is striking the horizon wire. Reading the scales where the index slides are located then gives the sun's altitude.

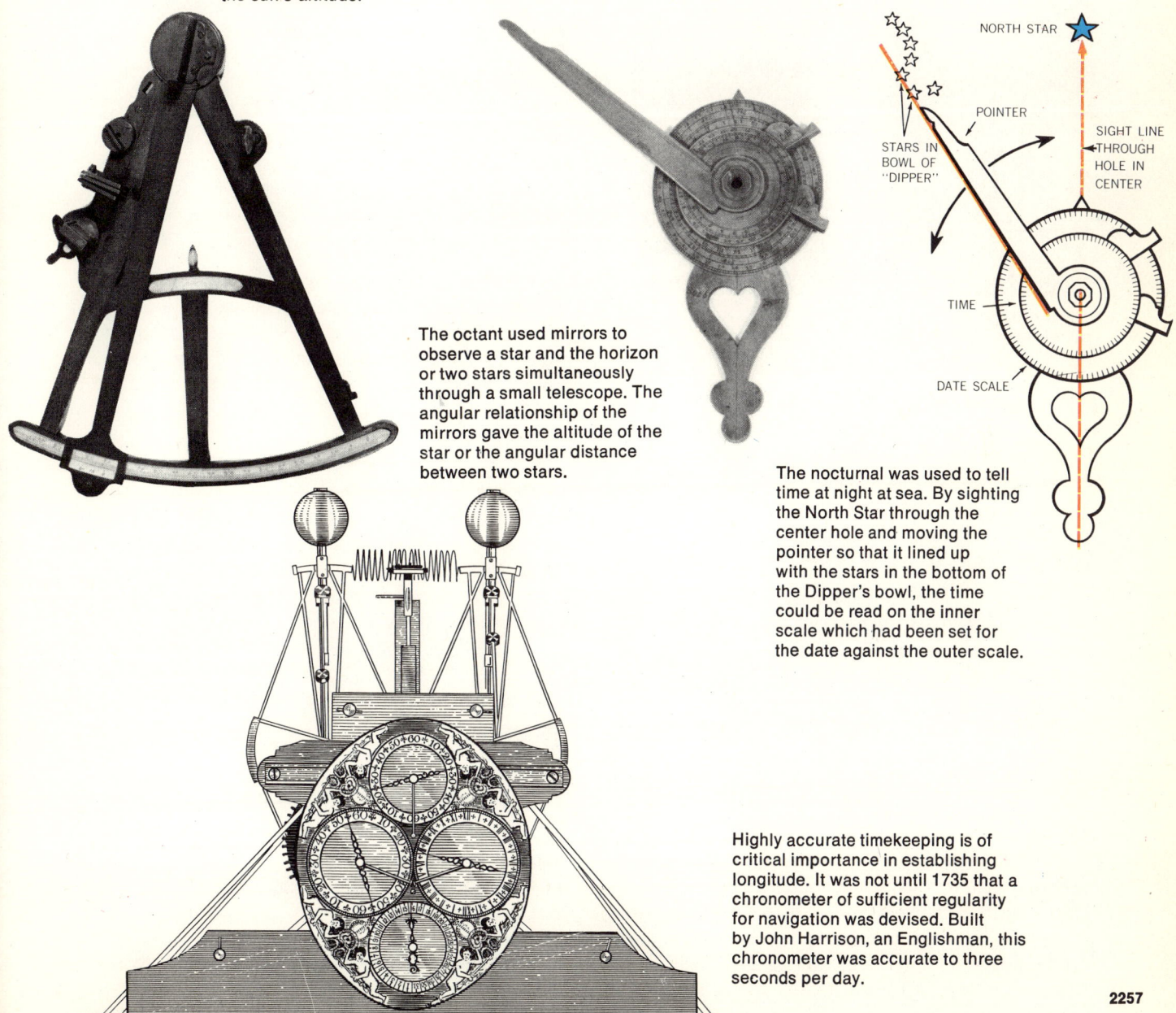

The octant used mirrors to observe a star and the horizon or two stars simultaneously through a small telescope. The angular relationship of the mirrors gave the altitude of the star or the angular distance between two stars.

The nocturnal was used to tell time at night at sea. By sighting the North Star through the center hole and moving the pointer so that it lined up with the stars in the bottom of the Dipper's bowl, the time could be read on the inner scale which had been set for the date against the outer scale.

Highly accurate timekeeping is of critical importance in establishing longitude. It was not until 1735 that a chronometer of sufficient regularity for navigation was devised. Built by John Harrison, an Englishman, this chronometer was accurate to three seconds per day.

The armillary sphere is a model of the solar system used to locate the stars precisely with reference to a position on the Earth's surface.

converter tube, which can be used to electronically brighten an image at the focus of a telescope or spectrograph, before it is photographed. All the large telescopes are now being fitted with these image intensifiers, shortening exposure times for ordinary objects and extending the range of possible observations both in intensity and in wavelength.

Measuring Instruments

A variety of measuring devices are available for reducing photographic observations to quantitative terms. A key instrument is the *measuring engine,* which uses a precision screw to measure precise positions on a plate. A modification of this, particularly useful for spectrograms, is the *microphotometer,* in which a small spot of light scans the film, and a photomultiplier tube measures the amount that gets through.

Blink-comparators make faint objects that move, such as high-velocity stars, comets, and asteroids, stand out from the background. These devices align two photographs taken under equal conditions at different times, and make them alternately visible.

Instruments for measuring angles in the sky date back to ones devised by the ancient Greeks and to the more practical medieval Arabian *astrolabe*. Today, precise telescopic divided-circle instruments such as the *meridian circle* are used for fundamental determinations of time and star positions, along with such modern instruments as the *photographic zenith tube* and the *Danjon astrolabe*. New instruments of this type are increasingly automated.

Other Telescopes

Only optical telescopes have been discussed here, but astronomers now use a battery of other devices to observe celestial sources. At long wavelengths, special infrared telescopes are being built; the longer wavelengths mean that the mirrors need not be of the same absolute accuracy. *Radio telescopes* have brought in an entirely new technology.

At shorter wavelengths, special devices are being built to observe the ultraviolet light that would be absorbed by the glass in an ordinary telescope. Special *x-ray telescopes* are now under construction using entirely new principles.

James Caplan

See also: Observatories, Planetariums, Radio astronomy, Regional space centers

Television

Television systems operate by changing the light reflected from a scene and the sound accompanying that scene into electromagnetic waves that can be transmitted by air or cable to a distant receiver which then reproduces the original scene or image on a screen.

In black-and-white television, each image is divided into very tiny elements of light, similar to the process in photography (*see*) in which the different light and shade values of a photograph are reproduced by a pattern of dots.

The lens of the television camera focuses the light rays reflected from an image onto the face of an Image Orthicon tube. The face of this tube is called the *signal plate* and is covered with a mosaic of photosensitive points. Each point corresponds to one picture element. When the light rays from the lens strike the plate, electrons are released in proportion to the strength or intensity of the light striking any one area. The brighter the light the more electrons are released. In this way, the entire surface acquires a positive photoelectric charge whose distribution matches the distribution of light in the image.

The electronic image is then transferred to another plate called a *target* where it is translated into high-frequency electromagnetic waves. This process

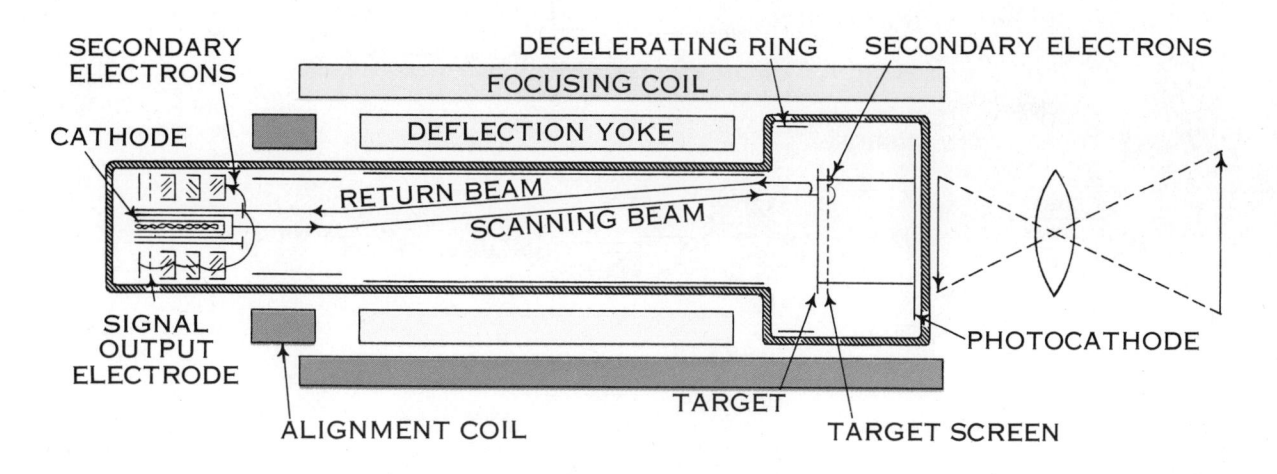

Diagram (top)

Labels: SECONDARY ELECTRONS · DECELERATING RING · SECONDARY ELECTRONS · FOCUSING COIL · CATHODE · DEFLECTION YOKE · RETURN BEAM · SCANNING BEAM · PHOTOCATHODE · SIGNAL OUTPUT ELECTRODE · ALIGNMENT COIL · TARGET · TARGET SCREEN

Orthicon Tube Features

"ANTI-GHOST" IMAGE SECTION—A specially designed image section used in certain RCA Image Orthicons. Provides proper geometry and suppresses highlight flare or "ghost" that occurs when field-mesh image-orthicon types are operated above the knee.

PHOTOCATHODES—Individually processed in each tube to provide maximum sensitivity and uniformity.

PRECISION CONSTRUCTION—Employed in the manufacture of certain RCA Image Orthicons. All tube parts including the envelope are precision made, precision spaced, and precision aligned. Provides tubes having excellent registration capability and uniformity of tube characteristics.

OPTICAL-GLASS FACEPLATES—Made of the finest optical-quality glass to eliminate optical distortion. Image orthicons having fiber-optics faceplates can also be provided.

TARGETS—Made of specially-selected optical glass free of blemishes. Thickness is held to 0.0001" tolerance to prevent resolution loss due to lateral charge leakage. Other image-orthicon types now available have new target materials which afford longer tube life.

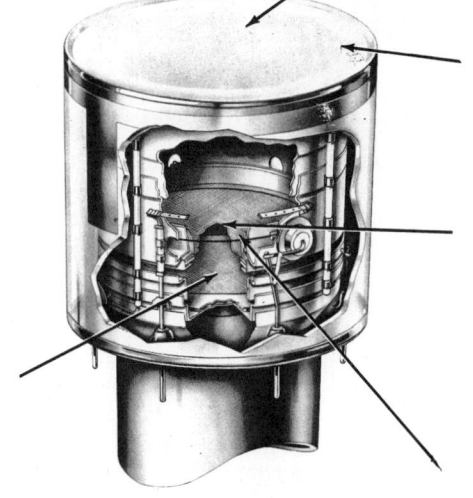

FIELD-MESH—A fine mesh screen employed in certain image orthicons which causes the scanning beam to approach the target perpendicularly at all points and prevents "beam-bending" due to charge pattern on the target. Provides a picture that is relatively free of unwanted bright edges or "overshoots" at the boundary of brightly illuminated portions of a scene. Improves dynamic registration in color pickup applications and provides superior picture sharpness.

MICROMESH—A delicate, precision, electroformed mesh having 750 openings per linear inch. Prevents mesh-pattern and moiré effects without the need for defocusing. Improves picture detail when used with aperture-correction to provide full response.

ORTHICON TUBE

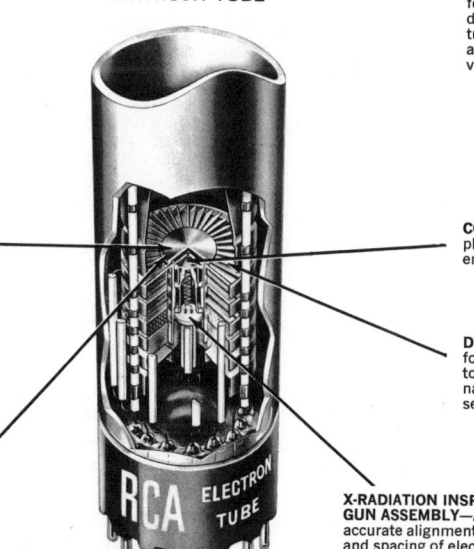

SUPER DYNODE—The first dynode of the multiplier section in non-field mesh tubes designed to eliminate "synode-burn" and consequently excessive "dark-shading."

CONTROL GRIDS—Gold-plated to reduce thermionic emission.

DYNODES—Precision formed, spaced, and aligned to assure uniformity of signal gain in the multiplier section.

HIGH-GAIN DYNODE—The first dynode of the multiplier section in field-mesh tubes designed to increase the output signal-to-noise ratio and signal-output level.

X-RADIATION INSPECTED GUN ASSEMBLY—Assures accurate alignment of parts and spacing of electrodes.

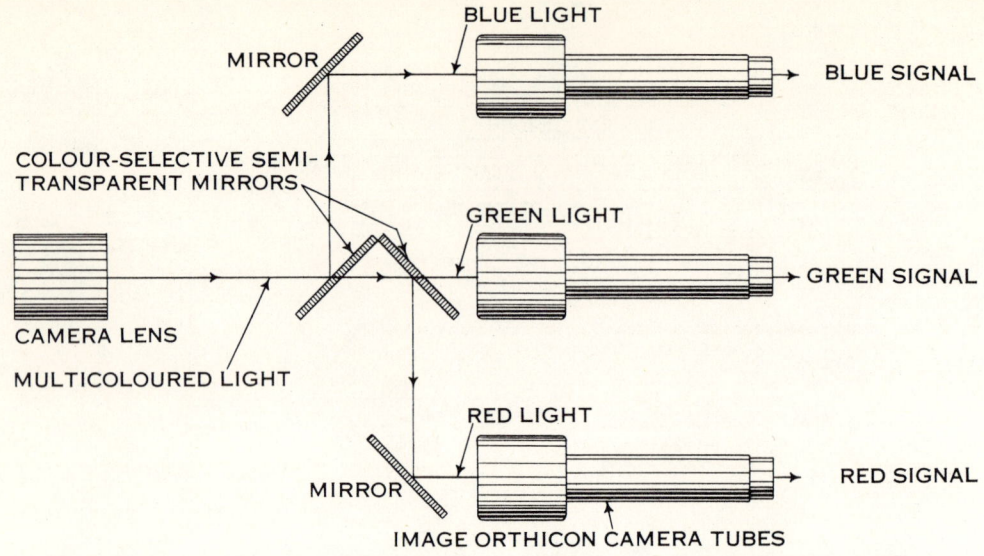

A schematic diagram shows selective separation of light in a color television camera. Multicolored light from the lens is separated into primary colors by color-selective and reflecting mirrors.

is initiated by an electron gun that shoots out an extremely narrow beam of negative electrons. The beam sweeps back and forth across the scene, scanning the target line by line. The beam takes 1/30 of a second to scan the entire target. The intensity of each photosensitive point is thus recorded 30 times per second. Each photosensitive point produces an electric impulse with a strength that corresponds to the strength of illumination at that point. An electron multiplier then amplifies this current to a usable strength so it can be transmitted as a video signal.

Thus, 30 complete pictures are transmitted each second, and the camera is able to register the small changes in light patterns that occur when there is rapid movement in a scene.

In a television receiver the incoming impulses are fed to a control electrode in the picture tube. The picture tube is actually a cathode-ray tube whose inside face is coated with a substance that glows when electrons strike it. The stronger the electron flow, the more the tube will light up.

The picture tube is adjusted so that the beam of electrons, which is synchronized with the beam in the camera tube, sweeps back and forth in straight lines across the screen. As in the camera tube, the beam travels across the face of the tube 30 times per second. In this way, a pattern of luminous points of varying intensity is produced on the screen, recreating the scene viewed by the camera.

Color Transmission

In a color-television transmitter, the picture signal is produced by three camera tubes. The light from the lens first strikes a separating mirror or prism that filters the light so that each camera tube picks up a different color from the scene. One camera tube selects the red light, another selects the green light, and a third selects the blue light. In this manner, the color television camera breaks down the scene into its three primary colors. Some color cameras also have a fourth camera tube which registers the scene in black-and-white.

The tube in a color-television receiver contains three electron guns that direct the red, green, and blue signals to the inner face of the picture tube. This area is coated with many thousands of phosphor dots, clustered in groups of three, which glow when the electron beam hits them. Each of the three dots reacts to a different color.

Behind the screen is a shadow mask that has extremely small and very accurately placed holes, similar to a sieve. These holes are so engineered that they align the stream of electrons from the red electron gun with the red-reacting phosphors, and green gun with the green-reacting phosphors, and the blue gun with the blue-reacting phosphors. The adjustment of the guns and the mask are most critical. If the electrons from the red gun do not strike the red phosphor dot, the red shades of the picture will not be seen. Since these color dots are so small and so close together, the eye brings them together into a true-to-life picture.

Television wavelengths are very short and are able to travel only in straight lines. As a result, the range of a video signal through the air is limited to but little more than the visual horizon. Today, however, that problem is being solved by transmitting the signals to a satellite in a geostationary orbit. From its high altitude the satellite can transmit video signals to roughly one-third of the Earth's surface. Coaxial cables can also be used for long distances, but even then the signal has to be reamplified at regular intervals to maintain its strength and clarity.

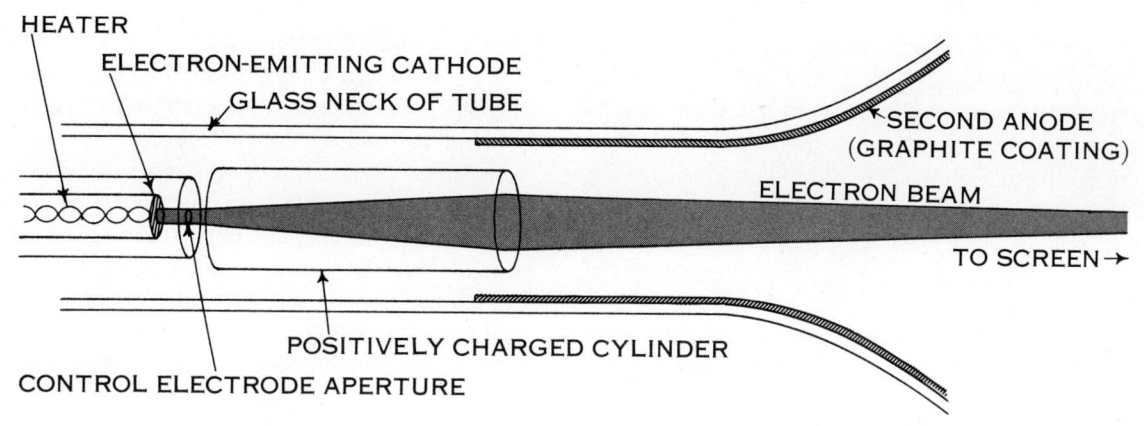

HEATER
ELECTRON-EMITTING CATHODE
GLASS NECK OF TUBE
SECOND ANODE (GRAPHITE COATING)
ELECTRON BEAM
TO SCREEN →
POSITIVELY CHARGED CYLINDER
CONTROL ELECTRODE APERTURE

Monochrome picture tube electron beam activates phosphors inside tube face to create pictures.

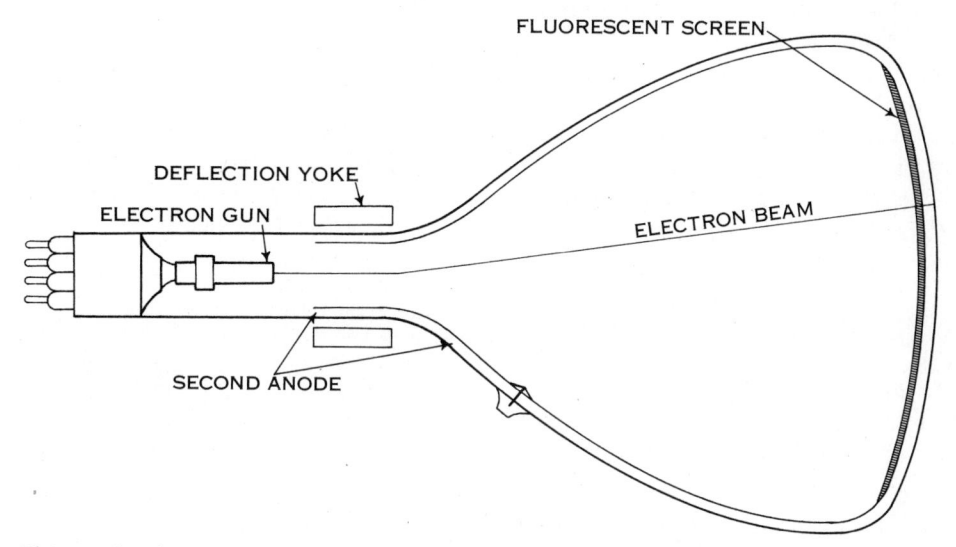

FLUORESCENT SCREEN
DEFLECTION YOKE
ELECTRON GUN
ELECTRON BEAM
SECOND ANODE

Picture tube electron gun generates and directs the electron beam toward the viewing screen.

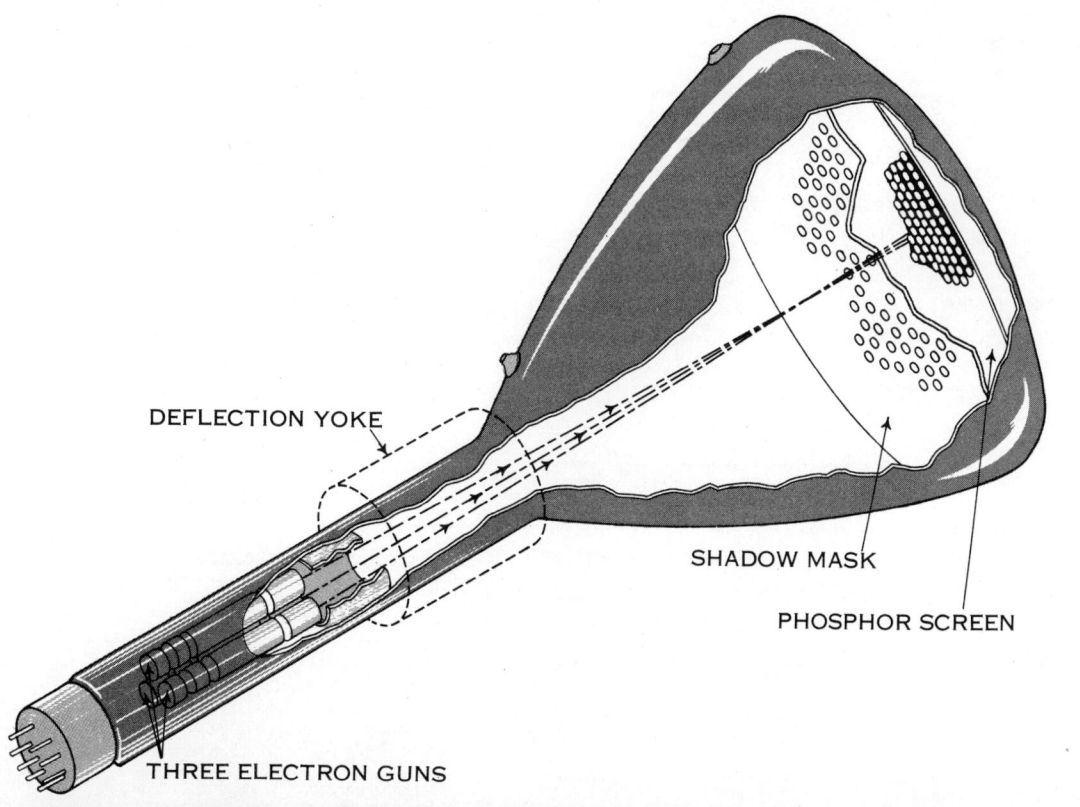

DEFLECTION YOKE
SHADOW MASK
PHOSPHOR SCREEN
THREE ELECTRON GUNS

Shadow mask in the picture tube sorts out color beams before they strike the phosphor screen.

2261

Television

Apollo Television

A portable television camera and transmitting equipment are scheduled to be on board the Apollo Lunar Module (*see*), the first manned spacecraft to land on the moon. Much research has gone into the planning of this system. Not only must the camera be extremely lightweight and rugged, but it must also function properly in the hostile environment of the moon's surface.

A standard black-and-white studio camera weighs as must as 85 to 100 pounds, while the smallest Vidicon camera used commercially weighs about 20 pounds. For use on the moon, engineers have designed a camera that is not only rugged but weighs only 7.25 pounds without optics. It is considered semiportable since it is connected to the spacecraft by a small power cable that provides the necessary 28 volts d.c. power. There is also a small coaxial cable to carry the video signal from the camera to the transmitter in the spacecraft.

The camera operates in much the same way as a commercial TV camera, although its weight limitation requires a different scanning format. In order to keep the weight down, it is necessary to use a minimum amount of power. According to communications theory, a low-power signal must use a very narrow bandwidth or range frequency to keep the "noise" in the system from obscuring the video signal. Therefore, this system uses only about 1/8 the bandwidth of a commercial television signal, or 500,000 Hertz (Hz) as compared to over 4,000,000 Hz. This narrow bandwidth necessitates another compromise: the scan rate must be slowed to 10 frames per second. The scan rate for commercial TV is 30 frames per second. As a result, this "slow-scan" camera will not read motion as distinctly as a commercial camera.

The camera can also take "still" pictures that are transmitted at the rate of only 0.625 frames per second. This mode of transmission is not intended to register motion but will be used to obtain high-resolution (1,280 lines per frame) pictures of inani-

AS-204 television camera weighing 4½ pounds will be carried on the first Apollo moon flight. The camera will relay live images of the Apollo Saturn mission astronauts back to Earth.

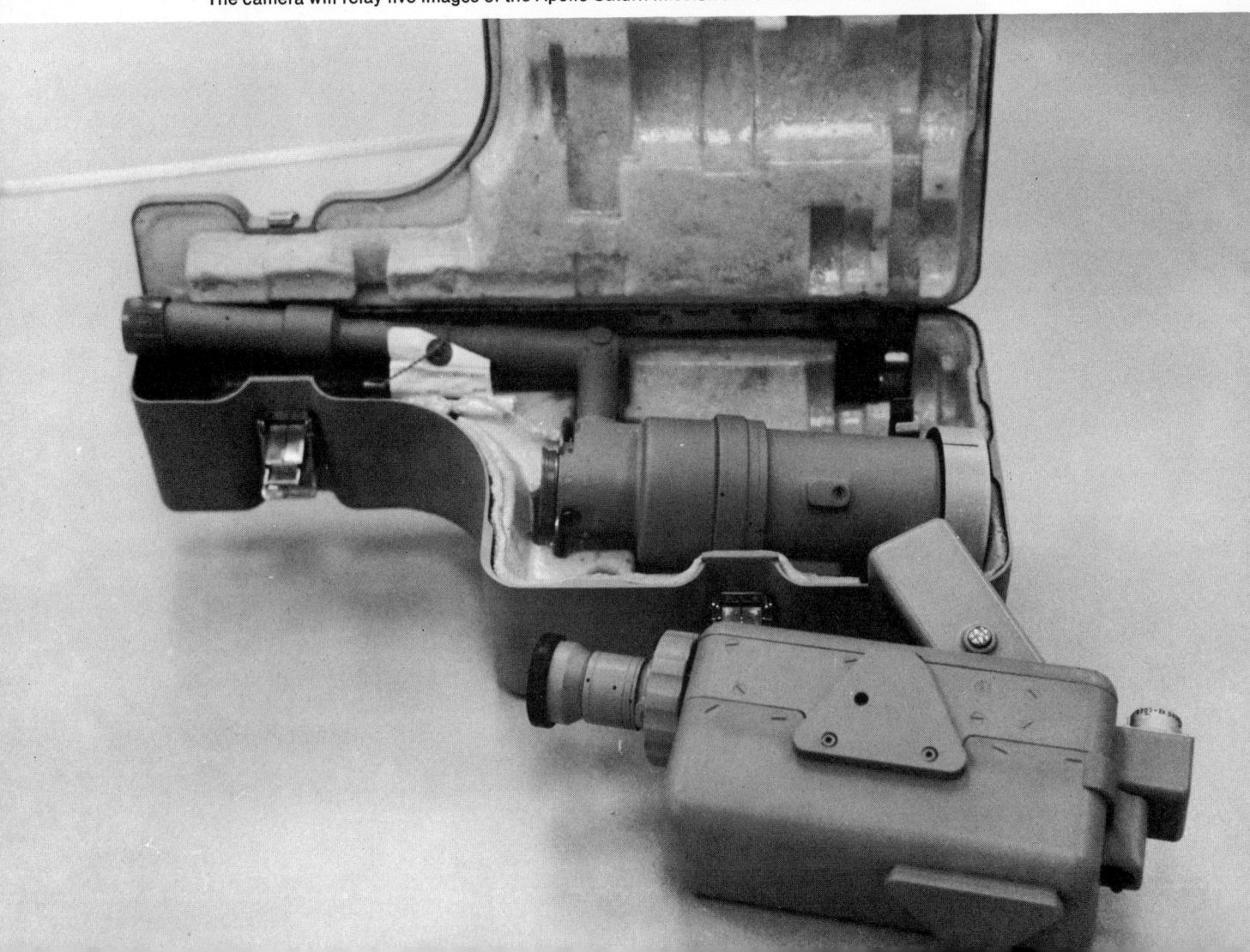

mate objects for detailed scientific study of them.

This camera must also be able to operate in a total vacuum where the electronic components of an average studio camera would arc severely and short out. Another requirement is the ability to withstand a wide range of temperatures at the same time. During operation, one side of the camera will be toward the sun and will have to endure temperatures of approximately 150° F, while the other (shadow) side of the camera is freezing at a temperature of approximately −130° F. In addition, the camera will be subjected to radiation effects that are screened from the average camera by the Earth's atmosphere.

Problems of reception must also be overcome since the transmitter on the moon is quite small compared to the average television station transmitter. By the time the signal has traveled through space for 238,800 miles and has penetrated the Earth's atmosphere, it has become very weak and difficult to isolate from all the "noise" near its frequency. A highly specialized antenna is needed to capture this weak signal and amplify it to a usable strength.

Even after the signal has been isolated and amplified, it is still a nonstandard signal that has to be converted to the standard 525-line-scan, 30-frame-per-second signal for transmission over standard commercial equipment.

For the Apollo program the signal will be received at Goldstone, California; Cape Kennedy, Florida; and Madrid, Spain. Each of these sites is equipped with an 85-foot dish antenna and a converter to standardize the signal. Whether or not the converted signal will be transmitted immediately to the Mission Control Center (*see*) at Houston, Texas, is a matter that will be decided as the need arises. Each site will have the capability of taping the signal so it can be stored for study.

TV Coverage of Spaceflight Activities

A demand for more extensive television coverage of spaceflight activities has existed since the early days of the Mercury program (*see*). Although the networks provided broad coverage of preflight and launch action on all Mercury flights, there was only one attempt to televise a picture from the spacecraft to the Earth. A "slow scan" mode of operation was used, and although the results were far below commercial standards, they generated a great deal of interest.

With the successful launch of the geostationary Early Bird communications satellite in April, 1965, it became feasible to televise commercially the landing and recovery of a spacecraft from the deck of a ship at sea.

Lunar pictures from a Ranger spacecraft are received as signals and converted into photographs by a television receiving display.

Accordingly, the three major networks pooled their resources and manpower to establish a Transportable Satellite Communications Earth Station on board the USS *Wasp,* the recovery ship assigned to the Gemini 7/6 mission. The antenna of the onboard station "locked on" to the Early Bird satellite. The satellite then retransmitted the signal from the *Wasp* to a permanent ground station at Andover, Maine. Normal ground transmission was then used to transmit the signal to the studios in New York so that a live broadcast could be made.

On December 16-18, 1965, the first live television coverage of an astronaut's recovery was made. Television viewers clearly saw the parachute descending and the spacecraft landing in the ocean with a tremendous splash.

Other Applications of TV

Television also has many applications in the fields of science, industry, and education. For instance, a scientist working with atomic materials must be protected by many feet of shielding. However, with closed-circuit television he can operate the most complex and intricate equipment by remote control (*see*) because he is able to see every move on the TV screen. A small remotely controlled television camera is placed in the dangerous area, and the signal from it is fed via coaxial cable to a monitor receiver easily visible to the scientist. In this manner, he can carry out the most dangerous experiments with no danger to himself.

In Houston, Texas, experiments in which traffic is controlled by television are currently being conducted. A number of the heaviest traffic areas are under constant television surveillance. When the monitoring officer at headquarters spots a disabled auto or an accident that could lead to a serious disruption of traffic, he can immediately dispatch the nearest police radio car to the scene. Frequently the police are able to prevent serious traffic problems in this manner.

Television can also be used to guide a missile accurately to its target. For example, the "memory" of the guidance system can be given an exact replica of what a television camera should see during the last two minutes as the missile approaches the target. The scene that is actually registered by the television camera in the missile is then automatically compared with this replica. Any difference between what the camera sees and what it is supposed to see in the target area will cause servo motors to actuate the guidance controls until an exact match is made. The camera will then be able to guide the missile to a perfect hit. Similarly, television can be used for navigation. This can be accomplished by matching stars or star fields and locking on to them to follow a preprogrammed track.

Remotely controlled television cameras in a robot aircraft can use this system to fly over enemy territory. In this way, a continuous picture of the enemy activity can be sent back without endangering personnel.

On November 5, 1967, an Applications and Technology satellite, ATS III, was launched into a geostationary orbit at 47°. This satellite carried a color-television transmitter that provided coverage for almost one-third of the total surface of the Earth. Shortly after achieving its final position, it began transmitting high-quality color pictures. Such pictures are of great value in studying worldwide weather forecasting. Environmental specialists also hope to use satellite television capabilities to help control the weather and to forecast worldwide food resources.

Although television has been in use for over 25 years, it is only now beginning to be refined and used as a tool to aid humanity. Robert S. Hart

See also: Communications satellites, Missiles, Radio, Receivers, Resolution, Space communications, Transmitters

Teller, Edward

Hungarian-American physicist
Born: January 15, 1908;
Budapest, Hungary

Dr. Edward Teller is popularly known as the father of the hydrogen bomb, but his contributions to nuclear weapons technology extend far beyond that one project.

Following undergraduate training in physics at the Institute of Technology in Karlsruhe, Germany, Teller received his doctorate at the University of Leipzig in 1930. He worked for two years with a research organization before receiving a Rockefeller award to study in Copenhagen. In 1935 he emigrated to the United States, and accepted a chair as professor of physics at George Washington University in Washington, D.C. In 1941 he became an American citizen.

Teller spent the years of World War II as a participant in the Manhattan Project (see). There he was responsible for planning and production for both atomic and hydrogen bomb research programs. Following the war he served with the University of Chicago Institute for Nuclear Studies, and as professor of physics at the University of California. He still holds the position of professor-at-large with that institution.

Throughout his teaching career, Teller has continued to contribute greatly to nuclear research projects. As chairman of the University of California department of applied sciences, and assistant director of the Los Alamos, New Mexico, Science Laboratory, he brought to fruition the theories that resulted in successful development of the hydrogen bomb (see) in 1952.

In addition to his professorial duties, Teller has served as associate director of the University of California's Lawrence Radiation Laboratory since 1954, and as the nation's leading advisor on matters related to nuclear energy. For his discoveries and research, he has received many national and international awards and honors. In recent years Teller has continued his nuclear research as well as investigating moral and ethical questions on the use of nuclear weapons. He is the co-author of four authoritative texts on nuclear research, *The Structure of Matter*

(1948), *Our Nuclear Future* (1958), *The Legacy of Hiroshima* (1962), and *The Reluctant Revolutionary* (1964), as well as numerous technical papers in his field.

Robert L. Parrish

See also: Nuclear energy

Telstar, *see* Communications satellites

Temperature control

Many forms of temperature control, both heating and cooling, are required by aircraft and spacecraft. These range from simple air-cooling methods for small reciprocating engines to complex environmental control systems (*see*) for manned spacecraft.

In between, controls must be exercised over the temperatures of such diverse items as the whirling blades of a jet turbine, the recirculating air in an airplane's cabin, and the immobile heat shield of a re-entering Command Module. Each involves its own peculiar problems; methods that work under one set of conditions often are useless elsewhere.

For all temperature control systems, one basic principle remains unchanged: heat from a warmer substance is absorbed by a cooler substance. It is hard to imagine using liquid oxygen (*see*) at −297°F as a heating agent, but when one is trying to warm liquid helium from −453°F to convert it into a gas at, say, −375°F, the liquid oxygen works quite well.

Conversely, it does not seem reasonable to suppose that extremely hot water can be used to cool an object, but that is exactly what happens in a water-cooled engine. The important factor is the *relative* temperature of the "hot" and "cold" objects involved. As long as there is a difference in the two temperatures, the "hot" item will get "cooler," and the "cold" item will get "warmer."

Surviving Re-entry

Most spectacular of the temperature control requirements imposed in the aerospace field is that of bringing a satellite, or spacecraft, safely back to Earth. An orbiting spacecraft has a velocity of about 17,500 mph at the moment of retrofire. Retrofire itself cuts only about 325 mph from that speed, or just enough to insure re-entry. But now an additional 17,000 mph must be lost before the parachutes are deployed, and it must be lost in less than 30 minutes.

Coming back into the atmosphere at nearly 5 miles per second, the spacecraft encounters ever-increasing resistance from the air. It is friction that puts on the "brakes," and friction alone cuts down the 17,000 mph of unwanted speed. At the same time this friction is being converted into heat. Only a few inches away from an astronaut's head, the temperature rises to between 3000° and 4000°F.

The astronaut is protected by the process of *ablation*, a unique means of controlling extreme temperatures under unusual conditions. Ablation (*see*) is the process of burning away, or charring, and is essentially a self-destructive means of cooling.

Ablative heat shields are used on all re-entry vehicles, whether spacecraft, satellites, or nuclear warheads. Silicon-base fiber glass combined with various plastic resins is the most common material used. Ablative materials have a high heat-reducing tolerance. When that limit is reached, they undergo three heat-reducing processes. The first two, sublimation and boiling, occur only at the surface of the material. Some of the heat shield surface *sublimates* converting directly from a solid to a gas and carrying off heat as the gas escapes. Some of it turns into a *boiling* liquid, also carrying off heat as the liquid blows away. The two processes mean that fresh surfaces constantly are being exposed to the heat. But most important, layers directly beneath the surface *absorb* tremendous quantities of heat as they turn into crisp, black char. The char itself is more heat resistant than the original material, thus creating a final buffer layer between exterior temperatures and the spacecraft cabin.

Keeping Astronauts Cool

Regulating temperatures within the spacecraft cabin itself involves far different problems. Heat given off by electronic equipment and by the astronauts must be largely eliminated, and cold creeping in from space must be controlled.

The primary heat source during Mercury program (*see*) one-man missions was the astronaut's body, which produced up to 1,000 BTU (British Thermal Units) per hour. Humidity in the form of perspiration at the rate of seven pounds per day also was taken into consideration.

Mercury designers settled on a heat exchanger (*see*) using water evaporation to maintain a temperature balance. Water in a space vacuum boils at about 35°F. Thus the water could absorb excess astronaut body heat by boiling and dissipating that heat into space.

With the advent of Gemini (*see*) and Apollo (*see*) such a simple method of controlling temperatures no longer was adequate. Apollo must use a combination of techniques, improved water boilers being just one, to meet the requirements of a three-man crew journeying to the moon.

A water glycol solution pumped through coils,

Spacecraft Radiator

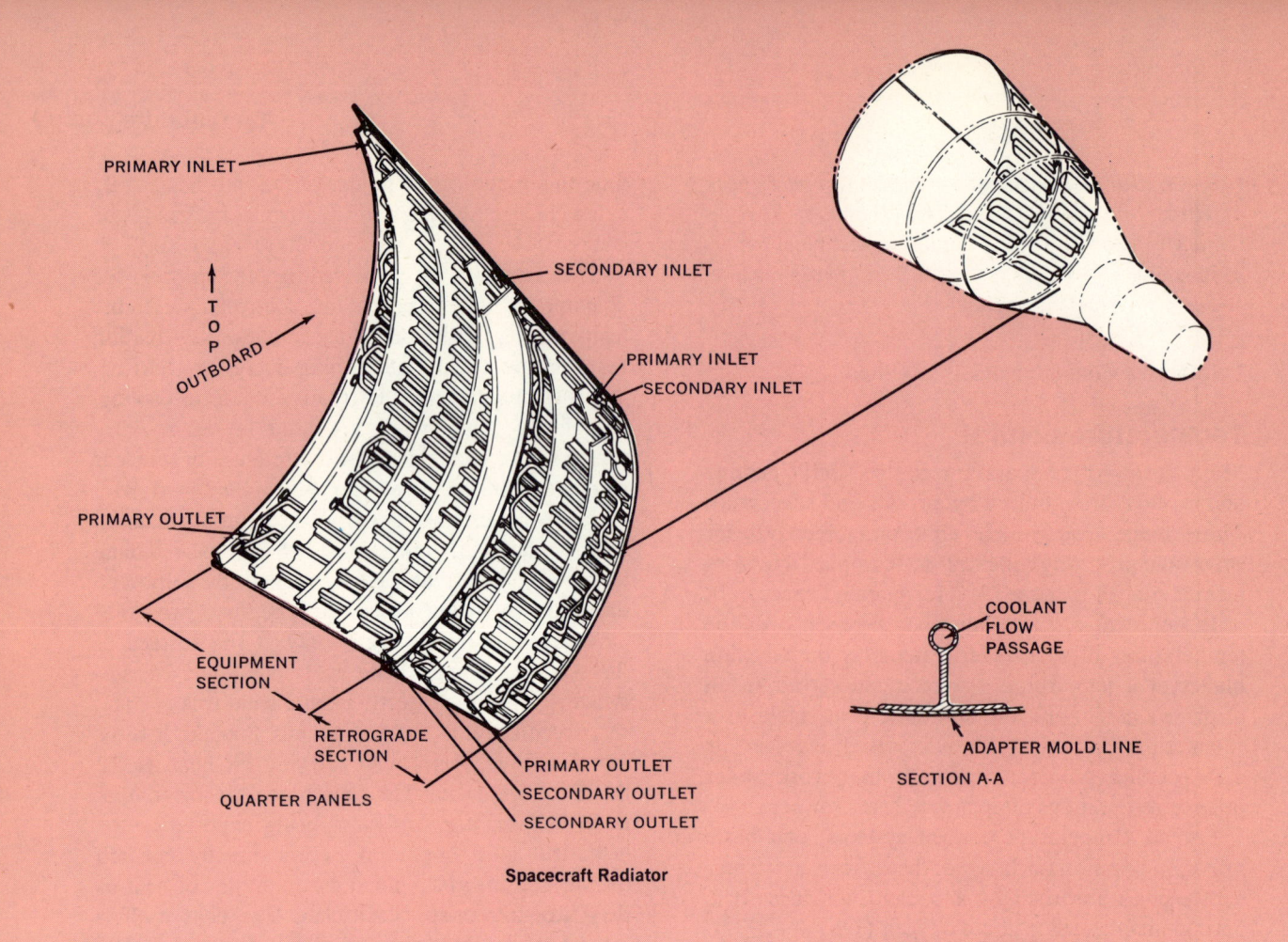

The spacecraft radiator is a basic element of the coolant subsystem of environmental control.

tubes, and channels in the spacecraft is the primary heat transfer agent. In this case, it is not correct to call it a *cooling* agent because it also is used as a *heating* agent.

Heat-producing electronic equipment is mounted to *cold plates,* thin-walled metal plates through which channels have been bored. Water glycol flowing through the channels is warmed by the equipment, thereby carrying away heat. More heat is absorbed from the cabin atmosphere and from the spacesuit circuit, both of which are picking up heat from body radiation, respiration, and equipment. In these respects, the water glycol is a cooling agent, but the heat it now carries must be reduced. Some of the heat is transferred to the icy cold oxygen being pumped into the cabin, warming the oxygen to a comfortable temperature. Some of it is lost by flowing through cold plates that must be warmed rather than cooled. The rest of the unwanted heat is dissipated through contact with a water boiler.

Although the system primarily is automatic, astronauts can control water glycol flow through various portions of the spacecraft. This allows them, for instance, to control temperatures in the cabin, or in their spacesuits (*see*).

Aircraft Cabin Temperatures

The comfort of an aircraft cabin is taken for granted by today's travelers. In most light aircraft the simplest of all cooling systems is used: a controllable vent which allows outside air to flow directly into the cabin. If heat is needed, it comes from another vent that draws air directly from the hot engine compartment. Simplicity is this system's primary virtue, but it is almost impossible to control cabin temperature with great precision.

The pleasure of flying on the modern turboprop and turbojet aircraft of today is largely due to the perfection of cabin pressurization and air conditioning. Most passengers cannot quite imagine a flight in which the aircraft stays at altitudes below 20,000 feet, or where they have to wear oxygen masks throughout the flight. Yet in the late 1930's such proposals were presented by aircraft designers.

Early attempts at cabin pressurization resulted in cabin temperatures ranging up to 150°F. The problem was that pressurizing air increases its tempera-

Temperature control

ture. The heat of pressurization is still used when additional heat is needed.

The four major components of the air conditioning systems used in commercial air transports (*see*) are the same basic components found in home air conditioners, including a source of compressed air, an intercooler, a water separation system, and an expansion turbine. The configuration of these components, their location in the aircraft, and the power source they use vary from plane to plane.

The compressor may be run in a variety of ways. On some aircraft a hydraulic motor is used, supplied from a branch of the engine's hydraulic system (*see*). Electrical and mechanical power takeoffs are used on other aircraft. On large turbojets or fan jets, compressed air may be bled off the engine compressors, either to be used directly or to power a separate turbine.

Since air becomes heated when it is compressed, the next step in the system must be to cool the air to a comfortable temperature. The intercooler performs this task and may be air-cooled itself by simply forcing air through passages in it, or by refrigeration. The water system reduces the humidity of the air to a comfortable level.

Cooling Aircraft Engines

Engine temperatures must be regulated because the heat generated by burning fuels, by a nuclear reaction, or by internal friction is high enough to melt or distort the engine. High temperature also can break down lubricating fluids and fuels. Heat generated by an internal combustion engine (*see*) can be dissipated by contact with a cool stream of air, or with a liquid coolant.

Comparatively few American aircraft engines have been liquid-cooled. Those that are cooled in this manner operate in the same way as a conventional automobile engine. The coolant, usually water or ethylene glycol, is pumped through jackets surrounding the cylinders. The flow rate is fast enough to carry away the heat before the liquid boils. The liquid then is circulated through a radiator (*see*) where it is cooled by the flow of air.

The major advantage of liquid cooling is that more heat may be transferred, from a given area of metal surface, to a liquid than to air. The primary disadvantage is that it requires another mechanical system which must be maintained, and adds weight to the aircraft.

Most designers prefer air cooling. Air-cooled engines need more surface area at the cylinder wall. This greater heat-transferring area is provided by welding fins to the outside of the cylinder walls. The

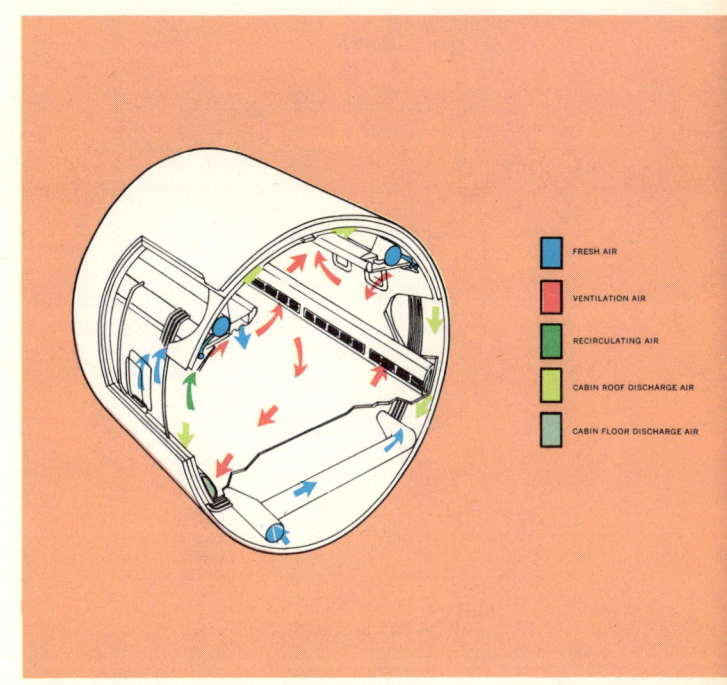

Air circulation system of the Concorde supersonic transport ensures passenger comfort.

Early water-cooled engines such as the Roberts four-cylinder model were efficient but heavy.

number and size of the fins depend on the amount of cooling required and the amount of air which will flow past the fins.

Airflow through the fins of many aircraft is controlled with shutters, or flaps, built into the cowling. These cowl flaps are adjusted to prevent too much airflow while the engine is warming up. They are opened to the proper setting for operating conditions at takeoff and cruise.

Temperature control

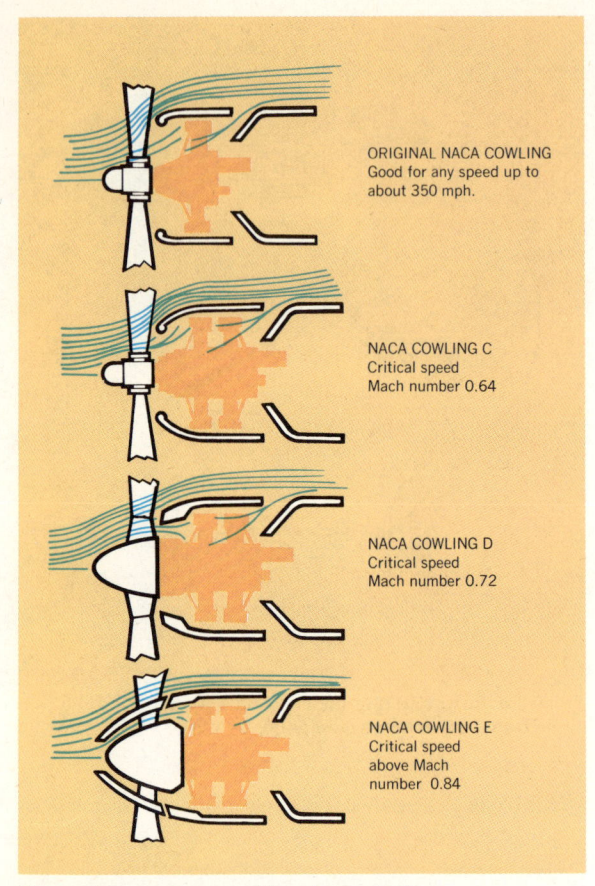

ORIGINAL NACA COWLING
Good for any speed up to about 350 mph.

NACA COWLING C
Critical speed
Mach number 0.64

NACA COWLING D
Critical speed
Mach number 0.72

NACA COWLING E
Critical speed
above Mach number 0.84

The engine cowling provides air circulation for temperature control as well as streamlining. Adjustable flaps control airflow.

More than cylinder cooling is required for an internal combustion engine. Ducts also are provided to carry air to the oil coolers, and in some aircraft to a cooler for air coming from the supercharger (*see*) to the engine. As the supercharger compresses air to feed combustion by the engine, the air is heated. To avoid premature detonation of the fuel-air mixture, compression heat must be removed.

Cooling Jets and Turbines

Jet and turboprop engines are air-cooled by mounting the engine in a shroud. Air flows between the engine and shroud from the front or intake end of the plane to the rear or exhaust end, where it is expelled with the engine's exhaust gases. The engine's tailpipe ends just inside the shroud which extends to the end of the fuselage (*see*), or nacelle. As the hot exhaust gases flow out of the tailpipe, they create a low-pressure area in the remaining length of the shroud. This sucks cooling air back from the intake end. Although this system prevents the heat of the engine from reaching the rest of the airframe, it does only part of the job. The combustion chambers or combustors, turbines, and lubricating systems also must be cooled.

The combustion section of the engine is made of a high-temperature alloy (usually cobalt or nickel base alloy). Air from the compressor enters the combustor liner through perforations called *thimble holes* and *louvers*. The thimble holes direct air into a boundary layer of comparatively cool air along the inner surfaces of the liner. This boundary layer acts as insulation to prevent overheating of the chamber walls.

The flow from the louvers is called *secondary combustion air* and keeps the flame away from the walls. This air then passes through a series of holes in the outer flange of the combustor liner. Here it is divided into a number of airstreams to cool the outer turbine casing and shroud and the base of the first-stage turbine. Some air is diverted into the turbine blades themselves to cool both the blades and the trailing edges of the blades. Other diverted air is directed against the flat surface of the turbine wheel near the hub to offset some of the forward motion of the compressor rotor and reduce the thrust loadings on the bearings.

The cooling air which was routed through various parts of the first-stage turbine is then routed to cool the second-stage turbine. It eventually joins the main gas stream and leaves through the nozzle.

Air is not the only cooling medium used in the jet engine. Jet fuel also is a convenient heat sink (*see*), and is used for this purpose on most modern planes. Fuel often is used for dissipating heat in the oil cooler. Since even the new synthetic oils cannot stand temperatures above approximately 450°F, the flow of oil through the lubricating system must be fast enough to prevent the temperature from rising too high. Since the oil itself acts as a coolant as it lubricates, the heat it absorbs must be dissipated. The oil cooler is ordinarily a typical liquid-to-liquid heat exchanger. It consists of a large number of passages arranged in a honeycomb pattern with the fuel and oil flowing through adjacent passages.

These cooling methods are very simple compared with the cooling systems which will be necessary for the advanced air-breathing engines of the future. One of the major difficulties in supersonic flight is that the entire engine is immersed in an air stream 600° hotter than conventional subsonic turbojet engines. As a result, the combustion system and turbine are forced to operate at temperatures which would soften ordinary materials. Turbine inlet temperatures, about 1600°F in subsonic engines, go above 2000°F in supersonic engines.

In the critical turbine area, experiments are underway using *impingement cooling* on the leading edges of the turbine blades. This is where the greatest heat input is encountered. The impingement system uses jets of air directed at the critical areas. *Convection cooling* (transfer of heat by circulation of heated liquid or gas) can be used in the midchord section of the blades along with fins to increase the surface area exposed to cooling air. *Film cooling,* in which air flows over the surface of the blade, is being studied for the trailing edges where it is difficult to locate cooling passages inside the blade.

Proper cooling is necessary for engine durability, which is the key factor in operating costs and is measured by the time between major overhauls of an engine. Current subsonic jets operate up to 10,000 hours between major overhauls. In fact, they are becoming so reliable that the major overhauls usual in the past are rapidly disappearing. Instead, problem areas are detected and corrected as they arise during routine maintenance. New engines for supersonic transports (*see*) and V/STOL aircraft (*see*) must be equally reliable in order to be economically practical.

Cooling Rocket Engines

Keeping rocket engine temperatures within safe limits is far more difficult than cooling the turbine or piston engine. This is because most of a rocket's operation is in space, where there is no atmosphere to carry away heat.

Two methods for cooling rocket engines are in common use. One is to route the fuel (*see*) or the oxidizer (*see*) through channels in the walls of the nozzle before they reach the injector and combustion chamber. Fuels such as kerosene (*see*) can absorb only a small fraction of the combustion heat without vaporizing, but sometimes this is enough.

The situation is improved when supercold liquid hydrogen with a temperature below −423°F is the fuel. This is the case, for instance, with the Saturn's S-IVB stage. Liquid hydrogen is an ideal heat sink and can absorb large quantities of heat as it passes through the walls of the engine nozzle.

The second method is to use an ablative liner for the nozzle throat. By carefully calculating the rate of ablation, and by correlating it with the desired firing time of the engine, a nozzle throat can be designed to provide a liner with just the right amount of protection.

The supercold liquid gases also are used to provide temperature controls in the form of heating. For instance, Apollo uses liquid oxygen in some instances to warm up liquid hydrogen, or nitrogen, until it becomes gaseous. The gas, still colder than −300°F, provides the pressure to force the liquid through valves and thus flow toward the combustion chamber.

It is obvious that in aerospace, there is more to temperature control than setting a thermostat.

Jim Schefter

See also: Aircraft propulsion systems, Electrical systems, Ignition systems, Life-support systems, Lubricants, Rocket propulsion systems, Space propulsion systems

Temperature gauges

Everyone is familiar with thermometers, both the kind used to tell how hot or cold the weather is and the kind used to tell whether or not one has a fever. Thermometers are temperature gauges, and many of them are used in aerospace vehicles. Airplane engine temperatures are very important, and the temperature of an astronaut's spacesuit is even more important. On unmanned satellites, the temperature of the equipment compartment is one of the most important measurements sent down to the ground by the telemetry system.

Principles of Operation

Most ways of measuring temperature make use of one of three different principles. The first and best known is that heat makes things expand. Galileo (*see*) used this principle when he made his *thermoscope,* which was a thin glass tube with a large bulb on the end. He warmed the bulb in his hands and then put the other end in a small dish of colored liquid. By heating the bulb in his hands he had warmed the air inside it and made it less dense than the air around it, so that atmospheric pressure pushed the colored liquid part way up the narrow tube. Then the liquid would move up and down as the air outside became colder or warmer. The trouble with this idea was that the liquid also moved up and down as the atmospheric pressure changed, like a barometer (*see*), and it was impossible to tell whether it was measuring temperature change, pressure change, or both. This was about 1600, and shortly afterward people began to make sealed glass thermometers of the kind in use today.

Another very common type of thermometer, the kind with a dial and a pointer, is also based on the principle that heat makes things expand. Added to it, however, is the knowledge that heat makes different things expand by different amounts. If strips of two different metals are soldered together, one will expand faster than the other as it warms up.

Temperature gauges

The only way it can expand is by bending both strips, with the longer one naturally on the outside. If one end is fastened and the other connected to a pointer, the pointer will move as the temperature changes and make the combined strip, called a *bimetal strip,* bend and straighten out. Bimetal strips are often used in thermostats like those in electric irons and toasters.

For most aerospace purposes it is easier to use the second principle, which is that many substances change their electrical resistance as the temperature changes. If a piece of material (usually a special metal alloy) is placed in an electrical circuit, the voltage in the circuit changes as the temperature of the material changes, and an ordinary voltmeter connected to the circuit becomes a temperature gauge. Of course, such a temperature gauge must be calibrated, which means that the voltage corresponding to certain temperatures must be measured. Then the dial of the voltmeter can be marked in degrees instead of volts.

Not long ago it was found that certain semiconductors (*see*) were very good for this purpose because their resistance changed very rapidly with temperature, and they could therefore be used to measure temperature changes with high accuracy. This kind of a temperature gauge is called a *thermistor*. Both kinds of electrical temperature gauges are very convenient for aerospace uses because the dial can be placed anywhere and simply connected to the sensitive element (and a power supply, of course) by wires.

The third principle is called the *thermocouple*. About 150 years ago it was discovered that if pieces of two different metals were connected at their ends, and if the two ends or junctions had different temperatures, an electric current would be generated. The greater the difference in temperature, the higher the voltage. It is easy to see that if one end is placed at a point where the temperature is to be measured, inside an engine, for example, while the other end remains outside at a more or less constant temperature, the voltage generated will depend on the inside temperature. Thermocouples are especially useful for measuring temperature differences.

Very high temperatures can be measured by a method called *optical pyrometry*. When a metal or a gas grows hotter, it changes color, as iron becomes red hot and then white hot. Very high temperatures can then be determined simply from the color. That is how scientists determine the temperatures of the sun and the stars.

Robert Drake Kennedy

Temperature scales

One of the early problems in the development of thermometers was the adoption of a standard scale so that a thermometer could be *calibrated,* or marked to show what temperature corresponded to a certain height of the liquid column. The temperature of a body is its relative ability to communicate heat to other bodies. If the body in question absorbs heat from another source, it is cooler than that source. If it transfers heat, it is warmer. Temperature scales permit the measurement of this quality.

The first thermometers depended upon the expansion and contraction, with temperature changes, of a known volume of air. The air was contained in a glass bulb, with a tube extension filled with water. The column of water, which communicated with a reservoir open to the atmosphere, moved up or down the tube with temperature changes.

The best these crude thermometers could provide was a very rough approximation of the temperature. In fact, if they were calibrated at all, they rarely indicated more than eight or ten levels. These levels were assigned numerical "degree" values and/or were labeled with descriptive captions ranging from *Most Extremely Cold* through *Cold, Temperate,* and *Warm* to *Intolerably Hot.*

Scales in Current Use

In time, alcohol and mercury thermometers very similar to those in use today were developed. These

Two types of temperature gauges: the bi-metal strip type and the resistance thermometer.

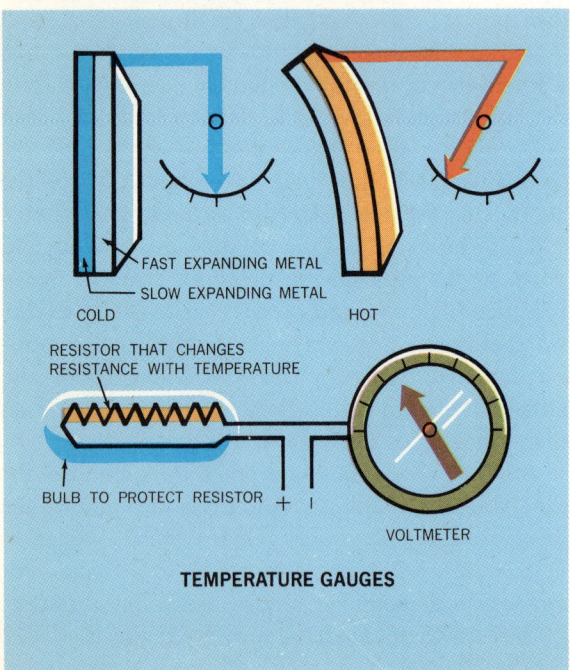

TEMPERATURE GAUGES

instruments permitted more precise measurements and encouraged the invention of more precise scales. The first to become well known was that of Gabriel Daniel Fahrenheit, a German-born resident of Holland, who described his system in 1724.

The *Fahrenheit scale* (°F) found ready acceptance because it was based upon two relatively stable reference points: the lowest temperature obtainable with a mixture of ice and common salt, and the normal temperature of the healthy human body. These two points were assigned the values of 32° and 96°, respectively, although the latter is now known to be 98.6°. Fahrenheit devised the mercury thermometer in order to measure the boiling point of water, which he observed at 212°. The Fahrenheit scale is still in common use in English-speaking countries.

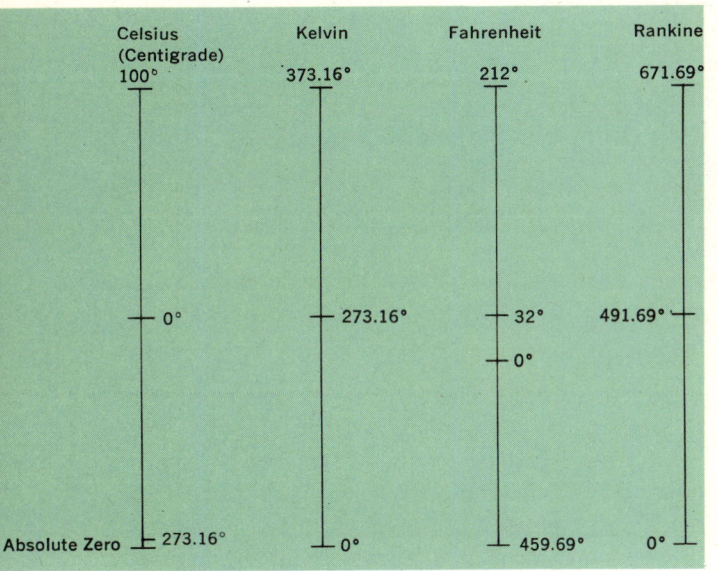

Four temperature scales are in use. The selection of one depends on the application, with Fahrenheit and Celsius used most commonly.

The next important temperature scale appeared in France in 1730, the invention of Rene-Antoine de Reaumur, a French naturalist. *Reaumur scale* used a single point of reference, the freezing point of water, and was divided by units up to 80°, the boiling point. The fluid used in the thermometer is a specified standard alcohol. The Reaumur scale is used today in French-speaking countries, the U.S.S.R., and in Central Europe.

The *Celsius,* or *centigrade, scale* (°C) was developed by Anders Celsius, a Swedish astronomer, about 1741. It contains 100 degrees between the two fixed points, the freezing and boiling points of water. It is commonly used in many European countries, and is the standard scale of science throughout the world.

The *Kelvin scale* (°K), also known as the *absolute* or *thermodynamic scale,* was invented by the Englishman William Thomson (Lord Kelvin) about 1854. It is identical in units with the centigrade scale, except that its zero point is absolute zero—the point at which all motion, even that of orbital electrons, theoretically ceases and heat no longer exists. Absolute zero is 273° below 0° centigrade, so 273°K is the same as 0°C. Kelvin chose to fix the ice (freezing point of water) to steam (boiling point of water) interval at 100°. A thermodynamic scale with the ice-steam interval 180° as in the Fahrenheit scale is called the *Rankine scale* (°R) and is used in engineering.

Dale D. Campbell

See also: Temperature control

Tensile strength

Tensile strength is the relative resistance of a metal to deformation under stress. It is expressed in pounds per square inch (psi), and the measurement is usually calculated from the amount of tension (stress) required to pull a test specimen apart divided by the original cross-sectional area of the material tested.

The term is most often used with another measurement, *yield point,* which means the tension on a test specimen at which point the specimen begins to tear apart and continues to the point of complete rupture even though no more stress is applied.

Another measure of material strength is the *yield strength,* that point at which a stressed piece of metal can no longer spring back to its original dimensions when a force exerted upon it is finally removed. This is also expressed in psi and usually refers to the amount of stress needed to create a .02 per cent change in the test specimen from its original shape.

Part of the design problem in aerospace is that yield or tensile strength changes with temperature. A block of maraging steel (steel heated to improve strength) at 70°F may have a yield strength of 237,000 psi. This falls to 112,000 psi at 1000°F and to 26,000 psi at 1200°F.

Tensile strength can vary from yield strength by a wide margin, as in Waspalloy, one of the superalloys which has a tensile strength of 190,000 psi, but a yield strength of only 124,000 psi.

Keith W. Bennett

See also: Alloys, Manufacturing, Materials, Nickel, Steels, Tolerances

TERMINOLOGY OF AEROSPACE

A selected listing of terminology which has developed as a result of aerospace technological advancement or which has a specific meaning in aerospace.

Abort	To cancel or cut short a mission.
Ace	A pilot who has scored five aerial victories.
Acquisition	Acquiring a spacecraft at ground stations for tracking purposes.
Angel	A radar echo caused by an unseen physical phenomenon.
Astronautics	The art or science of designing, building, and operating space vehicles and associated equipment.
Attitude	The position of a vehicle in relation to a reference point such as the horizon.
Backup	An item or system available to replace another, or a backup crew to replace a prime crew.
Bird	Any rocket, satellite, or aircraft.
Black box	Any unit, usually an electronic device, which can be mounted in a vehicle as a single package.
Blip	A spot of light on a radarscope.
Blackout	A loss of radio communications during re-entry of a spacecraft or of an aircraft in flight. Also refers to loss of consciousness due to insufficient oxygen supply during flight.
Boilerplate	A copy of a spacecraft used only for testing.
Breakoff phenomenon	The psychological feeling associated with being completely alone.
Burn	The period of a rocket engine firing.
CapCom	From **Cap**sule **Com**municator. Ground link, usually an astronaut with a manned spacecraft.
Cluster	Two or more engines bound together to function as one unit.
Command	A signal which initiates or triggers an action in the device which receives the signal.
Constant wear garment	An astronaut's underwear.
Countdown	The step by step process leading to a launching measured in hours, minutes, and seconds.
Data reduction	Transformation of observed values into useful, ordered, or simplified information.
Destruct	To deliberately destroy a rocket after it has been launched.
Diskey	From **Dis**play **Key**board. Apollo console for computer readouts.
Display	The graphic presentation of the output data of a device or system; a real-time readout.
Downrange	A direction away from the launch site and along a line of the test range.
Down the slot	Expression for a successful flight of a rocket.
Dump	To transmit stored information, usually from a satellite to a ground station.
Envelope	Conditions for an entire launching operation.
Eyeballs in, eyeballs out	Terms used to describe acceleration experience.
g or G-force	Acceleration or deceleration on an object measured at 32.2 feet per second.
Generation	Stages of development, or groups, such as first generation of astronauts.
Glitch	An unexplained malfunction or breaking of voltage.
Hack	An exact starting reference for time. Clocks are started for a mission at a time hack on command.
Hardware	Referring to the physical object, such as the actual engines, pumps, guidance system, or other spacecraft or rocket parts.
Hold	To halt the sequence of a countdown.
Home	The action of a missile in directing itself toward a target by sensing the target's heat or electrical activity.
Inject	To be placed into orbit.
Insert	To place an object into orbit.
LASER	**L**ight **A**mplification by **S**timulated **E**mission of **R**adiation.
Liftoff	The instant a rocket leaves its launching pad.
Lock on	A sensor, radar, or radio has singled out and remains fixed on one object.
Long count	Counting from one to ten and back. Used to test radio communications.
Mayday	International distress call.
Max Q	Maximum period of stress on a spacecraft or rocket.
Mate	To fit together stages or parts of a spacecraft.
Memory	The component of a computer which provides data or instructions previously recorded so as to make them bear upon an immediate problem.
Module	Spacecraft. The Command Module, Lunar Module, and Service Module as used in the Apollo program.
Nominal	Expected or uneventful, as in a nominal mission.
Pancake	A full-stall hard landing in an aircraft.
Pogo	Vibrations in a rocket booster, usually in the first stage.
Q	Dynamic pressure.
RADAR	**Ra**dio **D**etection **a**nd **R**anging.
Readout	The retrieval of data from a storage system, computer, receiver, etc. The readout may take the form of printed copy, pictures, illuminated numbers, etc.
Real time	Time in which reporting takes place; at this very instant.
Recovery	The finish of a space mission when the spacecraft and crew are recovered.
Scrub	To cancel a scheduled mission.
Shot	Firing of a rocket.
Slave	Any system under the control of another system.
Slip	A schedule postponement.
Software	Computations and data received from instruments used to program computers.
Soft landing	Landing at a slow speed to avoid crash or destruction.
Sophisticated	Complex and intricate; most highly advanced state-of-the-art.
Stage	A portion of a rocket containing its own fuel tanks and engines.
State-of-the-art	The present stage of development of a vehicle, process, or system.
Tanks	Term for astronaut monitor who watches propellant instruments in blockhouse during a manned space launch.
Trajectory	The path of a spacecraft.
T-time	Any specific time, minus or plus, with reference to zero or launch time during countdown.
Umbilical	Any line that carries electrical, communications, and oxygen connections from one place to another.
Velcro	A material consisting of a pile tape and a hook tape used in spacecraft to anchor items down in a weightless condition.
Window	A time period in which a rocket must be fired to achieve its objective.
X	Symbol for experimental.
Zap	To attack and destroy.

Terminology of aerospace

Understanding English is not enough sometimes—you have to know the jargon. For instance, suppose someone said, "Order an abort unless the *g*'s are damped out." Unless you were familiar with aerospace terminology, you wouldn't understand that the speaker said the mission was to be halted unless acceleration forces were eliminated.

In all professions a language develops which is different from the vernacular but thoroughly understandable to the people involved. Aviation and space jargon is a bit more complex because of the many words made from initials (*acronyms*) and from squeezing two or more words together, such as a verb and preposition combination.

In the early days of aviation, some airplane parts took the same name as those of birds, while others were named for their function. With the beginning of rocket and jet technology, the budding jargon emerged into full bloom. Acronyms came fast and furious, and although abbreviations are almost as old as writing itself, the space generation has adopted both as a time-saving shorthand. NASA itself has "invented" many of the words.

Harold R. Williams

Testing

Before an astronaut flies a spacecraft or a passenger rides in an airliner, many tests of the materials used, of the various sections or pieces of equipment, and of the complete vehicle will have been made and evaluated to prove that the craft is safe. The tests are intended to tell whether the test article works, how well it works, and how long it works.

The scope of present-day testing is a far cry from aviation's earliest days. Then, each flight of an airplane was really a test of its ability to hold together in flight. When aviation came of age in the 1920's and early 1930's, test pilots would put new planes through strenuous maneuvers designed literally to tear the wings off. If the aircraft survived these tortures, it was considered fit to fly.

Testing today still strains material and equipment to and even beyond their limits, but the tests are conducted under strict controls. They are completely monitored, with data recorded and analyzed scientifically. At one point in Apollo spacecraft testing, instruments pick up test data from 1,500 separate spacecraft and ground support activities at a rate of 25,600 samples *per second*.

Testing

Torture Tests

Tests to demonstrate that a piece of equipment will work properly in flight are done by putting the unit through its paces even before it is installed in the craft. For example, an airplane's landing gear is extended and retracted hundreds of times in an engineering laboratory. Control surfaces and hydraulic systems are exercised similarly before they are declared safe for installation in the new design.

Wing sections are buffeted for hours, even days, by scores of pneumatic hammers, are vibrated, and are twisted and bent. From the start of the test to its completion, gauges measure the results of the torture and transmit the data to recording devices for later analysis. From evaluation of the data, engineers can determine if the component will survive similar rigors in actual flight or, if not, what must be done to make the unit safe.

Safety *standards,* or the level to which each component or the entire vehicle must perform, are based on the most severe conditions the hardware will experience in use. But a safety *factor* exceeding the standard is designed into most units and the total craft. These safety factors are expressed in numbers such as one-and-a-half or two or three, for example, and represent the unit's ability to perform properly beyond the standard. A factor of two means the equipment is safe to conditions twice as severe as the worst predicted.

Mock-ups

Another technique of testing a craft's performance before it flies, and even before the flying version is built, is the use of mock-ups or dummies. Subscale models are used in wind tunnel tests to determine an airplane's or a spacecraft's aerodynamic shape and its probable structural integrity and heating characteristics. Usually, however, mock-ups are full-scale constructions. Often built of wood, they help designers to determine the proper location of instruments, or they verify passenger-seating arrangements and safety procedures.

Spacecraft testing especially employs mock-ups called *boilerplates.* They are test vehicles made of metal and are the same shape and size, often the same weight, as the actual flight article. In certain tests, the boilerplates themselves actually fly. Cheaper to build than the true spacecraft, boilerplates are proving invaluable to testing.

As a result of the Apollo fire at Cape Kennedy, the National Aeronautics and Space Administration (NASA) (*see*) is using fully equipped boilerplate spacecraft for flammability tests. By deliberately starting fires in the mock-ups, NASA technicians can tell which materials and systems are fireproof and which must be replaced or protected. They also can decide how best to arrange stored equipment so it will not contribute to the spread of a fire. The amount of energy required to start a fire, the speed at which the flames grow and spread, and the time they take to burn themselves out are recorded by sensing devices and on motion picture film.

Even before the tragic fire, boilerplate spacecraft were used extensively in NASA's testing programs. Mock-up Apollo (*see*), Gemini (*see*), and Mercury program (*see*) spacecraft all flew several suborbital missions to test such things as launch escape system

An F-4 Phantom undergoes drop tests *(left)* to evaluate landing gear reliability. The full-scale aircraft will also be subjected to static and cyclic fatigue, shock, vibration, and heat tests.
A Saab 105 is being placed in a climate chamber *(right)* where the cabin air system will be tested at very low temperatures simulating conditions at high altitudes.

Testing

operation, heat shield performance, structural integrity under pressure, and even the ability to float safely after impact in water.

Boilerplates are dropped at velocities of 40 to 50 feet per second into water and onto solid ground to test construction design, and from airplanes to check performance of the Earth-landing system's deployment devices and parachutes.

Environmental Testing

Because a spacecraft faces more severe conditions than an airplane, it must pass additional types of tests. In turn, the requirement for such tests has brought about new methods and facilities for testing.

During its climb to orbital altitude atop a powerful booster rocket, the spacecraft picks up vibrations and noise created by the engines of the launch vehicle (*see*). Vibration (*see*) could harm spacecraft equipment or even shake the ship to pieces. Excessive noise (*see*) could impair the astronaut's ability to do his job.

Components, such as a communications system, get a thorough going-over on *shaker tables,* vibrators which shake the equipment much harder and faster than the worst launch vehicle oscillations experienced. Each component goes through another shaking up after it has been installed and the complete spacecraft is vibrated. Contractor and NASA facilities are large enough to vibrate the entire Apollo spacecraft stack—Command, Service, and Lunar modules.

Special acoustic or sound chambers generate noise too intense for a human being to endure. The noise level reaching the cabin of the spacecraft, placed inside the chamber, is measured, recorded, and analyzed.

In space the ship faces new challenges. Its surface facing the sun is subjected to intense heat, its shaded side to extreme cold. In the test laboratory, technicians use a chamber fitted on one side with banks of heat-producing lamps, while the opposite wall holds tubing through which supercold liquid is forced. In this thermal simulation of space, the test article, instrumented with sensors (*see*) inside and out, bakes up to 400°F on one side and freezes to as much as 320° below zero on the other.

Space vacuum also poses a hazard which must be overcome by spacecraft design (*see*) and proven by ground tests. To permit the crew to perform its duties in space, the cabin is pressurized to about 5½ pounds per square inch (psi). The outside

A thermobasic cell *(left)* is used by Fiat for ground tests of equipment and components under conditions equivalent to the extremes found during flight. An anechoic chamber is used to test the antenna radiation pattern of an F-4 Phantom *(right)*.

Testing

pressure in space is zero. If the spacecraft hull were unable to contain the internal pressure, the astronauts would have to keep their spacesuits (*see*) pressurized. Movement would be difficult. If the craft could not sustain overpressures, it would split or burst.

Chambers large enough to hold the spacecraft and strong enough to contain a vacuum simulating an altitude greater than 200,000 feet are used to test spacecraft pressurization. The Apollo Command Module has demonstrated the ability to withstand more than 30 psi internal pressure.

Engine Testing

Although most spacecraft testing facilities are located at the manufacturer's plants and at the Manned Spacecraft Center (*see*), some specialized testing is conducted at sites such as the NASA White Sands Test Facility in Las Cruces, New Mexico. Here test stands hold the spacecraft engines for static firing under ambient and vacuum conditions. Instrumentation and photography record the engine's performance. Before any given type of spacecraft engine is approved for flight testing, it has completed its mission many times on the ground.

Launch vehicle engine systems go through the same kind of testing, much of it in the giant static test stands at the Marshall Space Flight Center (*see*). When booster and spacecraft are mated on the pad at Cape Kennedy, every component has been tested and retested, many of them as individual units and again as a part of the whole craft.

At the Kennedy Space Center (*see*), further test programs are conducted to determine electronic and functional integrity. The Vehicle Assembly Building on Merritt Island, designed and equipped for preflight testing, is the largest building in the world. It has to be, to allow spacecraft and rocket technicians to conduct the extensive tests while sheltering the vehicle.

Final preflight testing is carried out on the launch pad. Preliminary unmanned tests lead up to simulated countdown and launch demonstrations in which the spacecraft crew and the ground controllers and technicians go through the many procedures required for a real launch.

Flight Testing

As complete and exhaustive as ground tests are intended to be, the ultimate proof of airplane or spacecraft design and construction is in flight. And as complex as airplane flight testing might be, it still is straightforward compared to spacecraft flight tests.

Once an airplane earns approval for flight, a pilot takes off with it and puts it through a well-planned series of increasingly more difficult maneuvers (*see*), each monitored and recorded for postflight analysis. The wringing-out procedure takes weeks or months.

Spacecraft flight testing also is carried out in progressive steps, but when man first takes it into space, the ship already has proved its wings.

Unmanned flight testing substitutes instrumentation readings for visual observations and radioed commands for manual actions. The early flight tests of the Mercury capsule included missions by trained chimpanzees, but the primates were used to help predict man's reaction to space rather than to assist in testing the capsule.

NASA's current flight test philosophy is one of what is called *all-up testing* rather than the strict sequential steps in which the launch vehicle was flown in one test, the unmanned spacecraft and the launch vehicle in suborbital flight in a second, unmanned spacecraft in orbit in a third, then manned flight.

All-up testing places an almost fully equipped spacecraft on an untried booster, such as in the Apollo 4 mission. That flight in November, 1967, was the first by a Saturn V. With strong prospects

An Apollo spacecraft sits atop a *rocker* during testing of the guidance and navigation units. The response of gyroscopes is also monitored.

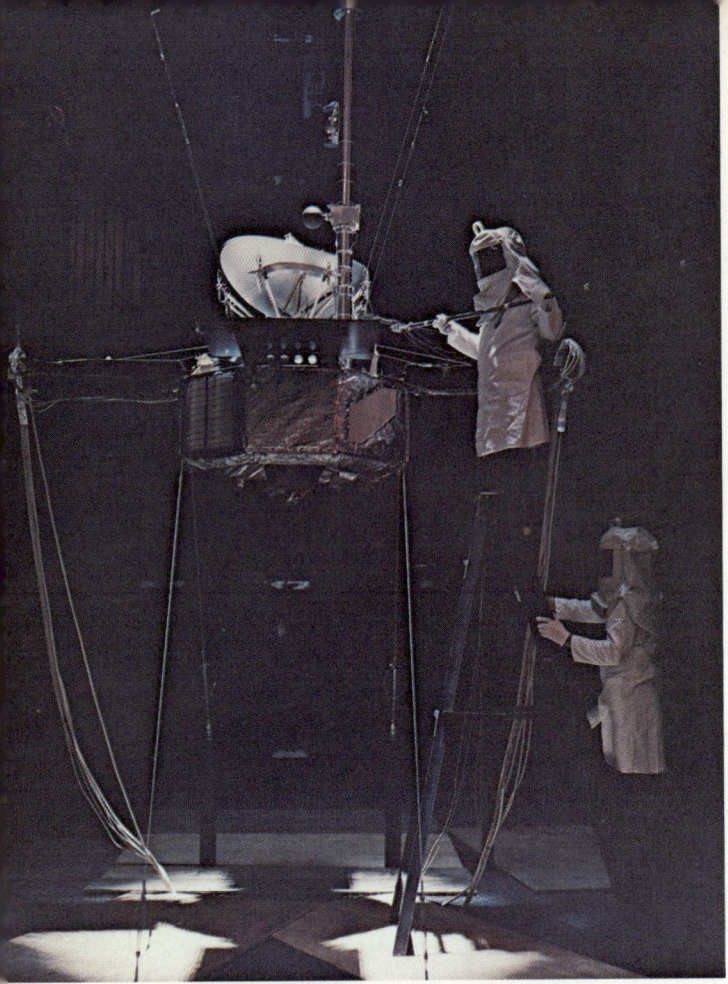

The Mariner 5 spacecraft is prepared for extensive tests in a space simulator *(above)*. A thrust of 1,500,000 pounds *(below)* streams from an F-1 rocket engine during a series of NASA tests.

of a successful launch, based on extensive testing as already discussed and on performance by the Saturn I, engineers decided to take advantage of the potentially good booster to test the spacecraft in flight as well. The plan represented a saving of time and money. The mission was a success.

Manned Flight

The ultimate goal of aircraft and spacecraft testing is *man-rating,* demonstrating that the craft is safe enough to carry human beings. In the case of a spacecraft, testing continues beyond man-rating. The first astronauts to fly the ship function just as test pilots do in an airplane.

As on the preceding unmanned flights, the many and complex spacecraft systems are instrumented to pick up data, which is telemetered to ground recording stations and to flight controller display consoles. Instrumented data also is stored on recorders in the spacecraft to be recovered after landing for postflight analysis.

Instruments, however, cannot replace the actions and the observations of a trained test pilot—the astronaut. His reports to engineers on the ground are vital to the test program. Only a man can determine how the spacecraft responds to its controls, or how easy or difficult equipment is to operate in space.

After the flight is completed, the astronaut continues to add data to the test program. He goes through a *debriefing* in which he recounts all the observations and experiences he gathered during the mission. Engineers question him at length, noting items and incidents that may not have shown up on instrument readings.

The spacecraft too contributes postflight data to testing. After recovery, it is thoroughly examined and disassembled. The condition of the heat shield, the outer shell, and the various individual components becomes part of the voluminous data on tests that started even before the spacecraft was built.

Modern aeronautical testing is based on precision —precise methods of testing, of gathering information on the test results, and of analyzing that data. Precise evaluation is the end product of the testing program, matching actual results with established standards. The result of testing evaluation is the construction of the safest, most reliable article that human engineering know-how can create.

J. W. Kroehnke

See Also: Apollo, Gemini, Manufacturing, Materials, Mercury program, Satellites, Test pilots and test flying

XB-70 Valkyrie cruises at Mach 3 with wingtips lowered. It is now making test flights in a NASA program with mission support from Edwards AFB.

Test pilots and test flying

There are two basic types of test flying: experimental or engineering flights and production testing. Experimental test flying includes first flights and exploratory testing of any new design, either aircraft or spacecraft. Production testing is limited to first flights and required routine test flying of aircraft that have already been developed and "debugged" and are in volume production.

In the early days of flying, the aircraft designer was usually his own test pilot. However, as aircraft became more complex and pilots more highly skilled, the dashing figure of the begoggled hero so popular in older motion pictures became a reality. It frequently took more nerve than engineering background to make first flights in many of the airborne contraptions of past years. Even today, some do-it-yourself builders act as their own test pilots. However, even with relatively simple aircraft and gliders, most first flights are now undertaken by pilots with extensive experience.

Test Pilot Schools

As aircraft and spacecraft have become ever more complex, so have the requirements for the experimental test pilot. Nearly all active experimental test pilots today are college graduates or graduates from one of the military test pilot schools, located at Edwards Air Force Base, California; Patuxent River Naval Air Station, Maryland; the RAF Empire School in London, England; or Epner at Istres in France.

Requirements for entrance to the USAF Aerospace Research Pilot School at Edwards Air Force Base (*see*) are typical of the other military schools. A pilot "must be no more than 32 years of age, possess a bachelor's degree in engineering, physical science, or mathematics, be serving on active duty as a pilot on flying status in the grade of major or below and have a minimum of 500 flying hours as aircraft commander or instructor pilot."

The Edwards AFB school, the first of its kind,

Test pilots and test flying

grew from the old USAF Experimental Flight Test Pilot School established on February 4, 1951. On October 12, 1961, the school was redesignated as the USAF Aerospace Research Pilot School and directed to develop the new kind of test pilot needed for aerospace vehicles. The course was divided into two sections: a five-month experimental test pilot phase covering the latest developments of testing aircraft and related aeronautical equipment, and a seven-month advanced phase to train personnel for manned space research programs. Application is voluntary, and classes are limited to 22 carefully chosen students.

"The school's aerospace mission is dynamic; changes in objectives, curriculum content, and training methods will certainly accelerate as man probes beyond the limits of the atmosphere and the boundaries of today's technology," states a USAF brochure. "What form these changes will take can not now be accurately predicted—even the planners who must translate tomorrow's vehicle possibilities into today's training have only a glimpse of the school's future."

Edwards Air Force Base

Nearly all civilian and military first flights of high-performance aircraft since 1946 have taken place at Edwards AFB, California. The 300,000-acre USAF Flight Test Center is located on the western edge of the Mojave Desert, 100 miles northeast of Los Angeles. First military use of the 44-square-mile dry lake, frequently cited as the world's finest natural landing field, dates back to 1931-1933 when Lt. Col. H. H. Arnold (*see*) was Commander of March Field at Riverside, California, about 80 miles south of the lake. The lake bed was first used

FAA test pilot Joe Tymcsyszyn at the controls of a Douglas DC-8 during an acceptance flight of the aircraft for Alitalia Airlines.

Instrument panel of Lockheed rigid-rotor helicopter during a steep turn demonstrating the unusually fine maneuverability of the craft.

as a bombing range where, in 1937, the entire Army Air Corps participated in a large-scale maneuver.

Early in World War II, the area was used as a training field for Lockheed P-38, Consolidated B-24, and North American B-25 bombers and crews. Bombing targets included a realistic 650-foot model of a Japanese Navy heavy cruiser of the Mogami class, dubbed the *Muroc-Maru*.

It was here that the first USAF jet aircraft, Bell's XP-59A, was flown in 1942. All known records of the famed X series of rocket supersonic aircraft have been made in the vicinity of the lake, beginning with the first supersonic flight on October 14, 1947, by Captain Charles Yeager (*see*) in the Bell X-1. Five years later, Major Yeager flew the Bell X-1A to 1,650 mph, twice the speed of sound.

Formerly called Muroc Dry Lake, Edwards AFB was renamed in 1950 in honor of Capt. Glen W. Edwards who lost his life while flight testing the YB-49 flying wing. Seven natural runways crisscross the 11-mile length of the dry lake, and a 15,000-foot concrete runway has been added that extends out into the lake. An estimated $3 billion in research aircraft and an untold number of lives have been saved by the lake. Research aircraft like the X-15 were designed to land on the surface of the lake with skids, making the aircraft less complex and lighter than if normal landing gear had been required.

Many first flights and virtually all flight test programs of modern jet transports have taken place at Edwards AFB. For example, first flights of both the Douglas DC-8 and DC-9 originated at the Long Beach, California, factory, but the first landings were made at Edwards AFB. Five DC-9's were involved in Federal Aviation Administration (FAA) certification at Edwards AFB with an initial flying phase of more than 3,200 operational tests prior to certification. Both Douglas and FAA pilots participated in this program and others of its type.

Development of the X-15 Program

Development of the X-15 experimental rocket research airplane is an outstanding example of the effort required before manned orbital flights could be undertaken. All X-15 flights have either taken off from Edwards AFB or landed there. The X-15 research program (*see*) dates back to 1952 when the National Advisory Committee for Aeronautics (NACA) (*see*), the forerunner of today's National Aeronautics and Space Administration (NASA) (*see*), initiated studies of problems which might be encountered in spaceflight.

Two years later, NACA detailed the X-15 as a manned vehicle to explore spaceflight to speeds of Mach 6 and altitudes to 400,000 feet. Since the X-15 was to be air-launched, length was limited to 50 feet and gross weight to 30,000 pounds. When no suitable rocket engines were available, a separate contract was made with North American Aviation (now North American Rockwell) to build three aircraft.

Later, Reaction Motors, Inc., was chosen to build a 50,000-pound-thrust rocket engine that could be throttled from 30 to 100 per cent in flight thrust variation, capable of 90 seconds operation at full throttle and weighing 618 pounds without fuel.

Two B-52's were modified to carry the X-15—and later the M-2 lifting body—to altitude for launch. A high range, 50 miles wide, 485 miles long, and unlimited in altitude, was developed. Sophisticated telemetry (*see*) and radar (*see*) were capable of picking up 600,000 items of data per minute and pinpointing the X-15 anywhere in its corridor. High-range ground stations were located at Wendover AFB, Utah; near Ely and Beatty, Nevada; and on the main NASA roof at Edwards AFB. The high range covers areas of sparse population and has many dry lakes suitable for emergency landings.

Test pilots scheduled to fly the X-15 practiced in F-104 fighter aircraft, with the landing gear extended, speed brakes open, and drag parachute out to simulate the rapid descent of the tiny 22-foot wing of the X-15. Pilots were subjected to high *g*-loads in a human centrifuge, and computers were developed to preplan pilot techniques to reach maximum speed and altitude.

North American completed the first X-15 late in 1958, and two small rocket engines, similar to those used in the X-1, were installed until a larger engine

Test pilots and test flying

could be completed. The first glide and rocket-powered flights were made by North American Aviation test pilot Scott Crossfield (see). On the third powered flight an explosion in the engine during the starting sequence caused Crossfield to shut down his engine, jettison his remaining fuel, and head for a landing on Rosamond Dry Lake immediately west of Edwards AFB. When the front landing gear touched the lake, it failed and caused the X-15 to break in two just aft of the instrument bay. The fuselage skidded about 1,500 feet, but the aircraft was later repaired.

Installation of the larger engine was followed by a series of successful flights by a number of NASA/USAF/Navy test pilots in which altitudes of 246,700 feet and speeds of 4,105 mph were achieved by the end of 1962. The late NASA pilot Joseph A. Walker (see) reached 354,000 feet (67 miles) in 1963. Major Pete Knight set an unofficial speed of 4,250 mph in 1966, surpassing a speed mark set by Walker 4½ years earlier.

Test pilot William H. Dana *(right)* in front of X-15 research plane. The portable air conditioner adds to the comfort of the test pilot while on the ground. John McKay *(below)* qualified for Astronaut Wings awarded to pilots for flying 50 miles above Earth.

Society of Experimental Test Pilots

A small group of pilots formed the Society of Experimental Test Pilots (SETP) in 1955. Organizational meetings were held at Palmdale, California, midway between Edwards AFB and the production test base at Palmdale. The group was "dedicated to assist in the development of superior airplanes and not to be used as an arbitrating group." SETP founders excluded production test pilots and restricted membership to pilots who were performing flights "that had never been done before." Currently there are more than 1,000 SETP members, an estimated one third of them actively participating in experimental flight test work. Many former experi-

Test pilots and test flying

mental test pilots continue to fly support missions in chase planes or to instruct in the test pilot's school. Virtually all SETP members, regardless of age, are actively engaged in some phase of aviation. When the first American team lands on the moon, it is probable that the astronauts will be members of SETP, described as the most exclusive group in the entire aerospace industry.

More than 10 per cent of the active SETP members have been killed in some phase of aircraft or spacecraft testing. Astronauts Grissom (*see*), Chaffee (*see*), and White (*see*) were all SETP members and frequent visitors at Edwards AFB. During the early Bell X-1 series, test pilot Jean (Skip) Zeigler was killed during top-off tests in the X-2 under a B-50 near Buffalo, New York. Later NASA pilot Joseph Walker climbed back into the B-29 launch aircraft after an explosion, and the X-1A was jettisoned to destruction over the Edwards AFB bombing range. Lt. Col. Frank K. Everest, Jr. (*see*), performed a similar feat when the X-1D caught fire just seconds before launch. Research disclosed that an impregnated leather gasket used for sealing a liquid oxygen joint and vent valves sensitive to shock or pressures in the presence of LOX (liquid oxygen) was causing these explosions.

In a calendar of events for Edwards AFB, there is the cryptic notation under June 8, 1966: "XB-70 experimental air vehicle number 2 piloted by North American Aviation test pilot Alvin S. White and AFFTC test pilot Major Carl S. Cross and an F-104 chase plane piloted by NASA's Joseph A. Walker collided over the Mojave Desert near Barstow, California, destroying both aircraft and killing Mr. Walker and Major Cross who was making his first XB-70 flight. Mr. White, who ejected successfully following the mid-air collision, received only minor injuries."

A subsequent issue of *Cockpit,* the monthly publication of SETP, contained the comment, "Somehow it is incongruous to imagine an old hand like Joe Walker involved in a mid-air the way it was reported. This encouraged a look at three-dimensional wake effects and material was found to suggest . . . the delta wing as having a flow field which can easily cause similar accidents in the future.

"A Wichita State University report showed that in the flow field at the trailing edge of a delta wing at high angle of attack . . . the vortex is rolled up to a position above and inboard of the wingtip at about 70% of semi-span. For a straight or swept wing we are used to the vortex only beginning to roll up at the wing tip. . . . Thus contrary to all past experience with straight or swept wings, flying in the immediate vicinity of a delta wing can produce a situation where an airplane is unsuspectingly and uncontrollably pulled into its vortex."

Rocket Propulsion

Companion testing facilities for rocket engine firing of over $150,000,000 in equipment have been erected at Luehman Ridge on the eastern edge of Edwards Dry Lake. The USAF Rocket Propulsion Laboratory is the largest tenant at Edwards. Original research in chemical and nuclear rocket propulsion systems are carried on here where test firings, both noisy and smoky, are undertaken without interfering with populated areas.

General Aviation Test Pilots

Engineering test pilots for less complex general aviation aircraft are normally required to have an engineering degree and at least 1,500 hours of flying experience. In addition to outstanding piloting skill, civilian companies desire technically qualified pilots who display salesmanship in verbal and written communications in trying to sell improvements as well as management ability in motivating engineers and experimental mechanics who work with them.

Production Test Pilots

In contrast, production test pilots are usually selected for their skill in the nuts-and-bolts part of airplane testing. Many of them have an A&P (airframe and powerplant) mechanics license or extensive practical skill in a fixed-base operation (*see*), corporate flying, or factory inspection work. Some have a military flying background with supplementary lightplane experience. In general, they are usually hired with more flying time than the engineering test pilot and, in some cases, they have 20 to 30 years of flying experience behind them.

Production pilots seldom make headlines or establish records. Complacency and boredom are their main complaints. Yet they have discovered minor discrepancies before a routine first flight that show an entire production line of two-place trainers with the ailerons hooked up backwards!

Tests of the M2 lifting body *(top left),* a half-cone glider with blunt nose and vertical tail fin, began in 1963. The M2-F1 and its successor, the M2-F2, are designs for aerospace re-entry vehicles. The Northrop F-5 *(top right)* at Edwards AFB in time-to-climb tests. A Douglas Skyrocket 558-2 drops from a B-29 *(bottom).* Three of the research aircraft were built and tested by Bill Bridgeman, a factory pilot.

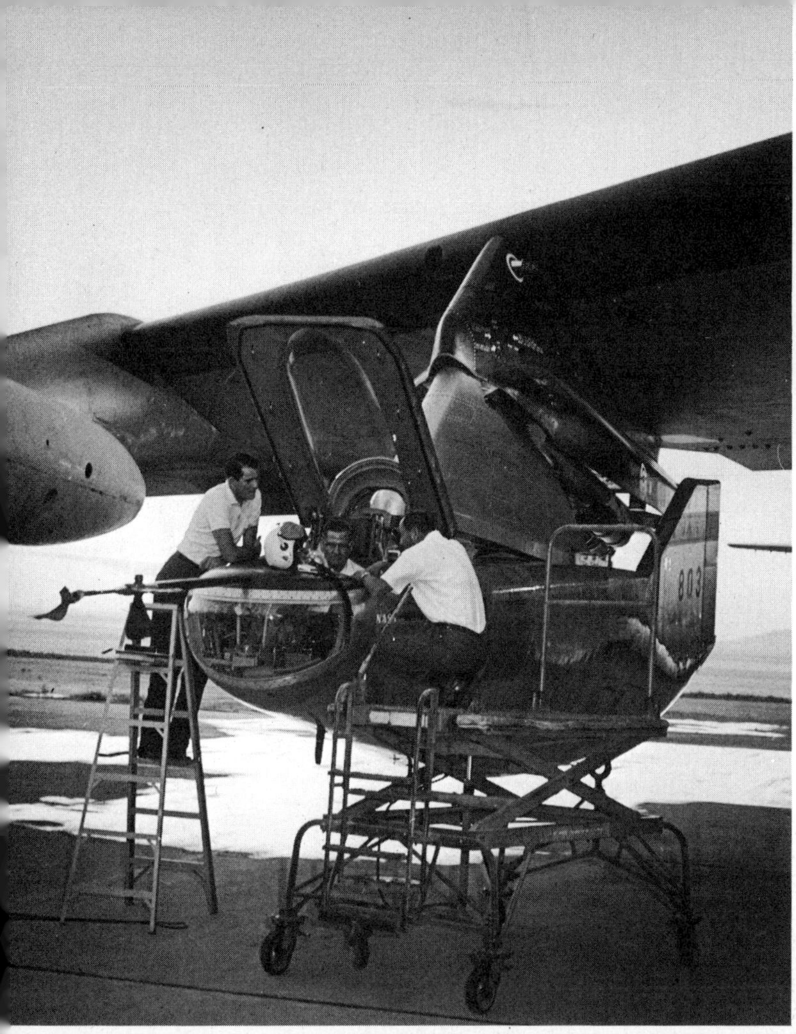
803

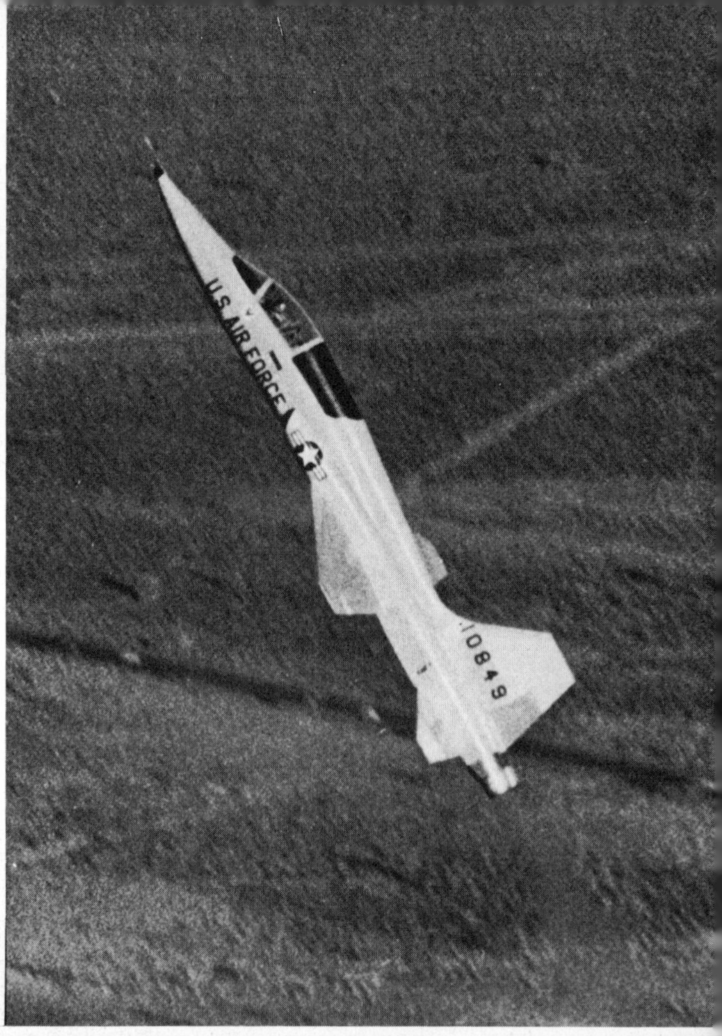
U.S. AIR FORCE
10849

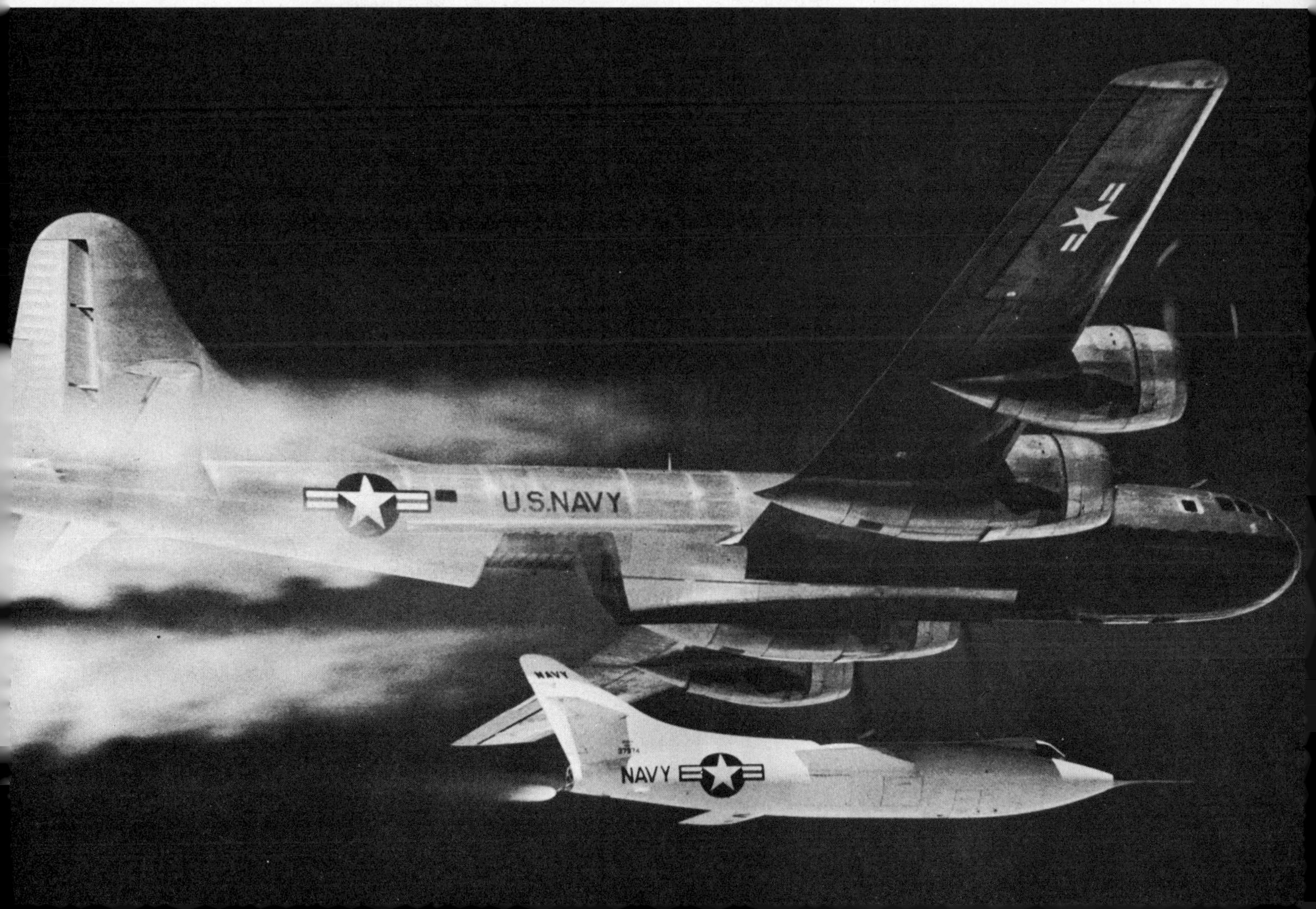
U.S.NAVY
NAVY
NAVY

Test pilots and test flying

Two production test pilots flying similar aircraft at the same time on *red line* (maximum safe speed) dives had elevator trim tabs slip from full nose-down position to full nose-up. One of the aircraft had its wings distorted so badly that they had to be junked.

Production test pilots naturally fly more than do engineering test pilots and will average as much as four hours a day in the air. Their one purpose is to get the airplane ready for the customer.

Many veteran pilots take up the usually routine job of production test flying after having flown the world over with either the military or the airlines. Most production test pilots are married and prefer to stay at home with their families rather than spend more than half their time away from home while flying for airlines. Most production test pilots prefer to do their own flying rather than act as flight instructors. However, some will give dual instruction after working hours at company-sponsored clubs.

Manufacturers frequently have a company policy to upgrade pilots from their own employee flying clubs to the position of production test pilot, starting with simple trainers. This not only offers an incentive for employees to improve their flying skills, but is also a morale booster. In addition, former factory workers usually make superior production test pilots because of their intimate knowledge of aircraft assembly techniques, particularly on aircraft that they once helped to build.

While pay scales differ with experience and the type of equipment to be tested (from simple trainers to complex multiengine executive aircraft), most production test pilots start at a salary equal to or better than that of an airline copilot. Factory pilots progress rapidly in flight experience since almost everyone is checked out in the complete line of aircraft manufactured. Nearly all test pilots are male, but there is no reason why a woman could not excel in production test flying.   Don Downie

See also: Edwards Air Force Base, X-15 research program, X-series aerospace vehicles

Test vehicles, *see* Testing

Tetrahedron

The tetrahedron is used at airports to indicate the wind direction and the runway in use for takeoffs and landings. It is located in a prominent place on the airfield in proximity to the runways so the pilot may observe it on the ground before takeoff and from the air before landing.

The tetrahedron is mounted to allow ease of rotation caused by the varying wind direction. However, it may be secured in any of several positions which correspond to the direction of the runways at a particular point. Usually constructed of aluminum tubing and the type of fabric used to cover aircraft, it can be lighted for night operations.

G. C. Chapman

See also: Airports, Aviation weather, Runways, Winds, Windsock

Tetrode, *see* Electronics

Theory of relativity, *see* Relativity theory

Thermal barrier

The thermal barrier is the region on the edge of the atmosphere where meteors burn up in fireballs in falling toward the Earth, as do spent rocket cases. If it were not for proper satellite design, both spacecraft and astronauts also might burn up.

The term *thermal barrier* is a misnomer. One might be led to believe that the thin air of the region is naturally hot, which it is not. The extreme heat is caused by the friction of objects hitting air at tremendous speeds. Heat is generated when the atom of any substance's molecules become active from being bombarded by already excited atoms. An object entering the atmosphere at 7 miles per second piles up molecules of air into clouds of excited atoms, which form a fireball around it and leave a brilliant trail behind. The fireball's center can have a temperature hotter than the surface of the sun.

The thermal barrier was a major problem in early development of intercontinental ballistic missiles. Streamlining had been used in previous aircraft design to gain speed and reduce aerodynamic drag. Early tests showed that in the thermal barrier too much heat was transferred to the body of a rocket. A blunt nose turned out to be the solution. It produced a strong bow shock wave ahead of the spacecraft which absorbed much of the heat when entering the atmosphere. It increased rather than decreased air resistance.

Two methods were explored for protection of the interior of the spacecraft. One was the heat sink method, using a highly conductive metal, such as copper, to absorb the heat, thus stroing it and keeping the metal from melting. A drawback to the heat sink was its weight. The other method was to cover the nose with an ablative material, such as fiber glass or Teflon, which would vaporize and melt away, but not enough to wear through the nose during flight.   John Howard

See also: Ablation, Heat shield, Heat sink, Reentry vehicles

Thermal protection systems, see Heat shields, Re-entry vehicles

Thermals

Thermals are rising air currents produced when the sun heats the Earth. As the Earth is heated, the air near the ground is also heated, making it lighter and more buoyant than the surrounding air over cooler patches of ground. The lighter air rises at speeds which may be as high as 20 feet per second to an altitude where its temperature is the same as the surrounding air. Technically, these are *convection currents* (*see*), but *thermals* which originated in soaring terminology, has become the accepted term for these air currents used to sustain soaring flight.

Thermals are produced most frequently on warm, sunny days over areas which retain the greatest amount of heat, such as sandy or rocky soils and plowed fields. Thermals are composed of large bubbles of air rather than columns. When the air near the ground is warmed enough to begin rising, cooler air moves in to take its place. This air begins heating and when warm enough rises to produce another bubble. The rate at which bubbles are produced depends on the air temperature and moisture content and ranges from a few minutes to over an hour.

Sanford Sasser, Jr.

See also: Sailplanes, Soaring

Thermistor, *see* Data acquisition and processing

Thermodynamics

Thermodynamics is a branch of theoretical mechanics that deals with the mechanical actions of heat energy (*see*), the relationship of heat and mechanical energy (*see*), and the conversion of one into the other. The applications of thermodynamic principles include the design of refrigeration systems, powerplants, and on a more theoretical level, the processes of biology, physiology, and astronomy (*see*).

Thermodynamics is based on the application of three general laws. The first is essentially the principle of the conservation of energy which states that energy (*see*) cannot be created or destroyed; it merely changes its form in the conversion from heat into mechanical energy or from mechanical energy into heat. The second states that in any system, heat will travel from a hot part to a cooler part, and that ultimately all parts of the system will reach the same temperature. The third deals with the measurement of energy at absolute zero.

Sanford Sasser, Jr.

Thornton, William E.

Scientist-astronaut
Born: April 14, 1929; Goldsboro, North Carolina
Status: Civilian

Dr. William Thornton was accepted for NASA astronaut training with the 11-man group named in August, 1967, following two years of research in aerospace medicine at the Aerospace Medical Division, Brooks Air Force Base, Texas. At that time Dr. Thornton was a captain in the U.S. Air Force.

Dr. Thornton received a B.S. degree in physics in 1952 from the University of North Carolina. Commissioned in the Air Force ROTC on the completion of his undergraduate work, he served as officer-in-charge of the Instrumentation Laboratory at the Flight Test Air Proving Ground, and later was consultant to Air Proving Ground Command.

Thornton was chief engineer in the electronics division of Del Mar Engineering Laboratories, Los Angeles, California, from 1955-59, when he returned to the University of North Carolina Medical School. He received a doctorate in medicine in 1963, and completed his internship at the Wilford Hall USAF Hospital, Lackland Air Force Base, Texas.

As an astronaut, Dr. Thornton's training schedule includes training in high-performance aircraft as well as classroom and field work in spaceflight.

He is married to the former Elizabeth Jennifer Fowler and they have two sons.

J. W. Kroehnke

See also: Astronauts

Thor rockets

The Thor intermediate range ballistic missile (IRBM) was developed originally to serve as a stopgap weapon system until the U.S. could complete and field the huge Atlas and Titan intercontinental ballistic missiles (ICBM) (*see*). The Thor since has become the most reliable and widely used long-range ballistic and space launch vehicle (*see*) in history.

Since its first unsuccessful launch on January 25, 1957, as part of a research and development project, the Thor has been launched more than 320 times, 250 of which were as a space booster. As of March, 1967, this rocket had established a record of 100 successful launches in a row.

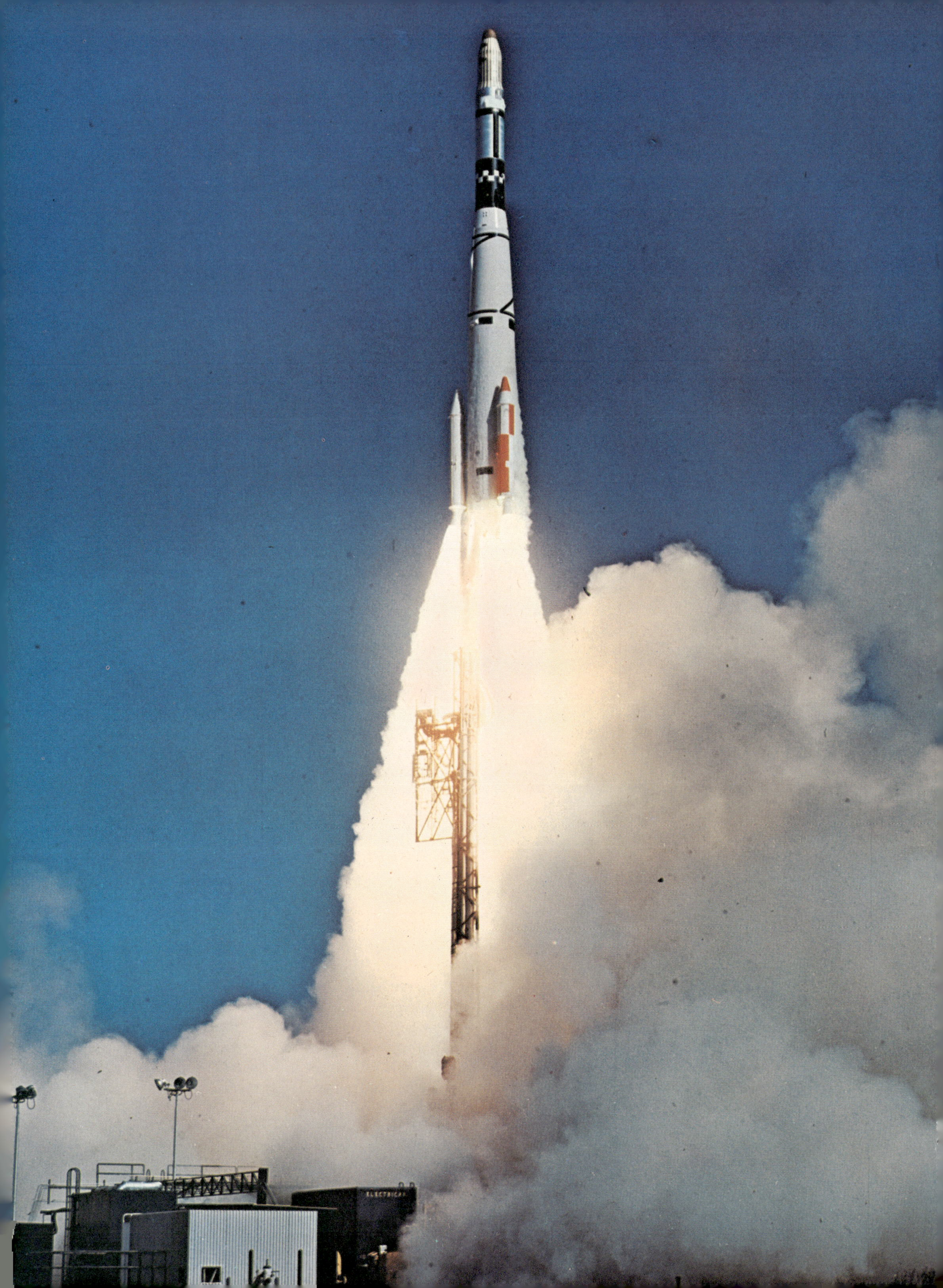

THOR VERTICAL TEST SPACE VEHICLE

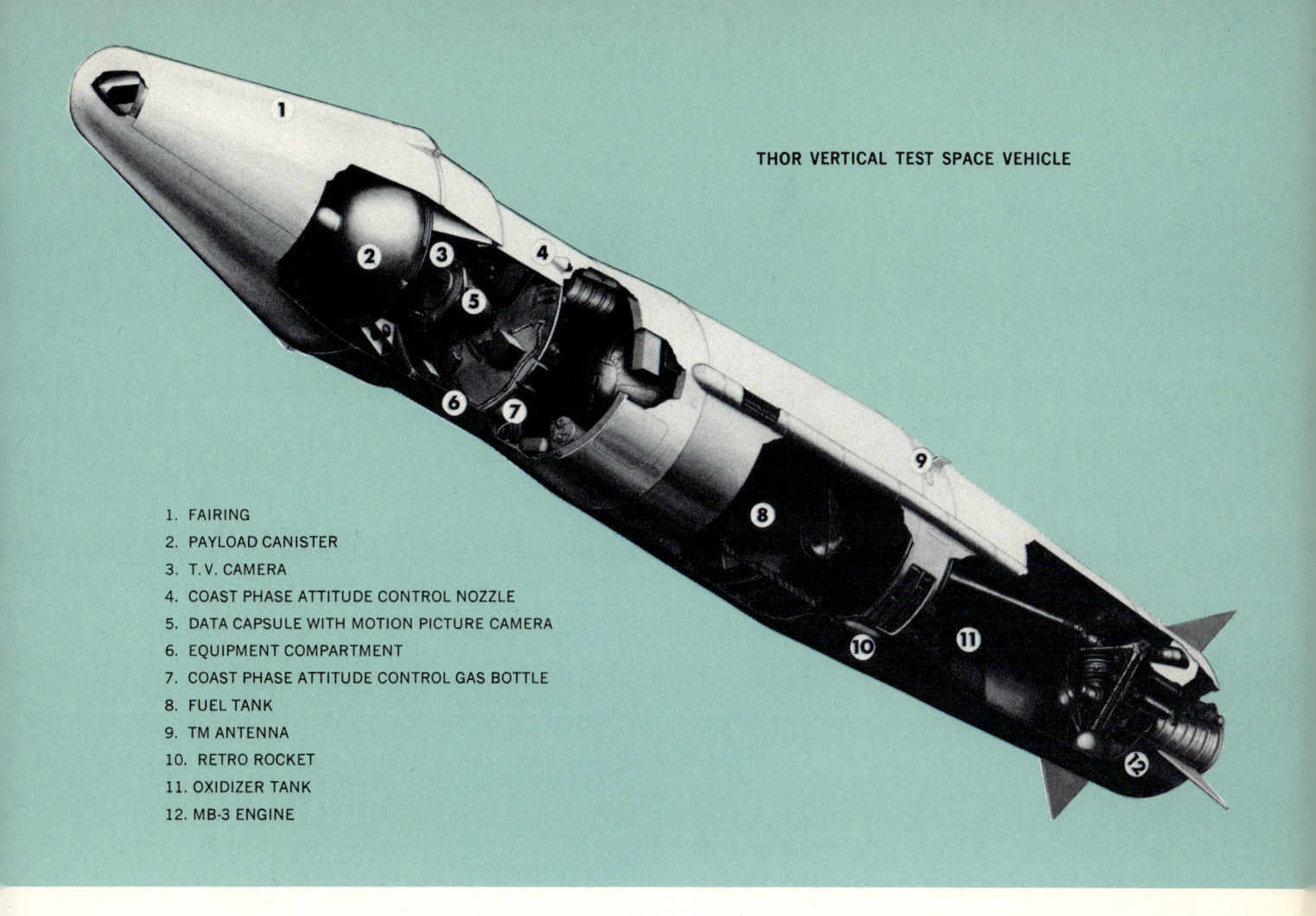

1. FAIRING
2. PAYLOAD CANISTER
3. T.V. CAMERA
4. COAST PHASE ATTITUDE CONTROL NOZZLE
5. DATA CAPSULE WITH MOTION PICTURE CAMERA
6. EQUIPMENT COMPARTMENT
7. COAST PHASE ATTITUDE CONTROL GAS BOTTLE
8. FUEL TANK
9. TM ANTENNA
10. RETRO ROCKET
11. OXIDIZER TANK
12. MB-3 ENGINE

The Thor program began on November 28, 1955, when the Pentagon authorized the rocket's development. Although the Atlas missile, the United States' first ICBM, was under development at that time, U.S. intelligence sources had indicated that the U.S.S.R. might have operational ICBMs before this country. Missile experts determined that by taking just one of the three engines being designed for Atlas, its nose cone (*see*) or re-entry vehicle (*see*), together with an available inertial guidance system (*see*), they could combine them into a smaller airframe and construct an operational IRBM in a relatively short period of time. The comparatively short-range Thor (1,500 nautical miles) was then to be deployed to Great Britain under the supervision of the Royal Air Force (*see*).

The first completely successful flight of the Thor vehicle occurred in September, 1957. From that point on, the missile met with significant achievement. Meanwhile, in a top-secret airlift called *Project Emily,* Thors quietly were placed aboard huge C-124 Globemaster transport planes at Long Beach, California, and flown directly to England. The RAF launch crews were trained at Vandenberg Air Force Base (*see*) in California.

By 1960 a force of 60 Thor missiles was operational in Great Britain. All 60 Thors have since been returned to the U.S. and converted into space launch vehicles.

Development and Expansion

Over the years, the power and stature of the Thor rockets have been expanded. Originally the liquid-rocket engines produced 165,000 pounds of thrust. When the Thor was converted into a space booster, the engines were uprated to produce 172,000 pounds of thrust. In 1963 a new version called the *Thrust Augmented Thor (TAT)* was introduced. In this version three solid-propellant, strap-on motors were added, increasing liftoff thrust to 330,000 pounds.

Another more powerful version of the Thor space booster joined the U.S. inventory in 1965. Called

More than two dozen launch vehicles are included in the Thor family which has earned the title of *Workhorse of the Space Age.* The Long Tank Thor, newest in the family, is 70 feet long and 8 feet in diameter. The Long Tank Thor can place a 3,000-pound payload in a low-altitude orbit.

Thor rockets

the *Long Tank Thor,* this version is 70 feet high as compared to the 56-foot height of the earlier models. Although the liftoff thrust was not increased, the burning time of the liquid engine is longer because of the increased propellant capacity. This, in turn, increases the payload capability 20 per cent.

Thor As a Launch Vehicle

During its long history, the Thor has accounted for an imposing list of space firsts. While still in the research and development stage as an IRBM, the Thor was chosen to boost Pioneer I and set a record by sending the craft 71,300 miles into space on October 11, 1958. This also was the first Air Force space launch and was conducted by the Ballistic Missile Division (AFBMD).

Since that time the Thor rocket has appeared in a number of increasingly more powerful configurations and has been teamed with almost every upper stage vehicle including the Able, the Able Star, the Delta, the Agena, the Altair, and the Burner II.

Thor placed the Explorer VI, the most sophisticated satellite of its day, into a highly elliptical Earth orbit; it gave scientists the first photographs of Earth from space; it orbited the Telstar satellites making possible the first transoceanic television transmission; and it launched Pioneer V, the first solar orbiting space vehicle, as well as the first Courier communications satellite, the first TIROS weather satellite, the first TRANSIT navigation satellite, and the first international spacecraft, the British designed Ariel satellite (*see*). It also launched the Echo, Nimbus, Syncom, and Early Bird satellites.

Teamed with the Agena rocket, the Thor vehicle launched the Discoverer I satellite, which was the first polar-orbiting satellite, the first satellite to achieve a precise circular orbit, the first to be stabilized in all three axes, and the first to maneuver on ground command as it circled the Earth. Later, the Thor rocket launched the Discoverer XIII, the first satellite from which a capsule re-entered the atmosphere and was successfully recovered.

The reliable Thor, affectionately called the "DC-3 of the space age," launched nuclear devices high into space over Johnston Island in the Pacific during the now historic Fishbowl series of high-altitude atomic tests. This important vehicle also serves as the core for the U.S. antisatellite weapon system.

Frank A. Burnham

See also: Agena rockets, Atlas missile and launch vehicle, Communications satellites, Discoverer project, Explorer satellites, Missiles, Navigation satellites, Pioneer, Rockets and rocketry, Weather satellites

Thrust

Rocket-engine thrust is a force created in the missile's thrust chamber where fuel and oxidizer are burned to form combustion gases. The thrust chamber includes the combustion chamber, where the burning occurs, and the nozzle, which gives velocity and direction to the combustion gas flow.

An engine's thrust is determined by the amount of combustion gas produced and by the velocity of the gas as it leaves the nozzle. As the velocity of the combustion gas is increased, the reaction force, or thrust, which propels the vehicle in the opposite direction, is also increased.

The thrust generated by a given engine depends on the weight of the vehicle and the external environment in which it will operate. Rocket engines operate more efficiently in space than in the atmosphere because atmospheric pressures and gravitational forces reduce thrust.

Peter V. Farwell

See also: Jet engines, Missiles, Rockets and rocketry

Thunderstorms, *see* Aviation weather, Weather

Thyratrons, *see* Electronics

Time

Any event, the recurrences of which can be counted, is a measure of time. Any recurring phenomena that can be assumed invariable may be used as a standard of time. An example is the periods of rotation of celestial bodies on their axes and the periods of revolution about their primaries, which can be counted and measured. The most convenient standard universally used until lately is the period of rotation of the Earth.

The period used in these measurements, called the *mean solar day,* is not the true period of rotation with respect to an inertial frame, but the period with respect to the mean position of the sun. Gravitational theory is used to define the day so that its ratio to the true period of rotation is absolutely fixed. The true period of rotation is 23 hours 56 minutes 4.0988 seconds of mean solar time. Mean solar time is determined by night-to-night observations of transits of stars across the meridian, stars whose times of transit can be precisely predicted from past observations. It has been shown in this century that the mean solar day is not an invariable unit of time but has a very irregular variation. The error in the day is about 1 part in 30,000,000. There is also a gradual increase in the length of our day due to tidal friction amounting to 1 part in 100,000,000 in a century.

In recent years the mean period of the Earth's revolution has come into use, but even this changes so that the mean period used is the value of the mean period in 1900.

What is meant by an invariable measure of time might best be defined by accepted laws of motion modified by the general relativity theory. For this reason the year has been substituted for the day, because the theory of rotation of the Earth, while satisfactory, is not adequate enough to be exact.

The theory of relativity has shown that in the most general sense, time and space are not mathematically distinguishable from each other. Time is not an independent variable in equations of motion so that one set of equations could not possibly be true for all observers. As long as observations are made from the Earth or any other place in the Earth's solar system, however, all observers may use the same equations without difficulty.

The fundamental unit of time is the mean solar second, which is 1/86,400 of a mean solar day. This is 1/31,556,925.975 of the tropical year 1900. Expressed in an equation:
86,400 seconds = 1,440 minutes = 24 hours = 1 day
The period of the Earth's rotation relative to fixed stars is called a *sidereal* day:
1 sidereal day = 86,164.09054 sec = 23 hr 56 min 4.09054 sec. The sidereal units have the same relation as the mean solar units for the mean solar day.

The *sidereal year* is the period of the Earth's rotation about the sun relative to the fixed stars and:
1 sidereal year = 365.2564 days = 31,558,150 sec

Another unit is the *tropical year*, which is the period of the Earth's orbital motion measured from equinox to equinox because of the precession of equinoxes:
1 tropical year = 365.2422 days = 31,556,930 sec

The *sidereal month* is the mean period of orbital revolution of the moon around the Earth relative to the fixed stars and is 27.32166 days. Another measure used is the *synodical month,* which is 29.5306 days and is the mean period of orbital revolution of the moon around the Earth relative to the mean sun.

Accurate measurement has always been the special province of astronomers, whose measurements have been the basis for the determination of time. Time is measured by the motion of a pendulum in the gravitational field of the Earth, the motion of a balance wheel of a watch or clock, the spinning of the rotor of a synchronous motor, the oscillations of a quartz crystal when placed in an appropriate electric field, or the electromagnetic energy emitted by atoms undergoing energy changes from one state to another. Since time is the measurement of something periodic, measurement of short and long times is especially important.

Short Times

In measurement, the second is a long period of time in many situations and must be further subdivided. A series of electronic oscillators may be built, each with a period shorter than the previous one. Periods as short as 10^{-12} seconds have been built. Using the laser or light amplifier it is possible to get even shorter periods that can be compared with the standard. The lifetime of some of the recently discovered strange resonances (particles) is about 10^{-24} seconds, approximately the time required for light (which moves at the fastest known speed) to cross the nucleus of hydrogen, the smallest known object. There may be still shorter times yet.

Long Times

Measurement of times longer than a day is easy; just count the days. If nobody is around to do the counting, nature has provided counters in tree rings, river-bottom sediments, carbon-14 and uranium half-life measurements, and several other methods. From these measurements it has been determined that the Earth started five billion years ago and the universe, at least in our part, began about ten or twelve billion years ago. To discover if earlier time has any meaning, one must consider relativistic effects.

The Twin Paradox

The twin paradox involves a hypothetical set of twins, Peter and Paul. When they are old enough to pilot a spaceship, Paul flies away at a very high speed, approaching the speed of light, and Peter, who is left on the ground, observes Paul moving so fast. From Peter's point of view, Paul's clock appears to run slower, his heartbeat seems slower, his thoughts seem slower, in fact, everything in Paul's spaceship, except the spaceship itself which is seen to move very fast, seems to the observer on Earth to go slower. Paul notices nothing unusual on his trip, but if he travels around for awhile and comes back, he will be younger than Peter, the man on the ground! This is correct, because time is relative to motion in space. It is one of the consequences of the theory of relativity which has been clearly demonstrated.

It is a paradox, however, because motion itself is relative to time and space. From Paul's point of view in space, Peter was the one actually moving, the one who should therefore age less rapidly. Logically, when they met, since each thought the other was moving, they should be the same age.

However, Paul must stop at the end of his trip and return to Earth to compare his clock with Peter's. The one who comes back must be considered to be the one that was moving. — Charles A. Velaer

See also: Greenwich mean time, Zulu time

Tin Goose, Ford Trimotor 4-AT

The Ford Trimotor was a large, high-wing aircraft having one motor mounted on the front of the fuselage and one suspended under each wing by a series of struts which also support the landing gear. Designed by William B. Stout and first produced by Henry Ford in 1925, the Trimotors were built with an all-metal corrugated covering and combined many of the design features of Fokker and Junkers aircraft.

The Trimotor was anything but beautiful and its ungainly appearance soon earned it the name of *Tin Goose*. But ungainly though it may have appeared to the originator of the name, the performance of the Tin Goose soon proved it to be reliable.

The Tin Goose contributed much to the early development of the airlines and was responsible in a large measure for their success. The assembly line production used by Ford made them available in larger numbers than any other aircraft. Their dependability made them attractive to the airlines while their safety made them reassuring to the public.

The Trimotor has been used in practically every application known to aviation. Besides its use with the airlines, it has been used as an executive aircraft and for barnstorming, crop dusting, freight hauling, flight instruction, and parachute operations, both military and fire-fighting. To complete the list of the Trimotor's versatility, it has been flown with wheels, skis, and pontoons, and has been flown upside down, looped, and rolled. In 1929 the Ford Company's advertising stated that the lifespan of the Trimotor was at least four years. Yet today, 40 years later, over a dozen Trimotors are still flying; supporting a legend of endurance and versatility that can be surpassed only by the DC-3. — Sanford Sasser, Jr.

See also: Commercial air transports

Tin Goose, Ford trimotor 4-AT
Specifications and Performance Data

Engines	three 300-hp Wright J-6 radials
Wingspan	74 ft.
Length	49 ft. 10 in.
Gross weight	10,130 lbs.
Maximum speed	130 mph.
Range	570 miles

Titanium

With a melting point of 3272°F which exceeds that of iron, and an atomic weight of only 48.1, titanium has long been regarded as an excellent lightweight but strong material for the aerospace industry (*see*).

Early problems of fabricating the metal presented difficulties. These were its relative scarcity and high cost (estimates range from four to five times the cost of aircraft-quality stainless steel) and the fact that it must be hot-worked, often at temperatures near 1000°F.

However, its desirability has offset these handicaps. The Boeing Aircraft Co. points out that the Boeing 727 went into service in 1964 with 1.84 per cent of its airframe weight in titanium; the Boeing 737 short-range jet went into service in 1967 with 2.16 per cent of its airframe weight in titanium; and the Boeing 747 Superjet will use 9.2 per cent of its airframe weight in titanium. Boeing also said that beginning in 1968 it was using 90,000 lbs. of titanium a month. Titanium is not used as a pure metal, but is alloyed with aluminum (*see*), vanadium, and tin or molybdenum.

European aircraft engineers show similar strong

interest in the light metal, and comment from abroad indicates that titanium is supplanting use of some of the aircraft steels in both airframe and engine applications. One estimate is that titanium usage will grow about 8 to 10 per cent per year, compared with a 5 to 6 per cent growth rate for stainless steel aircraft use. One aircraft designer in the U.S. indicates that he already uses titanium alloy rather than stainless steel for applications where operating temperatures do not exceed 700°F. Titanium parts have been used in much higher working temperatures, including use as jet engine parts. Tensile strength (*see*) of the alloys is about 120,000 psi to as much as 155,000 psi.

The metal continues to be costly. One source estimates the current price at about $10,000 per ton, but increased aircraft operating efficiencies tend to offset the high cost. Use of titanium in the rotor hubs of Sikorsky Marine Corps helicopters is estimated to have added the equivalent of 1,000 lbs. of lifting power.

The most common titanium alloy is 6 per cent aluminum and 4 per cent vanadium in a titanium base. This has been used in the Apollo program, and in high-performance rocket cases. Recently the General Electric Co. announced a beryllium (*see*) coating that would give a titanium alloy surface a hardness of about 400 per cent. This should further add to the metal's possibilities. — Keith W. Bennett

See also: Alloys, Metals and metallurgy

Titan rockets

The Titan series of Intercontinental Ballistic Missiles (ICBM) (*see*), first conceived as a backup vehicle for the Atlas ICBM in 1955, has matured into one of the most versatile groups of rockets in the history of the missile and space age.

The first rocket in the series, the Titan I, was the first ICBM to be placed in underground silos (*see*) protected from all but a direct nuclear blast. The Titan II, the configuration which is currently being used, is the United States' largest and most powerful ICBM. It has a range of more than 7,000 miles and can carry a warhead of several megatons.

The third and most famous member of the Titan series is the Gemini Titan Launch Vehicle (GLV). The GLV hurled 12 Gemini spacecraft into Earth orbit with great precision and 100 per cent success.

A more distant relative is the huge Titan III military space booster. According to the Air Force, the Titan III is the product of merging the storable liquid-fuel technology from the earlier Titan vehicles with the solid-propellant technology of the Minuteman ICBM. The Titan III was the first vehicle designed exclusively for use as a space booster. The Gemini Titan was simply modified for its manned space role from an ICBM.

In 1954 second thoughts about the ultimate reliability of the Atlas ICBM, the first U.S. ICBM ordered into development, were expressed by members of the Von Neumann advisory committee. Some engineers also voiced their lack of confidence in the Atlas vehicle because of its thin, pressurized "tin balloon" type of airframe. They felt it might not withstand the rugged *g*-loads inflicted on the missile during liftoff. The prospect of a two-stage missile in which more effective employment of available propulsion could be achieved was very attractive. Using a two-stage vehicle, it would be possible to achieve a greater total thrust, since one or more stages of the missile or booster could be ignited in space. Most of the burden of overcoming the combined forces of gravity and inertia would be shouldered by the powerful first stage of the rocket. As a result, when a RAND Corp. report suggested the feasibility of a true two-stage vehicle, the Air Force proposed that a second ICBM be developed to insure that an ICBM of sufficient sophistication would be available in the mid-1960's.

The decision to develop and deploy the Titan I came in early 1957. The Air Force Ballistic Missile Division (AFBMD) was made the executive manager of the program. During its very first research and development (R&D) launch on February 6, 1959, the Titan I became the first major missile to achieve 100 per cent success on the first try. Titan I recorded five consecutive successful test flights in the first five attempts.

Titan I

The Titan I was a 90-foot-long missile weighing some 200,000 pounds. A major portion of the airframe was constructed of integrally stiffened aluminum alloy panels that were machine-welded together to form the propellant tanks. The tank walls also formed the outer skin (airframe) for that portion of the missile. An interstage structure connected the first and second stages, and an adapter section provided the means for securing the re-entry vehicle, which contained the nuclear warhead, to the second stage. A kerosene-based fuel and liquid-oxygen oxidizer powered Titan I. The vehicle was not designed to be launched directly from its underground silo but was lifted by an elevator above the ground for firing. The Titan I had a radio-command guidance system and carried an old-style pencil-shaped re-entry vehicle.

Titan II

Development of a second version of the Titan ICBM, designated the Titan II, was announced by the Air Force on June 20, 1960. Titan II, which is still an active part of the U.S. ICBM deterrent force, differs from its predecessor in that it employs storable, hypergolic fuels (*see*). The oxidizer, nitrogen tetroxide (N_2O_4), does not need to be maintained at nearly 300°F below zero as did the liquid oxygen used in the Titan II. As a result, it can be stored aboard the missile indefinitely. The fuel, a blend of hydrazine and unsymmetrical dimethylhydrazine (UDMH) called *Aerozine 50,* and the oxidizer ignite upon contact with ane another thus eliminating complicated ignition systems. The Titan II features an all-inertial guidance system built by the AC Electronics Division of General Motors. The re-entry portion of the vehicle carries a multimegaton warhead and is manufactured by General Electric.

The Titan rockets, like the mythological giants for which they were named, are characterized by their huge size, their range, and destructive power. First conceived as an ICBM, the Titan has developed into a series of space boosters with a major role in manned space flight.

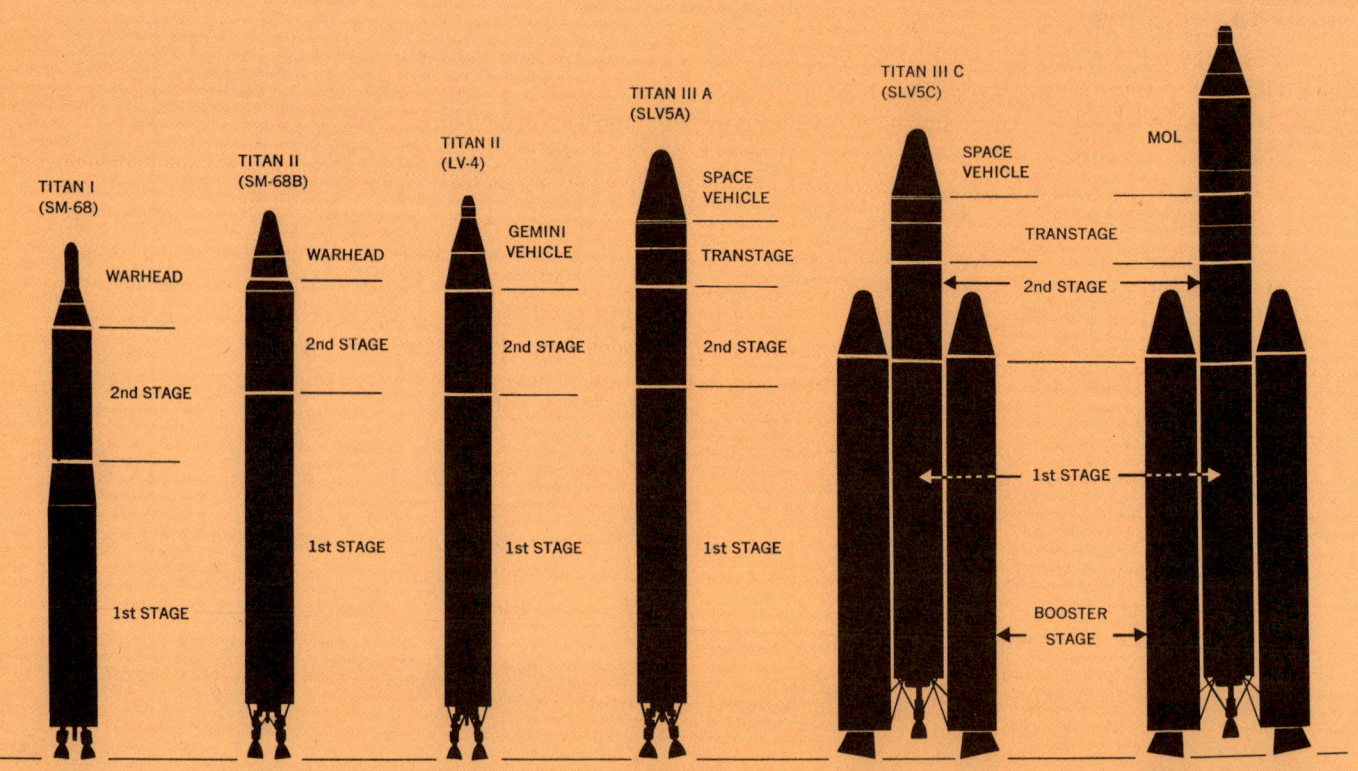

TITAN FAMILY OF MISSILES AND SPACE BOOSTERS

TITAN I (SM-68)	TITAN II (SM-68B)	TITAN II (LV-4)	TITAN III A (SLV5A)	TITAN III C (SLV5C)	TITAN III C (MOL CONFIGURATION)
WARHEAD / 2nd STAGE / 1st STAGE	WARHEAD / 2nd STAGE / 1st STAGE	GEMINI VEHICLE / 2nd STAGE / 1st STAGE	SPACE VEHICLE / TRANSTAGE / 2nd STAGE / 1st STAGE	SPACE VEHICLE / TRANSTAGE / 2nd STAGE / 1st STAGE / BOOSTER STAGE	MOL / TRANSTAGE / 2nd STAGE / 1st STAGE
HEIGHT 98 FT.	HEIGHT 103 FT.	HEIGHT 109 FT.	HEIGHT 124 FT.	HEIGHT 127 FT.	HEIGHT APPROX. 145 FT.

The Titan II also differs from the Titan I in that it was designed to be launched at a moment's notice directly from its underground silo. Titan II operational bases are situated at McConnell Air Force Base in Kansas, at Davis-Monthan Air Force Base in Arizona, and Little Rock Air Force Base in Arkansas. The vehicle became operational in June, 1963. A short time later the Titan II was selected by NASA for modification into the GLV. Although the Atlas vehicle had been successful in launching the Mercury spacecraft, the greater power of the Titan II was required for the heavier, two-man Gemini capsules. As in the Mercury program, the job of modifying and man-rating the Gemini launch vehicle was directed by the Air Force Space Systems Division (AFSSD, formerly AFBMD).

A comprehensive program to modify and test the Titan II for its manned role was established. A malfunction detection system (MDS) to sense problems in any of the vital booster systems and transmit this information to the astronauts so they could abort, a redundant flight control system which could take over if the primary system should fail, a redundant power system with added capacity to support the added electrical requirements, a redundancy in other critical systems, and more comprehensive instrumentation for checkout and flight were all added to the basic Titan II vehicle. The guidance system was converted to a radio-command system, and the vehicle's weight was reduced.

Frank A. Burnham

See also: Gemini, Missiles, Rockets and rocketry

Titan III

The Air Force Titan III is the first military space vehicle designed and built exclusively as a launch vehicle (*see*). This vehicle is also the only U.S. space booster which can be used for all five of the basic space missions: the Titan III can place a spacecraft into a low-altitude Earth orbit, a precise circular Earth orbit, a parking orbit, and a synchronous equatorial (geostationary) orbit, and can send a payload beyond the effective gravitational field of the Earth.

Other multistage launch vehicles, such as the Atlas/Agena and the Saturn 1B/Centaur, are achieved by combining various booster stages and upper stages. This process takes considerable time, effort, and expense. The Titan IIIC is the only "off-the-shelf" booster designed to support the full gamut of probable missions.

Currently, the Titan III series consists of five standard space launch vehicles (SSLV). The Titan III concept evolved from two independent studies which were conducted in 1961 to determine the feasibility of a standard space booster. Until that time, all space launch vehicles had been modified intercontinental range and intermediate range ballistic missiles (ICBM's and IRBM's) combined with various upper stages (Agena, Able, and Able Star). Although NASA's Saturn launch vehicle was being developed at that time, it was being designed as a special-purpose launcher for the Apollo program and did not have either the mission flexibility or the quick reaction time required for an all-purpose military booster.

Both the Phoenix Study conducted by the Air Force and the study conducted by the Institute of Defense Analysis (IDA) examined a large number of possible courses which could be followed in developing a standard workhorse launch vehicle in the 5,000- to 25,000-pound payload class.

The final decision to embark on the Titan III program was made by a joint Department of Defense-NASA committee, known officially as the Large Launch Vehicle Planning Group (LLVPG) or more popularly the Golovin Committee for its chairman, Dr. Nicholas E. Golovin.

Initial Development

The Titan III project was the first so-called billion-dollar program in which the contractors were almost exclusively awarded cost-plus-incentive-fee (CPIF) contracts. A CPIF contract is one in which the contractor is rewarded by payment over a target fee for good work (in the case of the Titan III for adherence to predetermined costs, schedule, and performance) and penalized for not meeting previously agreed levels.

To provide a solid base upon which to negotiate CPIF contracts, the Air Force Space Systems Division (AFSSD) assisted by the nonprofit Aerospace Corporation outlined in detail the complete system, the schedule, and the projected costs during a program definition phase which took place in 1962. In December of that year the actual 17-vehicle research and development program began.

The first member of the Titan III group to be built and test flown was the Titan IIIA. Although the A featured almost all the advanced features designed into the basic Titan III system, it was actually a stepping stone to the basic version, the Titan IIIC, and was not intended for ultimate operational use. The initial development program provided that five A's and 12 C's be constructed, but when the first four A models met with unparalleled success, the fifth flight was canceled. The fifth A vehicle will be

The Titan III-A with a third stage *space taxicab* as payload. The third stage, also called a *transtage,* is equipped with a rocket engine for maneuvering in space and is capable of carrying multiple payloads for ejection at selected points in its trajectory.

The Titan III, expected to be the "workhorse" booster of the space program, is launched carrying one of its many specialized payloads. The Titan is rated for both manned and unmanned payloads and is scheduled for both civilian and military missions in space.

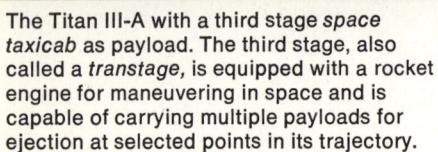

flown as a C and will launch multiple satellites as part of the Air Force Space Experiment Support Program (SESP).

Innovations in the Titans

The Titan IIIA was built and flown as a developmental vehicle to test the first and second liquid-fuel stages, the new all-inertial guidance system, a standard payload fairing, and the new third stage, called the *transtage* (transfer stage).

The noncryogenic storable oxidizer used in all three stages and the unique transtage are two of the features which give the Titan III its great mission flexibility. The fuel, a mixture of unsymmetrical dimethylhydrazine and hydrazine called *Aerozine 50,* and the oxidizer, nitrogen tetroxide (N_2O_4), do not need to be maintained at temperatures hundreds of degrees below zero as do liquid oxygen (*see*), liquid hydrogen, or liquid fluorine. They are also hypergolic, a property which enables them to ignite upon contact with one another so that a complex ignition system is not required. These fuels can be pumped aboard the vehicle and remain for long periods permitting the booster to be counted down and held, pending a requirement to launch on short notice. Thus, a Titan III can support a military contingency mission, whereas conventional cryogenic fuel vehicles cannot.

The capability of the transtage engines to be turned on and off in space, together with the extended operational life of the rocket's guidance system, enable the Titan III to move its payload from orbit to orbit, to change orbital plane, and to carry its payload to the synchronous corridor (21,000 miles) and maneuver it into a geostationary orbit so that the speed of the spacecraft in orbit matches the speed of the Earth's rotation. In this way, the satellite appears to remain stationary over a single spot on the Earth. The transtage's "switch engine" capability also permits the Titan III to carry a number of different satellites into space, placing each one in its assigned orbit.

The Titan IIIC, the basic vehicle in the series, differs from the A version in that it has two huge, five-segment, solid-propellant booster motors strapped on to the three-stage, liquid-free core vehicle (the Titan IIIA). The big solid motors are

The Titan III-C has been designated as the booster for the Manned Orbital Laboratory. With strapped on solid-propellant boosters its thrust on liftoff is 2.4 million pounds.

ignited at liftoff and provide 2.4 million pounds of thrust at sea level. The first liquid stage, which provides 470,000 pounds of thrust, is ignited in space for greater launch efficiency.

Three other versions of the Titan III have also been planned. The Titan IIIB and the Titan IIID are special-purpose versions of the vehicle designed to support classified military missions launched from Vandenberg Air Force Base (*see*) in California. Both the Titan IIIA and the Titan IIIC have been launched from Cape Kennedy exclusively. The B model is a modification of the A in which the transtage is removed and the Agena spacecraft is substituted. A radio-command guidance system is used instead of the inertial system. The D version is simply a B with two five-segment, solid booster motors. The Titan IIIB was first launched in 1966 and is operational today. Contracts for the D version were let in 1967.

The fifth version of the Titan III is the M, now being developed specifically for launching the Manned Orbiting Laboratory (MOL) (*see*). The M is the most powerful of all the Titan III vehicles. This rocket will have two seven-segment, solid booster motors capable of providing more than 3,000,000 pounds of thrust at liftoff. The Titan IIIM will not use the transtage for the seven MOL flights now programmed. The guidance system has not yet been selected. All Titan IIIM/MOL launches will be conducted from a new, $21 million launch complex now under construction at Point Arguello, California, and recently annexed by Vandenberg Air Force Base.

Payloads and Contractors

Titan III payloads have included 18 Initial Defense Communications System Satellites (IDCSS), a pair of advance Vela Nuclear Detection Satellites, five Lincoln Experimental Satellites (LES), a 21,000-pound inert flight-test payload, an Orbiting Spacecraft Carrying Amateur Radio (OSCAR IV), two gravity gradient experimental spacecraft, the Despun Antenna Test Satellite (DAS) and the huge Aerospace Research Support Program (ARSP) (*see*) space laboratory.

Prime contractors involved in the Titan III program include: Martin-Marietta Corp., system integration, airframe, assembly, and test; Aerojet General, liquid propulsion systems; United Technology Center, solid-propellant booster motors; AC Electronics Division of General Motors, inertial guidance system; Western Electric, radio-command guidance system; McDonnell-Douglas, standard payload shroud; and the Aerospace Corporation to provide systems engineering and technical direction for the executive program manager, the Air Force Space and Missile Systems Organization (SAMSO).

Frank A. Burnham

See also: Communications satellites, Inertial guidance systems, Nuclear detection satellites, Rockets and rocketry

Titov, Gherman Stepanovich

Cosmonaut
Born: September 11, 1935;
Verkhnee Zhilino, U.S.S.R.

As commander of spaceship Vostok 2, Gherman Titov circled the Earth on August 6-7, 1961. He is the second man to have looked on our planet from an orbiting spaceship and the first man who could say, "I have lived 17 days longer than each of you, for in 24 hours I have seen the sun rise and set 17 times."

Titov completed secondary school in 1953 and the Volgograd School for pilots in 1957. He also studied at the Zhukovsky Air Academy, and he was a member of the air force before becoming a cosmonaut in 1959. By that date he had flown 772 times.

While Yuri Gagarin (see) had opened the door to outer space for mankind, Gherman Titov proved that apart from merely existing in a spaceship's cabin and doing the simplest tasks, man could work most effectively in space. He was the first spaceman to take photographs from space, use manual controls, eat normally, sleep, take various biological and psychological tests, and perform physical exercises during spaceflight.

Gherman Titov is a "Hero of the Soviet Union." He is assistant editor-in-chief of *Aviatsia i Kosmonavtika* (Aviation and Space Flying), a Soviet Air Force monthly, and the author of numerous articles on spaceflight.
Novosti Press Agency

See also: Cosmonauts, U.S.S.R. aerospace activities, Vostok

Toftoy, Holger Nelson

U.S. Army Officer
Born: October 31, 1902; Marseilles, Illinois
Died: April 17, 1967; Washington, D.C.

From an early interest in Army ordnance and especially explosives, U.S. Army Major General H. N. Toftoy went on to direct the development of some of America's most successful missiles (see). As early as the end of World War II, he realized the potential of missiles, and organized the assembly of German V-2 rocket missile (see) technicians and captured equipment into a research project.

Toftoy was a student at the University of Wisconsin in 1922 when he received an appointment to the U.S. Military Academy. After graduating from West Point in 1926, he was assigned to the Army Air Service and sent to Texas for flight training. Defective eyesight led to reassignment to the Artillery the following year, however, and it was there that he developed a consuming interest in all types of ordnance. For five years he taught in that field at West Point, becoming noted as an authority on explosives and controlled mines.

During World War II Toftoy was given the job of clearing German mines from the harbors of France in preparation for the Normandy invasion. By war's end he had advanced to the post of chief of Army Ordnance Technical Intelligence. It was in that role that he formulated and put into action the Army's *Operation Paperclip,* under which 127 of Germany's top rocket scientists, components of some 100 V-2 rockets, and more than 30 tons of scientific documents were brought to the U.S. in 1945 to form the nucleus of the U.S. missile research and development programs.

From 1948 to 1952 Toftoy headed the rocket branch of the Army Ordnance research and development division, and in 1954 advanced to the post of Commanding General of Redstone Arsenal and its missile laboratories. Before his retirement from the Army in 1960, he had supervised development of some of the nation's most vital missile systems, including Honest John, Nike, Corporal, Nike-Ajax, Nike-Hercules, Hawk, Redstone, and Jupiter C, the system which put America's first satellite into orbit.

Since his retirement Toftoy has continued to contribute to rocket and missile advancements as an advisor and consultant to several aerospace corporations.
Robert L. Parrish

See also: Rockets and rocketry

Tolerances

Tolerances generally mean small variations in the dimensions of manufactured parts so that each will mate to another in the assembly of the vehicle. Another name for tolerances in manufacturing or design is *allowables.*

Tolerances became extremely important as objects were no longer made by hand but by machines. The critical aspect of tolerances increased when industrial societies adopted the mass production system of manufacture.

Historically, each individual craftsman developed his own set of tolerances which worked very well as long as the same man made all of the parts of the item involved; for example, the swordmaker who also manufactured the sheath or scabbard for each of his handmade swords. However, if one man in one city made the swords, and another man in another town made the scabbard, then each would have had to agree to a single set of tolerances, and the swordmaker's sword could only be so long, so wide, and just so thick to fit the scabbard made by the second man.

In machining a piece, the tolerance, or range of variation permitted to maintain a specified dimension, is called *dimensional tolerance*. It is either unilateral or bilateral. If *unilateral,* then the part involved will have a definite limit, say plus or minus 0.0003 inch. If a plus 0.0003 in., it cannot have a minus tolerance of 0.0003 in.; likewise, if a minus 0.0003 in., it cannot have a plus tolerance of 0.0003 in. If bilateral, the tolerance is given as a plus or minus dimension ($\pm$ 0.0003) and the part's final dimension must fall between these two limits.

Importance and Implementation

Tolerances are needed because in actual practice it is impossible to manufacture anything to an exact, precise dimension. Obviously, if very close tolerances are involved, the part becomes much more costly than if less rigid allowances can be accepted. This ability, normally called *accuracy,* has improved to the extent that today's aerospace engineer is quite capable of measuring dimensions in terms of light waves. However, even in the highly precise field of aerospace, this ability is by no means absolute. Thus, tolerances are extremely important in the design of aircraft, rockets, and spacecraft.

Since difficult tolerances also increase the cost of manufacture, designers compromise as much as possible whenever they can. The operation of a part, or a component, will determine the degree of manufacturing tolerance. But there are so many precision functions carried out routinely aboard an advanced aircraft or space vehicle that aerospace tolerances must be far more precise than those involved in the manufacture of automobiles.

Aircraft manufacturers today often use laser beams to measure the alignment of machines, and very sophisticated measuring devices check each part many times during its manufacturing cycle. Even when these components are being assembled, it is a common occurrence to see lasers (*see*) and other complex measuring instruments in constant use.

Tolerances also apply to other aerospace functions. Dimensions are not the only factors involved. Structures are built to very close strength and temperature tolerances, usually ordered by the type of operations expected of the structure. It may be designed to fly through the atmosphere at supersonic speeds, yet also be able to land as a normal aircraft after subsonic low-level flight.

The tolerances on each and every component are usually the result of the kind of performance the vehicle is intended to have. A tight plus-or-minus tolerance figure stems from the fact that the aircraft with a particular precision part will be flying at 2,000 mph. To hold up under the buffeting (*see*), temperatures, and vibration (*see*), imposed by this flight condition, the parts of the aircraft must fit tightly, and the only way this can be done is within the dimensional limitations of tolerances.

There is another kind of tolerance which the pilot or astronaut himself imposes both on the aircraft and on the mission involved. The airplane or space vehicle must not be allowed to exceed the tolerances of a human being. It cannot get too hot, nor can it impose forces beyond a certain degree, or the pilot's operating ability will be impaired.   John F. Judge

See also: Aerospace industry, Manufacturing, Production techniques, Quality control, Reliability and quality assurance

Ton mile

Ton mile refers to one ton of cargo moved one mile, and is used to express the amount of cargo handled in a given period.

See also: Commercial aviation, Passenger mile

Torque

Torque is a twisting force which tends to produce or stop rotation of a rigid body. The most significant torque-producing force in a propeller-driven airplane is created by the rotating propeller. In U.S.-built aircraft the rotation is clockwise as viewed from the cockpit (*see*) which then exerts a torque force that tends to rotate the airplane to a left along the longitudinal axis.

The basic aircraft is usually designed to partially counteract the torque force by rigging the left wing with a slightly higher angle of incidence, creating what is commonly called *wash in*. Since torque will vary with different power settings, control surface pressures and trim tabs (*see*) are used by the pilot as required.

The *P factor* of the aircraft is related to torque and may be defined as the asymmetrical thrust delivered by the propeller, especially by a single-engine aircraft when the flight attitude is changed. As long as the propeller axis coincides with the exact direction of the aircraft's motion, the thrust is uniform around its entire plane of rotation. However, when the airplane's attitude or direction of motion is changed, such as during takeoff and climb, the propeller blade as it descends on the right side of the aircraft will slightly increase its angle of attack (*see*) relative to the left or ascending side. This produces greater thrust which tends to turn the airplane

Torque

to the left. This *P factor* is increased as the angle of attack increases. The combined effects of torque and asymmetrical thrust are greatest during the initial takeoff and climb period. — Raymond J. Johnson

See also: Aerodynamics, Piloting techniques, Propellers

In a propeller-driven aircraft, the most significant force producing torque is created by the rotating propeller. When the propeller swings down to the right, it exerts a torque force that rotates the aircraft to the left.

1. PROPELLER ROTATION IS CLOCKWISE FROM PILOT'S POINT OF VIEW.
2. CLOCKWISE ROTATION OF THE PROPELLER IMPARTS A CLOCKWISE "TWIST" TO SLIPSTREAM.
3. THE LEFT SIDE OF THE AIRPLANE IS ACTED UPON BY AIR WHICH ACTS TO TURN THE AIRPLANE TO THE LEFT.

TORQUE

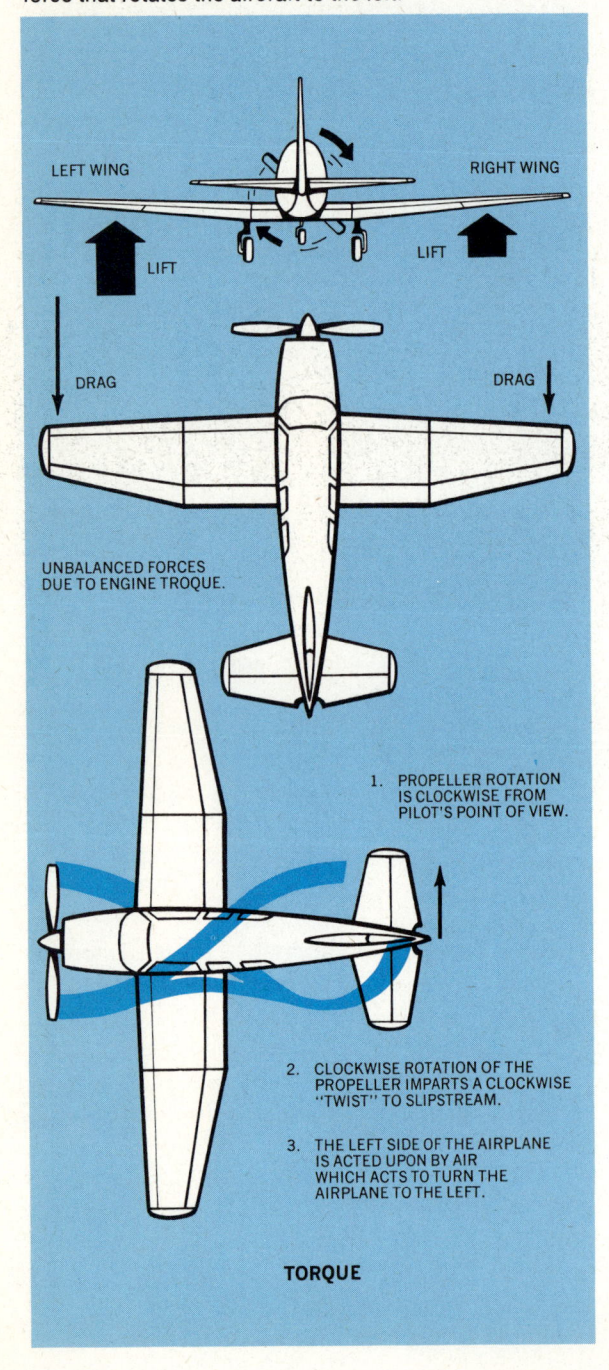

Townes, Charles Hard

American physicist
Born: July 28, 1915; Greenville, South Carolina

Dr. Charles H. Townes, provost and professor of physics at the Massachusetts Institute of Technology, has been a major contributor to U.S. aerospace technology development. An authority in nuclear and microwave technology and radio astronomy (*see*), he won the 1964 Nobel prize for physics.

Townes was educated at Furman and Duke universities and the California Institute of Technology before joining Bell Telephone Laboratories in 1939. His work there earned him an appointment at Columbia University. He was advanced to full professor and executive director of Columbia's radiation laboratory in 1950.

Dr. Townes served as a Fulbright lecturer in France and Japan in 1955-56. He returned home to pursue full-time research on microwave theory and later became vice president and director of research for the Institute of Defense Analysis. Townes also devised a method of measurements known as Masers (*see*). — Robert L. Parrish

Toxic fuels

All fuels currently used in aerospace can have a toxic effect on the human body. Aviation gasoline vapors can irritate the lungs and slow the brain's ability to function. Additives such as tetraethyl lead are quite toxic to the nervous system. To insure the safety of the passengers and crew, all cabins are properly sealed-off from the fuel supply. Exhaust fumes can be fatal to humans and proper safeguards must be taken to insure adequate protection.

Track

Track refers to a hypothetical line traced on the Earth's surface directly under a flying aircraft. On charts, the aircraft's track is indicated by lines connecting the plots of computed position. In denoting action, track refers to the observation of aircraft, spacecraft, or other moving objects by radar, gunsights, or optical instruments.

See also: Tracking systems and networks

VOLUME XII
ILLUSTRATIONS
COURTESY OF:

Adler Planetarium, Page 2256; 2257; 2258.
"Air Force Space Digest Magazine," Page 2223, TL; 2224.
American Telephone & Telegraph, Page 2143, R.
Beech Aircraft Corporation, Page 2157.
Boeing Company, The, Page 2168; 2169; 2176, T; 2178, T; 2191; 2192; 2193; 2194.
British Aircraft Corporation, Page 2183; 2184, T; 2185, TL; 2186, T; 2187, T; 2223, C.
British Aircraft Corporation/Sud-Aviation, Page 2184, B; 2185, TR, C, B; 2186, C, B; 2187, B; 2188; 2267, T.
California Institute of Technology and Carnegie Institution of Washington, Page 2245; 2249.
Cameron, Dr. A. G. W./Ezer, Dr. G., Page 2162, L.
Caplan, James, Page 2246; 2247; 2248; 2253, L.
Downie & Associates, Page 2277, R; 2278; 2281, TL, TR.
Ehricke, Dr. Krafft, Page 2105; 2106; 2107; 2108; 2109; 2110; 2199; 2238; 2239; 2240; 2241.
Engle, Eloise, Page 2219, TR.
Federal Aviation Administration, Page 2295; 2296.
Fiat, Divisione Aviazione, Page 2274, L.
Fiorio, Baron Franco, Private Collection, Arlington, Virginia, Page 2139.
Fisher Pen Company, Page 2137, R.
"Flying Magazine," Page 2171.
"Flying Review International Magazine," Page 2223, BL, BR.
General Precision Systems, Inc., Link Group, Page 2113, R.
Harvard College Observatory, Page 2174, L; 2253, R.
Hawker Siddeley Group Limited, Page 2202, BR.
Hughes Aircraft Company, Page 2208, C; 2209, R; 2211, T.
Jarrett Archives, Col. G. B. Jarrett, Page 2146.
Jet Propulsion Laboratory, Page 2209, L; 2216, C; 2234, T; 2276, T.
Kennedy, Robert Drake, Page 2270.
Kimmell, Steve/Johnson, Col. Raymond, Page 2140.
Kitt Peak National Observatory, Page 2254.

Kohn, Leo J., Page 2147; 2148; 2149; 2150; 2151; 2152.
Lick Observatory, Page 2250.
Lockheed-California Company, Page 2155, R.
Lockheed-Georgia Company, Page 2219, BL.
Lockheed Propulsion Company, Page 2122.
Lowell Observatory, Page 2161, B.
Marquardt Corporation, The, Page 2125.
Martin-Marietta Corporation, Page 2271; 2290, B; 2292; 2293.
McDonnell Douglas Corporation, McDonnell Division, Page 2113, L; 2117, B; 2202, TR; 2273, L; 2274, R; **Douglas Division,** Page 2165; 2201, T; 2281, B; 2284; 2285.
Mittauer, Richard T., Page 2216, T.
Mount Wilson and Palomar Observatories, Page 2162, R; 2251; 2252.
National Aeronautics and Space Administration, Page 2210; 2212, B; 2213; 2214; 2215; 2216, B; 2244; 2268; **Edwards Air Force Base,** Page 2279; **Langley Research Center,** Page 2218, C, B; **Lewis Research Center,** Page 2121; **Manned Spacecraft Center,** Page 2114; 2115; 2118, T; 2123; 2129; 2130; 2131; 2132; 2133; 2134; 2135; 2136; 2137, L; 2211, B; 2212, T; 2217; 2221; 2243; 2262; 2266.
National Air & Space Museum, Smithsonian Institution, Page 2138; 2144; 2145; 2267, B.
North American Air Defense Command, Page 2202, TL.
North American Rockwell Corporation, Page 2277, L; **Rocketdyne Division,** Page 2124; 2276, B; **Space & Information Systems Division,** Page 2275.
Novosti Press Agency, U.S.S.R., Page 2216; 2117, TL, TR; 2153, R; 2154; 2178, C; 2200.
Pasachoff, Jay M., Page 2173, BR.
Philco-Ford Corporation, Page 2203; 2207, BL, BR.
"Power To Fly," British Crown Copyright, Science Museum, London, Page 2170.
Quantas Airways, Limited, Page 2116, R.
Radio Corporation of America, Page 2259; 2260; 2261; 2263.
Runge, Fritz C., Page 2126; 2127.
SAAB, Page 2223, TR; 2273, R.
Sacramento Peak Observatory, Air Force Cambridge Research Laboratories, Page 2173, T; 2174, R; 2175.
Sanderson Films, Inc., Page 2227.
Slater, Col. Ralph, Page 2166, L.
SOVFOTO, Page 2153, L.
Sud-Aviation, Page 2178, B.
Swenson, Dr. G. W., Jr., Page 2173, BL.
Trans World Airlines, Inc., Page 2288.
United States Air Force, Official Photograph, Page 2155, L; 2176, B; 2201, B; 2208, T; 2220; 2229; 2230; 2233; **Edwards Air Force Base,** Page 2219, TL, TC, BR; **Offutt Air Force Base,** Page 2167; **Vandenberg Air Force Base,** Page 2290, T.
United States Army, Official Photograph, Page 2202, BL; 2207, TL, TR.
United States Department of Commerce, Environmental Science Services Administration, Page 2143, L.
United States Steel Corporation, Page 2164.
University of Michigan, Page 2161, T.
Williams, Harold R., Page 2272.
Whiting, Richard F., Page 2234, B.
Yerkes Observatory, Page 2255.

Key: T-Top, B-Bottom, R-Right, L-Left, C-Center.